COGNITIVE DEVELOPMENT IN INFANCY

This reader is one part of an Open University integrated teaching system and the selection is therefore related to other material available to students. It is designed to evoke the critical understanding of students. Opinions expressed in it are not necessarily those of the course team or of the University.

Cognitive Development in Infancy

A Reader edited by
John Oates and Sue Sheldon
at the Open University

Lawrence Erlbaum Associates, Publishers
in association with
The Open University

Reprinted 1991, 1993

Lawrence Erlbaum Associates Ltd., Publishers
27 Palmeira Mansions
Church Road
Hove
East Sussex, BN3 2FA
UK

British Library Cataloguing in Publication Data

Cognitive development in infancy: a reader
    1. Cognition in children   2. Infant psychology
    I. Oakes, John, *1946-* II. Sheldon, Sue
    III. Open University
    155.4'22   BF723.C5

    ISBN 0-86377-085-1 (Hbk)
    ISBN 0-86377-086-X (Pbk)

Typeset by Multiplex Techniques Ltd., Orpington
Printed and bound by BPCC Wheatons Ltd., Exeter

Contents

Preface   vii

I The Cultural and Biological Context   1

1. Connolly, K. (1981). Maturation and the ontogeny of motor skills. In
K. Connolly and H. Prechtl (Eds). *Maturation and Development*. London:
Heinemann, pp. 216–230.   3

2. Super, C. M. (1981). Cross-cultural research on infancy. In H. C. Triandis
and A. Heron (Eds), *Handbook of Cross-Cultural Psychology, Developmental Psychology, Vol. 4*. Boston: Allyn & Bacon.   23

II Infant Learning   49

3. Piaget, J. and Inhelder, B. (1966). *The Psychology of the Child* (translated by H. Weaver, published 1969). London: Routledge & Kegan Paul,
pp. 1–12.   51

4. Stamps, L. (1977). Temporal conditioning of heart rate response in newborn infants. *Developmental Psychology, 13*, pp. 624–629.   59

5. Siqueland, E. R. and De Lucia, C. A. (1969). Visual reinforcement of
non-nutritive sucking in human infants. *Science, 165*, pp. 1144–1146.   71

6. Watson, J. S. and Ramey, C. T. (1972). Reactions to response-contingent
stimulation in early infancy. *Merrill-Palmer Quarterly, 18*, pp. 219–227.   77

7. Rovee-Collier, C. K., Sullivan, M. W., Enright, M., Lucas, D., and
Fagen, J. W. (1980). Reactivation of infant memory. *Science, 208*, pp. 1159–1161.   87

III Perception to Cognition   93

8. Butterworth, G. (1986). Events and encounters in infant perception.
The New Psychologist, pp. 3–7.   95

9. Demany, L., McKenzie, B., and Vurpillot, E. (1977). Rhythm perception
in early infancy. *Nature, 266*, pp. 718–719.   105

10.   DeCasper, A. J. and Fifer, W. P. (1980). Of human bonding: newborns prefer their mothers' voices. *Science, 208*, pp. 1174–1176.   111

11.   Slater, A. and Morison, V. (1985). Shape constancy and slant perception at birth. *Perception, 14*, pp. 337–344.   119

12.   Quinn, P. C. and Eimas, P. D. (1986). On categorization in early infancy. *Merrill-Palmer Quarterly, 32*, 331–363.   131

IV   The Object Concept   163

13.   Piaget, J. and Inhelder, R. (1966). The construction of reality. In *The Psychology of the Child* (translated by H. Weaver, published 1969). London: Routledge & Kegan Paul, pp. 14–19.   165

14.   Bower, T. G. R. (1967). Phenomenal identity and form perception in an infant. *Perception and Psychophysics, 2*, 74–76.   171

15.   Bjork, E. L. and Cummings, E. M. (1984). Infant search errors: Stage of concept development or stage of memory development? *Memory and Cognition, 12*, 1–19.   177

V   Early Social Behaviour   217

16.   Bretherton, I., McNew, S., and Beeghley-Smith, M. (1981). Early person knowledge as expressed in gestural and verbal communication: When do infants acquire a "theory of mind"? In M. E. Lamb and L. R. Sherrod (Eds), *Infant Social Cognition*, Hillsdale, N. J.: Lawrence Erlbaum Associates Inc., pp. 333–373.   219

VI   Continuity   247

17.   Bornstein, M. H. and Sigman, M. D. (1986). Continuity in mental development from infancy. *Child Development, 57*, 251–274.   249

18.   Kagan, J. (1973). The importance of simply growing older. *New Society*, 14 June 1973, 610–12.   285

Author Index   293

Subject Index   303

Preface

This collection of papers has been selected to form part of an Open University third-level course, *Cognitive Development: Language and Thinking from Birth to Adolescence*. Its function in that course is to present an up-to-date review of the central areas of research and theory in the psychology of cognitive development in infancy, and, as such, will be of interest to people other than students on the course who wish to learn more about this important aspect of human development.

Two other Readers in the same course cover cognitive development from the immediate pre-school stage to the onset of adolescence (Richardson & Sheldon, 1987) and language development (Lock & Fisher, 1984). This period of infancy, from birth to about eighteen months, is arguably the most significant and momentous part of the whole life-span. For, in this brief space of time, a child makes the giant leap from being virtually helpless and apparently incompetent to taking the first small steps alone and uttering the first words. Walking and talking are the most obvious signs of the child's developing competence, but the end of the period of infancy is also marked by a whole range of other important achievements in motor and mental abilities.

But, despite the undoubted attraction of this period for psychologists, it remained enigmatic for a long time, because, without language, the most potent channel of communication, access to the infant's view of the world seemed effectively barred. This barrier was finally surmounted by the invention of several powerful new tools that capitalise on abilities that the infant does possess from birth and which can be pressed into service as communication media. Foremost among these abilities are looking, sucking and head-turning, all of which, when incorporated into carefully designed experimental methods, give us the possibility of seeing further and deeper into the infant's psychological being.

The 1960s ushered in a new era in the study of infancy: driven by the potential of the novel research tools, and by a new belief in infancy as a critical period for later development, research effort in the area burgeoned as never before and Western developmental psychologists generated such a plethora of research that the findings of these efforts are still being sifted, analysed and synthesised. For the picture that began to emerge in the 1960s was of the infant as far from helpless and incompetent, but rather as remarkably able and advanced in previously unsuspected ways. There developed a hope that the roots of later developments such as language, concept formation, social interaction and perception would be found in the new psychology of infancy. And indeed these hopes were largely realised in the boom of research that the era produced.

Even though the scale of this effort has not been sustained in the years that have followed, the impetus remains, and the most promising lines of study continue to be pursued with increasing sophistication of method and theory. This volume has been produced to show the major features of the new view of infancy that has opened up, and to signpost the paths along which research is continuing to offer new insights.

The first section sets the scene by considering the context of the development of cognition in infancy at two contrasting levels. In infancy, motor development is of particular interest, not only because it is the infant's motor behaviours that have been harnessed to the new methodologies, but also because cognition seems much more closely bound up with motor behaviours in these early months than later in the life-span.

Hence an understanding of the course of motor development and the theoretical issues that arise in conceptualising it are central to the field, and are well covered in the paper by Connolly (1981).

Of equal importance is the framework for development provided by the culture within which the infant grows up. The variety of child-rearing practices in different cultures, and the remarkable commonalities in infant development in these different conditions raise important and interesting questions which Super (1981) elaborates and addresses in his paper.

The second section focusses on the issue of how infants learn, and the papers here document the profound change from a concern with whether learning in infancy can be demonstrated at all, to an examination of the processes involved. The paper by Piaget and Inhelder (1966) that heads Section II provides an insightful framework for understanding how learning, with motor development, is part and parcel of the development of cognition.

The next set of readings takes us from a consideration of the perceptual world of the infant through to the central issue of the processes of concept formation. The first paper here, by Butterworth (1986), alerts us to the fact that perception serves cognition, and that it has to be seen in the light of both the content of the infant's natural environment and the cognitive demands of the infant.

One of the most intriguing areas in the study of early concept formation is the apparent lack in infants of any stable idea of objects in the world as having enduring identities. First highlighted by Piaget, as discussed in the extract from their writing on the subject, this notion has sustained a major research effort, and the other two papers here discuss central issues in the topic.

In common with theories of cognitive development at later ages, theories of infant development are now increasingly recognising the central importance of the social context for cognition. The paper in Section IV by Bretherton, McNew and Beeghley-Smith (1981) considers in depth the significance of this aspect.

In conclusion, the final two papers address the question of how infant cognition relates to later development. This is a theoretically complex and difficult area, and Bornstein and Sigman (1986) discuss different models that can be employed to embrace the empirical findings, while Kagan (1973) reminds us of the contribution that a cross-cultural perspective can offer.

The preparation of this Reader has involved the assistance of many people. Along with thanks for the help of Glyn Collis, Charles Crook and Alan Slater, who played a central role in selecting (and rejecting!) papers, we would like to thank George Butterworth for his attention both to the detail as well as the broader view this Reader is intended to convey.

John Oates
Sue Sheldon

REFERENCES

Lock, A. & Fisher, E. (1986). (Eds), *Language Development*. Beckenham: Croom Helm.

Richardson, K. & Sheldon, S. (1987). (Eds), *Cognitive Development to Adolescence*. London: Lawrence Erlbaum & Associates Ltd.

THE CULTURAL AND BIOLOGICAL CONTEXT

1 Maturation and the Ontogeny of Motor Skills

Kevin J. Connolly

The ability to make precise controlled movements is both commonplace and necessary for our everyday life. Observing the difficulties and constraints experienced by physically handicapped children shows clearly and often dramatically the essential importance of skilled motor behaviour. The ubiquity of skill often leads us to overlook its significance and to describe common actions as automatic. That some behaviour should be so common as to warrant the description automatic is not to suggest that it is unimportant; indeed such behaviours may be more important in adjusting to the varying demands of the environment than less common capacities.

For more than 50 years, motor development has attracted the attention of neurologists, psychologists, paediatricians and others interested in child development. The questions posed have varied both with the conceptual framework and the methods of investigation available. Much of the earlier work was concerned less with the processes involved in the observed changes than in describing their typical course and time of appearance. Implicit in the studies undertaken are assumptions about the causes and controls of development, and these change from time to time. For example, Gesell and Amatruda (1947) stated: "An examination of infant behaviour is essentially an examination of the central nervous system." This view embodies a central tenet of developmental diagnosis and points to a basic conceptual problem: the relationship between the developing brain and behaviour. It

Source: Connolly, K. & Prechtl, H. (Eds) (1981). *Maturation and Development*. London: Heinemann, pp. 216–230.

is unlikely that many would dispute the view that the "brain is the organ of behaviour" but in general our knowledge is so limited that psychology and neurology (and in particular developmental neurology) have proceeded largely independently in studying development. The conceptual problems are formidable; how, for example, might one envisage connections between brain development and, say, the acquisition of social skills? In the case of skilled motor performance, the connection seems more direct, but the nature of the relationship is nonetheless difficult to formulate.

IMPLICIT AND EXPLICIT ASSUMPTIONS

In general the young human infant has been seen as motorically immature. In one sense this is correct since the baby has a limited behavioural repertoire, limited at least in comparison with the normal two-year-old. But is this the best starting point? In some respects the newborn's behaviour is highly developed and he is capable of quite precise skilled motor actions; visual tracking of a moving stimulus (Barton, Birns & Ronch, 1971) and sucking, for example, which can be shaped by contingencies (Kaye, 1967). It is more useful to see the behaviour of the young infant not so much as impoverished or immature, but rather as adapted to a particular ecological niche. Within certain limits, the infant is anything but incompetent or helpless. It is important to appreciate that infancy, childhood and the processes of development themselves have been subject to evolutionary pressures and shaped by evolutionary forces.

To view the developing organism as an immature form of the adult is to apply a misleading model. The rules of behavioural organisation by which the infant operates are different from those of the mature organism. It has different tasks to fulfil and both its biological and cultural milieu are quite different from those of the adult. This position of course raises the problem of a comparative basis and calls into question assumptions of uniformity and direct causal connections between early and later behaviour. Not only the feasibility but also the logical basis of predicting from performance in infancy to status in middle childhood or adulthood are questionable. To assume that the child is no more than nature's way of making another adult leads us to an attenuated view of development. If the infant is qualitatively different from the adult, then what basis can we adopt for comparison, since to describe the infant's capabilities as some portion of the adult's would be to oversimplify and mislead.

MATURATION AND LEARNING

Child psychology has long recognised the importance of biological maturation as an important factor in development. Typically this has been gauged by using chronological age as an independent variable. This in turn implies that maturation as a process is uniform, invariant and can usefully be measured by the passage of time. In fact biological maturation is not a single, simple process and its connections with behavioural development are for the most part indirect and complex, and subject to variation from several sources. How then can these variables be related? It is unlikely that charting behavioural development and attempting to draw inferences about the central nervous system from changes in behaviour alone will prove very informative. First, biological and experiential factors reciprocally determine behaviour, they interact and probably covary. To conceptualise motor development as simply a process of unfolding is to oversimplify (Connolly, 1970). Second, the uniformity which has been presumed is doubtful. The stereotyped course of development which has often been referred to does not preclude variation, indeed were there not variation this would itself almost certainly indicate abnormality (Touwen, 1978). The available data do not support the view that motor development is stereotyped and to conclude from the generally low variation in time of appearance that identical processes and variables are at work is unwarranted.

Much of the previous research and theorising about motor development has focussed upon when in development (measured in terms of chronological age) various behaviours appear. The question of how they develop has received less attention. This concern for the product rather than the process of development has had consequences for the way in which the problems of motor development have been articulated. Gesell's (1954) maturation hypothesis has led to notions of maturation as a process of unfolding, in which the rate but not manner of change has been seen as variable. Uniformity rather than variability has been the overriding assumption, which in turn has led to the neglect of variations within individuals, between individuals and between behaviours. Consequently, important sources of information concerning developmental change have been neglected and appropriate theory has been rather narrowly formulated.

The development of motor behaviour in infancy and the acquisition of specific motor skills in childhood are not unrelated, though the nature of the changes involved at different points in development varies. In consequence, different processes will be involved and different factors will contribute to variability. All normal children raised in a wide variety of different cultures and physical environments learn to walk, but not all normal healthy children learn to write. Both are skilled motor actions and each has certain properties in common with the other, yet in some senses they are fundamentally different. In the case of walking, it seems consistent with the evidence to suggest that there are powerful biological predispositions common to all members of the species which, in a range of environments, result in the appearance of skilled motor behaviour. All normal children learn to walk and many to write, but these skills are learned in a rather different sense, though it is unlikely that the principles involved are completely different.

This raises the question of what is implied by the term "maturation". To say that walking is a consequence of maturation would not immediately be dismissed but if the same explanation were applied to writing it certainly would. The difference is that one is common to all children without specific tutoring and the other is not. Maturation is a name for many different growth processes and is not a *cause* of development, though it is often used as an explanatory and not a descriptive term. For example, distinctions have been drawn between maturation and learning, each being used in the sense of explanations for behavioural change. This confusion arises especially in trying to understand the development of those behaviours common to a species, such as walking, and those common to a culture, such as writing. Behaviour which is species-typical is not necessarily unlearned, and attempts to distinguish maturation from learning run the risk of falling back upon unsatisfactory definitions of maturation as that which is not dependent upon specific tutoring.

I shall use the notion of psychological maturation to refer to various competences and their associated performance which emerge as a result of the growth and development of the central nervous system in any reasonably normal and natural environment. Implicit in this is the idea of predisposition: in some manner which we do not yet understand the organism is programmed to produce the outcome. Without this it is difficult, if not impossible, to create a maturational competence simply through environmental intervention. Maturational competence of this kind *requires* certain environmental contributions and conditions. Variations in experience are often associated with the timing of the appearance of a given behaviour, and also with its quality. It is possible of course to interfere with the conditions and so retard or alter maturational sequences.

Maturation, then, is a complex set of processes which change at different rates over time and which are affected by many biological and experiential factors. The functions which these processes serve may be yoked together; not all will be present at birth and some will have served their purpose early in development. There is an implication that regular relationships exist between structures and actions, and competence gained at one point may be necessary for and may be incorporated into competence and performance at a later point. That a prior state must exist before a subsequent one will sometimes be the case and may lead to the description of behaviour as following a sequence of stages. However, the precise contribution of different factors will vary and it is likely that there will be different routes to the same end. The apparent invariances in order which have been described are almost certainly due to genetic mechanisms which have been fixed over the course of primate evolution. However, there is no necessity for closely dependent relationships to exist between all structures or all successive stages. This point has bearing upon a long-held preoccupation of many psychologists and others interested in child development, namely to predict future status from present status. The difficulty with this is in part a failure to appreciate the extent and significance of variation; the prediction of outcome requires not only a knowledge of the individual's past history but also a knowledge of the child's future encounters with a constantly shifting environment. In very broad terms predictions can be made, but there are logical limits to the extent to which this can be done.

PATTERNS AND SEQUENCES

If ultimately we are to understand behavioural development, then descriptive and analytical approaches are both essential. The way in which contemporary research and education has divided up the developmental sciences is not necessarily an accurate, or indeed helpful, division; "nature" does not read our textbooks. Conceptual analysis, theory building and hypothesis testing are valuable and essential. So too is a firm and detailed data base: we need to know the natural history of our organism and be familiar with the observed variation at a descriptive level. As a science progresses, so does the quality of the descriptive analysis given to the phenomena with which it is concerned. Most commonly this progress is associated with quantification, which gives more detailed and precise description. In broad and general terms there is an orderly sequence in the motor development of children and the nature and properties of this sequence are an important starting point.

Prone Progression

Before an infant can walk, usually he will develop some more primitive means of getting about. An early study of prone progression was made by Burnside (1927), who distinguished "hitching" from "crawling" and "creeping" in a small sample of nine babies, these being the commonest types of locomotion preceding walking. Crawling referred to any type of locomotion in which the body is prone; creeping indicated locomotion in which the body is raised from the floor but remains roughly parallel with it – usually on hands and knees; and hitching referred to locomotion in a sitting posture.

Ames (1937) who, like Burnside, analysed cine film of the motor activities of a series of infants, identified 14 stages of prone progression. An examination of individual differences among the 20 infants in the series suggested that the stages of prone progression flow into one another in essentially the same way for all children.

A more generalised picture of the stages of prone progression was presented by McGraw (1941), who investigated a sample of 82 infants. The nine stages on which every child could be rated, regardless of individual differences, were identified by McGraw as: (1) newborn posture and movements; (2) beginning spinal extension; (3) advanced spinal extension; (4) incipient propulsive movements in the anterior region; (5) incipient propulsive movements in the posterior region; (6) the assumption of a creeping posture; (7) deliberate but unorganised progression; (8) organised progression; and (9) integrated progression. Each of these phases was found to last between 30 to 35 days and the sequential aspects were thought to reflect the general cephalo-caudal developmental trend.

More recently, as part of a detailed descriptive analysis of developmental changes, largely during the first year of life but up to independent walking, Touwen (1976) has presented data on 51 infants. Locomotion in prone progression was one item which showed an evident developmental sequence. The overall time scale reported accords well with McGraw's earlier findings, though the more detailed results reveal some differences, largely finding less intra- and inter-individual overlap between consecutive phases. Although a developmental seqeunce has been identified and described, there are nonetheless substantial individual differences; some infants never reach the stage of creeping, some never progress in the prone position, and some progress only in a sitting position. The importance of postural control in the emergence of these functional behaviours is undoubtedly important (Touwen, 1976; Casaer, 1979).

The Development of Walking

In an early, and for its time very detailed, study of postural and locomotor development, Shirley (1931) identified five sequential phases in her sample of 25 infants. These were: (1) passive postural control; (2) active postural control; (3) active attempts at locomotion; (4) locomotion by creeping; and (5) complete postural control during walking. Shirley concluded that each of these stages was a prerequisite for the immediately succeeding stage, and that every baby proceeded from stage to stage in the same order.

McGraw and Breeze (1941), on the basis of observations of children from birth to five years, distinguished six distinct phases in the development of erect locomotion. These were: (1) the reflex stepping of the neonate; (2) the inhibitory or static phase; (3) the transitive phase: (4) deliberate stepping movements: (5) heel-toe progression; and, finally, (6) the integrated mature phase of erect locomotion. In his earlier paper, Burnside (1927) had reached similar conclusions, and he noted that the stability of the infant's body in the walking position depends upon body weight, the centre of gravity (which is fairly low in infants because the legs are proportionately shorter) and the basis of support, that is the area enclosed by the feet.

Certain relationships have been found between the emergence of independent walking and other developmental changes. Touwen (1971) found a close relationship between the mature phase of locomotion in the prone position and walking unsupported. Not surprisingly, Touwen (1976) has also reported a close relationship between standing without support and the development of independent walking; the maturation of postural control mechanisms must precede independent walking. These relationships between the appearance of prone progression and walking reflect the development of voluntary motor behaviour, which is based upon nervous system maturation.

The attainment of independent walking is not at all the same thing as the achievement of the mature walking pattern. The initial form of independent walking shown by the infant is characterised by steps with a wide base, hyperflexion of the hips and knees, and the arms are held in abduction and the elbows in extension. Typically, the pattern of movement is staccato. From this initial phase the width of the base gradually diminishes, a reciprocal arm-swing appears and both step length and walking speed increase. The staccato pattern gradually becomes smoother. In general, the development of walking appears to be complete by the time the child is five (Scrutton, 1969; Statham & Murray, 1971), though some authors argue that gait maturation is earlier (Burnett & Johnson, 1971). Sutherland, Olshen, Cooper and Woo (1980) have reported data from a study of 186 normal children aged between one and seven years. Using sophisticated techniques, they analysed a number of parameters throughout a walking cycle. Five important determinants of mature gait were identified, and important factors in their development were shown to be increasing limb length and greater limb stability. On these criteria, a mature gait pattern was evident at the end of the third year.

Reaching and Prehension

The capacity to reach and grasp are the fundamental components of manual skill. Visually directed reaching is one of the most striking developments during the first six months and it marks an important step towards the mastery of objects and tools. Like locomotion, reaching and grasping have been the subject of quite extensive investigations, but our knowledge of these processes remains limited.

Halverson (1931) investigated visually directed reaching in infants from four-and-a-half to twelve months. In contrast, Piaget (1952) and White, Castle and Held (1964) concentrated their attention on the period between the first and the fifth months and give a stepwise analysis, culminating in visually directed reaching at about five months. Whether visually directed reaching is present in the newborn and very young infant is still the subject of controversy. Bower, Broughton and Moore (1970a; 1970b) and Bower (1972) have claimed that visually directed reaching to an object does occur in the newborn under suitable conditions. When presented with a bright toy, reaching to within 5° to 10° of the target at a fairly high frequency was reported. However, Dodwell, Muir and Di Franco (1976) and Ruff and Halton (1978) were unable to replicate the findings. To a large extent these difficulties may reflect methodological problems and inadequacies, which are discussed in detail by McDonnell (1979). Although by no means unequivocal, there is evidence of reaching behaviour elicited by visual stimuli in the infant during the first month of life. DiFranco, Muir and Dodwell (1978) showed that many components of reaching are present in very young infants, but at that stage there is little evidence of the fine articulation characteristic of mature reaching.

Bower (1974) suggested that the early reaching which he observed was ballistic in nature, that is to say not subject to correction and adjustment during execution. Corrections could be made only between successive attempts. He suggested also that the infant's attempts at reaching were pre-adapted to attributes of the object, such as distance and size. Thus there is a distinction between visually triggered and visually guided reaching. McDonnell (1975) has argued that visually triggered reaching precedes visually guided reaching, and Hein, Held and Gower (1970) found that in animals whose movement was restricted, visually triggered but not visually guided extension developed.

Co-ordination between the hand and the eye, as in visually guided reaching, is evidence of the emergence of sensorimotor skill. Such action requires focussed attention, cognitive processing and flexibility of response, which is an important characteristic of skilled behaviour. Bruner and Koslowski (1972) argue that visually guided behaviour necessitates the correct sequencing of pre-adapted constituent acts, such as arm extension and flexion and the anticipatory adjustment of the posture of the fingers prior to contact. Also, the flexibility which such behaviour can show may require the inhibition of elements in the sequence or their reordering as a consequence of the available visual information. Between five and six months, most infants are capable of visually guided reaching to objects (McDonnell, 1975; Lasky, 1977).

Most of the investigations of reaching have involved reaching for stationary targets: von Hofsten (1979) and von Hofsten and Lindhagan (1979) have examined the reaching of infants to moving objects. From these studies it would appear that reaching for moving objects develops at the same time as visually guided reaching for stationary objects.

A response of the hand to stimulation of the palm has been described in a fetus at 10.5 weeks gestational age (Hooker, 1938; 1952). At 10.5 weeks there is incomplete synergistic flexion of the fingers, at 12 to 12.5 weeks the thumbs begin to be involved, and by 13 weeks there is often greater flexion of digits 3 to 5 than of the index finger. By 18.5 weeks a weak grasp is present. Twitchell (1965) has analysed the grasp reflex of the newborn and distinguished three kinds of automatic grasping response during the first four postnatal months: the traction response, the grasp reflex and the instinctive grasp reaction. Similarities and correlations between fetal and postnatal hand movement sequences have been noted by Humphrey (1969), but the relationship between reflex grasping and voluntary prehension, as Twitchell (1970) has pointed out, is not the simple one generally described.

Halverson (1931; 1937) made detailed observations on the components and development of voluntary manual activity and described both reaching and the prehensive pattern. Prior to 28 weeks the grip did not appear to involve thumb opposition in most of the sample, the object being clamped into the palm by flexion of the fingers. From about 36 weeks, Halverson claimed · that finger-tip grasping was the progressively preferred pattern.There is also a clear trend in the development of grasping for the object to move distally and radially with respect to the palm. In the early stages, at about 12 weeks, the object is often contacted with the ulnar border of the hand. As the thumb and index finger are progressively differentiated, there is a gradual use of the digits without involvement of the palm. Developmental changes in grip patterns have been investigated (Connolly & Elliott, 1972; Connolly, 1973) and it is apparent that the sequence of changes continues through the preschool years.

Lateralisation

It has usually been assumed that lateralisation of function is not present at birth, though the evidence now available would suggest that there is some lateralisation and that it develops from birth onwards. Corballis and Morgan (1978) have examined the evidence for a maturational left to right gradient and concluded that there is earlier or more rapid development on the left than on the right. If the leading side is damaged or in some way restricted, the gradient may be reversed so that growth occurs with the opposite polarity. In the case of sensorimotor activities, there is conflicting evidence which is difficult to evaluate because of methodological confusions and inadequacies (McDonnell 1979). de Schonen (1977) argues that without initial asymmetry in movement it is difficult to see how the differentiation of spatial control relative to a target could come about. Asymmetry and co-ordination are thus necessary conditions for the development of differentiation and complementary arm control.

TIMING AND VARIATION

The maturational hypothesis as we know it today derives primarily from Gesell's work. He considered behaviour to be an expression of the activity of the nervous system, and variations in behaviour were seen as a reflection of the degree of integrity of the child's nervous system. His concern with the development of behaviour was as a means of arriving at a diagnosis of the child's developmental status, and deviant behavioural development he interpreted as an indication of neurological impairment (Gesell, 1954). His work showed that the careful, systematic observation and testing of infants yields valuable information about their functional development, and it laid the foundations of developmental medicine (Gesell & Amatruda, 1947).

Norms and Timing

Developmental tests usually group the infant's behaviour into four or five broad categories, gross and fine motor performance being examples. Such grouping is crude, and inevitably overlaps occur between categories. The data generated from developmental tests tend to be of the "ages and stages" kind. Of the various tests and schedules available, the best are probably the Bayley Scales (Bayley, 1935; 1965; 1969). The motor scale has 81 items which were standardised on 1262 children, divided into 14 age-groups between 2 and 30 months. Another test which is frequently used is the Denver Developmental Screening Test (DDST) (Frankenburg & Dodds, 1967), the norms for which are based on 1036 American children aged between 1 month and 6 years. Both of these tests have now been standardised on samples of children in other countries; the Bayley Scales in the UK (Francis-Williams & Yule, 1967) and in Mexico (Solomons, 1980), and DDST in the UK (Bryant & Newcombe, 1979) and in Japan (Ueda, 1978). The primary purpose of these tests and other similar developmental schedules is as screening devices to identify infants with developmental problems which may be indicative of neurological impairment (Bryant, Davies, Richards & Voorhees, 1973, Camp, van Doorninck, Frankenberg & Lampe, 1977).

Variation and Atypical Development

Although the existence of variability in motor development has been acknowledged, the primary emphasis hitherto has been on similarity; normal development being presumed to be a circumscribed and predictable process. The maturation hypothesis is founded in a typological and not a population approach. Implicit in the notion of maturation lies the concept of the ideal type to which every individual is an approximation, and on the whole a close approximation. While the compiling of developmental schedules involves determining the extent of variability in a population, little attempt is made to understand or account for the existence of variability. To some degree the presumed identity or similarity reflects relatively crude methods of description and measurement: for example if independent walking is defined simply as the ability to take a number of steps without support, it does not allow one to say much about the nature or quality of the action. If we are to understand the processes of development, including the regularities in nature which call for explanation, it will be necessary to incorporate variability fully into our theorizing. The emphasis on stereotypy rather than variability will have to be adjusted, if not reversed; a point made in an important essay by Touwen (1978).

Variations in behavioural development can be grouped broadly into three sets; inter-individual variation, intra-individual variation, and extreme deviance which is usually associated with pathology. The differences between the three sets are not hard and fast, and the three are not mutually exclusive. Differences between individuals may be caused by many factors; genetic, physiological, nutritional, hormonal, and as a function of socialisation and experience. Intra-individual differences, when features of development normally linked in sequence and timing appear to be disconnected, may also be caused by any or several of a large array of factors. In some cases intra-individual variations, which imply temporary standstill, regression, or differences in rate within a single aspect of behaviour, may indicate pathology. Lundberg (1979) examined prospectively a series of cases showing dissociated motor development, defined as marked gross motor delay without any abnormal neurological signs, and contrasting with normal development of fine motor ability. Of the 78 children, who were first examined between 7 and 23 months, 10 became normal before 2 years. Of the remainder, 50 per cent were characterised at final follow-up by a number of clinical features, such as muscular hypotonia, while for the remaining 50 per cent no clinical condition was identified. Haidvogl (1979) has also reported a series of cases. It would be interesting to know in cases of dissociated motor development whether the appearance of rhythmical stereotypies in the legs and torso were delayed in comparison to stereotypies of the arms and fingers (see below).

There is no clear-cut division between normal and abnormal motor development; the normal range shades into the abnormal in much the same way as does intellectual capacity. Normal and abnormal may be defined statistically, or in terms of particular inabilities, or because a condition can be described. In the case of children whose development is slow, it is particularly difficult to decide upon abnormality, other than in an actuarial sense. In the case of children with motor deficits, or presumed motor deficits, it is particularly important to examine not only the physiological basis but also the whole matrix of their development. We also need much more detailed information about the course of development, both in populations and in individuals, before we can decide what constitutes being within the functionally normal range.

Sources of Variation

There are no doubt many causes of variation in motor development; constitutional, environmental and cultural. Although there has been very little investigation of genetic differences in motor development and motor performance, such evidence as is available, not surprisingly, indicates an effect.

McNemar (1933), in a study of 93 pairs of school-aged twins employing five tests of motor performance, found substantially higher within-pair correlations for identical (MZ) compared with fraternal (DZ) twins. Interestingly, the differences observed were maintained following practice. Similar results were obtained by Brody (1937); on all the comparisons made, MZ twins were more alike than DZ. Freedman (1965) used the Bayley scales to study the development of twins, and found the motor scale to more clearly differentiate MZ from DZ pairs. Genetic differences are likely to be an important source of variation in motor development, but the available data are sparse.

Events and conditions in pre- and perinatal life are also likely to contribute to variation in motor development. Rosenblith (1966) found a significant prognostic relationship between neonatal motor status and gross and fine motor development on the Bayley scales at eight months. Nutritional status also contributes effects, including specific nutritional deficits (Connolly, Pharoah & Hetzel, 1979). The effects of protein energy malnutrition are dependent upon the severity, timing and duration of the nutritional stress. Children given nutritionally adequate diets show some catch-up in growth and development, but there is also evidence of long-term detriment. Monckeberg (1968), in a 3- to 6-year follow-up of 14 severely malnourished children, after nutritional recovery found their motor development to be still retarded. Hoorweg and Stanfield (1976), in a carefully designed investigation, found evidence of what appeared to be permanent impairment of motor abilities in a sample of children aged between 11 and 17 years who had been admitted to hospital between 8 and 27 months of age in order to treat severe protein malnutrition. The relationship between motor performance, pre- and postnatal malnutrition and other pre- and perinatal events is undoubtedly complex and indirect; presumably such factors exert their effects on the development of the brain and they may manifest themselves subsequently in sub-optimal behavioural performance.

There is some evidence of differences in motor development being related to patterns of child-rearing, and also to social class, since child-rearing practices vary with social class. Neligan and Prudham (1969) reported a correlation between social class and the age of independent walking, children from lower social-class families tending to walk independently earlier. Hindley (1968), in a longitudinal study on the development of walking in samples of children from five European countries, found significant differences in the average age at which independent walking was achieved. The child's position in a family may also influence early motor development, first-born children tending to perform slightly better on motor tasks in infancy (Solomons & Solomons, 1964; Bayley, 1965).

The existence of ethnic differences in patterns of motor development has also received attention, though the amount of reliable data is sparse. Similarly, data from cross-cultural studies of motor development are restricted. Geber and Dean (1957) argued that African infants show precocity in early motor development, but methodological weaknesses make it difficult to interpret these data (Warren, 1972). However, the relative precocity reported by others has been related by Super (1976) to tasks specifically taught by caretakers, or which are incidental effects of daily caretaking practices: the infants were not found to be advanced on tasks which were not taught or practised. Solomons and Solomons (1975) reported data on motor development in three socio-cultural groups from Yucatan. No differences were found between the three groups on the Bayley motor scale but all were in advance of the USA norms between three and eight months. The authors suggest that this acceleration may be due to some culturally distinctive child-rearing practices, and comment that the infants were constantly held and carried. This practice may result in greater than usual vestibular stimulation, which an experimental study has shown to accelerate motor development (Clark, Kreutzberg, & Chee, 1977). The role of vestibular stimulation and its possible relationship to motor development via handling practices merits further investigation. Earlier cross-cultural studies of psychomotor development over the first two years have been reviewed by Werner (1972).

THE BIOLOGICAL SUBSTRATE

The human newborn customarily has been seen as an essentially reflex-bound creature who comes to display voluntary instrumental behaviour progressively over the first few months of life. In line with this view, an assumption of the maturation hypothesis has been that motor skills undergo some form of gradual transition from reflexive to voluntary control. The relationship of reflex to voluntary behaviour has itself been the subject of quite distinct opinions. Wyke (1975) advanced the view that for the first three months of its life the infant functions purely on the basis of reflexes. Bruner and Bruner (1968) argued that before voluntary programmed actions could become functionally effective, there must be a recession of reflex control over acts. Only following this could they be incorporated into a programme of instrumental action. This view has been challenged by Zelazo (1976), who argues that reflexes do not disappear but instead are incorporated into a hierarchy of controlled behaviour. The case is that the child develops the capacity to control reflexes, that is to activate as well as inhibit them, and they are then incorporated into a smoother, less stereotyped system of action.

Easton (1972) has perhaps gone furthest in suggesting that reflexes may underlie all volitional movements. In support of his view that reflexes, or co-ordinative structures as he calls them, provide the basic elements from which voluntary movements are constructed, he cites a number of observations. For example, that the tonic neck reflexes may be activated to aid voluntary effort (Hellebrandt, Schade, & Carns, 1962). The tonic neck reflex biases movement in the direction of gaze, and a shift in attention may thus elicit a reflex which permits a complex adjustment in direction without changing the organization of the reflexes involved. A sharply contrasting position is that adopted by Touwen (1978) who, in discussing sensorimotor development in infancy, argues that the reflex concept is an inappropriate basis on which to build an explanation of voluntary action. Touwen cites Sherrington's (1906) statement that a reflex is an artificial abstraction, and much of the disagreement may centre on the conception of a reflex. Leaving aside the suitability of the reflex as a "building block" for normal voluntary motor behaviour, there is no doubt that the nervous system possesses intrinsic properties which provide the basis for skilled movement. What these substrates are is a vitally important question which remains to be answered.

A possibility which has been largely overlooked in the heat of argument is that voluntary actions may emerge concurrently with and independently of the maturation of reflex functions. The evidence suggests that some instrumental activities are present from birth (for example eye movements and sucking) and others may be possible but occur infrequently because of central nervous system immaturity. A class of behaviours known for some time but which has attracted relatively little attention are the so-called rhythmical stereotypies. Gesell (1954) considered rocking to be a stage in prone progression, and Piaget (1952) labelled the infant's kicking and arm-waving movements "secondary circular reactions". Kravitz and Boehm (1971) suggested from their study of rhythmic habit patterns in infancy that these responses may provide a means of gaining more information about the maturation and development of motor skills. Thelen (1979), in an important and detailed study of these rhythmical movements over the first year of life, identified 47 patterns involving the legs, torso, head, arms and fingers. The responses were found to exhibit developmental regularities, as well as general constancy in form and distribution. Different groups of stereotypies had characteristic ages of onset, peak performance and decline. Also, the onset of stereotypies was found to be positively correlated with scores on the Bayley scales, the onset of stereotypies being predictive of the speed of motor development.

Although called stereotypies, perhaps unfortunately because of other connotations, the behaviours do show inter-individual differences and variation in their developmental course. Also, there is no reason to doubt that more detailed examination would reveal a rich variety in expression of the behaviours. Thelen (1980) has suggested, in a study searching for what determines the amount of stereotyped behaviour in normal infants, that they may be related to the amount of vestibular stimulation received, an interesting link with the work reported by Clark et al. (1977). These rhythmical behaviours appear to be quite characteristic movement patterns generated by the nervous system, and presumably they reflect the maturation of particular neuromuscular pathways. Are they an important step in the development of voluntary goal-directed activity? Their association with the emergence of voluntary actions, which Thelen's work reveals, indicates that they may well be. Indeed what they do suggest is the existence of central motor programmes (see Stein, 1978) capable of providing at least the initial temporal and topographical specifications necessary for the great range of skilled motor actions of which we become capable.

Our conception of the nervous system has changed dramatically over the past 25 years: we no longer see it as basically quiescent, becoming active only when stimulated by environmental events. It is a characteristic of the nervous system to generate activity, and our contemporary picture is of a complex hierarchy of simple movements which provide the elementary substrate for postural control and co-ordinated movement. Skilled motor actions involve the hierarchical recruitment and deployment of components into orchestrated programmes of goal-directed action. Much remains to be learned about the maturation of the nervous system and how behavioural development maps onto the changes; we are seeking to discover general rules of organisation and operation and not a Platonic ideal. What the building blocks of skilled action are is still the subject of controversy, but there are significant pointers which should be followed up by both biological and psychological investigations.

REFERENCES

Ames, L. B. (1937). The sequential patterning of prone progression in the human infant. *Genetic Psychology Monographs, 19,* 409–460.

Barton, S., Birns, B. & Ronch, J. (1971). Individual differences in the visual pursuit behaviour of neonates. *Child Development, 42,* 313–319.

Bayley, N. (1935). Development of motor abilities during the first three years. *Monographs of Society for Research in Child Development, 1.*

Bayley, N. (1965). Comparisons of mental and motor test scores for ages 1–15 months by sex, birth order, race, geographical location and education of parents. *Child Development, 36,* 379–411.

Bayley, N., (1969). *Manual for the Bayley scales of infant development*. New York: Psychological Corporation.

Bower, T. G. R. (1972). Object perception in infants. *Perception, 1,* 15–30.

Bower, T. G. R. (1974). *Development in infancy*. San Francisco: Freeman.

Bower, T. G. R., Broughton, J. M. & Moore, M. K. (1970a). Demonstration of intention in the reaching behaviour of neonate humans. *Nature, 228,* 679–681.

Bower, T. G. R., Broughton, J. M. & Moore, M. K. (1970b). The co-ordination of visual and tactual input in infants. *Perception and Psychophysics, 8,* 51–53.

Brody, D. (1937). Twin resemblances in mechanical ability, with reference to the effects of practice on performance. *Child Development, 8,* 207–216.

Bruner, J. S. & Bruner, B. M. (1968). On voluntary action and its hierarchical structure. *International Journal of Psychology, 3,* 239–255.

Bruner, J. S. & Koslowski, B. (1972). Visually preadapted constituents of manipulatory action. *Perception, 1,* 3–12.

Burnett, C. N. & Johnson, E. (1971). Development of gait in childhood, I & II. *Developmental Medicine and Child Neurology, 13,* 196–206, 207–215.

Burnside, H. L. (1927). Coordination in the locomotion of infants. *Genetic Psychology Monographs, 2,* 279–372.

Bryant, G. M., Davies, K. J., Richards, F. M. & Voorhees, S. (1973). A preliminary study of the use of the Denver Developmental Screening Test in a health department. *Developmental Medicine and Child Neurology, 15,* 33–40.

Bryant, G. M., Davies, K. J. & Newcombe, R. G. (1979). Standardisation of the Denver Developmental Screening Test for Cardiff children. *Developmental Medicine and Child Neurology, 21,* 353–364.

Camp, B. W., van Doorninck, W. J., Frankenburg, W. K. & Lampe, J. M. (1977). Preschool developmental testing in prediction of school problems. Studies of 55 children in Denver. *Clinical Pediatrics, 16,* 257–263.

Casaer, P. (1979). Postural behaviour in newborn infants. *Clinics in Developmental Medicine, No. 72.* London: S.I.M.P. with Heinemann; Philadelphia: Lippincott.

Clark, D. L., Kreutzberg, J. R. & Chee, F. K. W. (1977). Vestibular stimulation influence on motor development in infants. *Science, 196,* 1228–1229.

Connolly, K. J. (1970). Skill development: Problems and plans. In K. J. Connolly (Ed.), *Mechanisms of motor skill development*. London: Academic Press, pp. 3–24.

Connolly, K. J. (1973). Factors influencing the learning of manual skills by young children. In R. A. Hinde & J. S. Hinde (Eds), *Constraints on learning*. London: Academic Press.

Connolly, K. J. & Elliott, J. M. (1972). Evolution and ontogeny of hand function. In N. Blurton Jones (Ed.), *Ethological studies of child behaviour*. London: Cambridge University Press, p. 329.

Connolly, K. J., Pharoah, P. O. D. & Hetzel, B. S. (1979). Fetal iodine deficiency and motor performance during childhood, *Lancet, 2,* 1149–1151.

Corballis, M. C. & Morgan, M. J. (1978). On the biological basis of human laterality: I. Evidence for a maturational left-right gradient. *Behavioral and Brain Sciences, 2,* 261–269.

DiFranco, D., Muir, D. W. & Dodwell, P. C. (1978). Reaching in very young infants. *Perception, 7,* 385–392.

Dodwell, P. C., Muir, D. & DiFranco, D. (1976). Responses of infants to visually presented objects. *Science, 194,* 209–211.

Easton, T. A. (1972). On the normal use of reflexes. *American Scientist, 60,* 591–599.

Francis-Williams, J. & Yule, W. (1967). The Bayley Scales of Motor and Mental Development: An exploratory study with an English sample. *Developmental Medicine and Child Neurology, 9,* 391–401.

Frankenburg, W. K. & Dodds, J. B. (1967). The Denver Developmental Screening Test. *Journal of Pediatrics, 71,* 181–191.

Freedman, D. (1965). An ethological approach to the genetical study of human behaviour. In S. G. Vandenberg. *Methods and goals in human behavior genetics*. New York: Academic Press.

Geber, M. & Dean, R. F. A. (1957). Gesell tests on African children. *Pediatrics, 20,* 1055–1065.

Gesell, A. (1954). The ontogeny of infant behavior. In L. Carmichael (Ed.), *Manual of child psychology, 2nd. edn.* New York: Wiley.

Gesell, A. & Amatruda, C. (1947). *Developmental diagnosis, 2nd edn.* New York: Harper & Row.

Haidvogl, M. (1979). Dissociation of maturation: A distinct syndrome of delayed motor development. *Developmental Medicine and Child Neurology, 21,* 52–57.

Halverson, H. M. (1931). An experimental study of prehension in infants by means of systematic cinema records. *Genetic Psychology Monographs, 10,* 107–286.

Halverson, H. M. (1937). Studies of the grasping responses of early infancy, I, II & III. *Journal of Genetic Psychology, 51.* 371–392, 393–424, 425–449.

Hein, A., Held, R. & Gower, E. C. (1970). Development and segmentation of visually controlled movement by selective exposure during rearing. *Journal of Comparative and Physiological Psychology, 73,* 181–187.

Hellebrandt, F. A., Schade, M. & Carns, M. L. (1962). Methods of evoking the tonic neck reflexes in human subjects. *American Journal of Physical Medicine, 41,* 90–139.

Hindley, C. B. (1968). Growing up in five countries: A comparison of data on weaning, elimination training, age of walking and I.Q. in relation to social class from European longitudinal studies. *Developmental Medicine and Child Neurology, 10,* 715–724.

von Hofsten, C. (1979). Development of visually directed reaching: The approach phase. *Journal of Human Movement Studies, 5,* 160–178.

von Hofsten, C. & Lindhagan, K. (1979). Observations on the development of reaching for moving objects. *Journal of Experimental Child Psychology, 28,* 158–173.

Hooker, D. (1938). The origin of the grasping movement in man. *Proceedings of the American Philosophical Society, 79,* 597–606.

Hooker, D. (1952). *The prenatal origin of behavior.* Lawrence: University of Kansas Press.

Hoorweg, J. & Stanfield, J. P. (1976). The effects of protein energy malnutrition in early childhood on intellectual and motor abilities in later childhood and adolescence. *Developmental Medicine and Child Neurology, 18,* 330–350.

Humphrey, T. (1969). Postnatal repetition of human prenatal activity sequences with some suggestions of their neuroanatomical basis. In R. J. Robinson (Ed.), *Brain and early behaviour: Development in the fetus and infant.* London: Academic Press.

Kaye, H. (1967). Infant sucking behaviour and its modification. In L. P. Lipsitt & C. C. Spiker (Eds), *Advances in child development and behavior. Vol. 3.* New York: Academic Press.

Kravitz, H. & Boehm, J. (1971). Rhythmic habit patterns in infancy: Their sequences, age of onset and frequency. *Child Development, 42,* 399–413.

Lasky, R. E. (1977). The effect of visual feedback of the hand on the reaching and retrieval behavior of young infants. *Child Development, 48,* 112–117.

Lundberg, A. (1979). Dissociated motor development: Developmental patterns, clinical characteristics, causal factors and outcome, with special reference to late walking children. *Neuropädiatrie, 10,* 161–182.

McDonnell, P. M. (1975). The development of visually guided reaching. *Perception and Psychophysics, 18,* 181–185.

McDonnell, P. M. (1979). Patterns of eye-hand coordination in the first year of life. *Canadian Journal of Psychology, 33,* 253–267.

McGraw, M. B. (1941). Development of neuromuscular mechanisms as reflected in the crawling and creeping behavior of the human infant. *Journal of Genetic Psychology, 58,* 83–111.

McGraw, M. B. & Breeze, K.W. (1941). Quantitative studies in the development of erect locomotion. *Child Development, 12,* 267–303.

McNemar, Q. (1933). Twin resemblances in motor skills and the effects of practice thereon. *Journal of Genetic Psychology, 42,* 70–97.

Monckeberg, F. (1968). Effect of early marasmic malnutrition on subsequent physical and psychological development. In N. S. Scrimshaw, & J. E. Gordon (Eds), *Malnutrition, learning and behavior.* Cambridge, Mass.: MIT Press.

Neligan, G. & Prudham, D. (1969). Norms for four standard developmental milestones by sex, social class and place in family. *Developmental Medicine and Child Neurology, 11,* 413–422.

Piaget, J. (1952). *The origins of intelligence in children.* London: Routledge & Kegan Paul.

Rosenblith, J. F. (1966). Prognostic value of neonatal assessment. *Child Development, 37,* 623–631.

Ruff, H. A. & Halton, A. (1978). Is there directed reaching in the human neonate? *Developmental Psychology, 14,* 425–426.

de Schonen, S. (1977). Functional asymmetries in the development of bimanual co-ordination in human infants. *Journal of Human Movement Studies, 3,* 144–156.

Scrutton, D. R. (1969). Footprint sequences of normal children under five years old. *Developmental Medicine and Child Neurology, 11,* 44–53.

Sherrington, C. S. (1906). *The integrative action of the nervous system.* London: Constable.

Shirley, M. M. (1931). *The first two years: A study of twenty-five babies. Vol. 1. Postural and locomotor development.* Minneapolis: University of Minnesota Press.

Solomons, G. (1980). Standardisation of the Bayley Motor Scale of infant development in Yucatan, Mexico. *Developmental Medicine and Child Neurology, 22,* 580–587.

Solomons, G. & Solomons, H. C. (1964). Factors affecting motor performance in four-month-old-infants. *Child Development, 35,* 1283–1295.

Solomons, G. & Solomons, H. C. (1975). Motor development in Yucatecan infants. *Developmental Medicine and Child Neurology, 17,* 41–46.

Statham, L. & Murray, M. (1971). Early walking patterns of normal children. *Clinical Orthopedics, 79.* 8–24.

Stein, P. S. G. (1978). Motor systems, with specific reference to the control of locomotion. *Annual Review of Neurosciences, 1,* 61–81.

Super, C. M. (1976). Environmental effects on motor development: The case of "African infant precocity". *Developmental Medicine and Child Neurology, 18,* 561–567.

Sutherland, D. H., Olshen, R., Cooper, L. & Woo, S. L. Y. (1980). Development of mature gait. *Journal of Bone and Joint Surgery, 62A,* 336–353.

Thelen, E. (1979). Rhythmical stereotypies in normal human infants. *Animal Behaviour, 27,* 699–715.

Thelen, E. (1980). Determinants of amounts of stereotyped behaviour in normal human infants. *Ethology and Sociobiology, 1,* 141–150.

Touwen, B. C. L. (1971). A study on the development of some motor phenomena in infancy. *Developmental Medicine and Child Neurology, 13,* 435–446.

Touwen, B. C. L. (1976). *Neurological development in infancy. Clinics in developmental medicine, No. 58.* London: S.I.M.P. with Heinemann; Philadelphia: Lippincott.

Touwen, B. C. L. (1978). Variability and stereotypy in normal and deviant development. In. J. Apley (Ed.), *Care of the handicapped child. Clinics in developmental medicine, No. 67.* London: S.I.M.P. with Heinemann; Philadelphia: Lippincott.

Twitchell, T. (1965). The automatic grasping responses of infants. *Neuropsychologia, 3,* 247–259.

Twitchell, T. (1970). Reflex mechanisms and the development of prehension. In K. J. Connolly (Ed.), *Mechanisms of motor skill development.* London: Academic Press. pp. 25–62.

Ueda, R. (1978). Child development in Okinawa compared with Tokyo and Denver, and the implications for developmental screening. *Developmental Medicine and Child Neurology, 20,* 657–663.

Warren, N. (1972). African infant precocity. *Psychological Bulletin, 78,* 353–367.

Werner, E. E. (1972). Infants around the world, cross-cultural studies of psychomotor development from birth to two years. *Journal of Cross-Cultural Psychology, 3,* 111–134.

White, B.L., Castle, P. & Held, R. (1964). Observations on the development of visually directed reaching. *Child Development, 35,* 349–364.

Wyke, B. (1975). The neurological basis of movement. In K. S. Holt (Ed.), *Movement and child development. Clinics in developmental medicine, No. 55.* London: S.I.M.P. with Heinemann; Philadelphia: Lippincot, pp. 19–23.

Zelazo, P. R. (1976). From reflexive to instrumental behaviour. In L. P. Lipsitt (Ed.), *Developmental Psychobiology.* Hillsdale, N.J.: Lawrence Erlbaum Associates Inc.

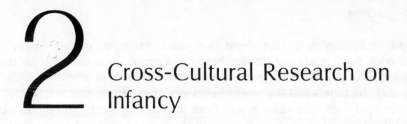

Cross-Cultural Research on Infancy

Charles M. Super

[. . .]

INTRODUCTION

The concept of infancy and the behavioral growth that characterizes it both have a strong central core in all cultures; at the same time, they are differentially sculpted in different contexts. Around the world, newborn babies enter life as the intense but relatively private focus of attention of a small number of people. They come equipped with essentially the same biological and social skills. In the succeeding months, they exhibit the same profound developments in their ability to attend to, understand, predict, engage, and manipulate their physical and social environment. They move, metaphorically, from organ to organism, from animal to human; along the way they pass markers apparently recognized by most societies. Around 3 or 4 months, for example, they "become a real person" to the American mother, and in Western Kenya the Kipsigis mother stops calling her baby a "monkey".

Nevertheless, children emerge from infancy as distinctly Irish, Egyptian, Rajput, Korean, Fijian, Yanamamo, Iroquois, or Azande, in their sounds and actions, their needs and skills. The concept of infancy is culturally divergent also. The English word "infant" is derived from Latin roots meaning without speech, and in their minds and textbooks most Europeans (including those transplanted to North America and other former colonies)

Source: Triandis, H. C. & Heron, A. (1981). *Handbook of Cross-Cultural Psychology, Vol. 4*. Boston: Allyn & Bacon.

think of infancy as lasting about two years. After this period, infantile behavior, such as wetting clothes, becomes a social embarrassment for the parents. Among the Kipsigis, however, infancy ends at about one year, roughly the time when the motor behaviors of particular parental interest are in operation. The child is safe from jealous witchcraft. The mother is no longer *saloita*, a "new mother," and she is freed from various prescriptions and proscriptions. A ritual traditionally marks the period of change.

This chapter is a brief review of the research literature on infant motor, mental, and social development outside of European, or Western, culture. Despite technical shortcomings in much of the work, we can sketch the major contours of initial status at birth, the emergence of important milestones, and variations in style, content, and use that appear around the universally developing abilities. Before applying the psychologist's microscope to particular behaviors, however, it is worthwhile taking a step backward to use the anthropologist's telescope. Infancy, when one inspects the obvious, does not exist in isolation. It is necessarily and profoundly enmeshed with other aspects of the culture, synchronically with the niche that is structured by daily life, and diachronically with events in the life cycle.

THE INTEGRATION OF INFANCY WITH THE LARGER CULTURE

Infancy has been of interest to anthropologists for two reasons. Historically their basic task has been the comprehensive description of life in other cultures, and classical ethnographies usually provide some information on infancy. Material artifacts such as cradleboards, or rituals such as those surrounding childbirth or kinship alignment provided common anchor points. As anthropological theory came to focus on individuals as the carriers of culture, however, the field of culture and personality emerged (Harris, 1968). The pioneering work of Mead (1930; Bateson & Mead, 1942) reflected the growing concern with the early acquisition of culture. During the formative years of psychological anthropology, as "culture and personality" has become, psychoanalytic theory was the most promising approach to understanding the effects of early experience. A number of studies attempted to link the typical child's socialization in a culture to the modal adult personality (Kardiner, 1944). The multicultural comparisons by Whiting and Child (1953) were seminal, both for their incorporation of learning theory and for their statistical method in which each culture provides a data point.

The integrative power of culture, connecting and structuring all aspects of human behavior, is the theoretical cornerstone of social anthropology; in the subdiscipline of psychological anthropology, John and Beatrice Whiting have drawn a developmental model for psychocultural studies that includes this perspective (J. Whiting, 1977). The physical environment and historical circumstances are seen in this theory to determine a society's maintenance systems, which include the social structure, economy, and household type. These maintenance systems, in conjunction with historically shaped value systems (Whiting, Chasdi, Antonovsky & Ayres, 1966), influence the number and identity of caretakers, feeding schedules, children's tasks, techniques of discipline, and other aspects of the child's environment (Barry & Paxson, 1971). Le Vine (1969; 1974; 1977) has elaborated the role of cultural values of the adults as both expressive and adaptive mediators of child care, and many variations can be found in the literature. Some groups, for example the Kwoma of New Guinea (Whiting, 1971) and Zinacantecans of Mexico (Brazelton, Robey & Collier, 1969), have conceptions of the dangers of witchcraft that influence the way they keep their infants close and private. Cultures differ in their typical view of the fragility of the newborn (de Vries & Super, 1979), the "naturalness" of crying (Rebelsky, 1973), and the value of encouraging babies in particular skills (Blount, 1972; Harkness & Super, 1977; Super, 1976).

The Whitings' theory, in agreement with most psychological views, postulates that the transaction between the environment, as previously described, and the universal, innate nature of human growth and development produces the personality and skills of the adult. Finally, adult personality is seen in psychological anthropology to contribute to the culture's projective-expressive systems, including religious and magical beliefs, rituals, art, recreation, and elements of folk theories of child development (Le Vine, 1980).

The issue of long-term consequences of variations in child care lies at the heart of traditional theory in both psychology and anthropology. Ethnographic studies of single societies often draw qualitative connections that are consonant with the long-standing Western belief in the unique importance of early experience. Spiro (1953), for example, draws a series of parallels between Ifaluk beliefs about ghosts who can both cause and cure sickness, on the one hand, and on the other the Ifaluk infant's experience of generally warm and permissive care during infancy, traumatically punctuated by morning baths in the very cold lagoon, and ended by severe rejection at the arrival of a new sibling.

Cross-cultural studies, in the narrow sense, have elaborated this line of inquiry by searching for statistically reliable relationships between a culture's typical infant care and adult projective-expressive systems. The Whiting and Child work (1953) on personality defenses has been mentioned. In addition, infant socialization has been related to the perceived nature of the gods (Lambert, Triandis & Wolf, 1959; Spiro & D'Andrade, 1958); common games (Barry & Roberts, 1972); musical rhythms (Ayres, 1973); physical violence (Prescott, 1975); and several aspects of adult mental functioning (Munroe, Munroe, & Whiting, 1973; Zern, 1970; 1972).

It remains to integrate this tradition in anthropology with more recent advances in lifespan psychology and the continuing debate about the long-term effects of early experience in humans (Clarke & Clarke, 1976). After all, a substantial amount of development intervenes between infancy and adulthood, and a variety of conditions can lead to continuity or discontinuity. These conditions could in theory include innate and stable neonatal dispositions that covary with mating group, for example genetic differences (Freedman, 1974); persistence of learned dispositions (Du Bois, 1944); lasting, environmentally induced effects on biological systems, such as hormones (Landauer & Whiting, 1964); sensitization to relearning (Campbell & Spear, 1972); stability in the environmental circumstances that elicit or structure particular behaviors (Super & Harkness, in press b); maturationally controlled behavioral transformations (e.g., changes at adolescence); arbitrary but socially patterned behavioral standards (Kagan & Moss, 1962); and institutionally imposed efforts to affect the course of development, such as schooling or initiation rites (Super & Harkness, in press a).

Even though several of these possibilities have been used to explain patterns of cultural variation in development, there is to date no concerted attempt to reevaluate the anthropological literature with regard to long-term mechanisms in developmental continuity and change. Anthropological theory, in short, has not caught up with the past two decades of developmental psychology. The particular advantage of an anthropological perspective applied to the study of infancy, on the other hand, highlights integrative and systematic aspects of the physical, social, and cultural environment that are often difficult to see from a monocultural position (Harkness, 1980). Recent publications by Chisholm (1980), Landau (1976), and Super and Harkness (in press b) present divergent uses of this larger perspective. As American psychology more generally awakens to the outside world, and as anthropology increasingly recognizes the advances in other disciplines, one can expect a greater frequency of transdisciplinary studies of infancy and infant development.

MOTOR DEVELOPMENT

A substantial portion of cross-cultural research on infancy is concerned with motor development; that is, with the attainment of motor milestones such as rolling over, the finger-thumb pincer grip, sitting, and walking. This reflects, in part, the early development in Western psychology of formal tests for these skills, and perhaps also their high visibility to the itinerant researcher who may fail to see more subtle aspects of behavior. A strong and recurring theme in this literature is the "precocity" of babies from traditional, nonindustrial societies: they may sit or stand, on the average, two, four, or more weeks before European and American norms. Particularly in the African case, this has been linked at times to reports of precocity at birth. A review of the current literature, however, indicates that, in fact, only some behaviors are advanced and they constitute a variable cluster that depends, at least primarily, on environmental factors.

Motor Behavior at Birth

Shortly after Geber's initial studies of advanced motor behaviors by Ugandan infants, reviewed in the following, she and Dean reported that the typical newborn in a Kampala hospital was comparable in level of maturity to a European infant of 4 to 6 weeks (Geber & Dean, 1957a). The frequent absence of primitive reflex activity was particularly significant, since the startle, Babinski, grasping, and several other reflexes are thought to disappear from the European infant's behavioral repertoire through inhibition by the rapidly maturing, higher cortical areas of the brain. These results fit smoothly enough with the picture of development initially described for the following months, and with other theories and preconceptions, that they were quickly accepted by many psychologists.

In retrospect, the Geber and Dean report is so flawed with regard to choice and administration of examination procedures, use of comparison groups, and data analysis and reporting that it is no longer convincing (Super, 1980; Warren, 1972). More importantly, several later studies have found no difference in neurological maturity between African groups and Euro-American norms or comparison samples. Warren and Parkin's study (1974), also carried out in Kampala, is the most thorough and it challenges both the facts and logic of the original report. The normal presence of neonatal reflexes has also been found by Griffiths (1969), Konner (1972), Freedman (1974), Vouilloux (1959a), Brazelton, Koslowski, and Tronick (1976), Keefer, Dixon, Tronick, and Brazelton (1978), and Super (unpublished data), using samples from South Africa, Botswana, Nigeria, Cameroon, Zambia, and Kenya. The very few reports that do not clearly support this view lack sufficient detail for adequate interpretation (Vincent & Hugon, 1962).

Some debate remains about possible qualitative differences in motor behavior between African and Caucasian newborns. Although the reports are not fully consistent, several researchers have characterized African infants as having greater muscular or postural strength, coordination, or control. The clearest report is by Keefer, Dixon, Tronick, and Brazelton (1978), who used the Brazelton Neonatal Assessment Scale (NBAS) to study Gusii newborns in a modernizing rural district in Western Kenya. They found superior muscle tone and control, as indicated by relatively smooth arcs of arm movements and strong, but not hypertonic tone in response to the examination. This characterization bears some similarity to Geber and Dean's (1957a) report of lesser flexion and less hypertonicity in Ugandan neonates, a finding that Warren and Parkin (1974) did not replicate. Coll, Sepkoski, and Lester (1978) found higher scores for a sample of American blacks on a summary scale that includes amount of hand-to-mouth activity and defensive movements to a cloth being put over the face. An earlier report, using different procedures, found no black-white differences in muscular tension, but did yield higher black scores on a summary that included motor reflexes (e.g., grasp, head turn), defensive reactions, and perceptual orienting items (Graham, Matarazzo, & Caldwell, 1956). In London, Hopkins (1978) reports black West Indian infants to be superior to a white English sample in general muscular tone and postural control.

There is no ready explanation for the pattern of specific differences and similarities in motor performance found in these studies. Given the methodological complexities of newborn testing, especially in non-Western settings, it has not been established what characteristics, if any, are particular to the "motoric style" of African babies. Since so many prenatal and perinatal factors can influence behavior in the first days of life, such as birth order, maternal anxiety, and routines of early care, and since few studies involve the same mating groups, the complexity of interpreting any result is formidable (Lester & Brazelton, in press; Super, 1980).

Outside Africa, there are only scattered reports of newborn motor behavior. In general, they find no group differences, lack meaningful data to support a claim of differences, or have failed to replicate. One possible exception is a set of studies from Latin America. In rural Guatemala, Ladino newborns were found to be lacking vigor and were disorganized in their motor behavior, which the authors attributed to the mothers' poor nutritional state. This interpretation is supported by a correlation within the sample between the socioeconomic background and level of motor organization (Brazelton, Tronick, Lechtig, Lasky, & Klein, 1977; Lasky, Lechtig, Delgado, Klein, Engle, Yarbrough, & Martorell, 1975). However, Coll, Sepkoski, and Lester (1977; 1978) tested infants of normal medical, and presumably nutritional, status in Puerto Rico and Florida, and also found the Puerto Rican newborns to be relatively low in motor maturity and muscle tone. Brazelton, Robey, and Collier (1969) (also Brazelton, 1972; 1977) examined five Zinacantecan neonates in the southern highlands of Mexico. They were similar to Caucasian-American infants in motor behaviors elicited by the examiner, such as being pulled up to a sitting position, but their spontaneous activity seemed more "fluid" and subdued in quality. Even though some writers have related this latter finding, as a population trait, to later motor development (see next section), it is also consistent with the picture presented by de Vries and Super (1979) as a probable outcome of testing in dark, quiet homes instead of in the standard hospital nursery context.

Motor Development After Birth

As indicated earlier, there is significant variation in the achievement of motor milestones among, as there is within, human groups. In accord with tradition, motor scores on the standard tests have usually been summed into Developmental Quotients, and scores over 100 were naturally given the traditional interpretation of precocity in the rate of motor development. More recent work has related the pattern of item attainment to specific environmental conditions, in a sense indicating the cultural bias of Developmental Quotients as a general measure of rate of growth. The majority of this work has been done in Africa, where enough environmental information is available to make the argument most clearly.

Despite serious methodological flaws in many of the studies (Super, 1980; Warren, 1972), it is now well established that African babies reared in relatively traditional ways achieve a variety of motor milestones, especially in the first year, before their European and American peers. The initial studies were by Geber and Dean in Uganda (Geber, 1956; 1958a; 1958b; 1958c; 1960; 1962; 1973; 1974; Geber & Dean, 1957b; 1958; 1964). At least partially similar results have been found in other Ugandan samples, as well as in Kenya, Tanzania, Zambia, Madagascar, Botswana, South Africa, Cameroon, Guinea, Nigeria, the Ivory Coast, and Senegal (Ainsworth, 1967; Kilbride, Robbins & Kilbride, 1970; Kilbride, 1976; Leiderman, Babu, Kagia, Kraemer, & Leiderman, 1973; Leiderman & Leiderman, 1974a; 1974b; 1977; Ssengoba, 1978; Super, 1973; 1976; Varkevisser, 1973; Goldberg, 1972; 1977; Konner, 1976; 1977; Ramarasaona, 1959; Liddicoat, 1969; Liddicoat & Griesel, 1971; Vouilloux, 1959a; 1959b; Naidr, 1975; Durojaiye, personal communication; Mundy-Castle & Okonji, 1978; Poole, 1969; Dasen, Inhelder, Lavallée, & Retschitzki, 1978; Bardet, Massé, Moreigne, & Senecal, 1960; Faladé, 1955; 1960; Lusk & Lewis, 1972; Moreigne, 1970; Valantin, 1970).

The skills on which African infants are most advanced, it appears, are the ones in which they have considerably more practice than American infants. There are qualitative reports of deliberate "teaching" of walking and sitting in a variety of African groups; for example, the Baganda of Uganda (Kilbride & Kilbride, 1975), the Wolof of Senegal (Faladé, 1955), and the Yoruba of Nigeria (Mundy-Castle & Okonji, 1978). Quantitative measures from individual interviews and observations in several East African groups indicate that a great majority of mothers think such teaching is important, and that the mothers or sibling caretakers are likely actually to carry out the practice every day in the few months before the particular skill is expected (Super, 1976). The training procedure, which may or may not have a unique name, consists of structured practice for the baby, such as providing cloth props while sitting or holding the baby's hands while standing. In addition to deliberate training, a number of traditional child care routines unintentionally provide practice. Among the Kipsigis of Kenya, for example, infants spend over 60 percent of their waking time sitting, often in someone's lap. This is considerably more often than a sample from metropolitan Boston (Super, 1976). Riding on the caretaker's back, another common position, likewise develops trunk, buttock, and thigh muscles more than does reclining in an American infant seat.

Less frequently, it seems, is there traditional support for prone behaviors. It is less often specifically taught, and since African babies are rarely lying down while awake (e.g., 10 percent Kipsigis vs. 30 percent Boston), they have less opportunity for incidental practice. Correspondingly, African infants are less often precocious in crawling, turning over, and other prone behaviors. This has been reported for the Baganda (Kilbride, 1976), the !Kung San (Konner, 1976), the Kipsigis (Super, 1976), and the Kikuyu (Leiderman, personal communication).

A causal interpretation of this patterning is supported by two kinds of reports. The logically weaker studies are correlational, in which the average age at crawling, for example, in a sample of societies is correlated with quantitative estimates of deliberate and incidental support. Super (1976) reports high cultural correlations of this sort, when there is adequate variation among groups. The more rigorous studies are experimental and indicate that specific training procedures, well within the species' normal range of experience, can significantly lower the age of walking and crawling in European and American samples, in some cases with a carry-over effect to other skills (Lagerspetz, Nygard, & Strandvik, 1971; Zelazo, Zelazo, & Kolb, 1972).

Attention to the patterning of item attainment in conjunction with the specifically relevant, environmentally orchestrated experiences contributes to the resolution of contradictory reports concerning the effects of culture change. Some studies have noted that infants from "modern," "elite," "urban," or "educated" families may not show advancement in the rate of motor development (Geber, 1956; 1958a; Super, 1976; Varkevisser, 1973; Vouilloux, 1959a; 1959b). This would be understandable if the daily care and training of infants in these families resembled the Euro-American pattern. Super (1976) provides evidence that this can be so. A few investigators (Poole, 1969) find no relationship between gross indicators of Westernization and motor development, and others (Janes, 1975; Leiderman et al., 1973) report higher scores in the less traditional families. Lacking specific information about the relevant environmental variables, it is not possible to re-evaluate each case, but there is no reason to think that conditions promoting early motor skills necessarily co-occur with economic or educational indices, especially under the variety of conditions that exist today in changing Africa. Super (1976) illustrates this with data from the village in which Leiderman et al. (1973) found infants from less affluent families to have lower motor scores: these families said they were less likely to give their babies special practice in walking and sitting.

For reasons that are not clear, standard psychometric tests of motor development usually contain more items sampling skills in which African babies are likely to receive practice than ones that are not particularly promoted. For progress in sitting and walking, for example, each skill has six items on the Bayley Motor Scale in the first year, compared to one for crawling. Consequently, these tests yield high Developmental Quotients in Africa, in the first 12 to 18 months. Changes in the content of motor tests accounts for a subsequent decline, and the cultural bias becomes more obvious. Walking items now include such skills as walking backwards, which is not particularly valued in traditional Africa; the rural child who has never seen a cup before may be less likely initially to drink from one. After weaning, nutrition, infectious disease, and parasites may become serious problems in some samples (e.g., Bardet et al., 1960; Ssengoba, 1978). Although the evidence is not as thorough on this point, it appears that healthy infants from urban, educated families show little decline after two years, with respect to Euro-American norms, as well as little precocity before age two (Geber, 1956).

Studies of motor development in Asia and the Americas indicate a similar picture of relatively rapid attainment of motor milestones in early infancy, accompanied by physically stimulating care, and followed by a relative decline. Within this generalization, however, significant variations in the timing and patterning of precocity and delay are reported. The level of documentation is not as complete as for Africa, especially with regard to the environmental factors that are implicated by the African work.

Babies from a range of social and economic levels in India have been shown to have developmental quotients well above 100 in the first year or two (Das & Sharma, 1973; Patel & Kaul, 1971; Phatak, 1969; 1970a; 1970b). There are some differences among subgroups (rural/urban; economic level) in the timing of decline in scores relative to American norms, and in the patterning of particular skills. Qualitative comments on infant care, in these groups and elsewhere in India, suggest the presence of both inadvertent support (e.g., back-carrying) and deliberate stimulation, by massage, of some aspects of motor development (Hopkins, 1976; Leboyer, 1976). There are, however, no quantitative figures that can be related to the modest discrepancies among Indian reports or to their common contrast with other groups.

Shorter periods of high Developmental Quotients occur in groups that appear to receive less stimulation. In Mysore, India, Venkatachar (Phatak,

1970a) found advancement in only two early motor areas, lasting six months, among infants from families who were economically advantaged and who, one can thus speculate, may have modified their care routines toward more Western models. In Guatemala (Wug de Leon, De Licardie, & Cravioto, 1964), sitting and prehension were found to be advanced in the early months, while later locomotion was delayed. Solomons and Solomons (1975) report a similar pattern in three Mexican samples and related the patterning to their observations on frequency of mothers' carrying the infants and discouraging independent activity on the cold or dirty floors. Low levels of stimulation and maternal emphasis on keeping infants calm and quiet have been related to relatively slow motor development in Southern Mexico, Guatemala, and Japan (Brazelton, Robey, & Collier, 1969; Arai, Ishikawa, & Toshima, 1958; Kagan & Klein, 1973). Other variations among ethnic groups have been reported for groups living in Hawaii, also attributed to child-rearing practices (Werner, Bierman, & French, 1971; Werner, Simonian, & Smith, 1968), and in Israel, where generational differences, corresponding to acculturation, support a similar interpretation (Ivanans, 1975; Palti, Gitlin, & Zloto, 1977).

Does the patterning of environmental stimulation account for all the variation among samples, or could the patterning be imposed on a more general advancement in some cases? One line of evidence suggests that a general advance in motor development may be possible. Experimental work with both laboratory animals and human beings demonstrates that "handling," mild stresses, and particular kinds of physical stimulation can substantially contribute to development. The most dramatic demonstration with human beings was made by Clark, Kreutzberg, and Chee (1977). They gave infants spinning rides in an office swivel chair, at a moderate speed, for a total of 80 minutes over a period of four weeks; the subjects subsequently showed advanced reflexive and gross motor behavior in comparison with a control group. Vigorous passive exercise such as stretching and massaging is given to infants in a number of African and Asian groups (Hopkins, 1976), and their daily life of being handled and carried probably constitutes a long-term analogue. Some comparative data are available on physical contact, presumably a rough index of tactile, vestibular, and muscular stimulation, and they indicate significantly higher levels in preindustrial samples. In the last half of the first year, for example, American infants are in body contact with another person about 30 percent of their waking hours, while comparable figures for Kipsigis (Kenya), !Kung (Botswana), Fijian, and Mayan (Guatemala) infants are about 60, 65, 57, and 64 percent (Super, 1980; Konner, 1973; Katz, personal communication; Rogoff, personal communication).

MENTAL DEVELOPMENT

Tools from the three major approaches to mental development in infancy have been applied in cross-cultural studies: (1) the traditional psychometric "baby tests"; (2) scales derived from Piaget's theory; and (3) measures of infants' visual attention to particular stimuli. For historical as well as theoretical reasons, studies using the baby tests emphasize individual differences, and their cross-cultural extension often focuses, therefore, on group differences. For analogous reasons, research in the other two traditions emphasizes the universal aspects of early mental growth. Nevertheless, studies of all theoretical persuasions indicate that normal infants in culturally normative care (e.g., not institutionalized) display the critical cognitive development at about the same time, the world over. This regularity can be seen as rather tight regulation or "canalization" of mental growth in a variety of circumstances (Scarr-Salapatek, 1976). On the other hand, group differences of a few months in average attainment are occasionally found, and this variation around the species' mean can seem impressive. Which aspect – commonality or diversity – is emphasized by a particular writer depends in part on the theoretical purpose of the moment. Both are true and both need explaining.

Mental Status at Birth

Many developmental psychologists think that the neonatal period may be too early to derive any good measure of mental status within the normal range. The detection of abnormal mental functioning in the opening weeks of life currently rests on neurological and more general behavioral items, essentially to assess the integrity of the central nervous system. Orientation and habituation to repeated stimuli sample behavior that can be acknowledged as fundamentally cognitive, and they can be elicited in newborns under carefully specified conditions that take into account the state of arousal, intensity and suddenness of stimulation, perinatal medication, ambient stimulation, hunger, and a number of other factors. It is doubtful, however, that individual differences on such measures indicate stable differences in mental development or potential.

Using the rather gross measures of neurological integrity and some indications of attentional behavior, cross-cultural studies find equivalence of mental functioning at birth in unstressed samples (with the exception, previously refuted, of Geber and Dean's claim regarding Ugandan newborns). The scattered group differences on particular items are probably best accounted for by medical and nutritional measures, conditions of testing, or chance variation. Of far greater interest in the comparative research are qualitative reports of early care that provide different opportunities and support for the use of the existing cognitive apparatus. The quiet, dark homes in which many infants are born in nonindustrial communities, with the constant companionship of the mother, stand out in this respect, although there are no substantial observations of early "cognitive" behavior in these settings.

Psychometric Baby Tests

Many of the items on the traditional baby tests form scales relevant to cognitive growth, such as the Bayley Scale of Mental Development and the Adaptive and Language schedules on the Gesell. The rationale of these scales appeals to face content and their coverage of the common "mental" accomplishments of infancy. Unlike the motor portions, however, the mental items are valued primarily not in their own right, but for what they are thought to index about some abstract quality of the infant's mental functioning. An item analysis of the mental index is therefore more difficult than one of the motor summary score, where general competence is directly expressed in a weighted average of competence in walking, sitting, and so on. In addition, we lack a taxonomy of functional equivalencies in environmental events to match with the equally unclear functional requirements of mental development, so it is more difficult to search for the connection between the test performance and the typical experiences of infants in a culture.

In fact, at some ages the various subscales of the traditional baby tests are highly correlated: for example, the correlation between the Bayley motor and mental scales ranges from 0.24 to 0.78 within the first two years. It is not surprising, therefore, that in cross-cultural application the subscales yield similar results. In general, children from disparate cultures master the test items at about the same time, but there are significant variations depending on the experiential supports provided by any particular culture. More obviously than for the motor test items, substantial lack of relevant experience can constitute overt inappropriateness or cultural bias of the test.

The most revealing analysis of experience and item performance does not directly involve cultural comparison but examines individual variation within a sample of Ugandan infants (Kilbride, 1976). A number of significant correlations, however, also correspond to sample differences. For example, performance on grasping and manipulative items was correlated with observed frequency in the supine position. At a more general level, the Kilbrides (1975) have related Baganda and American values toward social graces to the relative advances by the African infants in achieving the later smiling items on the Bayley Scale of Mental Development. In a similar but somewhat less theoretical vein, the Leidermans and their associates have related overall Bayley mental quotients to measures of "modernization" and plurality of caretakers (Leiderman et al., 1973; Leiderman & Leiderman, 1974a). Babies with richer and more educated parents, and those cared for by more than one caretaker (e.g., mother and older sister) tended to score higher.

It should be evident at this point that group comparisons of overall mental scores have rather limited meaning without detailed attention to the items that account for the differences and the environmental conditions that might relate to them. There is no shortage of evidence that performance on nonmotor scales of the baby tests can vary in both the pattern of timing of item attainment and in the overall score. Many of the reports previously cited concerning motor development in Africa include findings on mental scales. Faladé (1955), Geber (1958b), Ainsworth (1967), Liddicoat and Koza (1963), Lusk and Lewis (1972), Leiderman et al. (1973), and Kilbride (1976) all report high average scores for their African samples. This advance in mental scores is usually less than the motor precocity. Performance that does not average above American norms (although individual items may vary widely) has been found in other African samples by Massé (1969), Ramarasaona (1959), Theunissen (1948), Vouilloux (1959a; 1959b), and Falmagne (1962). It appears that in the first two years the verbal-vocal domain is most often found to develop at or below American norms.

Studies in India tend to show relatively high performance by upper class groups on the Gesell and Bayley mental scales, with infants from lower Socio-Economic Status (SES) and seriously deprived families, respectively, scoring at and below American norms (Athavale, Kandoth, & Sonnad, 1971; Kandoth, Sonnad, & Athavale, 1971; Patel & Kaul, 1971; Phatak, 1969; 1970a; 1970b; Uklonskaya, Puri, Choudhuri, Dang, & Kumari, 1960). Israeli studies reveal both kibbutz- and home-reared infants to average over 100 on the Bayley mental scale, and to be essentially similar to each other (Kohen-Raz, 1967; 1968). The acculturation, education, and ethnicity comparisons on adaptive, social, and language scales (Gesell) generally parallel the results for motor development: infants from educated families or those from North Africa tend to excel, at least in the first 18 months or so (Ivanans, 1975; Smilansky, Shephatia, & Frenkel, 1976). Arai et al. (1958) found Japanese babies to fall behind American norms for vocal and verbal behavior at about 4 months, although a large middle class sample was shown by Koga (1967) to generally excel on the Cattell Infant Intelligence Scale after the first year.

Class comparisons in Europe and the Americas produce a complex pattern of results, with higher SES samples usually scoring higher in the second year, but sometimes relatively poorly in the first year (Brown & Halpern, 1971; Curti, Marshall, & Steggerda, 1935; Grantham-McGregor & Hawke, 1971). Specifically ethnic comparisons, however, usually find no overall differences (Walters, 1967; Knoblock & Pasamanick, 1958; Bayley, 1965), although Rebelsky (1972) found large "deficits" in performance by Dutch infants on the Cattell scale. She attributes this fact to infants' adaptation to Dutch child-rearing techniques and goals.

Studies Using Piaget's Theory

Several studies of infant mental development in non-Western cultures use tests derived from Piaget's seminal observations on the emergence of intelligence in the opening years of life. From the Ivory Coast, Dasen and associates have recently reported on infants of 5 to 31 months from a rural agricultural village of the Baoulé people (Bovet, Dasen, Inhelder, & Othenin-Girard, 1972; Dasen, 1973; Dasen et al, 1978; Dasen, Lavallée, Retschitzki, & Reinhardt, 1977). These babies proceeded through a series of behaviors indicating intellectual growth remarkably similar to that originally described for Swiss children and replicated in detail in France by Lézine, Stambak, and Casati (1969), including, for example, the exploratory manipulations of a matchbox. There were some sample differences in the average age of passing particular test items: the Baoulé infants were a month or two early in the use of intermediary instruments and combining objects, and they were slightly delayed in one or two unrelated items. The French and Baoulé infants were equivalent in most other tasks concerning prehension, exploration, and object permanence.

Other studies generally project a similar picture of consonance in the sequence of early development, with some small sample differences in timing. Konner used the Einstein scales (Corman & Escalona, 1969) to examine infants of the !Kung San hunter-gatherers of Botswana. They progressed through initial prehension items apace with Corman and Escalona's American sample, but were advanced by a couple of weeks in the more complex visually guided reaching. In Lusaka, Zambia, Goldberg (1972; 1977) found a similar result for babies from lower income families, but no difference on the space or object permanence scales. All these authors interpret their findings as supportive of Piaget's general description of early mental accomplishment, and attribute the instances of advancement to differences in experience.

Goldberg (1972) and Dasen et al. (1978) point out, in addition, that the testing situation can be a very different experience for children reared in the traditional African manner. This is most obvious during the object permanence testing, when the baby is repeatedly frustrated by having the object taken away for use in the next test item, just after succeeding in retrieving it in the last item. The Ivory Coast group took particular efforts to avoid underestimating competence due to this problem (which raises the question of whether any of their relative advances might be artifactual), while Goldberg speculates that this testing problem accounts for the fact that her Zambian infants tended to perform better on the space scale than on object permanence, the reverse of the American pattern.

Subtle particulars of the testing situation were also thought by Kopp, Khoka, and Sigman (1977) to account for two small differences between their American and Indian samples. In New Delhi, the caretakers were more likely to offer comfort to a frustrated baby during the hidden objects procedure, whereas the American mothers were more likely to redirect the child's attention to the unsolved problem. Second, the Indian babies had slightly less success in using intermediary tools in the horizontal plane, which the authors attribute to their lesser experience in the prone position.

On all other tests there were no significant differences associated with nationality or, within samples, with socioeconomic status or modernization. A single report from Japan suggests no differences from American results on object permanence at 9 months (Takahashi & Hatano, 1976).

There are three reported instances of substantial delay in attaining object permanence. Hunt, Paraskevopoulos, Schickendanz, and Užgiris (1975) used a home-reared sample in Athens as one comparison group for an orphanage sample. The infants at home appeared to lag behind American babies by as much as six months on some of the more complex test items; but, as the authors point out, so many environmental and cultural differences overlap with the test results that it is difficult to draw a firm interpretation. In Guatemala, infants in a remote Mayan village achieved object permanence about three months later than expected, and a number of related measures showed similar delays (Kagan & Klein, 1973; Kagan, Kearsley, & Zelazo, 1978; Kagan, Klein, Finley, Rogoff, & Nolan, 1979). The delays were attributed to low levels of stimulation and little experience of variety in the first year. In a separate study, Lester, Kotelchuck, Spelke, Sellers, and Klein (1974) reported findings from a group of lower class Ladino infants who appear to lag substantially behind Corman and Escalona's (1969) New York sample. The lack of discussion about potential problems in testing, as well as lack of details on environmental supports for cognitive development, make it difficult to interpret these reported delays. Nevertheless, these studies warn that a simple maturational view of early development may not be adequate.

Studies of Infant Attention

The seminal work of Fantz (1958), on infants' distribution of attention to visual stimuli of varying complexity, introduced a new methodology to the study of infant cognition. From laboratory experiments in this tradition, developmental psychologists have made substantial gains in understanding the powers and limits of infants' abilities to notice, process, and store various kinds of information. A number of discrete findings have been replicated in other societies (Lasky, Klein, & Martinez, 1974; Yamada, 1978). The major generalization from the infant attention literature that has been subjected to cross-cultural replication is the developmental pattern of interest in models of human faces. A number of American studies indicate that babies around 4 months of age will show great interest in human masks, but this interest declines to a nadir in the last quarter of the first year. Attention to the same stimuli then increases for the next year or two, especially to masks that are distorted by having the major features (eyes, nose, mouth) rearranged. The theory used to account for these phenomena, drawn in part from the constructionist views emerging from the American discovery of Piaget, is that, in the early months, the infant is attracted by slight discrepancies between the stimulus and his or her still developing schema for what a face should look like. As the infant becomes more skilled in assimilating faces, the masks become less compelling. Late in the first year, however, the infant grows in ability to try to "understand" the discrepancies between the masks and real faces, and the distortions of the mask with scrambled features are particularly interesting (Kagan, 1970; 1971; Kagan, Kearsley, & Zelazo, 1978).

Figure 2.1 shows the results of similar studies with Ladino infants in Guatemala (Sellers, Klein, Kagan, & Minton, 1972), rural Mexicans (Finley, Kagan, & Layne, 1972), the !Kung San of Botswana (Konner, 1973), and Japanese subjects (Takahashi, 1973, and personal communication); the American results are also included (Kagan, 1970). Because of differences in procedures and detail of reporting, the comparisons are problematic: some plots are for the average first visual fixation over multiple presentations, others are for total fixation. The best available score was scaled to an arbitrary, common range of variation in constructing this figure. It is immediately evident that the curvilinear relationship of age and attention to human masks is replicated in these widely diverse settings. In the American, Mexican, and Guatemalan samples the increase in attention after the trough is greatest to the scrambled face. In the Japanese case, where the upturn is barely caught, a different distortion (a face with no features) attracted the greatest increase. Konner does not report this detail for the !Kung.

A close examination of Fig. 2.1 raises some interesting questions about the exact low point. Although the variations in procedures, measures, age of assessment, and context of testing render fragile any conclusion, it would appear that the trough of interest appears earlier in the Japanese and possibly the Guatemalan samples than in the American and !Kung ones. Kagan and associates have argued, from a large battery of measures used in more isolated Guatemalan (Mayan) samples, that low levels of variety and stimulation can result in a few months' delay in the ability to activate hypotheses about discrepancy; this should be reflected in the placement of the trough, but we lack an adequate combination of measures on the diverse samples used here to evaluate such an explanation for Fig. 2.1 (if, in fact, the differences exist). The unusual dip at 27 months in the !Kung infants' attention might be an artifact of the small number of subjects, or as Konner argues, a reflection of heightened fear of strange events at that age.

[. . .]

CONCLUSIONS

Cross-cultural studies of infant development have yet to fulfill their potential contribution. This is partly for their small number, but also because of their frequent methodological inadequacy. The interdisciplinary complexity of the enterprise places an unusual burden on the three tasks of any social

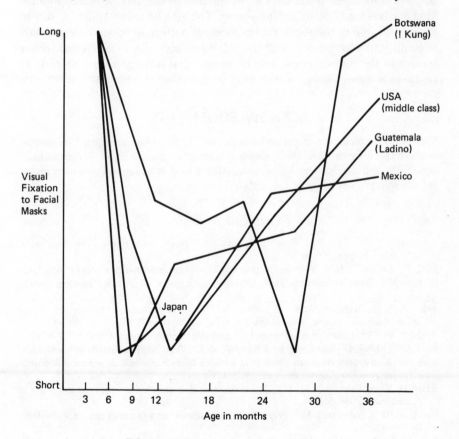

FIG. 2.1. Infants' attention to facial masks.

science. First, the accurate, quantitative description of infant behaviors under field conditions is noticeably more difficult than in the one-way-mirrored, wired-for-sound laboratory, but it still requires the technical skills of the psychometrician and the ethologist. Second, the theoretical perspectives of several disciplines are needed to conceptualize adequately the observed regularities and differences. Finally, understanding the causes and consequences of the regularities and differences can be treacherous without both the clinical insights of the ethnographer and the cold tools of the statistician.

Nevertheless, the literature as it stands already makes a substantial beginning toward sketching out the commonalities of our species' early ontogeny and the ways in which diversity is created around this core. The essential motor and mental competencies may become expressed in any particular behavior at slightly varying times, but they are strongly "built-in" in that they seem to develop similarly in all children in the diverse niches humankind has created for its infant young. The use of these abilities, still in infancy, to join in the social fabric becomes patterned in ways we are only beginning to recognize as cultural. Cultural diversity is as special to our species as the built-in plans, and it appears that infancy is not too early to study its workings also.

ACKNOWLEDGEMENTS

The author's research and preparation of this chapter were supported in part by funds granted by the William T. Grant Foundation, the Carnegie Corporation of New York, and the Spencer Foundation. All statements made and views expressed are the sole responsibility of the author.

REFERENCES

Ainsworth, M. D. S. (1967). *Infancy in Uganda: Infant care and the growth of love.* Baltimore, Md.: Johns Hopkins Press.

Arai, S., Ishikawa, J., & Toshima, K. (1958). Développement psychomoteur des enfants Japonais. *Revue de Neuropsychiatrie Infantile et d'Hygiène Mentale de l'Enfance, 6,* 262–269.

Athavale, V. B., Kandoth, W. K., & Sonnad, L. (1971). Developmental pattern in children of lower socio-economic group below 5 years of age. *Indian Pediatrics, 8,* 313–320.

Ayres, B. (1973). Effects of infant carrying practices on rhythm in music, *Ethos, 1,* 387–404.

Bardet, C., Massé, G., Moreigne, F., & Senecal, M. J. (1960). Application du test de Brunet-Lézine à un groupe d'enfants Ouolofs de 6 mois à 24 mois. *Bulletin de la Société Médicale d'Afrique Noire de Langue Française, 5,* 334–356.

Barry, H. III. & Paxson, L. M. (1971). Infancy and early childhood: Cross-cultural codes 2. *Ethnology, 10,* 466–508.

Barry, H. III. & Roberts, J. M. (1972). Infant socialization and games of chance. *Ethnology, 11,* 296–308.

Bateson, G. & Mead, M. (1942). *Balinese character: A photographic analysis.* New York: New York Academy of Sciences.

Blount, B. G. (1972). Parental speech and language acquisition: Some Luo and Samoan examples. *Anthropological Linguistics, 14,* 119–130.

Bovet, M. C., Dasen, P. R., Inhelder, B., & Othenin-Girard, C. (1972). Étapes de l'intelligence sensori-motrice chez l'enfant Baoulé: Étude préliminaire. *Archives de Psychologie, 41,* 363–386.

Brazelton, T. B. (1972). Implications of infant development among the Mayan Indians of Mexico. *Human Development, 15,* 90–111.

Brazelton, T. B. (1977). Implications of infant development among the Mayan Indians of Mexico. In P. H. Leiderman, S. R. Tulkin, & A. Rosenfeld (Eds), *Culture and infancy: Variations in the human experience.* New York: Academic Press.

Brazelton, T. B., Koslowski, B., & Tronick, E. (1976). Neonatal behavior among urban Zambians and Americans. *Journal of the American Academy of Child Psychiatry, 15,* 97–107.

Brazelton, T. B., Robey, J. S., & Collier, G. A. (1969). Infant development in the Zinacanteco Indians of Southern Mexico, *Pediatrics, 44,* 274–290.

Brazelton, T. B., Tronick, E., Lechtig, A., Lasky, R., & Klein, R. E. (1977). The Behavior of nutritionally deprived Guatemalan infants. *Developmental Medicine and Child Neurology, 19,* 364–372.

Brown, R. E. & Halpern, F. (1971). The variable pattern of mental development of rural black children: Results and interpretation of results of studies on Mississippi children aged one week to three years by the Gesell Developmental Scales. *Clinical Pediatrics, 10,* 404–409.

Campbell, B. A. & Spear, N. E. (1972). Ontogeny of memory. *Psychological Review, 79,* 215–236.

Chisholm, J. S. (1980). Development and adaptation in infancy. In C. Super & S. Harkness (Eds), Anthropological perspectives on child development. *New Directions for Child Development, 8,* 15–30.

Clark, D. L., Kreutzberg, J. R., & Chee, F. K. W. (1977). Vestibular influence on motor development in infants. *Science, 196,* 1228–1229.

Clarke, A. M. & Clarke, A. D. B. (1976). *Early experience: Myth and evidence.* New York: Free Press.

Coll, C., Sepkoski, C., & Lester, B. M. (1977). *Differences in Brazelton Scale performance between Puerto Rican and North American White and Black newborns.* Paper presented at the meeting of the Society for Research in Child Development, New Orleans.

Coll, C., Sepkoski, C., & Lester, B. M. (1978). *Differences in Brazelton scale performance between Puerto Rican and Mainland Black and Caucasian infants.* Manuscript submitted for publication, 1978.

Corman, H. H. & Escalona, S. K. (1969). Stages of sensorimotor development: A replication study. *Merrill-Palmer Quarterly, 15,* 351–362.

Curti, M. W., Marshall, F. B., & Steggerda, M. (1935). The Gesell schedules applied to one-two-, and three-year-old Negro children of Jamaica, B.W.I. *Journal of Comparative Psychology, 20,* 125–156.

Das, V. K. & Sharma, N. L. (1973). Developmental milestones in a selective sample of Lucknow children: A longitudinal study. *Indian Journal of Pediatrics, 40,* 1–7.

Dasen, P. R. (1973). Preliminary study of sensori-motor development in Baoule children. *Early Child Development and Care, 2,* 345–354.

Dasen, P. R., Inhelder, B., Lavallée, M., & Retschitzki, J. (1978). *Naissance de l'intelligence chez l'enfant Baoulé de Côte d'Ivoire.* Berne: Hans Huber.

Dasen, P. R., Lavallée, M., Retschitzki, J., & Reinhardt, M. (1977). Early moderate malnutrition and the development of sensori-motor intelligence. *Journal of Tropical Pediatrics and Environmental Child Health, 23,* 145–157. (Monograph)

de Vries, M. W. & Super, C. M. (1979). Contextual influences on the Brazelton Neonatal Behavioral Assessment Scale and implications for its cross-cultural use. In A. Sameroff

(Ed.), Organization and stability of newborn behavior: A commentary on the Brazelton Neonatal Behavioral Assessment Scale. *Monographs of the Society for Research in Child Development, 43,* (5–6, Serial No. 177), 92–101.

Du Bois, C. (1944). *The people of Alor.* Minneapolis: University of Minnesota Press.

Faladé, S. (1955). *Le développement psycho-moteur de jeune Africain originaire du Senegal au cours de sa première année.* Paris: Foulon.

Falmagne, J.-C. (1962). Étude comparative du développement psychomoteur pendant les six premièrs mois de 105 nourrissons blancs (Bruxelles) and 78 nourrissons noirs (Johannesburg). *Mémoirs de L'Academie Royale des Sciences d'Outre-Mer. Classes des Sciences Naturelles et Médicales, 13,* fasc. 5.

Fantz, R. L. (1958). Pattern vision in young infants. *Psychological Record, 8,* 43–47.

Finley, G. E., Kagan, J., & Layne, O. Jr. (1972). Development of young children's attention to normal and distorted stimuli: A cross-cultural study. *Developmental Psychology, 6,* 288–292.

Freedman, D. G. (1974). *Human infancy: An evolutionary perspective.* Hillsdale, N. J.: Lawrence Erlbaum Associates Inc.

Geber, M. (1956). Développement psycho-moteur de l'enfant africain. *Courrier,6,* 17–29.

Geber, M. (1958a). L'enfant africain occidentalisé et de niveau social supérieur en Ouganda. *Courrier, 8,* 517–523.

Geber, M. (1958b). Tests de Gesell et de Terman-Merrill appliqués en Uganda, *Enfance, 11,* 63–67.

Geber, M. (1958c). The psycho-motor development of African children in the first year, and the influence of maternal behavior. *Journal of Social Psychology, 47.* 185–195.

Geber, M. (1960). Problèmes posés par le développement du jeune enfant africain en fonction de son milieu social. *Le Travail Humain, 23,* 97–111.

Geber, M. (1962). Longitudinal study and psychomotor development among Baganda children. In *Proceedings of the Fourteenth International Congress of Applied Psychology* (Vol. 3). Copenhagen: Munksgaard.

Geber, M. (1973). L'environnement et le développement des enfants africains. *Enfance, 3–4,* 145–174.

Geber, M. (1974). La recherche sur le développement psychomoteur et mental à Kampala. *Compte-rendu de la XII Reunion des Equipes Chargées des Études sur la croissance et de développement de l'enfant normal.* Paris: Centre International de l'Enfance.

Geber, M. & Dean, R. F. A. (1957a). The state of development of newborn African children. *Lancet, 272(1),* 1216–1219.

Geber, M. & Dean, R. F. A. (1957b). Gesell tests on African children. *Pediatrics, 20,* 1055–1065.

Geber, M. & Dean, R. F. A. (1958). Psychomotor development in African children: The effects of social class and the need for improved tests. *Bulletin of the World Health Organization, 18,* 471–476.

Geber, M. & Dean, R. F. A. (1964). Le développement psychomoteur et somatique des jeunes enfants africains en Ouganda. *Courrier, 14,* 425–437.

Goldberg, S. (1972). Infant care and growth in urban Zambia. *Human Development, 15,* 77–89.

Goldberg, S. (1977). Infant development and mother-infant interaction in urban Zambia. In P. H. Leiderman, S. R. Tulkin, & A. Rosenfeld (Eds), *Culture and infancy: Variations in the human experience.* New York: Academic Press.

Graham, F. K., Matarazzo, R. G., & Caldwell, B. M. (1956). Behavioral differences between normal and traumatized newborns: II: Standardization, reliability, and validity. *Psychological Monographs, 70*(21, Whole No. 428).

Grantham-McGregor, S. M. & Hawke, W. A. (1971). Developmental assessment of Jamaican infants. *Developmental Medicine and Child Neurology, 13,* 582–589.

Griffiths, J. (1969). Development of reflexes in Bantu children. *Developmental Medicine and Child Neurology, 11,* 533-535.

Harkness, S. (1980). The cultural context of child development. In C. Super and S. Harkness (Eds.), Anthropological perspectives on child development. *New Directions for Child Development, 8,* 7–13.

Harkness, S. & Super, C. M. (1977). Why African children are so hard to test. In L. L. Adler (Ed.), Issues in cross-cultural research, *Annals of the New York Academy of Sciences, 285,* 326–331. Reprinted in L. L. Adler (Ed.), *Cross-cultural research at issue.* New York: Academic Press, in press.

Harris, M. (1968). *The rise of anthropological theory: A history of theories of culture.* New York: Crowell.

Hopkins, B. (1976). Culturally determined patterns of handling the human infant. *Journal of Human Movement Studies, 2,* 1–27.

Hopkins, B. (1978). *The early development of black and white infants living in Britain.* Paper presented at the meeting of the International Association for Cross-cultural Psychology, Tilburg.

Hunt, J. McV., Paraskevopoulos, J., Schickendanz, D., & Užgiris, I. C. (1975). Variations in the mean ages of achieving object permanence under diverse conditions of rearing. In B. Z. Friedlander, G. Sterritt, & G. E. Kirk (Eds.), *The exceptional infant II: Assessment and intervention.* New York: Brunner/Mazel.

Ivanans, T. (1975). Effect of maternal education and ethnic background on infant development. *Archives of Disease in Childhood, 50,* 454–457.

Janes, M. D. (1975). Physical and psychological growth and development. *Journal of Tropical Pediatrics and Environmental Child Health, 21,* 26–30.

Kagan, J. (1970). The determinants of attention in the infant. *American Scientist, 58,* 298–306.

Kagan, J. (1971). *Change and continuity in infancy.* New York: Wiley.

Kagan, J., Kearsley, R. B., & Zelazo, P. R. (1978). *Infancy: Its place in human development.* Cambridge, Mass.: Harvard University Press.

Kagan, J., & Klein, R. E. (1973). Cross-cultural perspectives on early development. *American Psychologist, 28,* 947–961.

Kagan, J., Klein, R.E., Finley, G., Rogoff, B., & Nolan, E. (1979). A cross-cultural study of cognitive development. *Monographs of the Society for Research in Child Development, 42,* Serial No. 180.

Kagan, J., & Moss, H. A. (1962). *Birth to maturity: A study in psychological development.* New York: Wiley.

Kandoth, W. K., Sonnad, L., & Athavale, V. B. (1971). Milestones in lower socioeconomic group. *Indian Pediatrics, 8,* 176–183.

Kardiner, A. (1944). Conclusions to the autobiographies. In C. Du Bois, *The people of Alor: A social-psychological study of an East Indian island.* Minneapolis: University of Minnesota Press.

Keefer, C. H., Dixon, S., Tronick, E., & Brazelton, T. B. (1977). *A cross-cultural study of face to face interaction: Gusii infants and mothers.* Paper presented at meeting of the Society for Research in Child Development, New Orleans.

Keefer, C. H., Dixon, S., Tronick, E., & Brazelton, T. B. (1978). *Gusii infants' neuromotor behavior.* Paper presented at the International Conference on Infant Studies, Providence, R. I.

Kilbride, J. E. (1976). *Mother-infant interaction and infant sensorimotor development among the Baganda of Uganda.* Unpublished doctoral dissertation, Bryn Mawr College.

Kilbride, J. E., & Kilbride, P. L. Sitting and smiling behavior of Baganda infants: The influence of culturally constituted experience. *Journal of Cross-cultural Psychology, 1975, 6,* 88–107.

Kilbride, J. E., Robbins, M. C., & Kilbride, P. L. (1970). The comparative motor development of Baganda, American white, and American black infants. *American Anthropologist, 72,* 1422–1428.

Knoblock, H., & Pasamanick, B. (1958). The relationship of race and socioeconomic status to the developmental of motor behavior patterns in infancy. *Psychiatric Research Reports, 10,* 123–133.

Koga, Y. (1967). *MCC baby test.* Tokyo: Dobunshoin.

Kohen-Raz, R. (1967). Scalogram analysis of some developmental sequences of infant behavior as measured by the Bayley Infant Scale of Mental Development. *Genetic Psychology Monographs, 76,* 3–21.

Kohen-Raz, R. (1968). Mental and motor development of Kibbutz, institutionalized, and home-reared infants in Israel. *Child Development, 39,* 489–504.

Konner, M. J. (1972). Aspects of the developmental ethology of a foraging people. In N. Blurton Jones (Ed.), *Ethological studies of child behavior.* Cambridge, England: Cambridge University Press.

Konner, M. J. (1973). *Infants of a foraging people.* Unpublished doctoral dissertation, Harvard University.

Konner, M. J. (1976). Maternal care, infant behavior and development among the !Kung. In R. B. Lee & I. DeVore (Eds), *Kalahari hunter-gatherers: Studies of the !Kung San and and their neighbors.* Cambridge, Mass.: Harvard University Press.

Konner, M. J. (1977). Infancy among the Kalahari Desert San. In P. H. Leiderman, S. R. Tulkin, & A. Rosenfeld (Eds), *Culture and infancy: Variations in the human experience.* New York: Academic Press.

Kopp, C. B., Khoka, E. W., & Sigman, M. (1977). A comparison of sensorimotor development among infants in India and the United States. *Journal of Cross-cultural Psychology, 8,* 435–452.

Lagerspetz, K., Nygard, M., & Strandvik, C. (1971). The effects of training in crawling on the motor and mental development of infants. *Scandanavian Journal of Psychology, 12,* 192–197.

Lambert, W. W., Triandis, L. M., & Wolf, M. (1959). Some correlates of beliefs in the malevolence and benevolence of supernatural beings: A cross-societal study. *Journal of Abnormal and Social Psychology, 58,* 162–169.

Landau, R. (1976). Extent that the mother represents the social stimulation to which the infant is exposed: findings from a cross-cultural study. *Developmental Psychology, 12,* 399–405.

Landauer, T. K., & Whiting, J. W. M. (1964). Infantile stimulation and adult stature of human males. *American Anthropologist, 66,* 1007–1028.

Lasky, R.E., Klein, R. E., & Martinez, S. (1974). Age and sex discriminations in five- and six-month-old infants. *Journal of Psychology, 88,* 317–324.

Lasky, R. E., Lechtig, A., Delgado, H., Klein, R.E., Engle, P., Yarbrough, C., & Martorell, R. (1975). Birth weight and psychomotor performance in rural Guatemala. *American Journal of Diseases of Children, 129,* 566–569.

Leboyer, F. (1976). *Loving hands: The traditional Indian art of baby massaging.* New York: Knopf.

Leiderman, P. H., Babu, B., Kagia, J., Kraemer, H. C., & Leiderman, G. F. (1973). African infant precocity and some social influences during the first year. *Nature, 242,* 247–249.

Leiderman, P. H., & Leiderman, G. F. (1974a). Affective and cognitive consequences of polymatric infant care in the East African Highlands. In A. D. Pick (Ed.), *Minnesota symposia on child psychology* (Vol. 8). Minneapolis: University of Minnesota Press.

Leiderman, P. H., & Leiderman, G. F. (1974b). Familial influences on infant development in an East African agricultural community. In E. J. Anthony & C. Koupernik (Eds), *The child and his family: Children at psychiatric risk* (Vol. 3). New York: Wiley.

Leiderman, P. H., & Leiderman, G. F. (1977). Economic change and infant care in an East African agricultural community. In P. H. Leiderman, S. R. Tulkin, & A. Rosenfeld (Eds), *Culture and infancy: Variations in the human experience.* New York: Academic Press.

Lester, B. M., & Brazelton, T. B. (in press). Cross-cultural assessment of neonatal behavior. In H. W. Stevenson & D. A. Wagner (Eds), *Cultural perspectives on child development.* San Francisco: Freeman.

Lester, B. M., Kotelchuck, M., Spelke, E., Sellers, M. J., & Klein, R. E. (1974). Separation protest in Guatemalan infants: Cross-cultural and cognitive findings. *Developmental Psychology, 10,* 79–85.

LeVine, R. A. (1969). Culture, personality, and socialization: An evolutionary view. In D. A. Goslin (Ed.), *Handbook of socialization: Theory and research.* New York: Rand McNally.

LeVine, R. A. (1974). Parental goals: A cross-cultural view. *Teachers College Record, 76,* 226–239.

LeVine, R. A. (1977). Child rearing as cultural adaptation. In P. H. Leiderman, S. R. Tulkin, & A. Rosenfeld (Eds), *Culture and infancy: Variations in the human experience.* New York: York: Academic Press.

LeVine, R.A. (1980). Anthropology and child development. In C. M. Super & S. Harkness (Eds), Anthropological perspectives on child development. *New Directions for Child Development, 8,* 71–86.

Lezine, I., Stambak, M., & Casati, I. (1969). *Les étapes de l'intelligence sensori-motrice.* Paris: Centre de Psychologie Applique.

Liddicoat, R. (1969). Development of Bantu Children. (Letter to the Editor). *Developmental Medicine and Child Neurology, 11,* 821–822.

Liddicoat, R., & Griesel, R. D. (1971). A scale for the measurement of African urban infant development: Preliminary report. *Psychologia Africana, 14,* 65–75.

Liddicoat, R., & Koza, C. (1963). Language development in African infants. *Psychologia Africana, 10,* 108–116.

Lusk, D., & Lewis, M. (1972). Mother-infant interaction and infant development among the Wolof of Senegal, *Human Development, 15,* 58–69.

Massé, G. (1969). *Croissance et développement de l'enfant à Dakar.* Paris: Centre International d'Enfance.

Mead, M. (1930). *Growing up in New Guinea: A comparative study of primitive education.* New York: William Morrow.

Moreigne, F. (1970). Le développement psycho-moteur de l'enfant Wolof en milieu Dakarois de 6 mois à 6 ans. *Revue de Neuropsychiatrie Infantile et d'Hygiène Mentale de l'Enfance, 18,* 765–783.

Mundy-Castle, A. C., & Okonji, M. O. (1978). Mother-infant interaction in Nigeria. Paper presented at the meeting of the International Association for Cross-cultural Psychology, Tilburg.

Munroe, R. L., Munroe, R. H., & Whiting, J. W. M. (1973). The couvade: A psychological analysis. *Ethos, 1,* 30–74.

Naidr, J. (1975). Psychomotoricky vývoj africkýchv dětí. *Ceskoslovenska Pediatrie, 30,* 173–176.

Palti, H., Gitlin, M., & Zloto, R. (1977). Psychomotor development of two-year-old children in Jerusalem. *Journal of Cross-cultural Psychology, 8,* 453–464.

Patel, N. V., & Kaul, K. K. (1971). Behavioral development of Indian rural and urban infants in comparison to American infants. *Indian Pediatrics, 8,* 443–451.

Phatak, P. (1969). Motor and mental development of Indian babies from 1 month to 30 months. *Indian Pediatrics, 6,* 18–23.

Phatak, P. (1970a). *Mental and motor growth of Indian babies (1–30 months).* Final Report, Department of Child Development, M. S. University of Baroda, Baroda, India.

Phatak, P. (1970b). Motor growth patterns of Indian babies. *Indian Pediatrics, 7,* 619–624.

Poole, H. E. (1969). The effect of Westernization on the psychomotor development of African (Yoruba) infants during the first year of life. *Journal of Tropical Pediatrics, 15,* 172–176.

Prescott, J. W. (1975). Abortion or the unwanted child: A choice for a humanistic society. *The Humanist, 35(2),* 11–15.

Ramarasaona, Z. (1959). *Psychomotor development in early childhood in the Tananarive region.* Report of the CSM Meeting of Specialists on the basic psychological structures of African and Madagascan Populations. London: CCTA/CSA Publication No. 51.

Rebelsky, F. (1972). First discussant's comments: Cross-cultural studies of mother-infant interaction: Description and consequence. *Human Development, 15,* 128–130.

Rebelsky, F. (1967). Infancy in two cultures. In F. G. Rebelsky & L. Dormon (Eds), *Child development and behavior* (2nd ed.). New York: Alfred A. Knopf, 1973. (Reprinted from *Nederlands Tijdschrift voor de Psychologie, 1967, 22,* 379–385.

Scarr-Salapatek, S. (1976). An evolutionary perspective on infant intelligence: Species patterns and individual variations. In M. Lewis (Ed.), *Origins of intelligence.* New York: Plenum.

Sellers, M. J., Klein, R., Kagan, J., & Minton, C. (1972). Development determinants of attention: A cross-cultural replication. *Developmental Psychology, 6,* 185.

Smilansky, E., Shephatia, L., & Frenkel, E. (1976). *Mental development of infants from two ethnic groups* (Research Report No. 195). Jerusalem: Henrietta Szold Institute.

Solomons, G., & Solomons, H. C. (1975). Motor development in Yucatecan infants. *Developmental Medicine and Child Neurology, 17,* 41–46.

Spiro, M. E. (1953). Ghosts: An anthropological inquiry into learning and perception. *Journal of Abnormal and Social Psychology, 48,* 376–382.

Spiro, M. E., & D'Andrade, R. G. (1958). A cross-cultural study of some supernatural beliefs. *American Anthropologist, 60,* 456–466.

Ssengoba, C. M. E. B. (1978). *The effects of nutritional status on the psychomotor development of rural Kenyan infants.* Unpublished doctoral dissertation, University of Michigan.

Super, C. M. (1973). Patterns of infant care and motor development in Kenya. *Kenya Education Review, 1,* 64–69.

Super, C. M. (1976). Environmental effects on motor development: The case of African infant precocity. *Developmental Medicine and Child Neurology, 18,* 561–567.

Super, C. M. (1980). Behavioral development in infancy. In R. L. Munroe, R. H. Munroe, & B. B. Whiting (Eds), *Handbook of cross-cultural human development.* New York: Garland Press.

Super, C. M. & Harkness, S. (in press, a). The development of affect in infancy and early childhood. In H. Stevenson & D. Wagner (Eds), *Cultural perspectives on child development.* San Francisco: Freeman.

Super, C. M. & Harkness, S. (in press, b). The infant's niche in rural Kenya and metropolitan America. In L. L. Adler (Ed.), *Cross-cultural research at issue.* New York: Academic Press.

Takahashi, K., & Hatano, G. (1976). *Mother-child interaction and cognitive development.* Paper presented at the meeting of the Japanese Psychological Association, Nagoya.

Takahashi, M. (1973). The cross-sectional study of infants' smiling, attention, reaching, and crying responses to the facial models. *Japanese Journal of Psychology, 44,* 124–134.

Theunissen, K. B. (1948). *A preliminary comparative study of the development of motor behavior in European and Bantu children up to the age of one year.* Unpublished master's dissertation, Natal University College.

Uklonskaya, R., Puri, B., Choudhuri, N., Dang, L., & Kumari, R. (1960). Development of static and psychomotor functions of infants in the first year of life in New Delhi. *Indian Journal of Child Health, 1960, 9,* 596–601.

Valantin, S. (1970). *Le développement de la fonction manipulatoire chez l'enfant senegalais au cours des deux premières années de la vie.* Unpublished doctoral thesis, Université de Paris.

Varkevisser, C. M. (1973). *Socialization in a changing society: Sukuma childhood in rural and urban Mwanza, Tanzania.* Den Haag: Center for the Study of Education in Changing Societies.

Vincent, M., & Hugon, J. (1962). L'insuffisance ponderale du premature africain au point de vue de la santé publique. *Bulletin of the World Health Organization, 26,* 143–174.

Vouilloux, P. D. (1959a). Étude de la psychomotoricité d'enfants africains au Cameroun: Test de Gesell et réflexes archaïques. *Journal de la société des Africainists, 29,* 11–18.

Vouilloux, P. D. (1959b). Test moteurs et réflexe plantaire chez de jeunes enfants camerounais. *Presse Médicale, 67,* 1420–1421.

Walters, C. E. (1967). Comparative development of Negro and white infants. *Journal of Genetic Psychology, 110,* 243–251.

Warren, N. (1972). African infant precocity. *Psychological Bulletin, 78.* 353–367.

Warren, N., & Parkin, J. M. (1974). A neurological and behavioral comparison of African and European newborns in Uganda. *Child Development, 45,* 966–971.

Werner, E. E., Bierman, J. M., & French, F. E. (1971). *The children of Kauai: A longitudinal study from the prenatal period of age ten.* Honolulu: University Press of Hawaii.

Werner, E. E., Simonian, K., & Smith, R. S. (1968). Ethnic and socioeconomic status differences in abilities and achievement among preschool and school-age children in Hawaii. *Journal of Social Psychology, 75,* 43–59.

Whiting, J. W. M. (1971). Causes and consequences of mother-infant contact. Paper presented at meeting of the American Anthropological Association, New York.

Whiting, J. W. M. (1977). A model for psychocultural research. In P. H. Leiderman, S. R. Tulkin, & A. Rosenfeld (Eds), *Culture and infancy: Variations in the human experience.* New York: Academic Press.

Whiting, J. W. M., Chasdi, E. H., Antonovsky, H. F., & Ayres, B. C. (1966). The learning of values. In E. Z. Vogt & E. M. Albert (Eds), *People of Rimrock: A study of values in five cultures.* Cambridge, Mass.: Harvard University Press.

Whiting, J. W. M., & Child, I. L. (1953). *Child training and personality.* New Haven, Conn.: Yale University Press.

Wug de Leon, E., De Licardie, E., & Cravioto, J., (1964). Operación Nimiquipalq VI: Desarrollo psicomotor del niño en una población rural de Guatemala. *Guatemala Pediatrica, 4,* 92–106.

Yamada, Y. (1978). Effects of stimulus novelty on visual and manipulative exploration in infancy. *Japanese Journal of Educational Psychology, 1,* 41–51.

Zelazo, P. R., Zelazo, N. A., & Kolb, S. (1972). "Walking" in the newborn. *Science, 176,* 314–315.

Zern, D. (1970). The influence of certain child-rearing factors upon the development of a structured and salient sense of time. *Genetic Psychology Monographs, 81,* 197–254.

Zern, D. (1972). The relationship between mother-infant contact and later differentiation of the social environment. *Journal of Genetic Psychology, 121,* 107–117.

II INFANT LEARNING

3 The Sensori-Motor Level

J. Piaget and B. Inhelder

If the child partly explains the adult, it can also be said that each period of his development partly explains the periods that follow. This is particularly clear in the case of the period where language is still absent. We call it the "sensori-motor" period because the infant lacks the symbolic function; that is, he does not have representations by which he can evoke persons or objects in their absence. In spite of this lack, mental development during the first eighteen months[1] of life is particularly important, for it is during this time that the child constructs all the cognitive substructures that will serve as a point of departure for his later perceptive and intellectual development, as well as a certain number of elementary affective reactions that will partly determine his subsequent affectivity.

SENSORI-MOTOR INTELLIGENCE

Whatever criteria for intelligence one adopts – purposeful groping (E. Claparède), sudden comprehension or insight (W. Köhler or K. Bühler), coordination of means and ends, etc. – everyone agrees in recognizing the existence of an intelligence before language. Essentially practical – that is, aimed at getting results rather than at stating truths – this intelligence nevertheless succeeds in eventually solving numerous problems of action (such as reaching distant or hidden objects) by constructing a complex

---

[1] Ages indicated in this reading are always average and approximate.

Source: Piaget, J. & Inhelder, B. (1966). *The Psychology of the Child*, (translated by H. Weaver, published 1969). London: Routledge & Kegan Paul, pp. 1–12.

system of action-schemes[2] and organizing reality in terms of spatio-temporal and causal structures. In the absence of language or symbolic function, however, these constructions are made with the sole support of perceptions and movements and thus by means of a sensori-motor coordination of actions, without the intervention of representation or thought.

Stimulus-Response and Assimilation

There certainly is such a thing as a sensori-motor intelligence, but it is very difficult to specify the exact moment when it appears. Actually, the question makes no sense, for the answer always depends upon an arbitrary choice of criterion. What one actually finds is a remarkably smooth succession of stages, each marking a new advance, until the moment when the acquired behavior presents characteristics that one or another psychologist recognizes as those of "intelligence". (All writers are in agreement in attributing this quality to at least the last of these stages, from twelve to eighteen months.) There is a continuous progression from spontaneous movements and reflexes to acquired habits and from the latter to intelligence. The real problem is not to locate the first appearance of intelligence but rather to understand the mechanism of this progression.

For many psychologists this mechanism is one of association, a cumulative process by which conditionings are added to reflexes and many other acquisitions to the conditionings themselves. According to this view, every acquisition, from the simplest to the most complex, is regarded as a response to external stimuli, a response whose associative character expresses a complete control of development by external connections. One of us,[3] on the other hand, has argued that this mechanism consists in *assimilation* (comparable to biological assimilation in the broad sense): meaning that reality data are treated or modified in such a way as to become incorporated into the structure of the subject. In other words, every newly established connection is integrated into an existing schematism. According to this view, the organizing activity of the subject must be considered just as important as the connections inherent in the external stimuli, for the subject becomes aware of these connections only to the degree that he can assimilate them by means of his existing structures. In other words, associationism conceives the relationship between stimulus and response in a unilateral manner: $S \rightarrow R$; whereas the point of view of assimilation presupposes a reciprocity $S \rightleftarrows R$; that is to say, the input, the stimulus, is filtered through a structure that consists of the action-schemes (or, at a higher level, the

---

[2]A scheme is the structure or organization of actions as they are transferred or generalized by repetition in similar or analogous circumstances.

[3]Jean Piaget, *The Origins of Intelligence in Children* (New York: International Universities Press, 1951; London: Routledge and Kegan Paul, 1953).

operations of thought), which in turn are modified and enriched when the subject's behavioral repertoire is accommodated to the demands of reality. The filtering or modification of the input is called *assimilation*; the modification of internal schemes to fit reality is called *accommodation*.

Stage One

The point of departure of development should not be sought in the reflexes conceived as simple isolated responses, but in the spontaneous and total activities of the organism (studied by E. von Holst and others). There are relatively fixed and predictable reflexes embedded in this total activity, but they can be viewed as a differentiation of this global activity, as we shall see. Some of these reflexes are developed by exercise instead of remaining unchanged or atrophying and are the points of departure for the development of schemes of assimilation.

On the one hand, it has been shown by the study of animal behavior as well as by the study of the electrical activity of the nervous system that the organism is never passive, but presents spontaneous and global activities whose form is rhythmic. On the other hand, embryological analysis of the reflexes (G. E. Coghill and others) has enabled us to establish the fact that reflexes are formed by differentiation upon a groundwork of more global activities. In the case of the locomotive reflexes of the batrachians, for example, it is an overall rhythm which culminates in a succession of differentiated and coordinated reflexes, and not the reflexes which lead to that rhythm.

As far as the reflexes of the newborn child are concerned, those among them that are of particular importance for the future (the sucking reflex and the palmar reflex, which will be integrated into later intentional grasping) give rise to what has been called a "reflex exercise"; that is, a consolidation by means of functional exercise. This explains why after a few days the newborn child nurses with more assurance and finds the nipple more easily when it has slipped out of his mouth than at the time of his first attempts.[4] The reproductive or functional assimilation that accounts for this exercise also gives rise to a generalizing assimilation (sucking on nothing between meals or sucking new objects) and a recognitive assimilation (distinguishing the nipple from other objects).

We cannot label these modifications of sucking acquisitions in a strict sense, since the assimilating exercise does not yet go beyond the preestablished boundaries of the hereditary apparatus. Nevertheless, the assimilation fulfills a fundamental role in developing this activity. This makes it impossible to regard the reflex as a pure automatism and also accounts for

---

[4]Similar reflex exercises are observed in animals too, as in the groping that characterizes the first efforts at copulation in Lymnaeae.

later extensions of the reflex scheme and for the formation of the first habits. In the case of sucking we observe, sometimes as early as the second month, the commonplace but nonetheless instructive phenomenon of a baby sucking his thumb. Fortuitous or accidental thumbsucking may occur as early as the first day. The more advanced sucking is systematic and dependent upon a coordination of the movements of arm, hand, and mouth. Associationists see here only an effect of repetition (but what is the source of this repetition, since it is not imposed by external connections?), and psychoanalysts already see a symbolic behavior by representative identification of the thumb and the breast (but what is the source of this symbolic or evocative power, well before the formation of the first mental images?). We suggest that this acquisition be interpreted as a simple extension of the sensori-motor assimilation at work as early as the reflex. It is quite clear that this is a genuine case of acquisition in a broad sense, since there exists no reflex or instinct for sucking one's thumb (indeed, the appearance of this activity and its frequency are subject to variation). But this acquisition is not a random affair: it is introduced into a reflex scheme that is already formed, extending it through the integration of sensori-motor elements hitherto independent of this scheme. Such integration already characterizes Stage Two. Although the child's actions seem to reflect a sort of magical belief in causality without any material contact, his use of the same means to try to achieve different ends indicates that he is on the threshold of intelligence.

Stage Two

Some such pattern characterizes the formation of the first habits, whether they depend directly upon an activity of the subject, as in the foregoing case, or seem to be imposed from the outside, as in the case of "conditionings". A conditioned reflex is never stabilized by the force of its associations alone, but only by the formation of a scheme of assimilation: that is, when the result attained satisfies the need inherent in the assimilation in question (as with Pavlov's dog, which salivates at the sound of the bell as long as this sound is identified with a signal for food, but which ceases to salivate if food no longer follows the signal).

But even if we use "habits" – for lack of a better word – to refer to acquired behavior while it is being formed as well as after it has become automatized, habit is still not the same as intelligence. An elementary "habit" is based on a general sensori-motor scheme within which there is not yet, from the subject's point of view, any differentiation between means and ends. The end in question is attained only by a necessary succession of movements which lead to it, without one's being able to distinguish either an end pursued from the start or means chosen from among various possible schemes. In an act of intelligence, on the other hand, the end is established from the outset and pursued after a search for the appropriate means. These means are furnished by the schemes known to the subject (or "habit" schemes), but they are used to achieve an aim that had its source in a different scheme.

Stage Three

The most interesting aspect of the development of sensori-motor actions during the first year of the child's life is that it not only leads to elementary learning experiences which are the source of simple habits on a level where intelligence, strictly speaking, is not yet observed, but it also provides a continuous series of intermediaries between habitual and intelligent reactions. Thus after the reflex stage (Stage One) and the stage of the first habits (StageTwo), a third stage (StageThree) introduces the next transitions after the beginning of coordination between vision and prehension – around four and a half months on the average. The baby starts grasping and manipulating everything he sees in his immediate vicinity. For example, a subject of this age catches hold of a cord hanging from the top of his cradle, which has the effect of shaking all the rattles suspended above him. He immediately repeats the gesture a number of times. Each time the interesting result motivates the repetition. This constitutes a "circular reaction" in the sense of J. M. Baldwin, or a new habit in the nascent state, where the result to be obtained is not differentiated from the means employed. Later you need only hang a new toy from the top of the cradle for the child to look for the cord, which constitutes the beginning of a differentiation between means and end. In the days that follow, when you swing an object from a pole two yards from the crib, and even when you produce unexpected and mechanical sounds behind a screen, after these sights or sounds have ceased the child will again look for and pull the magic cord. Although the child's actions seem to reflect a sort of magical belief in causality without any material connection, his use of the same means to try to achieve different ends indicates that he is on the threshold of intelligence.

Stages Four and Five

In a fourth stage (Stage Four), we observe more complete acts of practical intelligence. The subject sets out to obtain a certain result, independent of the means he is going to employ: for example, obtaining an object that is out of reach or has just disappeared under a piece of cloth or a cushion. The instrumental acts appear only later and they are obviously seen from the outset as means: for example, seizing the hand of an adult and moving it in the direction of the unreachable object, or lifting the screen that masks the hidden object. In the course of this fourth stage, the coordination of means and ends is new and is invented differently in each unforeseen situation (otherwise we would not speak of intelligence), but the means employed are derived only from known schemes of assimilation. (In the case of the object that is hidden and found again, the combination is also new, as we shall see in the next section. But the fact of seizing and moving a cushion corresponds to a habitual scheme).

In the course of a fifth stage (Stage Five), which makes its appearance around eleven or twelve months, a new ingredient is added to the foregoing behavior: the search for new means by differentiation from schemes already known. An example of this is what we call the "behavior pattern of the support". An object has been placed on a rug out of the child's reach. The child, after trying in vain to reach the object directly, may eventually grasp one corner of the rug (by chance or as a substitute), and then, observing a relationship between the movements of the rug and those of the object, gradually comes to pull the rug in order to reach the object. An analogous discovery characterizes the behavior pattern of the string, studied first by Bühler and then by many others: bringing the objective to oneself by pulling the string to which it is attached.

Stage Six

Finally, a sixth stage marks the end of the sensori-motor period and the transition to the following period. In this stage the child becomes capable of finding new means not only by external or physical groping but also by internalized combinations that culminate in sudden comprehension or *insight*. For example, a child confronted by a slightly open matchbox containing a thimble first tries to open the box by physical groping (reaction of the fifth stage), but upon failing, he presents an altogether new reaction: he stops the action and attentively examines the situation (in the course of this he slowly opens and closes his mouth, or, as another subject did, his hand, as if in imitation of the result to be attained, that is, the enlargement of the opening), after which he suddenly slips his finger into the crack and thus succeeds in opening the box.

It is at this same stage that one generally finds the well-known behavior pattern of the stick, first studied by Köhler in chimpanzees and later by others in the human infant. But Köhler, like Bühler, considers that there is an act of intelligence involved only in cases where there is sudden comprehension. He banishes groping from the domain of intelligence and classifies it with the behavior of substitution, etc. Claparède, on the other hand, saw groping as the criterion of intelligence, attributing the onset of hypotheses to an externalized groping. This criterion is surely too broad, since groping exists as early as the reflex and the formation of habits. But the criterion of *insight* is certainly too narrow, for it is by means of an uninterrupted succession of assimilations on various levels (Stages One through Five) that the sensori-motor schemes lead to those new combinations and internalizations that finally make immediate comprehension possible in certain situations. This last level (Stage Six) cannot therefore be separated from the others; it merely marks their completion.

4 Temporal Conditioning of Heart Rate Responses in Newborn Infants

Leighton E. Stamps

Temporal heart rate conditioning was evaluated in 32 newborn infants (16 experimental and 16 control) by examining responses to the unconditioned stimulus (UCS), in anticipation of the UCS, and in its absence. There was weak evidence, only in the females, of a conditioned anticipatory deceleration immediately before the UCS. Response differences between the experimental and control groups following the UCS and in its absence were also found.

There has been some question in the past as to whether the newborn infant can be classically conditioned (Sameroff, 1971). In the last several years, however, both classical reward and classical aversive conditioning of heart rate responses have been demonstrated in neonates. Clifton (1974), who used a delayed paradigm and an appetitive unconditioned stimulus (UCS), and Forbes and Porges (1972, reference note 1), who employed a trace procedure and an aversive UCS, both found conditioned heart rate responses in the absence of the UCS. These investigations did not, however, demonstrate conditioned anticipatory responses which are normally found in studies of adult heart rate conditioning. In a third study, Stamps and Porges (1975) used a trace paradigm and an appetitive UCS. This study did demonstrate anticipatory responses in addition to responses in the absence of the UCS. Relationships among the sex of the infant, the level of spontaneous heart rate variability, and conditionability were also shown. They found that females and high variability subjects were more likely to

Source: *Developmental Psychology* (1977) 13, 624-629. Copyright 1977 by the American Psychological Association. Reprinted by permission of the publisher and author.

exhibit conditioned responses than other infants. These studies indicate that newborns show classically conditioned heart rate responses similar to those seen in adults.

There have been very few attempts of any type of temporal conditioning with newborns. Several studies which have been described as temporal conditioning have dealt with the alteration of feeding schedules. Marquis (1941) and Bystroletova (1954) both reported changes in motor activity in anticipation of feeding. Krachkovskaia (1959), using a similar procedure, found an anticipatory rise in leukocyte count before feeding. All three of these studies leave a number of unanswered questions regarding the effects of digestive and metabolic processes which may account for the responses rather than conditioning. The remaining study of newborn temporal conditioning (Lipsitt & Ambrose; 1967, reference note 2) dealt with respiration, heart rate, and motility responses. Although the authors reported conditioning, this investigation is subject to methodological criticisms, primarily based on the lack of a control group. Thus, there do not seem to be any convincing demonstrations of newborn temporal conditioning. There is, however, evidence indicating that older infants can be temporally conditioned. Brackbill, Lintz, and Fitzgerald (1968) reported conditioned pupillary responses using a temporal paradigm with infants approximately two months old.

The association between spontaneous heart rate variability and conditioning, mentioned above, appears to be compatible with other research on heart rate variability. The level of variability has been related to the magnitude and consistency of heart rate responses during attentional tasks in both newborns and adults (Porges, 1973; 1974; Porges, Arnold, & Forbes, 1973; Porges, Stamps, & Walter, 1974). In the latter, heart rate variability was also related to behavioral performance on these tasks. Since one of the main components of classical conditioning is attention to environmental contingencies, the relationship between heart rate variability and heart rate conditioning is not surprising. The present study was designed to determine if the newborn can be classically conditioned using a temporal paradigm and if this type of conditioning is related to the heart rate variability and sex of the infant.

METHOD

Subjects

An original sample of 55 full-term human neonates was selected from the nursery of the West Virginia University Hospital on the basis of the following criteria: (1) age between 35 and 80 hours; (2) birth weight between 2700 and 4100 g; (3) Apgar ratings of 8.0 or more; (4) normal spontaneous or low forceps delivery; and (5) born from mothers who had not had histories of pregnancy or delivery complications. There were 32 subjects (16 male and 16 female) included in the analysis. The other 23 subjects were excluded because of difficulty in maintaining them in a quiet awake state due to sleeping (18) or crying (5). The mean birth weights were 3378 g for the experimental group and 3419 g for the control group. Mean ages for the experimental and control subjects were 54.8 hours and 57.7 hours, respectively. There were no significant differences between groups or sexes on either age or birth weight. The medication given to the mothers was similar for both sexes and groups. The majority received either a saddle block or pudendal anesthetic. Permission was obtained from the mother before any infant was tested.

Apparatus

The laboratory room temperature was maintained at approximately 80°F (27°C). The background noise level during testing consisted primarily of "white noise" set at 60dB. Heart rate responses were continuously recorded on a Grass model 7P polygraph, with a paper speed of 10 mm per second. A Grass model 7P4D Tachograph measured heart rate which was recorded by two Beckman Bio-Potential surface electrodes. The stimuli were programmed using punched film and were presented automatically. The UCS was a 2 seconds presentation of recorded buzzer, with an intensity of 90 dB (SPL) measured at the infant's head. The buzzer was presented through a speaker, placed 3 feet directly behind the infant.

Procedure

Subjects were randomly assigned to the experimental and control groups with the stipulation that each group have an equal number of males and females. Each subject was tested in one session lasting approximately 15 minutes. The testing was done either during the period between 4:00 and 5:00 p.m., prior to the 5:30 p.m. feeding, or between 8:00 and 9:00 p.m., before the 9.30 p.m. feeding.

Subjects were brought to the laboratory, awakened if necessary, and placed in a supine position. EKG electrodes were placed approximately over the right third and left tenth rib, and a ground electrode was placed on the right calf. The infant was left to rest quietly for 2–3 minutes while the polygraph was calibrated. Spontaneous heart rate was then measured for 30 seconds before the presentation of the first stimulus.

No trials were started unless the infant was in a "quiet awake" state (eyes open with no gross body movement). If the subject changed state, the procedure was stopped until he stabilized in the quiet awake state. If this did not occur within a few minutes, an attempt was made to quiet active babies and awaken sleeping babies. The testing session was interrupted for 9 of the 32 subjects (4 experimental, 5 control). For those 9 subjects, the mean number of interruptions was 1.2.

Each experimental subject received 22 2-second presentations of the 90 dB buzzer. The buzzer was presented every 20 seconds (onset to onset), except when a test trial occurred. In this case the buzzer was omitted to observe the effects of conditioning. Four test trials were interspersed among the stimulus presentations, occurring after the 7th, 13th 18th, and 22nd UCS. When a test trial occurred, there were 40 seconds between buzzer onsets.

The control group received 22 presentations of the UCS at randomized intervals of 10, 20 and 30 seconds (onset to onset). There were, however, several restrictions on this radomization. First, both the experimental and control subjects received test trials at the same time period within the testing session. Second, both groups received the same number of stimulus presentations before each test trial. Third, both groups received the last stimulus before the test trial at the same time period within the testing session.

Quantification of Data

Heart rate was obtained from a beat by beat readout of the tachograph. The heart rate reading for each 0.5-seconds measurement interval consisted of the heart rate in beats per minute calculated from the last completed interbeat interval. Conditioning was evaluated by responses to the UCS, in anticipation of the UCS, and in its absence. Each response was quantified over a 10-second period which included 20 0.5-seconds measurement intervals. The UCS response period began with UCS onset, the anticipatory response period began 10 seconds after the previous UCS onset, and the response period in the absence of the UCS began at the time when the UCS would normally have been presented. To determine anticipatory responses and responses to the UCS, 10 trials were examined (1, 2, 5, 6, 11, 12, 15, 16, 20, 21). These were then combined into five trial blocks. The particular trials were chosen in order to sample responses at five points during the testing session. Also, specific trials were omitted from the analysis for two reasons. First, trials immediately following a test trial were excluded. Second, in the control procedure, some of the stimulus presentations were only 10 seconds apart. These trials were also specifically omitted from the analysis for both groups because 10 seconds was not sufficient time for the heart rate to recover from the previous stimulus presentation. Responses made in the absence of the UCS were evaluated on the four test trials.

RESULTS

Spontaneous Heart Rate and Heart Rate Variability

Mean heart rate and heart rate variance were computed for a 30-second period (60 0.5-second intervals) prior to the onset of the first stimulus. An analysis of variance resulted in no significant differences between the experimental and control groups or between sexes on either heart rate or heart rate variance. The difference in variance between males and females, however, approached significance, with the females showing higher variability. $F(1, 28) = 3.8$, $p < 0.06$.

Responses to the UCS

For each subject, peak acceleration in response to the UCS was defined as the highest heart rate during any 0.5-second interval in the 10-second period following UCS onset. There were no significant differences between groups, between sexes, or across trials on this variable. When the total response over the 10-second period beginning with UCS onset was examined, a Group × Interval interaction was found, $F(19,532) = 1.68$, $p < 0.05$ (interval refers to 0.5-second intervals). As illustrated in Fig. 4.1, the experimental subjects exhibited a faster return toward prestimulus level than the control subjects following peak acceleration to the UCS. At UCS onset the heart rate of the experimental group was approximately 2.5 beats per minute lower than that of the control group. This difference may be indicative of an anticipatory response occurring prior to the UCS.

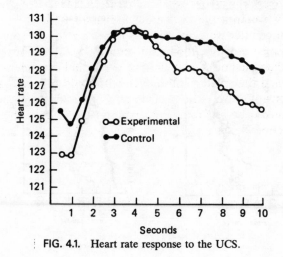

FIG. 4.1.   Heart rate response to the UCS.

FIG. 4.2. Acquisition of the anticipatory heart rate response by females.

Anticipatory Responses

An analysis of responses made in anticipation of the UCS yielded a Group × Sex × Trial Block × Interval interaction, $F(76, 2128) = 1.30, p < 0.05$. A test of simple effects indicated a Group × Trial Block × Interval interaction only in the females, $F(76, 2128) = 1.23, p < 0.05$. This interaction is shown in Fig. 4.2. There appears to be no difference between the experimental and control females on Trial Blocks 1 and 2. On Trial Blocks 3–5, however, the experimental females exhibited a lower heart rate than the control females. An analysis of trends was also done for each of the groups (experimental and control females) on each of the five trials blocks. Significant results were found only for the experimental females who exhibited responses characterized by a quadratic trend, on Trial Block 3, $F(1,7) = 6.66, p < 0.05$, and a cubic trend on Trial Block 4, $F(1,7) = 6.08, p < 0.05$.

Responses in the Absence of the UCS

In analyzing responses made in the absence of the UCS, a Group × Interval interaction was found, $F(19,532) = 1.70, p < 0.05$. A test for simple effects indicated that only the control subjects exhibited a change in heart rate across intervals, $F(19,532) = 4.08, p < 0.0001$. as seen in Fig. 4.3, the control subjects' heart rate appears to be decelerating while that of the experimental group seems to have stabilized.

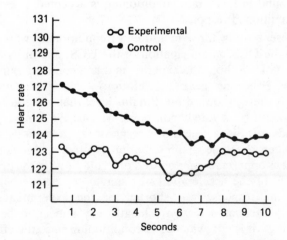

FIG. 4.3. Heart rate response in the absence of the UCS.

DISCUSSION

The interpretation of the conditioned heart rate response has often been questioned (Headrick & Graham, 1969). The difficulty occurs because the conditioned response is a deceleration, independent of the direction of the unconditioned response (UCR). In some cases, when the UCS is a noxious stimulus, the UCR will be an acceleration (Obrist, Webb, & Stutterer, 1969; Wilson, 1969). Since a conditioned response (CR) is usually defined as a response similar to the UCR, a heart rate deceleration would not always fit this definition. This interpretation is based on S–R theory (Hull, 1943) in which conditioning is said to involve an association between a stimulus (CS) and a response (UCR, CR). In cognitive learning theory, however, conditioning is defined as an association between stimuli (CS–UCS or in temporal conditioning, UCS-UCS), which is referred to as an S–S relationship (Bolles, 1972; Tolman, 1949). More specifically, an expectancy is learned during conditioning. The subject learns that one stimulus predicts the occurrence of a second stimulus and in this manner learns to expect a specific sequence of events. This latter interpretation has been used by several authors to explain the conditioned heart rate response (Clifton, 1974; Fitzgerald & Brackbill, 1976; Stamps & Porges, 1975). The heart rate deceleration in anticipation of the UCS could be described as a conditioned orienting response which prepares the infant to deal with the UCS. The deceleration in the absence of the UCS may also be an orienting response, which could be interpreted as a "searching" response for the missing stimulus. Both of these responses are based on a learned expectancy which is determined by the temporal contingency between stimuli (CS–UCS or UCS–UCS). Thus, according to cognitive learning theory, this type of S–S association found in heart rate conditioning is accepted as evidence of a classically conditioned response.

In the present study three measures of conditioning were examined: responses to the UCS, in anticipation of the UCS, and in its absence. In response to the UCS, both the experimental and control groups exhibited accelerations. Following peak acceleration, the experimental subjects showed a faster return toward prestimulus level than the control subjects. In studies of adult heart rate conditioning Wilson (1969) has reported that the magnitude of the acceleratory response to a noxious stimulus is attenuated when the time of presentation is predictable, as in classical conditioning, as opposed to randomized presentations. In the present study, the magnitude of the acceleration was similar for both groups, but the duration of the response was shorter for the experimental subjects. Although this attenuated response length may appear to be similar to Wilson's findings, it is not evidence of conditioning since the effect did not show a statistically significant development across trial blocks.

The second measure of conditioning was the response made during the anticipatory period, occurring 10 seconds before the UCS. A change in response across trial blocks was exhibited only by the females. The differences between the experimental and control females were most apparent on the last three trial blocks. These differences between groups are the result of an increase in rate across trial blocks by the control females. This finding may be due to an increase in the duration of response to the previous UCS or an increase in the arousal level in these control infants. This type of change seems to have been suppressed in the experimental subjects, possibly as a result of the predictability of the UCS presentations. Although these group differences may be a result of the experimental manipulation, tests of simple effects failed to identify a meaningful pattern of change across trial blocks which would have been indicative of acquisition. The argument for acquisition of an anticipatory response is strengthened, however, by the significant trends found only in the experimental females on Trial Blocks 3 and 4.

The relationships in the present study among the sex, heart rate variability, and conditionability of the newborn are very similar to the results reported by Stamps and Porges (1975). In both studies, females exhibited higher levels of spontaneous heart rate variability and were also more likely to exhibit conditioned responses than the males. This greater responsivity may have been due to the sex of the infant, the level of heart rate variability, or some interaction of the two.

The final measure used to evaluate conditioning was the response made in the absence of the UCS. The analysis of this period indicated that the heart rate of the experimental group had already stabilized, while the control subjects continued to exhibit a gradual deceleration. These results are similar to the responses to the UCS when the experimental group exhibited a faster return toward prestimulus levels than the control group. It was hypothesized that the experimental subjects would show further deceleration when the UCS was omitted. When an expected stimulus does not occur, the organism will usually exhibit an orienting response (Sokolov, 1963) which is characterized by heart rate deceleration. This type of response indicates that the subject has accurately perceived the time intervals between stimuli. Since a deceleration was not exhibited by the experimental subjects, the infants apparently did not accurately perceive the 20 seconds interval. The heart rate of the experimental infants, however, was lower than that of the control subjects throughout the period. This indicates that the experimental group exhibited a larger deceleration before this period in the trial and also that the lower heart rate resulting from the deceleration was sustained, at least until the end of the trial. These results are not, however, evidence for conditioning, since the response did not show development across trial blocks.

In the present study, only the females exhibited evidence of a conditioned anticipatory response. Group differences were found for responses to the UCS and in its absence, however, these responses did not show a trial effect. The results of this study seem to indicate that the temporally conditioned heart rate response in the newborn does not show the same stability as that of older subjects.

ACKNOWLEDGEMENTS

The author would like to express thanks to Stephen W. Porges for critically reading the manuscript and to Norah Gutrecht for facilitating research in the West Virginia University Hospital Newborn Nursery.

REFERENCE NOTES

1. Forbes, E. J., & Porges, S. W. (1972, October). *Heart rate classical conditioning with a noxious auditory stimulus in human newborns.* Paper presented at the meeting of the Society for Psychophysiological Research, Boston
2. Lipsitt, L. P., & Ambrose, J. A. (1967, March). *A preliminary report of temporal conditioning to three types of neonatal stimulation.* Paper presented at the meeting of the Society for Research in Child development, New York.

REFERENCES

Bolles, R. C. (1972). Reinforcement, expectancy, and learning. *Psychological Review, 79,* 394–409.

Brackbill, Y., Lintz, L. M., & Fitzgerald, H. E. (1968). Differences in the autonomic and somatic conditioning of infants. *Psychosomatic Medicine, 30,* 193–201.

Bystroletova, G. N. (1954). Obrazonvanie u novoorozhdennykh detei us lovnogo refleksa no vremi v sviazi s sutochnym ritmom kormleniia. (The formation in neonates of a conditioned reflex to time in connection with daily feeding rhythm.) *Zhurnal Vysshei nervnoi Deiatel'nosti, 4,* 601–609.

Clifton, R. K. (1974). Heart rate conditioning in the newborn infant. *Journal of Experimental Child Psychology, 18,* 9–21.

Fitzgerald, H. E., & Brackbill, Y. (1976). Classical conditioning in infancy: Development and constraints. *Psychological Bulletin, 83,* 353–376.

Headrick, M., & Grahm, F. K. (1969). Multiple-component heart rate responses conditioned under paced respiration. *Journal of Experimental Psychology, 79,* 486–494.

Hull, C. L. (1943). *Principles of behavior.* New York: Appleton-Century.

Krachkovskaia, M. V. (1959). Reflex changes in the leukocyte count of newborn infants in relation to food intake. *Pavlov Journal of Higher Nervous Activity, 9,* 193–199.

Marquis, D. P. (1941). Learning in the neonate: The modification of behavior under three feeding schedules. *Journal of Experimental Psychology, 29,* 263–282.

Obrist, P. A., Webb, R. A., & Sutterer, J. R. (1969). Heart rate and somatic changes during aversive conditioning and a simple reaction time task. *Psychophysiology, 5,* 606–723.

Porges, S. W. (1973). Heart rate variability: An autonomic correlate of reaction time performance. *Bulletin of the Psychonomic Society, 1,* 270–272.

Porges, S. W. (1974). Heart rate indices of newborn attentional responsivity. *Merrill-Palmer Quarterly, 20,* 231–234.

Porges, S. W., Arnold, W. R., & Forbes, E. J. (1973). Heart rate variability: An index of attentional responsivity in human newborns. *Developmental Psychology, 8,* 85–92.

Porges, S. W., Stamps, L. E., & Walter, G. F. (1974). Heart rate variability and newborn heart rate responses to illumination changes. *Developmental Psychology, 10,* 507–513.

Sameroff, A. J. (1971). Can conditioned responses be established in the newborn. *Developmental Psychology, 5,* 1–12.

Sokolov, E. N. (1963). *Perception and the conditioned reflex.* New York: McMillan.

Stamps. L. E., & Porges, S. W. (1975). Heart rate conditioning in newborn infants: Relationships among conditionability, heart rate variability, and sex. *Developmental Psychology, 11,* 424–431.

Tolman, E. C. (1949). There is more than one kind of learning. *Psychological Review, 56,* 144–155.

Wilson, R. S. (1969). Cardiac response: Determinants of conditioning. *Journal of Comparative and Physiological Psychology Monograph, 68* (1, Pt. 2).

5 Visual Reinforcement of Non-Nutritive Sucking in Human Infants

E. R. Siqueland and C. A. De Lucia

The development of learning tasks for the human infant, in which his behavior is made experimentally effective for producing changes in the exteroceptive environment, may provide important tools for studying the ontogeny of exploratory behavior over the first weeks and months of human life. In experiments with infants from three weeks to one year of age we began to explore the feasibility of using the sucking response as a conditioned operant to assess the infant's response to visual feedback as a reinforcing event. Sucking is a response that can be reliably elicited in most infants during the first days of life, and studies with newborns have suggested that sucking is a functionally adaptive response that may be influenced by nutritive reinforcement contingencies in the feeding situation (Sameroff, 1968). We created an artificial environment for the infant in which visual feedback was made experimentally contingent upon his emission of high-amplitude non-nutritive sucking responses.

Our apparatus consisted of a nipple and a pressure transducer which provided both polygraphic recordings of all sucking behavior and a digital record of sucking pressure in excess of 17 mm-Hg. Presentation of the projected visual stimulus was automatically programmed. Criterion amplitude sucks activated a power supply which was designed to increase the intensity of a 500-watt light source in a standard 35-mm slide projector. The reinforcing consequence was the opportunity to view on a rear projection screen a 35-mm slide. Transition from no illumination to maximum brightness of the projected visual stimulus occurred gradually, in direct

Source: *Science* (1969), *165*, pp. 1144–1146.

proportion to the infant's sucking rate ("conjugate reinforcement", Lindsley, 1963).

In the first experiment we studied the effects of visual reinforcement on the acquisition of high-amplitude sucking in 4-month-old infants. Groups of ten infants were randomly assigned to one of three experimental conditions. One group (base-line group) provided base-line reference data for spontaneous changes in the frequency of high-amplitude sucking over 10 minutes of testing in the experimental situation. For the other two groups a 15-minute conditioning procedure consisted of 2-minute baseline, 4-minute conditioning, 2-minute extinction, 4-minute reconditioning, and finally a second 3-minute extinction phase. For the sucking reinforcement group (SR group), presentation of the projected visual stimuli was experimentally contingent upon the occurrence of criterion sucking during each of the two 4-minute conditioning phases. For the last group (SW group) the occurrence of criterion sucking resulted in the discrete withdrawal of the projected visual stimuli, and each high-amplitude suck delayed the presentation of the visual stimulus for 5 seconds. For the last two groups, eight 35-mm chromatic slides (geometric patterns, cartoon figures, and human faces) were presented during each conditioning phase with a change of visual stimuli occurring every 30 seconds. During the base-line and extinction phase, infants sucked in the presence of a constant, dimly illuminated projection screen. All subjects were seated facing the projection screen on the lap of a female research assistant who held the nipple to the infant's mouth for the duration of the experimental procedures. A criterion amplitude suck was a positive pressure response of 18 mm-Hg or greater. Base-line reference data obtained from infants of this age had shown that approximately 35 per cent of the infant's normal non-nutritive sucking met our experimental criterion of a high-amplitude suck.

The mean rate of criterion sucks for each of the three groups in 1-minute blocks over base-line, conditioning, and extinction phases are shown in Fig. 5.1. The apparent reinforcing effects of visual feedback seen in the performance of the SR group reflect reliable differences ($p < 0.05$ or less for all comparisons noted; two-tailed tests) between the SR group and the other two groups during the initial 4-minute conditioning and the 2-minute extinction phases. One-way analyses of variance (Kruskal-Wallis) indicated that there were no overall differences between the base-line sucking for the three groups, but highly reliable differences between the sucking rates for these groups were obtained during the initial conditioning and extinction phases. Subsequent individual comparisons between the pairs of groups (Mann-Whitney U-test) indicated that the SR group responded at a higher rate than either of the other two groups during the first conditioning and extinction phases. Reliable differences between the high-amplitude sucking rates of the SR and SW groups were maintained over the reconditioning

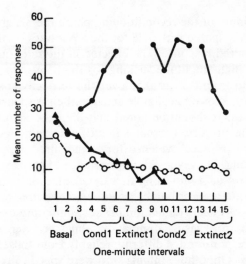

FIG. 5.1. Mean response rates for the three groups of 4-month infants over conditioning and extinction phases. Solid circles: sucking reinforcement group; open circles: stimulus withdrawal group; closed triangles: base-line group.

and final extinction phases of the experiment. A series of Wilcoxon matched-pairs tests were used to determine the statistical reliability of the apparent acquisition and extinction effects for the SR group over the conditioning and extinction procedures. This group demonstrated predictable shifts in sucking rate, indicating response acquisition and extinction effects over each of the two conditioning and two extinction phases of the experiment. Similar statistical tests with the SW group indicated negligible shifts in frequencies of criterion sucking over the conditioning and extinction phases.

The sucking data for the three groups were also analyzed with respect to changes in the proportion of criterion high-amplitude sucks relative to the total number of sucks emitted during each minute in the experimental situation. Selective reinforcement of high amplitude sucking should have resulted in progressively higher proportions of the infant's sucking behavior meeting the criterion for the conditioned operant. This analysis provided clear support for the conclusion that visual reinforcement resulted in a rapid conditioned response differentiation by the SR group. While there were negligible differences in the mean response ratios (the number of criterion amplitude sucks divided by the total number of sucks) for the three groups during base-line measures (range from 0.36 to 0.39), by the 4th minute of conditioning 0.70 of all sucks emitted by the SR group met the criterion of high-amplitude sucking. In contrast to this high proportion of criterion sucking for the sucking reinforcement group, mean response ratios for the base-line and SW groups were 0.30 and 0.24, respectively.

By the final minute of the reconditioning phase the SR group had a mean ratio of 0.85 as compared with 0.38 for the SW group. Furthermore, extinction of the acquired response was reflected in the ratio measures with the proportions of high-amplitude sucking for the SR group decreasing from 0.70 to 0.49 and from 0.85 to 0.56 over the respective extinction phases. The other groups showed negligible shifts in their response ratios over the extinction phases. It should be noted that the experimental procedure of withdrawing the projected visual stimuli contingent upon sucking (SW group) failed to produce evidence for an acquired suppression of high-amplitude sucking. However, the performance of this group does provide additional control data indicating that the changes in criterion sucking in the SR group were not attributable to either generalized arousal or specific eliciting effects of visual stimulation *per se*. Simply presenting infants with a changing pattern of visual stimulation while they were sucking did not result in their response rates differing reliably from those of the base-line control subjects. Only those infants who were specifically reinforced with visual feedback for emitting high-amplitude sucks (SR group) showed evidence of an acquired response differentiation. The reinforcing effectiveness of the visual feedback is seen in the fact that the learned response differentiation occurred quite rapidly, and by the end of 8 minutes of reinforced training these infants showed marked proficiency in their performance with better than 0.80 of their responses meeting the conditioned response criterion.

Additional evidence for the reinforcing effects of visual feedback on sucking behavior in human infants was obtained in a subsequent experiment with 12-month infants. While the first experiment showed that visual reinforcers could be employed to modify the topography of sucking in 4-month infants, the second experiment was designed to determine whether similar reinforcement procedures could be effectively employed to reestablish sucking in infants for whom non-nutritive sucking was no longer a stable response in their behavioral repertoire. Attempts to obtain base-line reference data on non-nutritive sucking with 12-month infants indicated that better than 60 per cent of the infants actively rejected the experimental nipple prior to completing a 5-minute base-line measure of sucking. The apparent aversiveness of the sucking task for these infants was reflected in the high frequency of such behaviors as "crying", "fussing" and attempts by subjects to push away the non-nutritive nipple. Thus, in the second experiment we studied the effectiveness of visual reinforcers in reestablishing sucking with 12-month infants. A second variable studied in this experiment was the effect of varying the amount of redundancy in the array of visual reinforcers on the reinforcing effectiveness of the visual feedback. Studies with infrahuman organisms have indicated that instrumental exploratory behavior increases with increasing amounts of change in the visual reinforcing event

(Berlyne, 1950; Menzel, Davenport & Rogers, 1961). Briefly, the second experiment compared the conditional sucking rates for two groups of ten 12-month infants who received visual reinforcers varying in the amount of redundancy. Both groups were presented with conditioning and extinction procedures similar to those employed with the SR group in the previous experiment. One group (high-redundancy group) received three replications of four chromatic stimuli as reinforcers over the two 4-minute conditioning phases (with a stimulus change each 30 seconds). The second group (low-redundancy group) was presented with a single replication of eight visual stimuli as reinforcers over these conditioning phases. The results showed that when sucking was made functional for visual feedback, both groups showed rapid acquisition of conditioned sucking during the initial 4-minute conditioning phase.

In contrast to a base-line reference group of 12-month infants, who averaged less than 15 sucks per minute over a 5-minute sucking measure, both of the experimental groups averaged better than 40 sucks per minute during the 4th minute of the initial conditioning phase. Although the two groups did not differ in their conditioned sucking rates during the initial 4-minute conditioning and 2-minute extinction phases, the effects of stimulus redundancy on the reinforcing effectiveness of the visual feedback was seen during the reconditioning and second extinction phases, with the high-redundancy group sucking at reliably higher levels than the low-redundancy group during both these phases. In contrast to the apparent satiation effects due to reinforcement which are reflected in the decreasing sucking rates for the former group during reconditioning (third and fourth replication of the set of four stimuli), infants receiving only the second replication of the set of eight stimuli during reconditioning (low-redundancy group) maintained highly stable rates of conditioned sucking. These results supported the prediction that the reinforcing effectiveness of visual feedback was reliably influenced by the amount of stimulus redundancy.

Our experiments provide support for the conclusion that effective reinforcement of motivated behavior in the young human infant is not limited to a restricted class of stimuli in his environment. In addition to nutritive reinforcers, there are other classes of stimuli, possibly in each of the sensory modalities, that are effective in strengthening instrumental behaviors in infants. Berlyne (1967) has suggested that any stimuli that are effective in "capturing the subject's attention" can have reinforcing value in suitable circumstances. The important developmental problem is the specification of stimulus parameters which distinguish positive and negative stimuli, and distinguish reinforcing and nonreinforcing stimuli for the developing infant in each of the sensory modalities. In subsequent experiments with infants we have found that visual feedback of the type employed in these experiments was effective in supporting motivated exploratory behavior with infants as young as 3 weeks of age. Furthermore, acquisition of conditioned sucking has been demonstrated when heterogeneous auditory feedback in the form of music and human voices was employed for reinforcement.

REFERENCES

Berlyne, D. E. (1950). *British Journal of Psychology, 41,* 68.

Berlyne, D. E. (1967). In D. Levin (Ed.) *Nebraska Symposium on Motivation,* University of Nebraska Press, Lincoln, p. 1.

Lindsley, O. R. (1963). *American Journal of Orthopsychiatry, 33,* 624.

Menzel, E. W., Davenport, R. K., & Rogers, C. M. (1961). *Journal of Comparative Physiological Psychology, 54,* 16.

Sameroff, A. J. (1968). *Journal of Experimental Child Psychology, 6,* 607.

6 Reactions to Response-Contingent Stimulation in Early Infancy

John S. Watson and Craig T. Ramey

When a stimulus consistently follows an individual's response, the situation is set for instrumental learning. If the stimulus is rewarding and the individual is capable of learning, the response should become more frequent. Thus, the traditional learning analysis would ask whether the response is affected by the situation (e.g., does the response become more frequent, stronger, etc.). In this paper, we shall ask this standard learning question in an analysis of the effectiveness of a special learning situation which was arranged for young infants. As a consequence of an unexpected reaction to this learning situation, however, we shall also consider the question of whether for the human infant the response-contingent stimulus is affected by its occurrence in early instrumental learning situations. In the concluding portion of this paper we will propose that the stimulus very likely is affected in that it appears to acquire the functional meaning of a "social stimulus" for the human infant.

The data we will discuss are from a short-term longitudinal study conducted at the Institute of Human Development. The study involved presenting two weeks of a special contingency experience to infants between their eighth and tenth weeks of life. Some previous research suggested that the human infant, under natural conditions, might be undergoing a deprivation of opportunity to engage in and adapt to contingency experiences. The combination of his short memory and the long recovery periods of his naturally effective motor responses could prohibit his becoming aware of otherwise manageable contingencies in his world. Prohibiting the exercise

Source: *Merrill-Palmer Quarterly* (1972), *18*, 219-227. Copyright 1972 Wayne State University Press.

of the available capacity for processing contingency information could deprive the infant of a formative intellective experience. It has been hypothesized that this "natural deprivation period" might exist for much of the first three months of life (Watson, 1966a; 1967).

The underlying objective of our research was to provide infants with manageable response-contingent stimulation within the first three months on the assumption that this would lower the effects of the natural deprivation period. Of necessity, then, the preliminary objective for this study was the development of a means to present manageable response-contingent stimulation to young infants in their homes which would allow them to exercise their capacity over some specified period of days.

METHOD

Apparatus

A special system (pictured in Watson, 1971) was constructed to provide the contingency situation. Basically, the apparatus was like a floor lamp which extended over the crib so that a visual display could be hung approximately 18 inches above the infant's head while he lay in his crib at home. The display was a rather simple set of three polyurethane forms, either three spheres or three rectangles, painted different colors and held in a fixed cluster by a wire frame. The display was hung from the shaft of an electric motor on the stand. This allowed electrical control of the display so that when activated it would rotate 90 degrees (this rotary movement lasted one second).

A pressure sensing pillow was developed so that small changes in pressure on the pillow would serve to operate the system. The electronic controls and an event counter were contained within an auxiliary sound-proof box. Thus, the system provided the infant with the possibility of controlling the rotation of the visual display by making very small movements of his head. It was assumed that such small movements could be made and repeated within sufficiently short periods of time to be within the memory limits of the infant and so be a contingency experience of which the infant could become functionally aware.

Subjects

Forty eight-week-old infants from the East San Francisco Bay Area served as Ss.[1] The Berkeley city birth records were used to preselect full term

---

[1]Two additional infants participated in the study but have been dropped from the analysis due to procedural irregularities. Both were in the experimental group. In one case the pillow was placed under the infant's back rather than head and in the other case the mother built a competing mobile as described later in the text.

babies who were being reared at home by their natural parents and whose fathers had at least completed college. Better than 90% of the families contacted agreed to participate in the study. These infants were randomly assigned to three groups, 18 to an experimental group and 11 each to two control groups. Each group was composed of approximately an equal number of each sex.

Procedure

The "contingency mobile" was placed in the homes of the 18 experimental infants. Mothers of the infants were instructed to hang the display and turn on the system for 10 minutes a day for 14 consecutive days. The instructions to the mothers of the 22 controls were the same as to the experimentals. In all cases the mothers were requested to expose their infants to the display at a time when the infants were peaceful and alert. They were instructed to record the event counter reading which indicated the number of times the system was activated during the daily session. The controls differed from the experimentals in that the display did not turn in response to pressure on the pillow. For half of the controls the display did not turn at all. This display was descriptively labelled the "stabile." For the other half of the control infants, the display did rotate periodically (at approximately a rate of once every 3 to 4 seconds), but the rotation was automatic and unrelated to pressure on the pillow. This display was descriptively labelled the noncontingent mobile or "auto-mobile."

As noted above, the number of pillow activations were recorded by the infant's mother at the end of each 10-minute exposure period. Thus, a record was available for each infant of the number of times he activated the system during exposure to the display on each of the 14 days.

RESULTS

Analysis of the home display records indicates that the infants who were able to control the movement of the display showed an increase in activations per 10-minute session across the 14 days of exposure (see Fig. 6.1). On the average, these experimental infants began with a rate of about 90 responses per session and this rate rose to about 135 per session in the final days (change in rate from days 1–2 to 13–14, $t = 3.72$, $p < 0.01$). The stabile control infants began with about 90 per session and ended with about 95 ($t < 1$, NS). The noncontingent controls began with about 80 and ended with about 90 per session ($t < 1$, NS). Comparison of the two control groups indicated they did not differ reliably either at the beginning (days 1–2, $t < 1$, NS) or in the final sessions (days 13–14, $t < 1$, NS), and this fact strongly suggests the turning of the display was not itself an elicitor of pillow activation either initially or after two weeks of exposure. It would

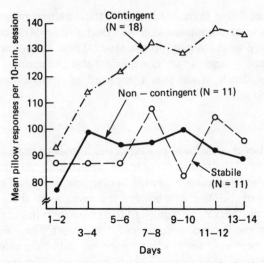

FIG. 6.1.   Pillow responses per ten-minute session across two weeks for the experimental and two control groups.

seem, then, that the rise in pillow activation evidenced by the experimental infants was due to the fact that their turning displays were contingent on their head movements on their pillows. They reacted to this response-contingent stimulation by learning to control it.

The adaptive instrumental reaction of these two-month-old infants across the two weeks of response-contingent stimulation is notable on two counts. First, it demonstrates that instrumental behavior or secondary circular reactions can be aroused and maintained in an infant's home environment at least one month earlier than Piagetian norms would indicate (Piaget, 1952). Second, the adaptive reaction also indicates the design of artificial situations to facilitate early control of response-contingent stimulation in the home is a very feasible art.

Possibly even more notable than the instrumental reaction, however, is a second type of reaction to the response-contingent stimulation as reported by the mothers of the infants. This reaction was not expected and was therefore recorded less systematically and objectively than would have been desirable. Nevertheless, the overall consistency of reports strongly suggests that the experimental infants had a very different "socio-emotional" reaction to their contingency mobiles than did the controls to their stabiles or noncontingent mobiles.

Although the idea to employ mobile-like structures as means to present contingent and noncontingent stimuli was inspired by the use of mobiles by Hunt and Uzgiris (1964) and Uzgiris and Hunt (1965) in their longitudinal study of the effect of recognition on infant attention, a trend reported in that study was not taken very seriously. Uzgiris and Hunt attempted to assess an hypothesis that "a stimulus pattern which moves predictably in response to the infant's efforts would be preferred over an equally familiar, but unresponsive one". Difficulties occurred in the presentation of responsive mobiles due to "a failure to anticipate the variety of infant cribs". Responsiveness of the pattern depended on the ability of the infant to shake his crib. Uzgiris and Hunt concluded that some cribs were too rigid and some were too bouncy so that in the latter case "the infant had no opportunity to establish a connection between his intentional movements and the swaying of the pattern, since it swayed practically all the time". But in a few cases (Uzgiris & Hunt, 1965, p. 10):

. . . where the cribs were moderately mobile, the infants developed what may be called a "relationship" with the responsive pattern: the infant's kicking would set the pattern in motion, which he then watched with signs of delight like cooing and laughing until the movement almost stopped, and then the infant would kick again, repeating such interaction for a considerable length of time. All the infants who developed such a relationship preferred the responsive pattern to the unresponsive one, but these cases were too few for a statistical test.

The observations of the present study would indicate that while Uzgiris and Hunt uncovered only a few cases of "socio-emotional" responding to the responsive mobile, those few infants were displaying a reliable reaction. Under the conditions of the present study, the appearance of this reaction was impressive.

We constructed 10 display systems; and, in order to ease scheduling problems, these systems were put into homes at the rate of 5 per week. This procedure had an unplanned advantage in that as we began to uncover hints of the rather special reaction of the first experimental Ss, we were able to inquire of our later experimental and control mothers about any noteworthy reactions on the part of their infants.

The first major suggestion of something unusual happening with the contingency mobile occurred when we arrived to pick up the system at the home of one of our first five experimental infants. The infant's mother reported that she had used the system again that day even though she had already completed the 14 day period. She said she hoped we didn't mind but she "had to get some work done in the kitchen". We had already noted the experimental mothers were showing a possibly greater interest in the study than the controls, but we had assumed that this, if it were a real difference, was probably due to the interest in the fact their babies were showing a learning capacity they had not anticipated. But this mother's choice to make additional "baby sitting" use of the contingency mobile implied that it had greater entertainment value than that possessed by the control systems.

With the remaining mothers in the study we began to inquire more fully about the attentional and expressive behavior of their infants to the exposure experience. All the infants were seen in the laboratory at the Institute of Human Development at the end of their two week exposure period. At the end of the laboratory session, mothers were interviewed. We asked mothers during this interview about the way in which they normally elicited smiling from their baby. We now inserted a casual inquiry as to whether the infant ever displayed any smiling or cooing behavior toward our mobile. The average response of experimentals can be summarized by an emphatic yes with answers of the following kind: "It was hysterical," and "Oh yes, a great deal". The response of the control mothers can be summarized by a passive yes as exemplified by answers such as "Yes, I think so," and "Yes, now and then". Two experimental mothers reported that their babies showed their first broad smiling and hearty cooing to the experimental mobile and then after a few days began displaying this kind of responsiveness to their parents.

One experimental mother reported "you have to see it, when he's with his mobile, you can't distract him, he loves it." With further inquiry it appeared that the experimental babies blossomed into smiling and cooing after a few days of exposure to the contingency mobile. There were only 3 exceptions to this pattern amongst the experimental Ss and there was only one control mother's report that resembled that of the experimentals. We took an opportunity to observe this control being exposed to his display. He did indeed show all the signs reported by experimentals including continuous smiling and cooing and intent fixation. It was also notable, however, that his activation rate on the pillow had progressed to a high rate across the two week exposure experience. He was in the noncontingent control group. The repetitive specificity of his head response to the display has led us to tentatively conclude that he may have become "superstitiously conditioned" due to an initial chance coordination between his rate of head movement and rate of periodic turning of the mobile.

The three exceptional experimental infants are also interesting. In the first case, when asked about the attending and expressive behavior the mother said, "a little, but not at all like to his old mobile." When asked further about her infant's "old mobile," the mother reported that it was just a regular mobile that they had hung up when the baby was 4 to 5 weeks old. She went on to say that after a few days he had become very excited over his mobile and began smiling and cooing a great deal at it. At this point we thought we had uncovered the perfect exception to the rule. Fortunately we thought to ask whether the infant had been able to affect the movement of the mobile by his own movement. The mother answered, "Oh yes, you see he was in a cradle and the mobile was attached to the side so that when he moved so did the mobile." She said that in the beginning they jiggled the mobile for him but that soon he began doing it on his own. In the other two exceptions, one showed no indication that he learned to operate the mobile – that is, his activation rate did not increase across sessions. The other did produce a daily activation record which indicated learning but the infant's method of activating the pillow was by way of strenuous arching of her body which may have had a prohibitive effect on the occurrence of smiling and cooing.

A final anecdote worth reporting is that of an experimental mother who, after a week of using our mobile, was inspired to construct one of her own. She attached strings to her infant's feet and arranged pulleys so that his kicking made a hanging display rotate and jiggle. The rate of movement to our experimental mobile dropped off during the last week of exposure and the mother reported a loss of interest in our mobile. We observed the infant with our mobile and noted that he kicked a good deal and then began to get upset. We asked her how much she was exposing her infant to the mobile she constructed. She reported that she attached the infant to it about 5 to 6 times a day for about 15 minutes to a half hour at a time on the average. In one session she said the infant had kept his mobile going for one and a half hours straight with great laughter and vocalization. She further reported that the baby now seemed to sleep better, be more alert while awake, and no longer needed his pacifier. We then tried to caution this mother that she might be engaging in "too much of a good thing." We suggested that she reduce the times a day she used this system of entertainment because her son might be missing an opportunity to learn about other things in his world.

DISCUSSION

These observations suggest that "socio-emotional" behavior arises in the context of repetitive experience with a specific contingent stimulus. How else are we to understand the vigorous smiling and cooing to the contingent mobile when in fact those behaviors – that is, the smiling and cooing – had no instrumental value for making the mobile turn? The observations further imply that it may well be the repetitive occurrence of a contingent stimulus which first elicits vigorous smiling and cooing and high attentional regard.

This "social" reaction raises the possibility that the method by which evolution may have guaranteed special responsiveness and attentional deployment toward members of the same species for humans may not have been by way of an instinctive response to the physical characteristics of the face stimulus (Fantz, 1961; Watson, 1966b), or by the association of this face stimulus with rewarding caretaking activities (Gewirtz, 1965), or by association with distal receptor stimulation (Walters & Parke, 1966). Rather, it may be that social responsiveness and high attentional deployment are set to occur for any repetitive contingent stimulus and its context. Under natural circumstances, it would seem more than likely that the first repetitive contingency experience of the human infant will occur within responsive interactions between himself and his caretaker. However, considering the existing evidence that the contingency memory limit of the young infant is about seven seconds (Watson, 1967), it seems unlikely that the contingency situation which releases hearty smiling and cooing is to be found in major caretaking activities. If it is true that to become aware of a contingency (i.e., to recognize a stimulus as being response-contingent) the infant must control the stimulus twice within at most seven seconds, situations such as crying-brings-comfort or kicking-brings-food are unlikely to generate contingency awareness. We are led to speculate, therefore, that the natural generic "social situation" is some form of playful interaction, between infant and caretaker.

CONCLUSION

Whether initial contingency experiences occur naturally or in the "artificial" context of a responsive mechanical system (e.g., the contingency mobile), the infant's reactions to the response-contingent stimulation appear to be of two kinds. The infant reacts intellectually by moving forward to what Piaget (1952) describes as the sensory-motor stage of secondary circular reactions. Additionally, he reacts "socio-emotionally" by displaying vigorous smiling and cooing in the contingency situation. It is clear that both of these reactions are significant events in the development of the human infant. It should be equally clear that providing infants with mechanically arranged contingency experiences must be pursued with caution. Until we more fully understand the social and intellective effects of providing response-contingent stimulation in early infancy, it would seem only reasonable to approach this form of early stimulation as an unknown quantity which might be either beneficial or harmful, depending on the amount and timing of its presentation.

ACKNOWLEDGEMENTS

Portions of this paper were initially reported at the Biennial Meeting of the Society for Research in Child Development, Santa Monica, 1969.

REFERENCES

Fantz, R. (1961). The origin of form perception. *Scientific American, 204,* 66–72.
Gewirtz, J. (1965). The course of infant smiling in four child-rearing environments in Israel. In B. Foss (Ed.), *Determinants of infant behavior, III.* New York: Wiley, pp. 205–260.
Hunt, J. & Uzgiris, I. (1965). *Cathexis from recognitive familiarity: An exploratory study.* Paper presented at the Convention of the American Psychological Association, Los Angeles, Cal.

Piaget, J. (1952). *The origins of intelligence in children.* (Margaret Cook, Translator) New York: International University Press.

Uzgiris, I. & Hunt, J. (1965, March). *The effect of recognition on infant attention: A longitudinal study.* Paper presented at the Society for Research in Child Development. Minneapolis, Minn.

Walters, R. & Parke, R. (1965). The role of the distance receptors in the development of social responsiveness. In L. Lipsit & C. Spiker (Eds), *Advances in child development and behavior, 2.* New York: Academic Press, pp. 59–96.

Watson, J. S. (1966a). The development and generalization of "contingency awareness" in early infancy: Some hypotheses. *Merrill-Palmer Quarterly, 12,* 123–135.

Watson, J. S. (1966b). Perception of object orientation in infants. *Merrill-Palmer Quarterly, 12,* 73–94.

Watson, J. S. (1967). Memory and "contingency analysis" in infant learning. *Merrill-Palmer Quarterly, 13,* 55–76.

Watson, J. S. (1971). Cognitive-perceptual development in infancy: Setting for the seventies. *Merrill-Palmer Quarterly, 17,* 139–152.

7
Reactivation of Infant Memory

C. K. Rovee-Collier, M. W. Sullivan, M. Enright, D. Lucas, and
J. W. Fagen

Rutgers University, New Jersey, U.S.A.

Three-month-old infants learned to activate a crib mobile by means of operant
footkicks. Retention of the conditioned response was assessed during a cued
recall test with the nonmoving mobile. Although forgetting is typically complete after an 8-day retention interval, infants who received a reactivation
treatment – a brief exposure to the reinforcer 24 hours before retention testing
– showed no forgetting after retention intervals of either 2 or 4 weeks. Further,
the forgetting function after a reactivation treatment did not differ from the
original forgetting function. These experiments demonstrate that (1) "reactivation" or "reinstatement" is an effective mechanism by which early experiences can continue to influence behavior over lengthy intervals and (2) memory deficits in young infants are best viewed as retrieval deficits.

The pervasive influences of early experiences on later behavior have been
extensively documented, as have early memory deficits or "infantile
amnesia" (Beach & Jaynes, 1954; Schachtel, 1947). Considered jointly,
these phenomena pose a major paradox for students of development: How
can the effects of early experiences persist into adolescence and adulthood
if they are forgotten during infancy and early childhood? Campbell and
Jaynes (1966) proposed a resolution to this paradox in terms of reinstatement, a mechanism that maintains a memory which would otherwise be
forgotten through occasional reencounters with the original training conditions over the period of development. Any given reencounter, however,
would be insufficient to promote new learning in organisms lacking the
early experience. Spear (1973) attributed the efficacy of reinstatement procedures to improved retrieval produced by the reactivation of a sufficient

Source: *Science* (1980), *208*, pp. 1159-1161. Copyright 1980 by the AAAS.

number (or kind) of existing but otherwise inaccessible attributes of the target memory. He hypothesized that reexposure to stimuli from the original training context, which had been stored as attributes of the memory, could prime or arouse other attributes that represented the original experience, increasing their accessibility and, thus, the probability of their retrieval.

"Reinstatement" or "reactivation" has been demonstrated in young and adult rats (Campbell & Jaynes, 1966; Spear & Parsons, 1976; Mactutus, Riccio & Ferek, 1979) and in grade-school children (Hoving, Coates, Bertucci & Riccio, 1972). We now report that a reactivation treatment can alleviate forgetting in 3-month-old infants after a retention interval as long as 4 weeks and that the forgetting function after a reactivation treatment is similar to the function after original training.

Our procedures were modeled after those of animal memory studies in which the experimenter trains a specific response in a distinctive context and later returns the subject to that context to see if the response is still produced. Because the retrieval cues are contextual and response production is assessed before reinforcement is reintroduced, the procedure is analogous to a test of cued recall (Spear, 1973).

In our studies, footkicks of 3-month-olds were reinforced by movement of an overhead crib mobile. The infant controlled both the intensity and frequency of the mobile movement by means of a ribbon connecting the ankle (Plate 1) with the hook from which the mobile hung. This procedure, "mobile conjugate reinforcement," produces rapid acquisition and high, stable response rates attributable to the contingency and not to behavioral arousal (Rovee-Collier & Gekoski, 1979). During nonreinforcement phases (baseline, retention tests, extinction), the mobile remained in view but was hung from a second mobile stand with no ribbon attachment and could not be activated by kicks.

Infants received three procedurally identical sessions in their home cribs. The first two were training sessions, spaced by 24 hours; the third followed a lengthy retention interval. Each session consisted of a 9-minute reinforcement phase preceded and followed by a 3-minute nonreinforcement period. In session 1, the initial 3-minute period defined the baseline; in sessions 2 and 3, it was a long-term retention test of the effects of prior training. Total footkicks during this test (B) were expressed as a fraction of the infant's total kicks during the 3-minute nonreinforcement phase at the conclusion of the preceding session (A), which was an immediate retention test. The ratio B/A indexed the extent of an infant's forgetting from one session to the next. Ratios of ≥ 1.00 indicated no forgetting, and < 1.00 indicated fractional loss.[1]

---

[1]Because operant levels are typically doubled or tripled during acquisition, retention ratios of 0.30 to 0.40 usually indicate performance at operant level. A 3-minute period of nonreinforcement at the conclusion of initial training sessions does not typically extinguish responding in infants 11 to 13 weeks of age.

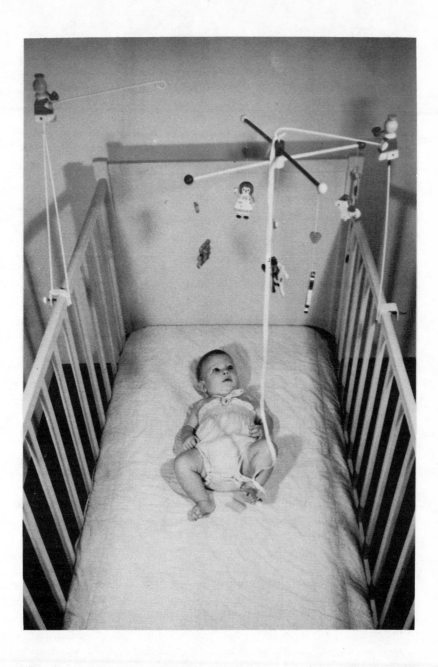

PLATE 1   An infant during a reinforcement phase with the ankle ribbon attached to the same suspension bar as that from which the mobile hangs. The empty mobile stand, clamped to the crib rail at the left, will hold the mobile during periods of nonreinforcement. (Photograph by Breck P. Kent.) (See also Plate 2, overleaf.)

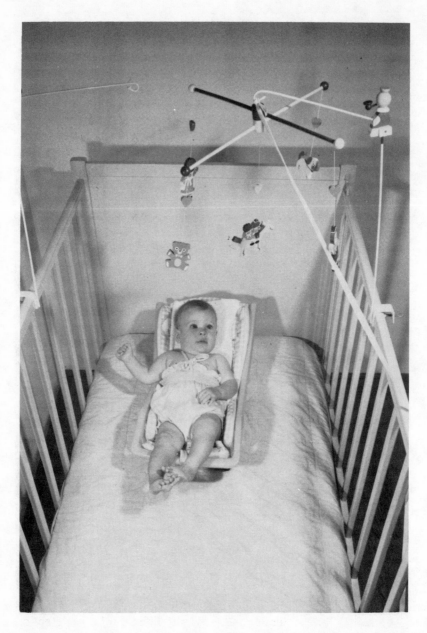

PLATE 2   The same infant (as in Plate 1) during a reactivation treatment. The mobile and ribbon are attached to the same suspension hook, but the ribbon is drawn and released by the experimenter (not shown), concealed from the infant's view at the side of the crib. Also not shown is the empty stand, positioned as before. The infant will be exposed to the reinforcer (the moving mobile) for only 3 minutes, 24 hours before retention testing. (Photograph by Breck P. Kent.)

A reactivation treatment was administered 24 hours before session 3. It consisted of a 3-minute exposure to the reinforcer (mobile movement) in a context identical to that of session 2 except that (1) the ribbon was not connected to the ankle but was draped over the side of the crib, where it was drawn and released by the experimenter at a rate corresponding to each infant's mean response rate during the final 3 minutes of acquisition in session 2; and (2) the infant was in a reclining seat (Plate 2), which minimized footkicks and altered the topography of those which did occur.[2] These changes, as well as the brevity of the reminder, precluded the opportunity for new learning or practice during a reactivation treatment. Footkicks were recorded by the experimenter and, independently, by a second observer present for at least a third of the sessions and naive with respect to group assignment and session number. Pearson product-moment reliability coefficients were > 0.95 for all studies reported here.

In study 1, retention of conditioned footkicks was assessed 2 weeks after training. Infants [mean $(\overline{X})$ age = 88.4 days, standard error (S.E.) = 3.3] were tested in three groups of six each: (1) a reactivation group received a 3-minute reminder 13 days after session 2 (24 hours before session 3); (2) a no-reactivation group received training but no reactivation treatment prior to session 3; and (3) a familiarization/reactivation control group received a procedure identical to that of the reactivation group except that infants in this group were removed from their cribs during the reinforcement phases of sessions 1 and 2 and thus had no training before session 3. The rates at which their reminders occurred were matched to those of the reactivation group.

Infants in this control group showed no change in response rate either within or across sessions (all t's < 1). Thus, infants of this age do not simply become more active over the 2-week interval, and their footkicking during the session-3 cued recall test is not a result of either elicited familiarity reactions or the reactivation treatment per se. The acquisition curve of this group in session 3, when reinforcement was introduced for the first time, was indistinguishable from the session-1 learning curves of the other two groups. An analysis of variance with repeated measures over sessions and blocks confirmed that response rates of the reactivation and no-reactivation groups did not differ during training (Fig. 7.1A). A 2 by 2 analysis of variance over retention ratios yielded a significant group-by-sessions interaction: Although 24-hour retention ratios did not differ, the 14-day retention ratio of the reactivation group significantly exceeded that of the no-reactivation group ($p < 0.01$), whose ratio reflected a return to baseline performance of session 1 (Fig. 7.1B). The retention ratio of the reactivation group

---

[2]During the reactivation treatment, infants produced responses at a rate of 0 to 2 kicks per minute: operant levels are typically 8 to 11 kicks per minute. In the infant seat, infants rarely exhibit the vertical leg thrusts characteristic of conditioned responding: rather, their movements seem to be postural adjustments or horizontal squirming.

was as high as in the 24-hour measure. Thus, both prior training and a reminder are prerequisite for reactivation.

In study 2, we repeated the procedure with 18 infants ($\overline{X}$ age = 76.9 days, S.E. = 2.0) but doubled the length of the retention interval. The reactivation group (N = 9) received a reminder 27 days after training, and retention was assessed the next day. A significant group-by-sessions interaction ($p < 0.03$) again confirmed the superior retention of the reactivation group in session 3 relative to that of the no-reactivation group (N = 9), which received no reminder during the retention interval (Fig. 7.1B). As before, the groups had not differed during training (Fig. 7.1A) or in 24-hour

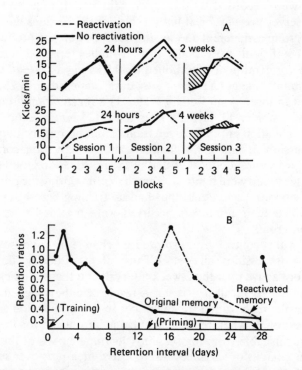

FIG 7.1. (A) Mean kicks per minute during training (sessions 1 and 2) and an identical session (session 3) occurring either 2 or 4 weeks after the completion of session 2. Blocks 1 and 5 are nonreinforcement phases; performance during long-term retention tests (block 1, session 2 or 3) is expressed as a fraction of the infant's performance during immediate retention tests (block 5, session 1 or 2, respectively). The reactivation group received a reminder 24 hours before the 2- or 4-week session; the facilitating or priming effect of the reactivation treatment is indicated by the hatched area, session 3.

(B) Retention ratios after 2 days of training (solid line) or 2 days of training plus a reactivation treatment (broken line); priming occurred 13 days after training for all points connected by broken lines or 27 days after training for the single data point at the 28-day retention interval. Each data point represents at least five infants.

retention performance. The 28-day ratio of the no-reactivation group reflected performance equivalent to their session-1 baseline level. The retention ratio (0.96) of the reactivation group is remarkable in view of the relatively young age of the infants during training and the relatively large portion of their lives that 4 weeks constitutes.

In study 3, we determined the course of forgetting following a reactivation treatment. Twenty infants ($\overline{X}$ age = 90.0 days, S.E. = 1.3) received a reactivation treatment 13 days after training as described for study 1; however, session 3 now occurred 3, 6, 9, or 15 days (N = 5 per interval) after the reminder. This corresponded to 16, 19, 22, or 28 days, respectively, after the completion of training. The session-3 retention ratios, along with those of the six infants tested 1 day after a reactivation treatment in study 1, were compared with retention ratios describing the original forgetting function. [We had previously obtained this function from 69 infants in a number of different experiments (Rovee & Fagen, 1976; Sullivan, Rovee-Collier & Tynes, 1979; Gekoski, 1980) carried out according to the same procedure as that used with the no-reactivation groups of this report.] At least five infants per retention interval contributed data 1, 2, 3, 4, 5, 7, 8, or 14 days after training (Fig. 7.1B). The no-reactivation group of study 2, tested after a 28-day retention interval, was also a control group for the reactivation group tested 15 days after the reminder (28 days after training).

Figure 7.1B is a composite of retention ratios of all groups tested after 2 days of training only ("original memory" function) or after 2 days of training plus a reactivation treatment ("priming") given either 13 (studies 1 and 3) or 27 (study 2) days after training ("reactivated memory" function). A one-way analysis of variance over all data points except that of the study-2 reactivation group indicated that ratios differed reliably as a function of retention interval ($p < 0.025$) and provided the error term for individual comparisons between means (Duncan's multiple range test). The latter indicated that the apparent increase above 1.00 in retention ratios in each function (Fig. 7.1B) was reliable: also, ratios of groups tested 8 (original memory function) and 19 (reactivated memory function) days after training did not differ from ratios of no-reactivation groups tested after retention intervals of 14 and 28 days, respectively. Regression analyses indicated that retention was a linear decreasing function of time since either training ($p < 0.005$) or priming ($p < 0.005$). Although the linear model provided a relatively poor fit in each instance, the intercepts and slopes of the two functions did not differ (t's < 1). Thus, forgetting of a reactivated memory followed the same temporal course as forgetting of the original experience.

Our findings confirm Campbell and Jaynes' (1966) proposition that reinstatement is a potent mechanism through which experiences of early infancy can continue to influence behavior. An infant's reencounters with contextual aspects of prior training or an earlier experience can prime or recycle the remaining memory attributes and enhance access to them, alleviating forgetting which otherwise appeared complete weeks earlier. Moreover, a reencounter with the original context can maintain access to the target memory with the same efficacy as original training. Our findings also implicate reinstatement as the mechanism which, during infancy, facilitates the acquisition of the vast amount of learning characteristic of that period of development.

More generally, our findings support a distinction between availability and accessibility of information in memory and imply that failures to observe retention in infants should be discussed in terms of retrieval failures rather than memory deficits (Spear, 1973; Spear & Parsons, 1976). We think that procedures that improve accessibility to important retrieval cues will radically alter current views of infant memory (Cohen & Gelber, 1975; Kagan, 1979; Ramsay & Campos, 1978) and that conditioning procedures, which permit a direct assessment of retention in infants, offer a promising means by which to bridge the gap between human and animal memory research.

ACKNOWLEDGEMENTS

Study 1 of this research formed a portion of a dissertation submitted by M.W.S. to Rutgers University in partial fulfillment of the requirements for the Ph.D. J. Davis and L. O'Brien assisted in the data collection. Supported by NIMH grant 32307 to C. K. R.-C.

REFERENCES

Beach, F. A. & Jaynes, J. (1954). *Psychological Bulletin, 51,* 239.

Campbell, B. A. & Jaynes, J. (1966). *Psychological Review, 73,* 478.

Cohen, L. B. & Gelber, E. R. (1975). In L. B. Cohen, & P. Salapatek (Eds.), *Infant Perception: From Sensation to Cognition, 1,* 347. New York: Academic Press.

Gekoski, M. J. (1980, April). Paper presented at the meeting of the Eastern Psychological Association, Hartford, Conn.

Hoving, K. L., Coates, L., Bertucci, M., & Riccio, D. C. (1972). *Developmental Psychology, 6,* 426.

Kagan, J. (1979). *The Sciences, 19,* 6.

Mactutus, C. F., Riccio, D. C., & Ferek, J. M. (1979). *Science, 204,* 1319.

Ramsay, D. S. & Campos, J. J. (1978). *Developmental Psychology, 14,* 79.

Rovee, C. K. & Fagen, J. W. (1976). *Journal of Experimental Child Psychology, 21,* 1.

Rovee-Collier, C. K. & Gekoski, M. J. (1979). *Advances in Child Development and Behaviour, 13,* 195.

Schachtel, E. G. (1947). *Psychiatry, 10,* 1.

Spear, N. E. (1973). *Psychological Review, 80,* 163.

Spear, N. E. & Parsons, P. J. (1976). In D. L. Medin, W. A. Roberts, & R. T. Davies (Eds.), *Processes of Animal Memory, 135,* Hillsdale, N. J.: Lawrence Erlbaum Associates Inc.

Sullivan, M. W., Rovee-Collier, C. K. & Tynes, D. M. (1979). *Child Development, 50,* 152.

III   PERCEPTION TO COGNITION

8 Events and Encounters in Infant Perception

George Butterworth

INTRODUCTION

Developmental psychologists have become fond of announcing how very much cleverer the human infant is than was ever realized. Of course, the truth is that it is not babies who have become cleverer but the psychologists who study them. The aim of this paper is to show how new sophisticated theories of perception have provided a framework for a reappraisal of long cherished assumptions of the perceptual abilities of very young babies.

Until the early 1970s much research on infant visual perception was carried out using static stimuli such as checkerboards, schematic faces, or geometric designs. A lot was learned from these studies about infants' visual acuity, preference for patterned over plain stimuli, colour vision and other psychophysical parameters. Nevertheless, these studies imposed a particular theory of perception on the baby and ignored the fact that in the real world we must obtain information about the environment from an ever changing, dynamic flux of stimulation that impinges on all the senses. "Frozen" perception in a single modality is the exception, not the rule, in life, and yet psychologists assumed that the static case was somehow the simplest and most appropriate for measuring the abilities of babies.

DYNAMIC APPROACHES TO PERCEPTION

There has been a strong tradition of "dynamic" perception in adult psychology, especially in the ecological psychology of James J Gibson (1979) of Cornell University in the USA and Gunnar Johansson of Uppsala in Swe-

Source: *The New Psychologist* (1986), pp. 3–7.

den. This approach is known as "event perception" (Johansson, Von Hofsten and Jansson, 1980). Johansson et al point out that the shift from static to dynamic models of perception in the adult literature coincided with a move away from the assumption that visual perception depends upon the analysis of cues contained within a frozen retinal image towards an analysis of the flow of sensory stimulation. Information can be generated by the moving objects in the environment, by the movements of the perceiver, or by the interaction of movements of object and observer. On the dynamic theory visual perception occurs by means of information available in the flux of stimulation.

Within this flux certain transitions reliably specify events in the environment and others specify the actions of the perceiving organism. Recently, the theoretical rationale for this approach has been further elaborated and more formal definitions have been offered. Warren and Shaw (1985) distinguish between "events" and "encounters" in perception. "Events" are defined in terms of the minimum units of persistence and change contained within the flow of visual information at the retina which specify the objective properties of the environment and which do not involve the activities of the observer. For example, one object may occlude another through its own motion as it passes across a particular point of observation but the observer's own activities need not be involved in generating this sensory transformation in the visual array. "Encounters", on the other hand, actively involve the observer: they are events that contain information derived from, or implicated in, the control of action (in Gibson's 1979 terminology such functional properties of sensory stimulation are called "affordances"). Hence, the reference to "events" and "encounters" in the title of this article.

EVENTS IN INFANT PERCEPTION

The dynamic approach to infant perception has been pioneered by Eleanor Gibson, and her students at Cornell, by Claus von Hofsten in Sweden, and by Tom Bower at the University of Edinburgh in Scotland. A rapidly growing number of studies has shown that even the youngest infant reveals remarkable abilities once the investigator takes a dynamic approach to perception.

When we observe one object occlude another we experience the event as a temporary disappearance of the hidden object, rather than an annihilation of it. The "permanence" of the object is one of the fundamental outcomes of event perception; the perception of permanence ensures continuity and coherence of experience through the many vanishings and reappearances of things in the field of view.

Bower (1967) was the first to suggest that babies perceive permanence. Infants aged seven weeks were conditioned to suck on a nipple in the presence of a large red ball. The ball was then made to disappear by slowly moving a screen in front of it. Babies continued to suck, evidence that they perceived the conditioned stimulus to be "present" but invisible. When the ball was made to vanish suddenly by an arrangement of mirrors, so that it appeared to have been annihilated, a condition that leads to the perception of impermanence among adults, then babies ceased to suck, as if the conditioned stimulus has ceased to exist. Thus, even very young babies may perceive that objects are permanent through the dynamic transitions in visual information that occur as one object occludes another.

Further evidence that infants extract information for permanence from the dynamic transitions in visual information obtained through movement has been obtained quite recently. Kellman and Spelke (1983) used the habituation method to investigate infants' perception of occlusion. Four-month old babies were repeatedly shown a display that looked like a swinging pendulum with its centre covered but which actually comprised two separate elements in common motion behind a screen. The decline in their attention (habituation) over repeated trials was measured. Then the occluding screen was removed and babies were shown one of two displays, either the two separate objects in common motion or a complete pendulum. The results demonstrated that four-month old babies perceived the partially hidden display as a whole object moving behind the screen. When the occluding object at the centre was removed babies showed renewed interest in the display, as if they were not expecting to see two disconnected objects. In the control condition, where a single moving pendulum was revealed behind the screen, babies showed no recovery of attention. Their low level of attention to the unoccluded display showed that they had all along perceived the rod as complete and this was simply one further instance of the same event. The fact that dynamic information was responsible for perception of completion of the rod was demonstrated when the experiment was repeated with the same stimuli presented as stationary displays. Under these static conditions the babies showed no evidence of discriminating between the complete and incomplete rod. It appears that the rigid motion of the two parts leads the infant to perceive them as a single connected rod that is partially hidden.

A recent study by Granrud et al. (1984) with babies aged five months shows the importance of dynamic information for depth perception in the young baby. This study capitalized on the tendency of babies, when given a choice, to reach and touch the nearest of several objects or surfaces presented simultaneously. A randomly moving display of dots was generated by computer and shown on a television screen. By clever computer programming it was possible to create the appearance of depth at an edge by continuous deletion of one part of the visual texture by the remaining texture on the screen. That is, the picture on the TV screen gave the appearance of one moving surface sliding behind another and the position of the "uppermost" surface could be varied from the left to right or centre of the screen. Infants would reach to touch the part of the TV screen where the moving surface appeared nearer to them, as specified by the occlusion of one textured surface by another.

Babies will also reach for the nearer of two real objects so long as there is information available for relative motion of the nearer to the further object. Kellman and Spelke (1983), showed that babies use relative movement to derive depth information when a further object is made to move behind a nearer and they preferentially reach for the nearer object. With common movement of both foreground and background objects babies show no preference for the nearer part when they reach. Information from relative movement therefore informs the infant that objects are at different distances.

All these studies of event perception support the hypothesis that babies use dynamic information obtained from the relative movements of objects in the perception of a world of spatially connected, separately moveable, whole, permanent objects in the first five months of life.

BIOLOGICAL MOTION

A line of research originating in Johansson's laboratory in Uppsala concerns the perception of biological motion. Biological motions are mechanically complex, animate movements such as walking or the movements involved in emotional expression.

Johansson developed a method of studying the dynamic visual information implicated in biological motion perception known as "point light walkers". Point light walkers are created by placing lights or luminous tape on the head, torso and limb joints of a person dressed in black who is then filmed in the dark while traversing a path normal to the observer's line of sight. Adults viewing the filmed dots in motion report a compelling experience of seeing a human figure walking. In fact, adults can recognize the characteristic patterns of movement of their friends, and they can often tell the gender of the walking person, just from the moving points of light (Cutting and Proffitt, 1981). The same luminous points seen when stationary do not reveal anything to the perceiver (nor does a single frame of the film of the point light walker) which shows that the information is carried in the dynamic transitions of the moving display.

Recent evidence shows that babies of from four to six months are sensitive to biomechanical motions specified by point light displays. Infants prefer to look at a display showing a walking motion than one in which the same number of dots simply move randomly (Fox and McDaniel, 1982; Bertenthal, Proffitt, Spetner, & Thomas, 1985). Thus it would appear that infants may be able to extract information about biological motion from moving points of light. Bower (1982, p. 273) discusses an intriguing extension of this line of research. In a study of toddler's perception of point light walkers it was discovered that babies prefer to look at a point light walker display of a baby of their own gender than at a display of an infant of the opposite sex. The films were made in the standard way and showed a boy or girl toddler walking bending and picking up an object. Bower suggests that gender typical differences in skeletal articulation may underlie this preference for the same sex display. There does seem to be a tendency for little boys to bend and pick up objects from the waist, while little girls bend at the knees. Perhaps the sex difference in babies' selective attention to biomechanical movement is based on little studied spontaneous differences in movement patterns such as these.

Eleanor Gibson and her students have also examined the potential of an event analysis for aspects of social perception. Walker, Owsley, Megaw-Nyce, Gibson and Bahrick (1980) showed that babies can distinguish between elastic and rigid motions of an object early in the first year of life. They showed that babies perceive the difference between elastic deforming movements, as when a sponge is squeezed repeatedly, and rigid movements of the same object – as, for example, when it rotates but is not deformed. The authors suggest that elastic motion may be discriminated from rigid motion because the external boundary and the interior texture of the object undergoes systematic deformation in the former case, whereas only the external boundary is transformed within the retinal array in the latter case. That is, information is available in the light projected to the retina for a discrimination between rigid and elastic objects and babies can make use of it. Walker (1982) has gone on to demonstrate that babies perceive the unity of visual and auditory expression of emotion using the preference method with films and sound tracks of animate happy or sad faces. It could be said that the elastic motions of the face and the intonations of the voice specify an emotional event to the baby.

INTERSENSORY EVENTS

As the previous example shows, not only do babies perceive events specified within a single modality; there is also evidence that they are sensitive to intersensory information. One of the earliest studies to show intersensory coordination was by Wertheimer (1961) who showed that an infant only eight minutes old would turn her eyes toward a sound played softly in one ear or the other. This early demonstration of an innate link between vision and audition has since been supported by a wide variety of research (see Butterworth, 1981 for a review) and again, a striking ability to extract information from the dynamic properties of sensory stimulation is revealed.

Kuhl and Meltzoff (1982) carried out a study in which four-month old babies were simultaneously presented with two video-recorded faces to left and right. One face was shown repeating the vowel 'i' and the other repeating the vowel 'a'. However, the baby heard only one sound track, to correspond with one of the visually presented vowels, in a randomly counterbalanced experiment. It was found that babies preferred to look at the face that matched the sound track, suggesting that they detect an intersensory correspondence between the auditory and visual information for the vowel sound. In a related series of studies, Meltzoff and Moore (1977), Meltzoff (1981) and Vinter (1984) have carried out extremely interesting research on imitation in newborn babies that may also be implicated in mechanisms of speech perception and production. These authors have shown that neonates will selectively imitate mouth opening, tongue protrusion and lip pursing movements. Imitation of "invisible" movements such as these may involve the same abilities as lip reading, and this could be important in the acquisition of language. The dynamic approach shows that babies' speech perception may profitably be investigated as an inter-modal event.

Many further examples of infant event perception are reviewed by Gibson and Spelke (1983); just one further instance will be mentioned here. Spelke, Born and Chu (1983) have carried out an extensive series of studies which reveal that babies are sensitive to the common rhythmic properties of events in vision and audition. Babies were simultaneously shown two films projected to left and right of the midline. In both films an object moved up and down in a rhythmic sequence with abrupt changes in the direction of movement from up to down and a single sound track was played of an abrupt noise. Babies prefer to look at the film where the sound track undergoes an abrupt transition at the same moment as the abrupt change in the visual direction of movement. That is, abrupt transitions in the patterning of auditory or visual stimulation are perceived as relating to the same event. The evidence suggests that event perception is not a modality specific process; rather it occurs by gathering of information from many sensory channels each attesting to the same external reality.

ENCOUNTERS IN INFANT PERCEPTION

An "encounter" is defined as an event that is particularly relevant to the perceiver's intentions or actions. Again, there is a great deal of evidence to show that even tiny babies are sensitive to the affordances of events. Some of the best known examples come from the study of "looming" with newborn babies. Looming is produced by accelerated expansion of a delimited portion of the visual field, as when an object rapidly approaches toward an observer. For example, an object can be presented moving toward an infant on a collision course, or so that it veers off to one side. When the looming object is on a collision course very young babies will raise their hands, move their heads backward and make "defensive" movements to the oncoming visual stimulus. When the looming object is on a miss path, the same babies simply sit and watch the object move by without making any defensive movements. Of course, no harm is allowed to befall the baby in these studies. That the response is specific to visual information has been shown by using a shadow caster to present the looming stimulus. Babies make defensive responses to the shadow so there can be little doubt that the response is to visually specified information rather than air movements, noise or other factors (Bower, Broughton & Moore, 1970.)

In the looming studies, only a portion of the visual field expands in relation to the remainder and this specifies an impending collision. When the whole visual field is in motion another event is specified: movement of the observer in a stable visual space. A number of studies have been carried out using the "moving room" technique, in which the whole visual environment is made to move in relation to the baby. Infants are tested inside a small room comprising three walls and a ceiling which can be moved above a rigid floor. Babies stand, sit or are seated with support in the room which is then moved relative to the infant so that the end wall comes toward or away from the baby. This movement of the room produces a flow pattern of visual information which corresponds to that which would ordinarily occur if the baby sways backwards or forwards. Several studies have demonstrated that babies maintain a stable standing or sitting posture through sensitivity to the visual flow pattern. They lose balance when standing or sitting in the moving room and their loss of balance is always appropriate to the direction of instability specified by the misleading visual flow, (Lee & Aronson, 1974; Butterworth & Cicchetti, 1978). In fact, this information may even be important in gaining head control, one of the earliest postures to be mastered by the infant. Pope (1984) showed that babies gain control of their heads with respect to the stable visual surroundings at least as early as the second month of life. Thus, dynamic transitions giving rise to a total flow of the visual array serve to specify the movement of self and babies use this dynamic information to gain control of the succession of postures and the motor milestones they achieve in the first 18 months of life.

Another example of the importance of dynamic information in the control of action comes from studies of the catching skills of very young babies. Von Hofsten (1982) reviews a series of studies in which he has shown that infants will manually intercept an object moving within reach on an elliptical trajectory. Babies will adapt the speed of their reach to the speed of the moving object. Even the newborn baby will attempt an interception, although obviously the very young infant is not as spectacularly successful in catching the moving target as the nine-month old. This example of eye-hand coordination in the baby again shows that event perception is not modality specific. Visual information for object movement specifies the possibility of encountering the object on a conjoint kinaesthetically specified trajectory of the arm.

These examples show that visual perception is very important in the development and control of reaching and locomotion in the sighted baby. But what about the baby who cannot make use of this information through blindness? It is worth noting that theoretical advances stemming from the dynamic approach to perception offer the possibility of constructing prosthetic devices in which information that is unavailable through vision may nevertheless be substituted in another modality. Bower (1977) reported one such case in which a congenitally anopthalmic baby was equipped with a sonar device. The sonar was worn on the head and it projected a continuous stream of ultrasound onto the environment. Reflections of the sound were converted electronically to audible sounds which convey information about the properties of objects. For example, the texture of an object is reliably specified by the clarity of the echoed signal (a hard object produces a clear sound, a soft one a fuzzy sound), the amplitude of the signal specifies the size of the object (loud big, soft small), the direction of the object is given by differences in time of arrival of the stereo signal at the ears. After some practice in using this device the baby was able to reach and grasp objects, to place the arms as if to break a fall when lowered toward a surface and would even play peek a boo with his mother with great pleasure as his head movements brought her in and out of the field of the sonic guide. The dynamic approach to infant perception not only helps us to understand better the abilities of the normal infant; it also offers the possibility of developing new methods of helping those with sensory handicaps.

CONCLUSION

The study of infant perception has entered a new era. The move from static to dynamic theories of perception has revealed so much about the perceptual world of the very young baby that there is no going back to the old theory of limited perceptual abilities. No doubt science proceeds by making simplifying assumptions, and 'static' perception may intuitively have seemed the appropriate way to study the naive human. However, dynamic perception has to be the simpler case, as far as the developing infant is concerned. Johansson (1985) said that his own studies of event perception led him to the conclusion that sensory systems are most efficient under conditions that are exceedingly complex to describe mathematically. By the same token, we may conclude that early infant perception is most efficient in the complex dynamic case. The apparently simple, static, two-dimensional, visual stimulus is actually atypical of the spatio-temporal world to which the infant is biologically pre-adapted. The static case actually requires an analysis akin to that involved in explaining picture perception. Perception in the baby is not pre-adapted for comprehending pictures. Rather, it is based on events and encounters of adaptive significance from whatever modality the information is derived. It is from this dynamic spatio-temporal perspective on perception that exciting insights have come which hold such promise for further study of the perceptual world of the young baby.

REFERENCES

Bertenthal, B.I., Proffitt, D. R., Spetner, N. B., & Thomas, M. A. (1985). The development of infant sensitivity to biomechanical motions. *Child Development 56,* 531–543.

Bower, T. G. R. (1967). The development of object permanence: some studies of existence constancy. *Perception and Psychophysics 2,* 411–418.

Bower, T. G. R. (1977). Blind babies see with their ears. *New Scientist, 255–257* (February).

Bower, T. G. R. (1982). *Development in Infancy.* Freeman: San Francisco (second edition).

Bower, T. G. R., Broughton, J., & Moore, M. K. (1970). Infant responses to approaching objects: an indicator of response to distal variables. *Perception and Psychophysics 9,* 193–196.

Butterworth, G. E. (1981). The origins of auditory-visual perception and visual proprioception in human infancy. In R. D. Walk, & H. L. Pick Jr. (Eds), *Intersensory Perception and Sensory Integration.* Plenum Press: New York.

Butterworth, G. E. & Cicchetti, D. (1978). Visual calibration of posture in normal and motor retarded Down's syndrome infants. *Perception 7,* 513–525.

Cutting, J. E. & Proffitt, D. R. (1981). Gait perception as an example of how we may perceive events. In R. D. Walk, & H. L. Pick Jr. (Eds), *Intersensory Perception and Sensory Integration.* Plenum Press: New York.

Fox, R., & McDaniel, C. (1982). The perception of biological motion by human infants. *Science, 218,* 486–487.

Gibson, J. J. (1979). *The Ecological Approach to Visual Perception.* Houghton-Mifflin: Boston.

Gibson, E. J. & Spelke, E. (1983). The development of perception. In J. H. Flavell, and E. Markman (Eds), *Cognitive Development.* Volume 3 of P. Mussen (Ed.), *Handbook of Child Psychology.* Wiley: New York.

Granrud, C. E., Yonas, A., Smith, I. M., Arterberry, M. E., Glicksman, M. L., & Sorkness, A. C. (1984). Infants' sensitivity to accretion and deletion of texture as information for depth at an edge. *Child Development 55,* 1630–1636.

Johansson, G. (1985). About Visual Event Perception. In R. E. Shaw, and W. H. Warren (Eds), *Persistence and Change.* Lawrence Erlbaum Associates Inc., New Jersey.

Johansson, G., Von Hofsten, C., & Jansson, G. (1980). Event perception. In M. R. Rosenzweig, and L. W. Porter (Eds), *Annual Review of Psychology:* 27–63.

Kellman, P. J. & Spelke, E. S. (1983). Perception of partly occluded objects in infancy. *Cognitive Psychology, 15,* 483–524.

Kuhl, P. K. & Meltzoff, A. N. (1982). The bimodal perception of speech in infancy. *Science 218,* 1138–1141.

Lee, D. & Aronson, E. (1974). Visual proprioceptive control of standing in human infants. *Perception and Psychophysics, 15,* 529–532.

Meltzoff, A. N. (1981). Imitation, intermodal coordination and representation in early infancy. In G. E. Butterworth (Ed.), *Infancy and Epistemology: An Evaluation of Piaget's Theory.* Harvester: Brighton.

Meltzoff, A. N. & Moore M. K. (1977). Imitation of facial and manual gestures by human neonates. *Science, 198,* 75–78.

Pope, M. J. (1984). *Visual Proprioception in Infant Postural Development.* Unpublished Ph.D thesis, University of Southampton.

Spelke, E. S., Born, W. S., & Chu, F. (1983). Perception of moving, sounding objects by four month old infants. *Perception 12,* 719–732.

Vinter, A. (1984). *Imitation, Representation et Mouvement dans les Premieres Mois de la Vie* Unpublished Ph.D. thesis, University of Geneva.

Von Hofsten, C. (1982). Foundations for perceptual development. In L. Lipsitt, and C. K. Rovee-Collier (Eds), *Advances in Infancy Research 2,* 241–261, Ablex: New Jersey.

Walker, A. (1982). Intermodal perception of expressive behaviour by human infants. *Journal of Experimental Child Psychology, 33,* 514–535.

Walker, A., Owsley, C. J., Megaw-Nyce, J., Gibson, E. J., & Bahrick, E. (1980). Detection of elasticity as an invariant property of objects by young infants. *Perception 9,* 713–718.

Warren, W. H. & Shaw, R. E. (1985). Events and encounters as units of analysis for ecological psychology In R. E. Shaw, and W. H. Warren (Eds), *Persistence and Change.* Lawrence Erlbaum Associates Inc., New Jersey.

Wertheimer, M. (1961). Psychomotor coordination of auditory and visual space at birth. *Science, 134,* 1692.

9 Rhythm Perception in Early Infancy

L. Demany, B. McKenzie, and E. Vurpillot

The chief characteristic of rhythm is the subjective grouping of objectively separate events. In a rhythmic sequence of identical tone-bursts, adults do not perceive the repetition of a single sound, but a recurring configuration which has temporal form. Such a sequence is organised according to the Gestalt law of proximity (Koffka, 1963, Fraisse 1956; 1974). Organisation of temporal form has never been studied systematically in pre-verbal infants. We present here results suggesting a precocious achievement of this function and contrasting with previous research (Bower, 1955; 1967), which failed to demonstrate organisation of spatial form by babies in accordance with the proximity law.

We adopted an habituation paradigm in which infants received auditory reinforcement contingent upon their visual fixation on a simple patterned-figure: a black outline-square on a white background. The infants themselves initiated the presentation of sound by looking at the figure and terminated it by looking away. After several such fixations, the auditory reinforcement was changed from one sound sequence to another. Any resulting increase in time of fixation on the visual stimulus was an index of discrimination.

Sequences of tone-bursts were presented by a loudspeaker placed directly behind the stimulus figure at a distance of 40 cm from the infant. The tone-bursts, 40 ms in duration, were derived from a tape-recording of a consonant chord produced by an electronic organ, with 270 and 1,620 Hz as dominant frequencies; intensity was 63 dB, about 25 dB above the

Source: *Nature* (1977), *266*, pp. 718–719.

ambient noise level. The stimulus figure subtended a visual angle of 8° and was positioned 20° to the left of midline. Fixation, as assessed by the corneal reflection technique (Maurer, 1975), was observed from directly in front of the infant, through a small hole in the screen containing the figure. The infant was judged to be fixating when, his eyes being turned to the left, the stimulus reflection was clearly observable over the right of the pupillatory opening. Duration of fixation, to the nearest tenth of a second, was recorded manually by a switch which simultaneously operated sound-emission and an event-recorder. In previous research, a high inter-observer reliability has been obtained for this measure (McKenzie & Day, 1971).

The first experiment was designed to demonstrate discrimination between the rapid, quite different sequences, S1 and S2, shown in Fig. 9.1. A regular pulse of tone-bursts, S1, was changed to an irregular sequence, S2. The two sequences had the same mean density of sound. We tested two samples, each of 10 infants, with mean ages of 71 d (s.d. 12) and 107 d (s.d. 6) respectively. Three fixations without sound reinforcement were followed by 12 fixations reinforced by S1 and then three fixations reinforced by S2. Median fixation times are shown in Fig. 9.2a. A significant increase in fixation time followed the change in reinforcement ($F = 10.37$, $p < 0.005$), indicating discrimination of the two sequences. No main or interaction effect was associated with age.

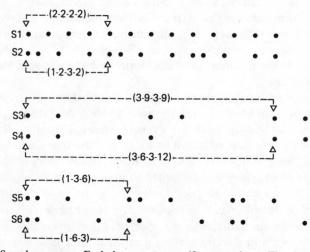

FIG. 9.1. Sound sequences. Each dot represents a 40-ms tone-burst. The shortest onset-to-onset interval was calibrated as 97 ms. All intervals were multiples of this unit. Their relative magnitudes in each sequence are given in brackets. Arrows delimit the period of each sequence. For example, the period of S2 is a succession of 1, 2, 3 and 2 time units (that is 97, 194, 291 and 194 ms). A sequence started always at the beginning of its period, and terminated when visual fixation ended (experiment 1) or after completion of the period in progress at that instant (experiments 2 and 3). Scale bar represents 1 s.

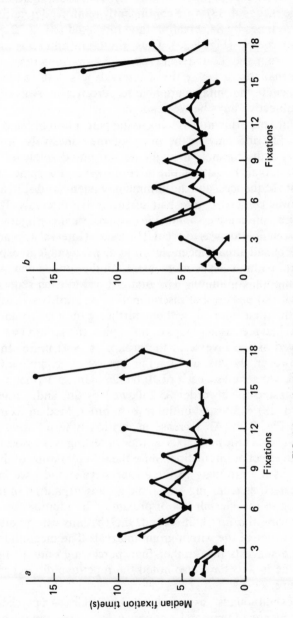

FIG. 9.2a and 9.2b. Median time of fixation in experiments.

Figure 9.2a. Median time of fixation in experiments 1 and 2. In experiment 1 (▲), there was no sound reinforcement for fixations 1-3. S1 was presented contingently with fixations 4-15, and S2 with fixations 16-18. In experiment 2 (●), there was no sound reinforcement for fixations 1-3, S3 was presented contingently with fixations 4-12, and S4 with the final three fixations. The duration of the first fixation after change of reinforcement was compared with the mean duration for the preceding three fixations.

Figure 9.2b. Median time of fixation in experiment 3. No sound reinforcement was associated with fixations 1-3. For Group 1 (●), S5 was presented contingently with fixations 4-15 and S6 with fixations 16-18. For Group 2 (▲), the order of sequence presentation was reversed. The duration of fixation 16 was compared with the mean duration for fixations 13, 14 and 15.

107

In a second experiment, we studied discrimination of slower rhythms, using the sequence S3 and S4 depicted in Fig. 9.1. The visual fixations of 10 infants (mean age 69 d; s.d. 18) were contingently reinforced nine times by S3 and then three times by S4. Fixation time increased ($t = 3.72$, $p <$ 0.005) when S4 replaced S3 (Fig. 9.2a). Thus, the 6-unit intervals of S4 were discriminated from the 12-unit intervals of S4 or from the 9-unit intervals of S3; alternatively, a new ratio of intervals was detected in S4. In any case, we conclude that infants are able to perceive intervals of six units (582 ms) as subjective links between sounds.

The aim of the third experiment was to examine perception of temporal form in sequences differing only in the order of their intervals. In the preceding experiment, discrimination might be attributed solely to the detection of a new interval. In experiment three, however, the same intervals were used in both sequences, and the minimum segment for distinguishing between them was composed of a pair of successive intervals. Thus, the grouping of three consecutive sounds into a perceptual configuration was mandatory if discrimination was to occur. The longest interval appearing in S5 and S6 (Fig. 9.1) had already been shown to be perceptible in experiment two. Therefore, within each reinforcement, all the sounds may have been linked in a temporal continuum. The first interval in each seqeunce was the same in order to ensure that discrimination was not based solely on a difference in this first interval, without further grouping. To adults, the sequences sound like recurring groups of three pips, the groups (●● ●) in S5 being perceived as the inverse of the groups (● ●●) in S6. In all emissions of S6, however, the first and final groups were incomplete (see Fig. 9.1). We tested two samples, each of 10 babies. Group 1 (mean age 69 d; s.d. 12) was tested in the order S5 followed by S6, and Group 2 (mean age 70 d.; s.d. 18) was tested in the reverse order. Median fixation times are shown in Fig. 9.2b. An increase in fixation time followed the change in sequence ($F = 11.81$, $p < 0.005$); order of testing was associated with no reliable main effect or interaction. Since the differentiating of these new sequences entails the grouping of three successive sounds, we infer that they were perceived as recurring "rhythmic groups"organised in temporal form according to the Gestalt law of proximity. In addition, it may be noted that, following the first half-second, the rhythms can be distinguished only by the order of the within-group intervals. The magnitude of the novelty response suggests that, rather than perceiving only a single, very brief change, the infants have also noted the repetitive difference in within-group structure.

A succession of several sounds was apprehended by babies as a psychological unit. This phenomenon of temporal grouping is, of course, not peculiar to rhythm perception. Language comprehension, for example, requires a similar process, since a semantic unit must be grasped as a whole, despite its sequential character. In the results reported here, perceived structure rests on a purely temporal variable: the relative values of the intervals between sounds. These results indicate that skills of temporal analysis and synthesis, prerequisites for operating with the sequential dimension of language, are present well before the stage of speech, and suggest that the early experience of time is more complex than is generally assumed.

ACKNOWLEDGEMENTS

We thank the staff and mothers of the infant centres: "Enfance et Famille", Paris, and "P.M.I. Georges Braque", La Courneuve. D. Demany designed and constructed the electronic equipment.

REFERENCES

Bower, T. G. R. (1965). *Psychonomic Science, 3*, 323–4.
Bower, T. G. R. (1967). *Perception Psychophysiology, 2*, 74–6.
Fraise, P. (1956). *Les Structures Rythmiques.* Publications Universitaires de Louvain.
Fraise, P. (1974). *Psychologie du Rythme.* Presses Universitaires de France, Paris.
Koffka, K. (1963). *Principles of Gestalt Psychology.* New York: Harcourt, Brace & World.
McKenzie, B. & Day, R. H. (1971). *Journal of Experimental Child Psychology, 11*, 366–375.
Maurer, D. (1975). In L. B. Cohen, & P. Salapatek, (Eds) *Infant Perception: From Sensation to Cognition, 1*, 1–76. New York: Academic Press.

10 Of Human Bonding: Newborns Prefer their Mothers' Voices

Anthony J. DeCasper and William P. Fifer

Abstract. By sucking on a nonnutritive nipple in different ways, a newborn human could produce either its mother's voice or the voice of another female. Infants learned how to produce the mother's voice and produced it more often than the other voice. The neonate's preference for the maternal voice suggests that the period shortly after birth may be important for initiating infant bonding to the mother.

Human responsiveness to sound begins in the third trimester of life and by birth reaches sophisticated levels (Eisenberg, 1976), especially with respect to speech (Eimas, 1975). Early auditory competency probably subserves a variety of developmental functions such as language acquisition (Eisenberg, 1976; Friedlander, 1970) and mother-infant bonding (Bell, 1974; Brazelton, Tronick, Abramson, Als & Wise, 1975; Klaus & Kennel 1976; DeChateau 1977). Mother-infant bonding would best be served by (and may even require) the ability of a newborn to discriminate its mother's voice from that of other females. However, evidence for differential sensitivity to or discrimination of the maternal voice is available only for older infants for whom the bonding process is well advanced (Miles & Melvish, 1974; Mehler, Bertoncini, Baurière & Jassik-Gershenfeld, 1978). Therefore, the role of maternal voice discrimination in formation of the mother-infant bond is unclear. If the newborn's sensitivities to speech subserves bonding, discrimination of and preference for the maternal voice should be evident near birth. We now report that a newborn infant younger than 3 days of age can not only discriminate its mother's voice but also will work to produce her voice in preference to the voice of another female.

Source: *Science* (1980), *208*, pp. 1174-1176. Copyright 1980 by the AAAS.

The subjects were ten Caucasian neonates (five male and five female).[1] Shortly after delivery we tape-recorded the voices of mothers of infants selected for testing as they read Dr. Seuss's *To Think That I Saw It On Mulberry Street*. Recordings were edited to provide 25 minutes of uninterrupted prose, and testing of whether infants would differentially produce their mothers' voices began within 24 hours of recording. Sessions began by coaxing the infant to a state of quiet alertness.[2] The infant was then placed supine in its basinette, earphones were secured over its ears, and a nonnutritive nipple was placed in its mouth. An assistant held the nipple loosely in place; she was unaware of the experimental condition of the individual infant and could neither hear the tapes nor be seen by the infant. The nipple was connected, by way of a pressure transducer, to the solid-state programming and recording equipment. The infants were then allowed 2 minutes to adjust to the situation. Sucking activity was recorded during the next 5 minutes, but voices were never presented. This baseline period was used to determine the median interburst interval (IBI) or time elapsing between the end of one burst of sucking and the beginning of the next.[3] A burst was defined as a series of individual sucks separated from one another by less than 2 seconds. Testing with the voices began after the baseline had been established.

For five randomly selected infants, sucking burst terminating IBI's equal to or greater than the baseline median (t) produced only his or her mother's voice (IBI $\leq t$), and bursts terminating intervals less than the median

---

[1]The infants were randomly selected from those meeting the following criteria: (1) gestation, full term; (2) delivery, uncomplicated; (3) birth weight, between 2500 and 3850 grams; and (4) APGAR score, at least eight at 1 and 5 minutes after birth. If circumsized, males were not observed until at least 12 hours afterward. Informed written consent was obtained from the mother, and she was invited to observe the testing procedure. Testing sessions began between 2.5 and 3.5 hours after the 6 a.m. or 12 p.m. feeding. All infants were bottle-fed.

[2]Wolff, 1 (1966). The infants were held in front of the experimenter's face, spoken to, and then presented with the nonnutritive nipple. Infants failing to fixate visually on the experimenter's face or to suck on the nipple were returned to the nursery. Once begun, a session was terminated only if the infant cried or stopped sucking for two consecutive minutes. The initial sessions of two infants were terminated because they cried for 2 minutes. Their data are not reported. Thus, the results are based on 10 of 12 infants meeting the behavioral criteria for entering and remaining in the study.

[3]With quiet and alert newborns, nonnutritive sucking typically occurs as bursts of individual sucks, each separated by a second or so, while the bursts themselves are separated by several seconds or more. Interburst intervals tend to be unimodally distributed with modal values differing among infants. (K. Kaye, 1977). A suck was said to occur when the negative pressure exerted on the nipple reached 20 mm-Hg. This value is almost always exceeded during nonnutritive sucking by healthy infants, but is virtually never produced by nonsucking mouth movement.

produced only the voice of another infant's mother.[4] Thus, only one of the voices was presented, stereophonically, with the first suck of a burst and remained on until the burst ended, that is, until 2 seconds elapsed without a suck. For the other five infants, the conditions were reversed. Testing lasted 20 minutes.

A preference for the maternal voice was indicated if the infant produced it more often than the nonmaternal voice. However, unequal frequencies not indicative of preference for the maternal voice per se could result either because short (or long) IBI's were easier to produce or because the acoustic qualities of a particular voice, such as pitch or intensity, rendered it a more effective form of feedback. The effects of response requirements and voice characteristics were controlled (1) by requiring half the infants to respond after short IBI's to produce the mother's voice and half to respond after long ones and (2) by having each maternal voice also serve as the nonmaternal voice for another infant.

Preference for the mother's voice was shown by the increase in the proportion of IBI's capable of producing her voice; the median IBI's shifted from their baseline values in a direction that produced the maternal voice more than half the time. Eight of the ten medians were shifted in a direction of the maternal voice (mean = 1.90 seconds, a 34 per cent increase) (sign test, $p = 0.02$), one shifted in the direction that produced the nonmaternal voice more often, and one median did not change from its baseline value (Fig. 10.1).

If these infants were working to gain access to their mother's voice, reversing the response requirements should result in a reversal of their IBI's. Four infants, two from each condition, who produced their mother's voice more often in session 1 were able to complete a second session 24 hours later, in which the response requirements were reversed.[5] Differential

---

[4]The tape reels revolved continuously, and one or the other of the voices was electronically switched to the earphones when the response threshold was met. Because the thresholds were detected electronically, voice onset occurred at the moment the negative pressure reached 20 mm-Hg.

[5]Two infants were not tested a second time, because we could not gain access to the testing room, which served as an auxillary nursery and as an isolation room. The sessions of two infants who cried were terminated. Two other infants were tested a second time, but in their first session one had shown no preference and the other had shown only a slight preference for the non-maternal voice. Their performance may have been affected by inconsistent feedback. Because their peak sucking pressures were near the threshold of the apparatus, very similar sucks would sometimes produce feedback and sometimes not, and sometimes feedback would be terminated in the midst of a sucking burst. Consequently, second session performances of these two infants, which were much like their initial performances, were uninterpretable.

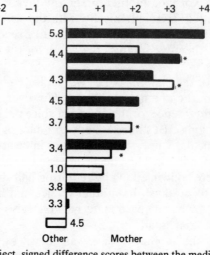

FIG. 10.1.   For each subject, signed difference scores between the median IBI's without vocal feedback (baseline) and with differential vocal feedback (session 1). Differences of the four reversal sessions (*) are based on medians with differential feedback in sessions 1 and 2. Positive values indicate a preference for the maternal voice and negative values a preference for the nonmaternal voice.Filled bars indicate that the mother's voice followed IBI's of less than the baseline median; open bars indicate that her voice followed intervals equal to or greater than the median. Median IBI's of the baseline (in seconds) are shown opposite the bars.

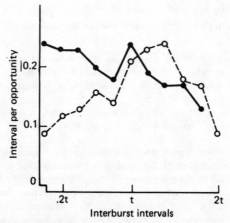

FIG. 10.2.   Interburst interval per opportunity when the maternal voice followed intervals less than the baseline median (solid line) and intervals equal to or greater than the median (dashed line). The IBI's are represented on the abscissa by the lower bound of interval classes equal to one-fifth the baseline median (t).

feedback in session 2 began immediately after the 2-minute adjustment period. The criterion time remained equal to the baseline median of the first session. For all four infants, the median IBI's shifted toward the new criterion values and away from those which previously produced the maternal voice. The average magnitude of the difference between the medians of the first and reversal sessions was 1.95 seconds.

Apparently the infant learned to gain access to the mother's voice. Since specific temporal properties of sucking were required to produce the maternal voice, we sought evidence for the acquisition of temporally differentiated responding. Temporal discrimination within each condition was ascertained by constructing the function for IBI per opportunity: IBI's were collected into classes equal to one-fifth the baseline median, and the frequency of each class was divided by the total frequency of classes having equal and larger values (Anger, 1956). When IBI's less than the baseline median were required, the likelihood of terminating interburst intervals was highest for classes less than the median (Fig. 10.2), whereas when longer intervals were required, the probability of terminating an IBI was maximal for intervals slightly longer than the median. Feedback from the maternal voice effectively differentiated the temporal character of responding that produced it: the probability of terminating IBI's was highest when termination resulted in the maternal voice.

Repeating the experiment with 16 female neonates and a different discrimination procedure confirmed their preference for the maternal voice[6]. The discriminative stimuli were a 400-Hz tone of 4 seconds duration (tone) and a 4-second period of silence (no tone). Each IBI contained an alternating sequence of tone-no-tone periods, and each stimulus was equally likely to begin a sequence. For eight infants, a sucking burst initiated during a tone period turned off the tone and produced the Dr. Seuss story read by the infant's mother, whereas sucking bursts during a no-tone period produced the nonmaternal voice. The elicited voice remained until the sucking burst ended, at which time the tone-no-tone alternation began anew. The discriminative stimuli were reversed for the other eight neonates. Testing with the voices began immediately after the 2-minute adjustment period and lasted 20 minutes. Each maternal voice also served as a nonmaternal voice.

During the first third of the testing session, the infants were as likely to suck during a stimulus period correlated with the maternal voice as during one correlated with the nonmaternal voice (Table 10.1). However, in the last third of the session the infants sucked during stimulus periods associated with their mother's voice approximately 24 per cent more often than during

---

[6]Three other infants began testing with the voices, but their sessions were terminated because they cried. Their data are not included. This study is part of a doctoral thesis submitted by W.P.F.

TABLE 10.1

Stimulus Associated with Maternal Voice	First Third		Last Third	
	$\overline{X}$	S.D.	$\overline{X}$	S.D.
Tone	0.97	0.33	1.26	0.33
No tone	1.04	0.31	1.22	0.19
Combined	1.00	0.32	1.24	0.27

Mean ($\overline{X}$) and standard deviation (S.D.) of the relative frequency of sucking during a stimulus associated with the maternal voice divided by the relative frequency of sucking during a stimulus associated with the nonmaternal voice. A ratio of 1.0 indicates no preference.

those associated with the nonmaternal voice, a significant increase [$F(1, 14) = 8.97$, $P < 0.01$]. Thus, at the beginning of testing there was no indication of stimulus discrimination or voice preference. By the end of the 20-minute session, feedback from the maternal voice produced clear evidence of an auditory discrimination; the probability of sucking during tone and no-tone periods was greater when sucking produced the maternal voice.

The infants in these studies lived in a group nursery; their general care and night feedings were handled by a number of female nursery personnel. They were fed in their mothers' rooms by their mothers at 9:30 a.m. and at 1:30, 5:00, and 8:30 p.m. At most, they had 12 hours of postnatal contact with their mothers before testing. Similarly reared infants prefer the human voice to other acoustically complex stimuli (Butterfield & Siperstein, 1972). But, as our data show, newborns reared in group nurseries that allow minimal maternal contact can also discriminate between their mothers and other speakers and, moreover, will work to produce their mothers' voices in preference to those of other females. Thus, within the first 3 days of postnatal development, newborns prefer the human voice, discriminate between speakers, and demonstrate a preference for their mothers' voices with only limited maternal exposure.

The neonate's capacity to rapidly acquire a stimulus discrimination that controls behavior (Siqueland & Lipsett, 1966; Kron, 1967) could provide the means by which limited postnatal experience with the mother results in preference for her voice. The early preference demonstrated here is possible because newborns have auditory competencies adequate for discriminating individual speakers: they are sensitive to rhythmicity (Condon & Sander, 1974), intonation (Eisenberg, Cousins & Rupp, 1966; Morse 1972), frequency variation (Eisenberg, 1976; see also footnote 6), and phonetic components of speech (Butterfield & Cairns 1974; DeCasper, Butterfield & Cairns, 1976). Their general sensory competency may enable other maternal cues, such as her odour (MacFarlane, 1979) and the manner in which she handles her infant (Burns, Sander, Stechler & Julia, 1972; Thoman, Korner & Bearon-Williams, 1977), to serve as supporting bases for discrimination and vocal preference. Prenatal (intrauterine) auditory experience may also be a factor. Although the significance and nature of intrauterine auditory experience in humans is not known, perceptual preferences and proximity-seeking responses of some infrahuman infants are profoundly affected by auditory experience before birth (Gottlieb, 1971; Hess, 1973).

ACKNOWLEDGEMENTS

Supported by Research Council grant 920. We thank the infants, their mothers and the staff of Moses Cane Hospital where this work was performed, and A. Carstens for helping conduct the research.

REFERENCES

Anger, D. (1956). *Journal of Experimental Psychology, 52,* 145.

Bell, R. (1974). In M. Lewis, & L. A. Roserblum, (Eds) *The Effect of the Infant on its Caregiver.* New York: Wiley.

Brazelton, T. B., Tronick, E., Abramson, L., Als, H., & Wise, S. (1975). *Ciba Foundation Symposium, 33,* 137.

Burns, P., Sander, L. W., Stechler, G., & Julia, H. (1972). *Journal of American Academic Child Psychiatry, 11,* 427.

Butterfield, E. C. & Cairns, G. F. (1974). In R. L. Schiefelbusch & L. L. Lloyd, (Eds) *Language Perspectives: Acquisition, Retardation and Intervention.* Baltimore: University Park Press.

Butterfield, E. C. & Siperstein, G. (1972). In J. Bosma, (Ed.) *Oral Sensation and Perception: The Mouth of the Infant.* Springfield Ill.: Thomas.

Condon, W. S. & Sander, L. W. (1974). *Science, 183,* 99.

DeCasper, A. J., Butterfield, E. C., & Cairns, G. F. (1976, April). Paper presented at the fourth biennial conference on *Human Development,* Nashville.

DeChateau, P. (1977). *Birth Family Journal, 41,* 10.

Eimas, P. D. (1975). In L. B. Cohen, & P. Salapatek, (Eds) *Infant Perception: From Sensation to Cognition, Vol 2,* 193, New York: Academic Press.

Eisenberg, R. B. (1976). *Auditory Competence in Early Life: The Roots of Communicative Behavior.* Baltimore: University Park Press.

Eisenberg, R. B., Cousins, D. B., & Rupp, N. (1966). *Journal of Auditory Response, 7,* 245.

Friedlander, B. (1970). *Merrill-Palmer Quarterly, 16,* 7.

Gottlieb, G. (1971). *Development of Species Indentification in Birds: An Inquiry into the Prenatal Determinants of Perception.* Chicago: University of Chicago Press.

Hess, E. H. (1973). *Imprinting.* New York: Van-Nostrand-Reinhold.

Kaye, K. (1977). In H. R. Schaffer, (Ed.) *Studies in Mother-Infant Interaction.* New York: Academic Press.

Klaus, M. H. & Kennel, J. H. (1976). *Maternal Infant Bonding.* St Louis: Mosby.

Kron, R. E. (1967). In J. Wortis, (Ed.) *Recent Advances in Biological Psychiatry.* New York: Plenum.

MacFarlane, A. (1975). *CIBA Foundation Symposium, 33,* 103.

Mehler, J., Bertoncini, J., Baurière, M., & Jassik-Gershenfeld, D. (1978). *Perception, 7,* 491.

Miles, M. & Melvish, E. (1974). *Nature, (London), 252,* 123.

Morse, P. A. (1972). *Journal of Experimental Child Psychology, 14,* 472.

Siqueland, E. R. & Lipsitt, L. P. (1966). *Journal of Experimental Child Psychology, 3,* 356.

Thoman, E. B., Korner, A. F. & Bearon-Williams, L. (1977). *Child Development, 48,* 563.

Wolff, P. H. (1966). *Psychological Issues, 5,* 1.

11 Shape Constancy and Slant Perception at Birth

Alan Slater and Victoria Morison

Abstract. Two experiments are described the object of which was to investigate whether perception of shape at birth is determined solely by proximal (retinal) stimulation, or whether newborn babies have the ability to perceive objective, real shape across changes in slant. In experiment 1 looking at (ie preference for) one stimulus, a square, when paired with either of two trapeziums, was found to change in a consistent manner with changes in slant, indicating that these changes in stimulation are detected and can cause considerable changes in looking behaviour. In experiment 2 newborns were desensitized to changes in slant during familiarization trials, and subsequently strongly preferred a different shape to the familiarized shape in a new orientation. This suggests that the real shape had been perceived as invariant across the retinal changes caused by the changes in slant, and further suggests that shape constancy is an organizing feature of perception which is present at birth.

INTRODUCTION

A large body of research exists relating to infants' ability to detect invariant or constant properties of objects over spatial and temporal transformations to the optic array. Among the questions asked are whether, and when, some of the constancies occur in infancy, and what is the role of learning in their development. One of the visual constancies investigated, and that which is the focus of the present research, is shape constancy, that is the ability to perceive an object as being the same shape despite changes in its orientation relative to the observer. Evidence for shape constancy in early infancy was reported by Bower (1966). Eight-week-old infants were conditioned to respond to a rectangle in a specific orientation, and they

Source: *Perception* (1985), *14*, pp. 337–344.

subsequently gave more responses to this rectangle when it was presented at varying orientations than to a trapezium of identical retinal shape presented in the frontoparallel plane. Using a similar transfer or generalization of learning paradigm, but with the different response measure of habituation/dishabituation of visual attention, Caron, Caron and Carlson (1979, p.716) familiarized three-month-old infants to a shape varying in slant and found greater recovery to a different shape than to the same shape in a new slant "indicating that the constant real shape . . . had been perceived across rotational transformations".

These findings suggest that shape constancy is present in early infancy, at least by two months of age. Even this early an attainment, however, leaves open the question of whether or not learning is involved. E J Gibson (1970, p.104) has expressed the critical question succinctly with respect to size constancy, and her remarks are equally applicable to shape constancy: "Does this mean that *no* learning is involved in the development of size constancy? Definitely not, since even eight weeks gives a lot of opportunity for visual experience". In order to disentangle the contributions of innate abilities, maturation, and learning it is therefore appropriate to look for the presence of perceptual constancies at birth.

In the experiments described here preferential looking and habituation/dishabituation procedures were used to investigate two interrelated questions with respect to shape constancy: (1) whether newborns can detect *differences* in the orientation or slant of the same shape (experiment 1); and (2) whether they can perceive a *constant* shape across changes in orientation (experiment 2). The second of these questions properly constitutes what may be called a "constancy experiment". Strictly speaking, the first question may be considered an irrelevance: ". . . it has never been required to show that in constancy experiments subjects discriminated among the different positions or proximal 'shapes' of an object presented at variable distances or orientations" (Walker et al. 1980, p. 713). However, it seems reasonable to suggest that answers to both questions contribute more to our understanding of the origins of shape constancy and slant perception than answers to either question alone. For reasons discussed below it was necessary to obtain answers to question (1) before the constancy experiment proper could be carried out. The experiments are presented after description of the general method.

GENERAL METHOD

Subjects

Subjects were selected from the maternity ward of the Royal Devon and Exeter Hospital, Heavitree, Devon, and were tested after their midday feed; throughout testing they were in the behavioural state of alert inactivity (Ashton, 1973). Seventy subjects were used in the first experiment (thirty-six males, thirty-four females; mean age 2 days 8 hours, range 6 hours to 9 days), and twelve in the second (seven males, five females; mean age 1 day 23 hours, range 6 hours to 5 days 23 hours). A further thirty-eight babies were seen but could not be used as subjects because of fussing or crying ($N = 6$), sleeping ($N = 5$), and complete position bias on paired-stimulus preferential looking trials or on post-habituation trials ($N = 27$).

Stimuli

Three stimuli were used: these are shown in Fig. 11.1. All stimuli were painted matt black. The square had sides 5 in long, and when shown in the frontal plane it subtended a visual angle of 23 deg at the viewing distance of 12 in. The width, and maximum and minimum heights of the large trapezium were, respectively, 11.5, 8, and 3.75 in, and of the small trapezium they were 2.5, 6, and 4.2 in. The large trapezium was constructed so that when it was slanted 60° away from the frontal plane, it gave the retinal image of the square in frontal plane at the viewing distance of 12 in. The vertical axis of rotation of the large trapezium is indicated by the dotted line in Fig. 11.1. The small trapezium, when shown in frontal plane, gave the retinal image of the square rotated through 60° at the viewing distance of 12 in.

FIG. 11.1.   The square and two trapeziums used as stimuli in experiment 1, shown in frontal view (0°). The vertical axis of rotation is indicated by the dotted line.

The small trapezium was only used in experiment 1 and was only presented in frontal plane. The square and large trapezium were presented in several orientations. These orientations are described throughout in degrees of angular rotation from the fronto-parallel plane as the infant viewed it, and in an anticlockwise direction as viewed from above. With respect to the frontal plane, the square at 0° and 180° is retinally equivalent, while the large trapezium at 0° is the left/right mirror image of itself at 180°. For either stimulus any two orientations that sum to 180° (i.e. 30° and 150°, 60° and 120°, etc.) give retinal mirror images.

Apparatus

The stimuli were presented against a background screen of matt white curtain material, and were illuminated by striplights placed behind and to both sides of the infant. The luminance levels of the white background and of the black figures were, respectively, 113 and 9 cd m^{-2}. To present the stimuli, horizontal holder arms (either one or two, as necessary) painted matt white were projected in front of the screen above the infant's line of sight. At the end of each arm was a similarly painted vertical rod from which the stimulus was suspended, with the vertical axis of rotation 9 inches in front of the screen and 12 inches from the infant's eyes. This rod could rotate and a marked protractor attached to its top allowed speedy and accurate change of slant position. A Rustrak four-channel event recorder was used, in association with a millisecond timer, to record the infants' fixations.

Procedure

Each subject was brought to the experimental room, on the maternity ward of the hospital, and seated upright on one experimenter's knee, with his/her eyes 12 in from the axis of stimulus rotation and in a horizontal plane coincident with the midline of the stimulus. Eye position was monitored throughout the experimental trials, and was maintained by use of a reference marker which was an extension to the horizontal holder arm. The procedures differed for the visual preference studies of experiment 1 and for the habituation trials of experiment 2: these details are given under the separate experiments.

The observers who recorded the infants' fixations were always naive as to the purpose of the experiments. For the paired-stimulus trials of forty-two subjects two independent observers recorded the infants' fixations on the stimuli. The interobserver agreement was high (Pearson $r = 0.84$).

EXPERIMENT 1

Introduction

A number of stimulus dimensions affect preferential looking in newborn babies. These dimensions include linearity, dimensionality (two or three dimensions), movement, contrast, and spatial frequency (Fantz & Miranda, 1975; Slater & Sykes, 1977; Slater, Morison & Rose, 1984a; 1984b; Slater, Earle, Morison & Rose, 1985). The purpose of the experiment was to see whether preferences existed between the square and the two trapeziums, and whether preferential looking was affected by changes in stimulus slant. No particular hypotheses were entertained.

Method

There were seven paired-stimulus preferential looking conditions, in each of which the square was paired with one of the trapeziums. Ten subjects were tested in each condition. The stimulus slants varied across conditions as described below. The vertical axes of the stimuli were positioned 19.5° to either side of the straight-ahead position. Stimulus distance and orientation were therefore arranged to be correct with respect to the appropriate lines of sight.

The seven conditions divide into two parts, distinguished by whether the square was paired with the small or the large trapezium. The conditions were: (I) the small trapezium in frontal plane paired with the square – (a) in frontal plane, (b) at 30° (150°), (c) at 45° (135°), (d) at 60° (120°); (II) the large trapezium at 60° (120°) paired with the square – (a) in frontal plane, (b) at 30° (150°), (c) at 60° (120°). Each stimulus pairing was shown for two trials, each trial continuing until 20 seconds of looking had accumulated. Each stimulus changed its left/right position from trial I to trial II, and also its orientation to give mirror-image reversals, as indicated above in parentheses; within a condition, position and orientation were counterbalanced across subjects.

These pairings were chosen because they allow quantification of changes in preferential looking that may result from systematic changes to the slant of one of the paired stimuli. Note that the paired stimuli of condition Id, and also those of IIa, give equivalent retinal images. If preferences are determined solely by the retinal features of the stimuli, no stimulus in either of these conditions should be preferred.

Results

The results are presented in Fig. 11.2, expressed as the mean percentage of time spent looking at the square in each condition; in this figure the dotted line through 50% represents equal preference for the paired stimuli. A highly systematic effect was found, such that as the slant of the square shifted from the frontal plane through more extreme slants, it became progressively less preferred. This shift in preferential looking was significant both for the pairings with the small trapezium (conditions Ia–Id; Jonckheere trend test, $S = 334$, $p < 0.001$, two-tailed) and for those with the large trapezium (conditions IIa–IIc; Jonckheere trend test, $S = 228$, $p < 0.001$, two-tailed). Several of the individual pairings gave preferential looking that was significantly different from 50% looking (condition Ia, $t_9 = 7.27$, $p < 0.001$; Id, $t_9 = 3.6$, $p < 0.01$; IIa, $t_9 = 2.62$, $p < 0.05$; IIc, $t_9 = 11.92$, $p < 0.001$. All p two-tailed).

Discussion

Changes to the slant of the square affected its attention-holding properties, or salience, when it was paired with either of the two trapeziums, and it is clear from the results that the newborns were responding both to the distal and to the proximal properties of the stimuli. The results can most parsimoniously be described in terms of the interaction of two variables. First, stimulus orientation affects preferential looking. The small trapezium at 0°/180° gives the same retinal image as the square at 60° (120°), condition Id, and the retinal image of the large trapezium at 60°(120°) is the same

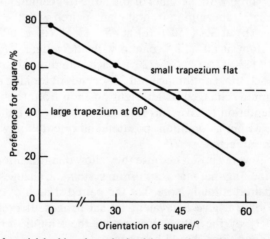

FIG. 11.2. Preferential looking data obtained in experiment 1. As the orientation of the square shifts progressively away from the frontal plane the square becomes less and less preferred when paired with either trapezium.

as that of the square at 0°, condition IIa. In both of these pairings the stimulus at 0° (180°) was significantly preferred. Second, size has an effect. The square at 0° was preferred to the small trapezium at 0° (180°) condition Ia. It might be that the square was preferred either because it is the largest stimulus, or because it approximates some optimal retinal (or real) size. To distinguish between these possibilities a final condition was run, with the square at 0° paired with the large trapezium at 0° and 180°. Ten additional subjects were tested, and a strong preference for the square was found (72.4% of the fixation time was spent viewing this stimulus, $t_9 = 4.88$, $p < 0.001$, two-tailed). Thus, the square in frontal plane seems to be the optimally preferred of these stimuli.

Exactly why these stimulus preferences should emerge is not clear. What *is* clear, however, is that newborn babies can perceive and respond to small (as little as 15°) changes to the orientation of the same figure (in this case, the square). Whether they can perceive a shape as being the *same* shape, independently of its slant, is the focus of the next experiment.

EXPERIMENT 2

Introduction

In this experiment each infant was given familiarization trials with one stimulus (either the square or the large trapezium), the stimulus being in a different slant from trial to trial. After this familiarization period the square and the large trapezium were shown for two paired test trials, with the familiarized stimulus in a different slant from any shown earlier. A similar procedure was used with three-month-old infants by Caron et al. (1979). The small trapezium was not used in this experiment as slanting it away from the frontal plane made its retinal width very small. The "ideal" stimulus pairing on the test trials would be the square at 0° and the large trapezium at 60° (120°), since these give equivalent retinal images. This pairing could not be used because of a methodological problem associated with testing newborn subjects; this is described next.

In other research we have found that "natural" preferences that exist for one of two paired stimuli cannot be changed by habituating newborns either to the preferred or to the nonpreferred member of the pair (Slater *et al.*, 1985). The pairing of the square at 0° and the large trapezium at 60° (120°) gives a significant preference for the square (67.13% of the looking time was spent viewing the square, condition IIa, experiment 1). To see whether this preference could be changed by prior exposure to one or other stimulus, the following pilot study was carried out. Six newborns were habituated to the stationary trapezium at either 60° or 120°, and six to the stationary square at 0°. A further four newborns were habituated to the trapezium changing in slant during the habituation trials, and eight to the square, similarly changing in slant. An infant-controlled habituation procedure was used (Slater, Morison & Rose, 1982; 1983). For all subjects the post-criterion test trials which followed habituation were paired presentation of the trapezium at 60° (120°) and the square at 0°. Those subjects who were habituated to the trapezium gave a significant preference for the novel square on the post-criterion trials (the square attracted 69.3% of the looking time, $t_9 = 3.67$, $p < 0.01$, two-tailed). However, those subjects who were habituated to the square itself also preferred the square on the post-criterion trials (62.9% of the looking time, $t_{13} = 2.48$, $p < 0.05$, two-tailed). Thus, a reliable preference for the square was found in all conditions, and this could not be changed by previous familiarization to one or other stimulus.

It is not at present clear why these natural preferences cannot be changed. However, it does mean that these particular orientations of trapezium and square cannot be used on the post-familiarization trials of an habituation experiment. The post-criterion pairings used in this experiment were of the square at 30° (150°) and the trapezium at 60° (120°) – no "natural" preference exists for either of these stimuli in these orientations (condition IIb, experiment 1).

Method

Twelve newborns, seven males and five females, were used as subjects. Each baby was given six familiarization trials to a shape whose orientations were different from trial to trial. Six subjects were familiarized to the square in the following orientations: (a) frontal, 0°; (b) 45°; (c) 120°; (d) frontal, 180°; (e) 60°; (f) 135°. Six subjects were familiarized to the trapezium in the following orientations: (a) frontal, 0°; (b) 75°; (c) 135°; (d) frontal, 180°; (e) 45°; (f) 105°. Different subjects in each of the familiarization conditions were presented the stimulus in a different orientation on trial a and subsequent trials, but with the orientation sequence maintained across subjects; thus the first subject in each condition received the stimuli in the order a, b, c, d, e, f; the second subject the order b, c, d, e, f, a; . . . ; the sixth subject the order f, a, b, c, d, e. This order of stimulus presentation (rather than, say, a random order) was chosen in order to maximize slant differences from trial to trial. Note that for the square (but not the trapezium) slants of 0° and 180° are identical. In order to ensure that each subject had the same exposure to the familiarized stimulus in each of its slants each trial continued until 25 seconds of looking had accumulated, at which point the stimulus orientation was changed to the next in sequence, and the next trial began. Each subject therefore looked at the familiarized stimulus for a total of 150 seconds. The looking time of 25 seconds per trial was chosen to be about the time newborns spend fixating stimuli that change from trial to trial, in infant-controlled trials (Slater et al., 1984a).

The familiarization trials were followed by two test trials. In one the square at 30° was paired with the trapezium at 120°, and in the other the square at 150° was paired with the trapezium at 60°. These orientations are different from any shown during the familiarization trials. Each trial continued until 20 seconds of looking had accumulated, and each stimulus changed its left/right position from the first trial to the second trial.

Results

Each subject looked at the stimulus for the same amount of time (150 seconds) on the familiarization trials. To accumulate this looking time the subjects took, on average, exactly twice the time (300 s, $s = 98.3$ s, range 217–480 s): this is the time elapsed from the start of the first look on trial a to the end of the last look on trial f. One variable of interest is the speed with which the subjects responded to the changed stimulus on familiarization trials b to f. On average the subjects looked at the stimulus 8.1 seconds ($s = 3.4$ s) after its orientation had been changed. Thus, this value of 8.1 seconds is the average intertrial interval.

The dependent variable of most interest is the time spent looking at novel and familiar stimuli on the post-familiarization test trials. These results, presented for individual subjects, are given in Table 11.1. Every one of the subjects spent more time looking at the novel shape in the test trials. The novelty preferences were about the same for those subjects familiarized to the square as for those familiarized to the trapezium, and overall 71.9% of the time (28.75 seconds out of a possible 40 seconds) was spent viewing the novel stimulus.

TABLE 11.1
Novelty Preferences of Experiment 2

Subject	Sex	Familiarized stimulus	Novelty preference/%	Subject	Sex	Familiarized stimulus	Novelty preference/%
1	M	square	73.8	7	F	trapezium	63.8
2	M		63.8	8	M		81.3
3	M		72.5	9	F		87.5
4	F		55.0	10	F		95.0
5	F		77.5	11	M		66.3
6	M		63.8	12	M		62.5
Average			67.7	Average			76.1
Overall average							71.9

DISCUSSION AND CONCLUSION

The results from the preference studies of experiment 1 demonstrate that newborn babies can discriminate small (15°) changes to the slant of the same stimulus, as indexed by changes in preferential looking. The reliable preferences for the novel shape that were found in the test trials of experiment 2 indicate that the newborn subjects were desensitized to the changes in slant of the stimulus shown on the familiarization trials, and that they were able to extract the constant, real shape of this stimulus. Their novelty response on the test trials was to the new shape, rather than to the familiarized stimulus in its new slant.

Although E J Gibson has acknowledged that learning may be involved in the development of shape and size constancy (see Introduction), she has also suggested (1969, p.366) that such constancies may be present in the perceptions of very young infants:

> I think, as is the case with perceived shape, that an object tends to be perceived in its true size very early in development, not because the organism has learned to correct for distance, but because he sees the object as such, not its projected size or its distance abstracted from it.

The present results certainly suggest that newborn babies have the ability to extract the constant, real shape of an object that is rotated in the third dimension. Shape constancy, therefore, would appear not to be a perceptual construct that is acquired by the learned abstraction of shape from its associated variables of slant and retinal image, but is an organizing feature of perception which is present at birth.

ACKNOWLEDGEMENTS

This research was supported by Grant C00232114 from the Economic and Social Research Council to the first author. We are indebted to the staff of the maternity ward of the Royal Devon and Exeter Hospital, Exeter, and to all the subjects' mothers for their help and cooperation. Mrs H Perry was one of the observers of infants' fixations.

REFERENCES

Ashton, R. (1973). The state variable in neonatal research: a review. *Merrill-Palmer Quarterly of Behavior and Development, 19,* 3–20.

Bower, T. G. R. (1966). The visual world of infants. *Scientific American, 215,* (6) 80–92.

Caron, A. J., Caron, R. F., & Carlson, V. R. (1979). Infant perception of the invariant shape of objects in slant. *Child Development, 50,* 716–721.

Fantz, R. L. & Miranda, S. B. (1975). Newborn infant attention to form of contour. *Child Development, 46,* 224–228.

Gibson, E. J. (1969). *Principles of Perceptual Learning and Development.* New York: Appleton-Century-Crofts.

Gibson, E. J. (1970). The development of perception as an adaptive process. *American Scientist, 58* 98–107.

Slater, A., Earle, D. C., Morison,. V., & Rose, D. (1985). Pattern preferences at birth and their interaction with habituation-induced novelty preferences. *Journal of Experimental Child Psychology, 39,* 37–54.

Slater, A., Morison, V., & Rose, D. (1982). Visual memory at birth. *British Journal of Psychology, 73,* 519–525.

Slater, A. Morison, V., & Rose, D. (1983). Perception of shape by the newborn baby. *British Journal of Developmental Psychology, 1,* 135–142.

Slater, A., Morison, V., & Rose, D. (1984a). Habituation in the newborn. *Infant Behavior and Development, 7,* 183–200.

Slater, A., Morison, V., & Rose, D. (1984b). Newborn infants' perception of similarities and differences between two- and three-dimensional stimuli. *British Journal of Developmental Psychology, 2,* 287–294.

Slater, A. M. & Sykes, M. (1977). Newborn infants' visual responses to square wave gratings. *Child Development, 48,* 545–554.

Walker, A. C., Owsley, G. J., Megaw-Nyee, J., Gibson, E. J., & Bahrick L. E. (1980). Detection of elasticity as an invariant property of objects by young infants. *Perception, 9,* 713–718.

12 On Categorization in Early Infancy

Paul C. Quinn and Peter D. Eimas

The research literature on the abilities of infants to categorize information from the domains of vision and speech is reviewed. The evidence suggests that infants are able to categorize their experiences, and that their categorical representations follow the same fundamental principles that govern the categorical representations of adults. Consideration is given to some of the difficulties that are encountered when the attempt is made to extrapolate from the categories and underlying concepts that are available to infants to those that exist in adults.

A major goal of cognitive psychology in past and recent years has been to understand the concepts and processes of categorization that give organization to our mental lives. This organization arises in that concepts permit us to respond in an equivalent manner to the members of a group of noticeably different objects or events (Bruner, Goodnow, & Austin, 1956), thereby eliminating the otherwise overwhelming variation that exists in the objects and events that populate our physical world. Concepts, in essence, permit adaptive encounters with the environment, particularly by helping us to comprehend new experiences at a relatively small cost to our cognitive resources. As Smith and Medin (1981) note in the opening sentence of their review of concepts and categories (p. 1) : "Without concepts, mental life would be chaotic".

Because the terms *concept, category* and *categorization* often mean different things to different people, it will be helpful to describe how these

Source: *Merrill-Palmer Quarterly* (1986), *32*, pp. 331-363. Copyright 1986 Wayne State University Press.

terms are used in this paper: The term *concept* refers to a mental structure or representation that defines how a set or class of entities, events, or abstractions are related. A *category* is the extension of a concept, made up of the entities of the natural world, including those objects and events that exemplify abstract, knowledge-based conceptual representations. The term *categorization* refers to the processes that are involved in determining categorical membership; it is a means by which knowledge directs our interactions with the environment.

It has long been recognized that our efforts to understand the nature of human concepts would be incomplete unless knowledge was obtained about the origins and development of concepts and categories. The following quote from Hull (1920, p. 5–6) illustrates this longstanding concern with conceptual development:

> A young child finds himself in a certain situation, reacts to it by approach say, and hears it called "dog". After an indeterminate intervening period he finds himself in a somewhat different situation, and hears that called "dog" also. Thus the process continues. The "dog" experiences appear at irregular intervals . . . At length the time arrives when the child has a "meaning" for the word dog. Upon examination this meaning is found to be actually a characteristic more or less common to all dogs and not common to cats, dolls and "teddy bears".

It is possible to interpret this view as implying that younger children may not be able to recognize a previously unseen dog as a member of the category *dogs* until they hear the label *dog* associated with different dogs over a period of time. Hearing the same label applied to different instances of the category *dogs* is presumed to prompt the child to seek out the characteristics common to all dogs that make them different from cats. An alternative interpretation that is possible (and indeed likely, given our present state of knowledge) assumes that some of the abilities involved in recognizing that dogs are alike in ways that cats are not are present before hearing the category names applied to these animals. The label *dog* would then be an indicant of knowledge, rather than a means for its acquisition. If this is true, it is important that we understand any existing abilities of prelinguistic infants to categorize the things of their environment, as it is from these abilities that the complex categories of the adult presumably develop. As Bower (1974, p. 235) points out, "Only when we understand the beginnings of a process, when it is simple and relatively undifferentiated, can we hope to understand its more complex manifestations". In addition, studying the processes of categorization in infants should provide some insight into the manner in which some of the biological and experiential determinants of human cognition interact during the earliest years of development.

The present paper reviews the evidence on categorization from the domains of vision and speech, which, as we hope to show, strongly suggests that infants possess complex and sophisticated processes for categorizing and representing their experiences with the environment. In addition, we consider the structural form that underlies the categorical representation of infants. As is well known, the view of the nature of concepts and categories has undergone a major revision in the past 15 years, due in large part to the research of Rosch and her collaborators (Mervis & Rosch, 1981; Rosch, 1978). They have shown that our conceptual representations are better described by prototypic structures rather than by lists of necessary and sufficient features, although, not surprisingly, the former view of conceptual structures is not wholly adequate – it cannot accommodate all of the experimental findings (Armstrong, Gleitman, & Gleitman, 1983; Murphy & Medin, 1985). Nevertheless, it does appear true at this writing that prototypic structures exist and serve to guide the processes of categorization in a wide variety of tasks. We examine the extent to which this conclusion applies to the categorical representations of infants. In the final part of our discussion, we consider some of the difficulties that are encountered when one attempts to extrapolate from the categories and their underlying concepts in young infants to those that exist in adults or even in children of 4 and 5 years of age.[1]

THE CATEGORIES OF INFANTS

In this section of the paper, research is reviewed on four different aspects of infant categorization of visual information: (1) dot patterns, (2) schematic faces, (3) hue, and (4) orientation. These particular bodies of research were selected because of their focus not only on the processes of categorization in early infancy, but also on the nature of the categorical representation. In addition, data are available from both adult and infant observers, thus allowing for intriguing comparisons. We also review, briefly because of

---

[1] In focusing our discussion as we do, we seek to provide a consideration of the problem of categorization in infants in a somewhat different perspective than has been the case in most past reviews. These reviews have often been concerned with a single aspect of categorization behavior in infants (Eimas, 1975) or primarily with methodological and taxonomic problems (Bornstein, 1984, and Reznick & Kagan, 1983). In contrast, our goals are to illustrate the principle findings in the area of infant categorization behavior, to relate these findings to the adult literature on categorization and concepts, and to note the difficulties that exist in providing a bridge between the categories and concepts of infants and those of adults.

numerous existing reviews, research on the categorization of speech in infants and the possible nature of the categories of speech.[2]

The Domain of Vision

In that much of the work to be reviewed in the present section involves, procedures that are somewhat idiosyncratic to research with infants, it will be informative to describe them for readers who are unfamiliar with the methodologies required to examine the mental life of infants. In a typical investigation, infants are first familiarized with different exemplars from a category. If, over the course of the familiarization trials, infants' looking (as most commonly measured in fixation time) declines or *habituates*, it is assumed that the infant has formed and stored in memory some representation of the stimuli. A subsequent test phase capitalizes on the finding that infants prefer novel to familiar stimuli (Fantz, 1964). The test phase can be conducted in one of two ways: (1) in the paired preference procedure, infants are presented with both a novel exemplar from the familiar category and a novel exemplar from a novel category; (2) in the serial habituation procedure, infants are presented with a novel exemplar from the familiar category followed by a novel exemplar from the novel category, or conversely. In either case, categorization may be inferred if the infant generalizes habituation to the novel exemplar of the familiar category and

---

[2]In considering the parsing of the environment into categories, we believe that there are cognitive prerequisites that must be solved at least partially before categorization routines can be effective. One of the most important, we believe, is the segmentation of the environment into coherent entities, that is, into bounded objects, events, and patterns. This aspect of human cognition is necessary for categorization, we believe, in that it provides the elements over which category membership may be assessed. The recent work of Spelke and her colleagues strongly suggests that the parsing of the environment into coherent entities, as least in the case of objects, begins early in life, aided by powerful initial, most likely innate, constraints (for reviews of this work, see Spelke, 1982 and 1985; and for example, Starkey, Spelke and Gelman, 1983, for evidence that two-dimensional patterns are also seen as individual elements). We believe that these constraints help to solve the nontrivial problem of how a child with little or no formal tuition arrives at an adultlike view of the world, despite there being an indefinite number of ways to segment the flux of contiguous and partially overlapping surfaces arriving at the visual sensorium.

Whereas adults' perception of objects appears to be guided by certain Gestalt principles of perceptual organization such as similarity (of surface features) and good continuation (Wertheimer, 1958), Spelke and her colleagues have shown that infants about 3 months of age construct the objects of their world around two perhaps more basic principles: the *common movement* and *connected surface* principles. In following the common movement principle, young infants group together surfaces that move together. In adhering to the principle of connected surface, infants perceive adjoining surfaces as constituting a single object, whereas surfaces that are separated laterally or in depth are seen as two separate entities. Only somewhat later (at about 6 months of age) do the more common Gestalt principles of similarity of form and good continuation begin to be used to further guide the perception of objects.

dishabituates to the novel exemplar of the novel category. This pattern of habituation followed by dishabituation indicates that the representation of the familiarization stimuli was categorical in that the infant perceived the novel exemplar of the familiar category as an instance of the familiar category, whereas the novel exemplar from the novel category is recognized as a non-instance (but see Reznick & Kagan, 1983). In addition, it must be shown that the generalization of habituation from the familiar exemplars to the novel exemplar from the same category did not occur simply because of an inability to discriminate between one or more of the familiar exemplars and the novel exemplar from the same category.

A second manner of assessing categorization in infants has been used often for stimuli that vary continuously along some physical dimension (e.g., hues and speech sounds). For these kinds of stimuli, categorization has been inferred on the basis of nonmonoticities in discrimination performance along some relevant dimension, showing that exemplars from the same hue or speech category are more difficult to discriminate than are exemplars from different categories. Of course, if the discriminability of the members of a category is not better than would be expected by chance, then categorization is a consequence of an inability to discriminate among certain members of a continuum. This process of categorization is quite different from that which enables us to respond in an equivalent manner (and perhaps even to experience perceptual constancy) in the face of discriminable differences among the members of a category. As we shall see, however, categorization does not appear to arise in any instance solely from an inability to discriminate.

Dot patterns.   One of the earliest accounts of how prototypes might be used to recognize new instances of a category was provided by Posner and Keele (1968; 1970) and later expanded upon by Homa and his associates (Homa & Chambliss, 1975; Homa, Cross, Cornell, Goldman, & Schwartz, 1973). The general procedure of their experiments involved subjects learning to classify exemplars of several categories of random dot patterns that are generated by distorting category-defining prototypes. The prototypes consisted of sets of nine dots that formed random shapes or coherent, known shapes (e.g., triangle, the letter A). Distortions were generated by moving each dot in a prototype small distances in a random direction. After subjects learned to classify instances that were generated from each prototype, their ability to classify each of the following was compared: (1) old exemplars that had been encountered during the learning phase of the experiment, (2) new exemplars that had not previously been encountered, and (3) the initial prototype which also had not been encountered during the learning phase. Posner and Keele (1968) found that immediately after learning, subjects performed better with the old exemplars and the original prototype as compared with the new exemplars. If a delay of 1 week is imposed between learning and testing, performance with the old exemplars decreases, but remains stable for the new exemplars as well as the original prototype (Posner & Keele, 1970). This pattern of results supports the notion that subjects had not only retained specific information about individual exemplars, but had also generated some central tendency of the exemplars encountered during learning: the prototype. Recognition of new instances could be based on their similarity to either the old exemplars or the newly constructed prototype. With time, the exemplar-specific information is lost and subjects rely primarily on the constructed prototypic representation as the basis for recognizing new instances of the category.

Homa and his associates (Homa et al., 1973; Homa & Chambliss, 1975) expanded upon Posner and Keele's original prototype formulations. Homa et al. found that when the number of instances from a particular category to be classified during the learning phase of the experiment was increased, performance improved for the prototype and new exemplars and decreased for the old exemplars in the transfer test. In addition to this effect of category size, Homa and Chambliss found that the number of categories subjects learned also facilitated performance with the prototype and new exemplars while hindering performance with the old exemplars in the transfer phase of the experiment. On the basis of these findings, Homa et al. and Homa and Chambliss proposed that the prototype is a dynamic entity which gradually evolves as one has more and more experiences with members of the category and with members of contrast categories. In extrapolating this view to natural categories, they have argued that as children come into contact with increasing numbers of exemplars from the category *dog*, for example, they gradually begin to build a list of features which are common to many members of this category. At the same time, children are also having experiences with exemplars from contrast categories like *cat* and *rabbit*, allowing them to register which of the most common features serve to distinguish dogs from cats and rabbits. The prototype thus becomes a list of the most common features that are also distinguishing features (see also Rosch & Mervis, 1975).

Using the adult research just described as a guide, Bomba and Siqueland (1983) asked whether 3- and 4-month-old infants could form a categorical representation from sets of dot patterns and, if so, whether this representation had a prototypic structure. Using a paired preference procedure, Bomba and Siqueland presented infants with different exemplars which were "square-like," "triangle-like," or "diamond-like" in their appearance. The exemplars were random dot distortions, generated from a symmetrical form (either a square, triangle, or diamond) that was defined as the prototype of the category. After familiarization with different exemplars from one form category, infants were presented with the previously unseen prototype from the familiar form category, paired with the prototype of one of the two remaining novel form categories. Infants looked longer at the novel category prototype, thus indicating that the previously unseen prototype from the familiar category was recognized as a member of that category. Bomba and Siqueland also found that infants could discriminate between the exemplar most similar to the prototype and the prototype itself; consequently, the generalization of habituation to the prototype of the familiar category in the original experiment did not occur simply because of an inability to discriminate.

In additional experiments, Bomba and Siqueland (1983) investigated the possibility that infants formed a prototypical representation of the sort proposed by Posner and Keele and Homa and his associates. After familiarization with a range of exemplars from one form category, infants were tested with the previously unseen prototype of that category and one of the previously seen exemplars. Bomba and Siqueland hypothesized that if a prototype were abstracted during familiarization and used in decisions regarding category membership, then it should actually be seen as more familiar than the previously seen exemplar. This result was not observed when the unseen prototype and the familiar exemplar were presented immediately after familiarization. When a delay was imposed between familiarization and testing, however, infants looked significantly longer at the familiar exemplar compared with the previously unseen prototype. This *prototype effect* also was observed when the number of exemplars from a common category presented during familiarization was increased. Thus, it seems that, like adults, infants show a greater reliance on prototypical information when a delay is imposed between category learning and a transfer test and when the number of instances to be classified during learning is increased, a mode of information processing that is efficient in a world of infinite variation.[3]

In a recent series of studies, Quinn (1985) extended the work of Bomba and Siqueland (1983) by investigating the acquisition of two categories during a single experimental procedure. Quinn's work was undertaken in part to understand the formation of categories under conditions that begin

---

[3]It should be mentioned that at least one exemplar-based model of representation also can account for the prototype effects observed in both infant and adult subjects (Medin & Schaffer, 1978). This model accommodates typicality effects by assuming that subjects attend more readily to or put more weight on the most frequently occurring features found among the experienced instances of a category. In this way, typical exemplars come to dominate the representation. We would argue that whereas the prototype effects reported in the present paper and elsewhere are not incompatible with an exemplar model like that proposed by Medin and Schaffer, they do, at the very least, pose serious problems for the class of exemplar models that contain no room for abstraction (e.g., the proximity model described by Reed, 1972). Such models also do not restrict the number of exemplars in the representation, a most serious shortcoming (Smith & Medin, 1981).

to approximate those that occur in the natural environment. In this situation, infants are presented with exemplars from more than a single category in a short period of time, and most likely in a haphazard fashion. And although we cannot completely replicate such conditions in the laboratory, we can begin to see the consequences of presenting exemplars from more than a single category on the formation of categories and their structure.

Using the paired-preference procedure and form category stimuli like those used by Bomba and Siqueland (1983), Quinn familiarized 3- and 4-month-old infants with six exemplars from a single form category or six exemplars from each of two form categories. For infants receiving information about two categories, the order of presentation of the patterns was quasi-random, with the constraint that no more than three exemplars from the same category be presented in succession. Both groups of infants were then administered the standard test of categorization in which a novel member of the familiar category was paired with a novel member of a novel category. The infants familiarized with two categories were tested on only a single category in order to equate the testing conditions across the two groups. Both groups of infants showed a reliable preference for the novel category item, thereby providing evidence for categorization. Interestingly, infants exposed to exemplars from two categories showed a somewhat higher novelty preference than did the infants who received information from only one category, despite the increased attentional and memorial demands in the former condition. On the basis of these results, Quinn speculated that presenting the infant with contrasting category information facilitates the categorization process by allowing the infant to see not only how common category members are alike, but also how they may be distinguished from the members of the contrasting category.

In a second experiment, Quinn asked whether there might be a different or more efficient manner of representation that accompanied the better categorization found among infants who saw exemplars from two categories. As in the previous experiment, infants were familiarized with exemplars from a single category or exemplars from two different categories. In the preference test phase, however, infants were given a prototype test in which a previously seen exemplar was paired with the novel prototype from the familiar category. The infants who observed patterns from two categories were administered two prototype tests, one for each of the familiar categories. If infants represented the category information in terms of exemplars, then the previously seen exemplar should be perceived as more familiar and thus not looked at preferentially. But if infants abstracted a prototype and were using it to represent the category information, then the novel prototype should be perceived paradoxically as the more familiar stimulus. Infants who saw patterns from a single category showed a reliable preference for the novel prototype, indicating recognition of the familiar exemplar. Infants who received information from two categories, in contrast, displayed a significant preference for the old exemplars from each of the familiar categories, indicating that they recognized the novel prototypes as more familiar. On the basis of these findings, Quinn concluded that the former infants represented the category information in terms of exemplars, whereas the latter infants represented the same information in terms of prototypes. This finding is consistent with the idea that infants store specific exemplars when confronted with small amounts of category information, but rely on prototypes to represent larger amounts of category information (Sherman, 1985, and the discussion later in this section).[4]

There is another, earlier study by Husaim and Cohen (1981) on the ability of infants to form more than a single categorical representation. They adopted an operant head-turning technique to examine 10-month-old infants' ability to acquire two contrasting, ill-defined categories. The stimuli were not dot patterns, but rather schematic line drawings of animals, which differed along four, binary-valued dimensions. Each value along each dimension was associated with one or the other value along the other dimensions, but with a probability less than 1, hence the ill-defined nature of the categories. After being trained to respond differentially to different exemplars of the two categories, infants were found to transfer learning to new exemplars from the two categories. Learning was transferred most frequently to prototypic stimuli made up of the modal dimensional values. The pattern of responding in the transfer test was interpreted by Husaim and Cohen as evidence that infants were using two or three independent dimensions in learning these categories. This argument rests on the assumption that infants divide their attention among the different dimensions and perceive them separately. Kemler (1981), however, has questioned this assumption and pointed out that the infants' classifications could have been based on one wholistic dimension, namely, the amount of contour in the stimulus. Although the question of which dimensions are used as a basis

---

[4]It is interesting to note that the categories in the studies by Bomba and Siqueland (1983) and Quinn (1985) were constructed with nonrandom, "good" form prototypes, whereas some of the categories used by Posner and Keele (1968; 1970) were constructed from random prototypes. Rosch (1973) has shown that form categories structured around perceptually salient, natural prototypes (e.g., good forms such as squares or triangles) are learned faster than categories organized around non-natural prototypes. Furthermore, even when a non-natural, distorted form was designated as the prototype and the good form as a peripheral category number, the good form was remembered as the best example of the category. Thus, it would be of considerable interest to learn if early category acquisition and prototype abstraction are more difficult for categories that are more arbitrarily structured. An answer in the affirmative would suggest that the "naturalness" of at least some categories (form, and possibly color and orientation as well) result from highly configural stimuli that can be easily stored and retrieved even by the young infant's processing system, rather than the result of differential experience in naming, identifying, and remembering good forms as opposed to more arbitrary ones.

for classification remains unresolved, the work of Husaim and Cohen, like that of Quinn, is important in demonstrating that infants can acquire a second category in a single, relatively brief experimental session, and that both categories are represented by prototypic structures.

Schematic Faces.   A number of researchers have used schematic faces to investigate how individuals abstract a central tendency from a set of specific experiences. Schematic faces can be characterized by values along a number of dimensions of similarity (e.g., nose length, eye separation). Observers may count or average the dimensional values when forming a prototype. If subjects average these values, then the prototype consists of the *mean* values for the different dimensions that characterize all instances of a category. If subjects count dimensional values, the prototype consists of the *modal* values for the different dimensions that characterize all instances of a category. Depending on the discriminability of the dimensional values presented during a familiarization session, subjects recognize faces composed of the mean or modal dimensional values as the most familiar (Goldman & Homa, 1976; Neumann, 1974). If the faces are composed of dimensions with highly discriminable values, then subjects are likely to recognize the modal prototype as more familiar. If the faces are composed of dimensions with minimally discriminable values, then subjects are likely to recognize the mean prototype as more familiar.

Strauss (1979) investigated whether 10-month-old infants represent a category of similar schematic faces with a mean or modal prototype. He presented infants with faces that varied along the dimensions of face length, nose length, nose width, and amount of separation between the eyes. Two familiarization conditions that differed in terms of the discriminability of the different dimensional values (low or high) were used. After familiarization, infants were given one of three recognition tests: (1) the mean prototype paired with a face consisting of completely novel dimensional values; (2) a modal prototype paired with the totally novel face; or (3) the mean prototype paired with the modal prototype. Strauss reasoned that if one of the prototypes had been abstracted during familiarization, then it would be perceived as more familiar than either the totally novel face or the other prototype. The results for the two familiarization conditions were similar. Infants looked less at the mean prototype when it was paired with either the totally novel face or the modal prototype. When presented with the totally novel face and the modal prototype, infants showed no significant preference for either face. These findings were taken as evidence that infants formed a prototype based on the average values along the dimensions of the familiar faces.

One apparent difference between adults and infants in the categorization of schematic faces is that infants form a mean prototype when the dimensional values are highly discriminable, whereas adults form a modal prototype. Of course, it was with adult observers that the discriminability values were determined. It may well be that 10-month-old infants would find this same set of dimensional values less discriminable than did the adults, and thereby providing an explanation for the difference between these two groups of observers. But there is another possible explanation. Sherman (1985) found evidence for the formation of modal prototypes by 10-month-old infants with a very similar set of stimuli. It is important to note, however, that she presented very few exemplars during the familiarization period and her stimuli varied along only three dimensions. Thus, with lesser amounts of information, infants appear to be able to retain information about specific exemplars and the frequency with which the component features appear. With greater amounts of information, it appears that infants may enter the features into an averaging process to obtain a mean prototypic representation. Quinn's (1985) data are consistent with such an explanation. A single category consisting of six exemplars was represented in terms of exemplars, whereas two categories with six exemplars each were represented as prototypes (see Homa et al., 1973; and Neumann, 1974, for findings with adults that are also consistent with this explanation).[5]

In a second study, Strauss (1981, as described by Cohen & Younger, 1983) familiarized 10-month-old infants with a set of schematic faces similar to those used in his earlier study. Infants were then given a recognition test, with the previously unseen mean prototype paired with a familiar face. Infants looked significantly more at the familiar exemplar than the previously unseen mean prototype. Consistent with the findings of Bomba and Siqueland (1983) regarding form categories, it appears that infants can construct a prototype from a range of experiences with similar schematic faces and recognize it as more familiar than a previously seen exemplar.

---

[5]It is of interest that the infant's shift from an exemplar to a prototypic representation with an increase in both the amount and variability of information presented fits well with predictions from distributed models of memory proposed by Knapp and Anderson (1984) and McClelland and Rumelhart (1985). These models are attractive in at least two respects. First, from a neurophysiological perspective, they are realistic in that the processing of information is constrained by known physiological properties of individual neurons. Second, from a developmental perspective, these models are economical in the sense that they require a minimum of "built in" knowledge in order to function. It is tempting to speculate that models of this nature may well describe the means by which young infants represent information categorically.

The work with schematic faces has provided a second data base on which to compare categorization in adults and infants, and shows that both groups represent a set of similar experiences in terms of a central tendency. Being able to represent our experience as a central tendency early in life is advantageous. First, it frees cognitive systems from having to keep a record of all instances of featural values, and second, it allows for a prototype that would require very little updating, both of which, if true, provide for considerable cognitive economy.

Hue.   Rosch (1973; 1975a) has argued that hue categories for adult observers are organized around perceptually salient natural prototypes. These natural prototypes are the common focal colors that Berlin and Kay (1969) found to be the best examples of color categories, despite very marked differences in the manner in which the languages of their observers encoded color space. A focal color may thus serve as a prototypical representation for a color category by being a "best" exemplar against which one could compare the relative "goodness" of other category members when making decisions regarding the category membership of incoming stimuli. These focal colors may be biologically given in that they correspond well with the points of unique hue that are derived from the physiologically-based, opponent processing of colors (e.g., unique blue occurs where the red-green opponent process is neither excited nor inhibited, Kay & McDaniel, 1978).

One form of evidence used to support the claim that hue categories have an internal structure in the form of a natural prototype is the learning of color terms by Dani natives (Rosch, 1973). These people do not have terms for the basic hue categories in their natural language. They divide up the color spectrum into two categories, light and dark, based on brightness rather than hue. When they were asked to learn names for different exemplars from different color categories in a paired-associated learning task, they learned the names of the natural prototype faster than the names for other exemplars of the category, even when the natural prototype was presented as a peripheral exemplar of a constructed category during training. Further, when looking at the naming errors over all the different exemplars from a category, category names appeared to be more difficult to acquire when the natural prototypes were presented as peripheral members of the category than when they were presented as central members. This finding seems to indicate that it is more difficult to learn color terms when taught with a set of exemplars that do not reflect the natural structure of the color space. Rosch (1975b, p. 184) summarizes the implications of these findings: "When category names are learned, they tend to become attached first to the salient stimuli, only later generalizing to other, physically similar instances. By this means these natural prototype colors become the foci of organization for categories".

To the extent that the internal structure of a hue category is derived from biology, one might expect it to be present and operating early in life. Using this adult work as a guide, the following questions might be asked about infants: (1) Do infants categorize hue information? (2) Is the representation of a hue category organized around a natural prototype?

The question of whether infants categorize hue information was first addressed by Bornstein, Kessen, and Weiskopf (1976). After habituation to an exemplar from the blue category (480 nm), 4-month-old infants were presented with either an exemplar from the familiar blue category (450 nm) or an exemplar from a novel green category (510 nm). They found that infants generalized their habituation to the novel blue hue and dishabituated to the novel green hue, even though both stimuli were 30 nm away from the habituation stimulus. In a second experiment, however, Bornstein et al. failed to reveal evidence of discrimination between the two exemplars from the blue category. Using rate of processing as an index of discrimination, they found that infants who were presented with an alternating series of two exemplars from a single category (450 nm and 480 nm) habituated just as rapidly as a group of infants who were given successive presentations of a single wavelength (480 nm). Both of these groups of infants habituated more rapidly than a group of infants who were presented with an alternating series of exemplars (450 nm and 510 nm) from two different categories. The assumption here is that if infants are sensitive to the variation in the blue category, they should not habituate as rapidly as infants who received a single entity. That they did so would seem to indicate that the generalization of habituation from one blue exemplar to a second blue exemplar occurred because of an inability to discriminate between the two. In a later study with 4-month-olds, however, Bornstein (1983) demonstrated that some within-category discrimination is possible for hue categories. In this study, infants who were given successive presentations of a single member of the blue category (476 nm light) habituated more rapidly than infants who were presented with six different members of the blue category (455, 470, 476, 480, 484, and 490 nm lights). Both of these groups were found to habituate more rapidly than a group of infants who were presented with hues from the different hue categories of green, blue, yellow, and red. It appears that infants are capable of discriminating between members of the same hue category, although not as well as they can discriminate between members of different hue categories, and thus the categorization of hue is not simply a consequence of a failure to discriminate.

As just noted, there is some evidence that the natural prototypes of adult hue categories correspond well with the unique hues derived from the physiologically based opponent processing system (Kay & McDaniel, 1978). If these physiological mechanisms are operating early, one might speculate that the hue categories of the infant are organized around these natural prototypes. Recall that for the categories of dot patterns and schematic faces, a prototype consisted of some index of central tendency of the familiar exemplars. But the natural prototype for hue endorsed by Rosch (1973; 1975a) suggests that one will not average the wavelengths of light that one is familiarized with to form a prototype. Rather, the natural prototype is the focal hue given to us by our biology. Although an appealing view, it awaits confirmation with infant observers.

Orientation.   The orientation of a visual stimulus is another continuum that may be represented by a very few highly salient values, whose perception may have a biological determination (Essock, 1980; Essock & Lehmkuhle, 1982; Essock & Siqueland, 1981; Quinn & Lehmkuhle, 1983a). Rosch (1973) has provided evidence that near main axis orientations are perceived in relation to the main axes (90° and 0°), whereas oblique orientations are perceived in relation to the 45° and 135° diagonals. (Note: All orientation values are expressed in degrees counterclockwise from horizontal.) This evidence suggested to Rosch that vertical, horizontal, and the two diagonals may serve as "cognitive reference points" along the orientation continuum against which the relative verticality, horizontality, or obliqueness of a visual stimulus is judged. This interpretation implies that there are four general categories of orientation that may have prototypic structure.

Bomba (1984) has examined infants' categorical representations of the orientation of squarewave gratings. Four-month-old infants were familiarized with a small range of oblique orientations around 112.5°. A second group of infants were familiarized with obliques around 104.5°. In a test phase, both groups of infants generalized their habituation to another oblique (135°) and dishabituated to a non-oblique (vertical or 90°). Bomba also found that this generalization of habituation from a range of oblique stimuli to another oblique stimulus was not a consequence of an inability to discriminate between them. Infants were able to discriminate orientations of 112.5° and 135° as well as 104.5° and 135°. Bomba has interpreted the equivalence in responding to a range of discriminably different oblique orientations on the same side of vertical as evidence that infants partition the orientation continuum into a wide oblique and narrow non-oblique (vertical and horizontal) categories.

Quinn, Bomba, and Siqueland have recently performed several experiments that follow from the initial finding that infants can acquire a category of oblique orientations to one side of vertical (Quinn & Bomba, 1986; Quinn, Siqueland, & Bomba, 1985). Quinn and Bomba have found that 4-month-old infants who are familiarized with a range of oblique orientations around 112.5° will generalize habituation to a 45° stimulus. This generalization of habituation occurred despite the ability to discriminate between 112.5° and 45°. These results suggest that infants form a more general oblique category than do adults, incorporating both left and right slanted oblique orientations into a single representation.

Quinn et al. (1985) have investigated the effects of memory on within- and between-category discrimination of orientation. More specifically, they employed the paired preference procedure to examine how a delay between familiarization and test will affect the ability of 2- and 3-month old infants to discriminate between the main axis stimulus pair (90° and 0°) and two oblique stimulus pairs (22.5° and 112.5°; 45° and 135°). Although the physical difference between these pairs of stimuli is the same, the work of Quinn and Bomba suggests that infants perceive horizontal and vertical as members of different categories, whereas the members of the oblique stimulus pairs are perceived as members of a general oblique category. The data indicated that the three stimulus pairs were equally discriminable when the test phase immediately followed familiarization. With a 3-minute delay between familiarization and test trials, however, the novelty preference score, the indicant of the ability to perform the horizontal-vertical discrimination, remained significantly above chance, whereas this same score for the two oblique discriminations fell to chance. This categorical-like pattern of responding appears to foreshadow the superior memorial abilities that young children display for horizontal-vertical stimulus pairs compared with oblique stimulus pairs on delayed matching to sample tasks (Bryant, 1969; 1973; Harris, LeTendre, & Bishop, 1974; Williamson & McKenzie, 1979; and see Pisoni [1973] for comparable findings in the domain of speech).

Bornstein (1982) reported the results of an unpublished study investigating the possibility that a category of near vertical orientations may have internal structure. Four-month-old infants were familiarized with a number of exposures of a stimulus oriented 5°, 10° and 15° to the left and right of a vertical (90°) orientation. In a test phase, infants were found to look less at the stimulus oriented to 90° as compared with a familiar oblique or a novel 7° deviation from the 90° orientation. This pattern of responding suggests that infants had abstracted a prototype, the vertical orientation, from experience with a number of near vertical orientations. Moreover, these results suggest that Rosch's (1975a) "cognitive reference points" for the orientation continuum are established very early in life.

In summary, evidence has been presented that is consistent with the idea that the categorization of dot patterns, schematic faces, hues, and orientation is well within the capacity of infants during the first year of life. Moreover, as is true for adults, infants organize and represent the categorical information in the dot patterns, schematic faces, and at least the orientations around the vertical orientation by prototypes. Although categories of hue for adults also seem to be organized around a prototype, the structure of hue categories of infants has not yet been investigated.[6]

The Domain of Speech

A basic issue in the categorization of speech sounds is how a nearly continuous acoustic signal that is marked by considerable variation in its physical properties is perceived as discrete phonetic segments by an adult listener. One type of acoustic variation is that which arises from such sources as phonetic context, speaker, rate of speech, and intonation. Adults are able to perceive the phonetic similarity of the members of the categories of speech that may vary along any or all of these dimensions. Kuhl (1979; 1980; 1983) examined the ability of 6-month-old infants to perceive the similarity among acoustically distinct tokens of the same phonetic category. More specifically, she investigated infants' ability to respond equivalently to tokens from the same phonetic category that have different intonation contours and are spoken by different speakers: a man, a woman, and a child. In one experiment, infants were trained to turn their heads in the direction of a visual reinforcer when a repeating background token from one phonetic category (*a*) was changed to a token from a different phonetic category (*i*), the vowel sounds in the words *pot* and *pit*, respectively. Once training was complete, acoustic variation in the two categories was introduced either gradually or abruptly, and the infants' responses to these new exemplars were assessed. These infants were found to generalize their head-turning response successfully to novel tokens from the target phonetic category when irrelevant variations in intonation contour and speaker identity were introduced into both the background and target phonetic categories. One might question whether this successful response generalization occurred because the infants were simply not sensitive to the irrelevant variations within the phonetic categories. Although Kuhl did not address this question, there is evidence that infants can discriminate between intonation patterns (Morse, 1972) and between male and female voices, and even form equivalence classes on the basis of this information (Miller, Younger, & Morse, 1982). This evidence is at least suggestive that the tokens from Kuhl's phonetic categories were discriminable. Kuhl (1980; 1983) also has provided evidence for the formation of equivalence classes

---

[6]It is possible, of course, that some infants may have formed representations of the experimental categories prior to the experimental sessions. Given the environments of infants, it would not be surprising to learn that representations for women or verticality or some colors existed before testing. Although it would be of interest to know if this were true, the existence of such representations prior to the experiment, which may have aided the categorization of the experimental materials, does not alter the major conclusion of these studies: processes for categorizing and representing environmental information are available to infants before they reach 6 months of age.

for additional phonetic contrasts, both vocalic and consonantal. This perceptual equivalence for different members of a phonetic category is apparently achieved without formal training and with little productive competence.

Another type of acoustic variation that has been extensively studied is that which arises from the inherent variation in the processes underlying the production of speech, even for a short utterance by a single speaker in a given phonetic context. In the typical experiment investigating the way this form of acoustic variation is perceived, mature listeners are asked to identify stimuli that vary along an acoustic dimension relevant to a particular phonetic distinction. Voice onset time (VOT) is one such dimension. VOT is defined as the time between the release of the sound and the onset of quasi-periodic energy that represents vocal fold vibration or voicing. It is a sufficient cue to distinguish voiced stop consonants (b, d, g), from voiceless stop consonants (p^h, t^h, k^h) in syllable initial position. The voiced stops (b, d, g) are the initial sounds in the nonsense syllables *bah, dah,* and *gah,* whereas the voiceless stops (p^h, t^h, k^h) are the first sounds in the syllables *pah, tah,* and *kah.* For example, when VOT is varied through a number of acoustically equal steps between 0 and 100 msec, a range sufficient to produce the contrast between the voiced and voiceless labial stops in the syllables (ba) and (p^ha), listeners typically classify all stimuli with VOT values less than 25 msec as members of the category (ba) and those stimuli with VOT values greater than 25 msec as members of the category (pa) (Lisker & Abramson, 1970).

In a corresponding discrimination task, Abramson and Lisker (1970) found that two stimuli separated by equal differences in VOT were better discriminated when they were from different phonetic categories than when they were from the same phonetic category, the *category boundary effect* (Wood, 1976), which is indicative of categorical-like perception. As Liberman, Cooper, Schankweiler, and Studdert-Kennedy (1967, p. 442) have noted: "One does not hear steplike changes corresponding to the changes in the acoustic signal, but essentially quantal jumps from one perceptual category to another" although in some situations and tasks, within-category differences are perceptible to adults and infants (Miller & Eimas, 1983; Repp, 1984). Given the discriminability of members of the same phonetic category, the categorical perception of speech as evidenced by the category boundary effect cannot be a consequence solely of an inability to discriminate. Additional processes that permit listeners to listen through the perceptible variation in the signal must contribute to the categorization of speech. Categorical-like perception has been demonstrated for a variety of acoustic dimensions specifying a number of phonetic distinctions (for reviews, see Pisoni, 1978; Repp, 1984).

More than a decade ago, Eimas, Siqueland, Jusczyk, and Vigorito (1971) showed that infants as young as one month also perceived the variation in

VOT in a categorical manner. They used a high amplitude sucking procedure in which sucking responses of a critical amplitude resulted in a single presentation of a simple speech pattern, for example, the syllable (*ba*), consisting of the voiced stop consonant (*b*) plus the vowel (*a*). Typically, infants increase their sucking rates with this form of contingency and then show a decrease in responsivity, perhaps as a result of satiation. When the sucking rate decreases by a set amount (or in some studies when a fixed period of time has passed) the stimulus is changed, to a voiceless stop consonant (p^h) plus the vowel (*a*) or to an acoustic variant of the original voicing category. Compared to an appropriate control group in which the stimulus is not changed, the infants for whom the second stimulus was drawn from a different voicing category showed an increase in sucking, whereas infants who received an acoustic variant of the same voicing category as the first stimulus showed virtually the same decline in sucking as did the control infants. In the years since this initial study, there have been numerous demonstrations with infants of categorical-like perception for the acoustic information underlying a number of phonetic distinctions based on differences in place of articulation, manner of articulation, and voicing (for the most recent reviews of this work, see Aslin, Pisoni, & Jusczyk, 1983; Eimas, Miller, & Jusczyk, in press; Jusczyk, 1981). As Eimas et al. (in press) have noted, "It would seem that the infant comes to the world endowed by our human biology to be able to distinguish and categorize virtually all of the information that is relevant to phonetic categorization in natural languages".

The just quoted statement should not be taken to mean that experience with the sounds of the parental language plays no role in the development of the phonetic categories of the adult. Cross-language studies have shown that many languages, but not English, divide the VOT continuum in syllable-initial position into three categories, the prevoiced (which does not occur in English), voiced, and voiceless, with the boundary locations at approximately the same VOT values. A number of other languages divide the VOT continuum into only two categories, and interestingly these languages often differ markedly in where the boundary location is situated along the VOT continuum. These differences across languages and others are, however, not in evidence during early infancy. The Kikuyu language, for example, does not use the voiced-voiceless distinction with bilabial stops, the contrast between (*b*) and (p^h), as do some languages such as English. Streeter (1976), however, has shown that young infants born into Kikuyu-speaking environments discriminate the information relevant to the voiced-voiceless distinction in bilabial stops. In addition, infants born into English-speaking environments, as well as Spanish-speaking ones, have been shown to discriminate VOT values that signal three voicing categories (Aslin,

Pisoni, Hennessy, & Perey, 1981; and Lasky, Syrdal-Lasky, & Klein, 1975, respectively), even though only two categories are present in English and Spanish (Abramson & Lisker, 1970; 1973; Lisker & Abramson, 1970). Finally, Werker and Tees (1984) have found that the parental language begins to exert its influence in the second half-year of life. They have shown that 6-month-old infants who are able to discriminate between two phonetic contrasts not present in the parental language lose this ability by 12 months of age. Such evidence suggests that infants are ready relatively early in life to distinguish between the information relevant to phonetic distinctions that occur in the parental language and those that do not occur. But how this capacity is translated into a lessening of discriminative abilities for information that is not relevant in the sound system of the parental language is not yet known.

The categorization of the sounds of speech is actually more complex than we have described in that usually many cues exist for a single phonetic distinction and these cues enter into perceptual trading relations (see Repp, 1982, for a review of this literature). Two cues enter into a perceptual trading relation if one acoustic property may substitute (i.e., compensate) for another property, within limits of course. That is to say, the manner in which the variation in one acoustic property is mapped onto the categories of speech is determined in part by the stimulus value along a second acoustic property. The consequence of a perceptual trading relation is that there is not an invariant range of values that specifies a particular phonetic category or a single value that marks the boundary between two phonetic categories; the acoustic properties literally trade with each other. VOT, for example, is itself a complex acoustic property composed of a number of covarying cues or properties for the voicing distinction, including the aspiration in the higher formants, the interval between the onset of speech and the onset of the first formant (F1), and the onset frequency of F1. Experimentation has shown that each of these properties may play a functional role in signalling the contrast between voiced and voiceless stops and that these properties enter into perceptual trading relations (see Lisker, Liberman, Erickson, Dechovitz, & Mandler, 1977, and Summerfield & Haggard, 1977, for the most complete studies of these effects).

In a recent experiment, Miller and Eimas (1983) showed that for 3- and 4-month-old infants, as for adult listeners, the spectral information given by the onset frequency of F1 enters into a trading relation with the temporal information provided by VOT. This was evidenced by a boundary shift along the VOT continuum for the $(d) - (t^h)$ distinction from a lower value of VOT to a higher value as the onset frequency of F1 was decreased, a pattern of results closely approximating that obtained with adults by Lisker et al. (1977). Furthermore, Eimas (1985) showed that the temporal and spectral information for the distinction between the words *say* and *stay* is perceptually equivalent as it is for adult listeners (Best, Morrongiello, & Robson, 1981; Fitch, Halwes, Erickson, & Liberman, 1980).

An early view of speech perception assumed that adult phonetic category assignments were made on the basis of which side of a naturally-given boundary value a speech sound falls (see Pisoni, 1978, for discussion of this view). This view has recently been challenged by the suggestion that the phonetic categories of the adult may be represented by prototypes (Eimas et al., in press; Miller, Connine, Schermer, & Kleunder, 1983; Oden & Massaro, 1978; Repp, 1977; Samuel, 1982) and that the phonetic boundary along a continuum lies at the intersection of two prototypic structures. As was the case in the visual modality, prototype theory in the speech modality assumes that membership in a category is graded, rather than all or none. It should be noted that the idea of a perceptual trading relation leads to a conception of categorical representations that are inherently prototypic in structure. As in a family resemblance structure, there is apparently no single cue value or even single cue that defines the categories of speech; rather, the presence of one cue value along one dimension allows values of other cues to vary and conversely. Thus, even though this phenomenon has a separate name in the speech literature, it is analogous to the idea of prototypic structures in other domains of categories and concepts.

In support of a prototypical representation for a phonetic category, Samuel (1982) has shown that some members of a phonetic category are actually perceived as better examples than others. Furthermore, of particular relevance for the present discussion is the strong evidence of Miller et al. (1983) for a prototypical representation of phonetic categories, obtained by means of a selective adaptation procedure that presumably operates at an auditory level of processing (Roberts & Summerfield, 1981). Inasmuch as this auditory level of processing is most likely available to the infant, the findings of Miller et al. led Eimas et al. (in press, ms., p.30) to speculate that "the speech categories of the prelinguistic infant also have internal structure that is based on category prototypes". Data at least consistent with this view have been presented very recently by Grieser and Kuhl (1983), who found that the formulation of equivalence classes in 6-month-old infants was affected by the "goodness" of the training stimulus.

One might ask from where do the prototypes of speech arise. The evidence on infants' division of acoustic continua into auditory categories appropriate for later phonetic categories demands that the processing systems underlying the perception of speech come pretuned. Perhaps through evolution the structure of our perceptual system for speech became predisposed (that is, particularly sensitive) to certain modal production values of these categories (Lisker & Abramson, 1964). Of course, it is also possible (but less probable, cf. Liberman & Mattingly, 1985) that the evolutionary process worked in the opposite direction; the natural dispositions of the auditory system may have shaped the evolution of the human vocal tract and thus the acoustic consequences of speech production. In either event, the situation for speech would be similar to that for hue in that the prototypic structures for hue and speech may have their basis in the innately organized neurophysiological hardware of the systems that mediate their perception. It will be of interest to learn the extent to which future research corroborates these views concerning the biological basis for the prototypic structure of the categories of speech.

If the prototypic structure of speech is a result of the actual hardware of the perceptual systems, one might well ask if there is a theoretical problem created by the fact that languages do not place boundaries at the same loci. For example, the Spanish and English voiced/voiceless boundary occurs at two different places. Jusczyk (1984) and Eimas et al. (in press) have suggested that this may result from the existence of multiple cues and the differential weightings given to the various cues for a phonetic contrast in different languages. Such a view requires that the prototypic structure of speech be malleable enough to allow for changes in the weighting of different acoustic cues that signal a phonetic contrast. With increasing experience with the sounds of the parental language, the acoustic information that is most important in signalling a phonetic contrast will come to be weighted most heavily in the internal representation of the child's developing phonology.

HISTORICAL PERSPECTIVES AND CURRENT ISSUES

We have reviewed the evidence from a variety of tasks using both visual patterns and speech that were designed to inform us of the principles by which infants categorize information in their environments. This evidence strongly indicates that the processes of categorization are available very early in life, and, most interestingly, supports the contention that a number of significant characteristics of these processes are remarkably like those that characterize the processes of categorization in adults. Thus, for example, the many studies of categorization in the visual domain with dot patterns, schematic faces, and information for orientation, have shown that not only do infants and adults form categorical representations, but that the structure of these representations are prototypic in nature. The conclusions to be drawn from studies of speech perception are likewise similar for adult and infant listeners. Categorical representations are characteristic of speech processing, and the categories appear to have prototypic structures. Moreover, the specifics of the processes of categorization are highly similar, as evidenced, for example, by the fact that both groups use multiple cues in the categorization of speech, and in a manner that indicates that these cues have entered into perceptual trading relations.

It would seem, as we have tried to show, that our abilities to categorize information arise from a rich set of biological constraints that are aided in their operation by an equally rich set of environmental constraints. For both hue and the categories of speech, we have suggested that the disposition to categorize the relevant information and the resulting prototypic structures are a consequence of the neurophysiology of the perceptual systems. There is also evidence for an inherent neurophysiological bias favoring horizontal and vertical orientations over oblique orientations that may help to explain the more finely tuned vertical and horizontal categories of infants as compared to their oblique categories (see Essock & Lehmkuhle, 1982, and Quinn & Lehmkuhle, 1983, for discussions of this possible neural basis). We have also noted that the manner in which the neurophysiologically based, distributed memory systems proposed by Knapp and Anderson (1984) and McClelland and Rumelhart (1985) may provide a means by which infants could represent information categorically as the amount of information (i.e., the number of exemplars) increases. Of course, as we know from developmental studies of speech perception (Werker & Tees, 1984), these initial dispositions of our neurophysiology must be sufficiently malleable in order to reflect important and consistent experiential differences. Unfortunately, we understand very little of the processes that yield the effects of experience, especially in human perceptual systems.

What we conclude from this review of the literature is that young infants are highly competent processors of information, able to appreciate the structured nature of their environment and able to form categorical representations. Moreover, processes underlying the formation of categories, are surprisingly sophisticated and quite similar in their functional characteristics to those processes that serve the categorization of information at maturity. Interestingly, the view that the categorization process and the underlying representations are precocious is in direct opposition to the view of those who pioneered the study of conceptual development in children. Vygotsky (1962) and Bruner, Olver, and Greenfield (1966) concluded from their empirical investigations that the categorical structures and conceptual representations of children were qualitatively different from those that are present at maturity.

How Vygotsky and Bruner et al., among others, arrived at this conclusion stems in part, we believe, as do Carey (1982) and Fodor (1972), from the metatheoretical model of concepts that at least implicitly guided much of their research. This framework, known as the *classical view of concepts*, assumes that concepts are defined and represented by sets of features that are singly necessary and jointly sufficient (see Smith & Medin, 1981, for a comprehensive discussion of this view). Adherence to this view resulted in decades of studies on concept formation in which the observer's task was to discover the rules, i.e., the classical definitions, that permitted a large set of stimuli to be assigned correctly to categories (e.g., Hull, 1920; and see Bruner, Goodnow, & Austin, 1956, and Bourne, Ekstrand, & Dominowski, 1971, for discussions of this literature). Developmental studies attempted to compare the conceptual structures that were inferred from the categories that children and adults constructed during the course of an experiment. In the task developed by Vygotsky, children and adults were presented an array of blocks that varied in such dimensions as color, height, shape, and size. At the beginning of the task, each participant was given an example of one category (e.g., large, tall, red, square) and was then asked to find the other members of it as well as the members of other categories. The categories all had classical definitions, and thus one category might consist of all large and tall blocks. Adults, typically, discover the correct categories and the process of discovery in an orderly and logical attack on the problem. But children do not readily discover the correct categories and, in the course of trying, form categorical structures that Vygotsky called *complexes*. Actually, Vygotsky identified a number of different categorical structures that he took to represent different stages of conceptual thought. However, we will consider only complexive structures and the corresponding stage of development as they are most relevant to the present discussion. Complexes are chains of blocks in which subgroupings of blocks are linked by a single attribute and this attribute changes during the course of the experiment. Thus, a child might use size to link the block presented by the experimenter with his or her first selection and then use shape to link the second selection to the first and so on.

Bruner et al. (1966) obtained evidence for complexive thinking with more natural objects and somewhat different tasks. In one situation, children were asked to describe the ways in which different items from a common superordinate category were similar. Like Vygotsky's subjects, these children link some items by one attribute and other items by different attributes. Consider the response of one child for items from the category *food* as reported by Bruner et al. (1966, p. 76): "Banana and peach are both yellow, peach and potato are round, potato and meat are served together, meat and milk come from cows".

Examples of what has been taken as the consequences of complexive thinking appear at least until the beginnings of adolescence. Now, given the (implicit) belief that concepts have by nature a classical definition and the ease with which adults form categories based on classical definitions, then it is not difficult to understand how Vygotsky and Bruner et al. interpreted the performance of children as the product of a qualitatively different (i.e., inferior) mind. Although there is little dispute about the behavior of the children, the interpretation of Vygotsky and Bruner et al. has been seriously challenged. It is possible, as Gelman (1978) has noted, that the children's poor performance may have resulted from a failure to comprehend fully the instructions and the nature of the task (see, Markman, Cox, & Machida, 1981, for evidence that supports this contention). It also could have occurred because of stimulus preferences or response biases that determine the sequential selection of the items. Either possibility could well mask any similarities in conceptual structures that might exist in children and adults. An even more telling criticism, however, has been offered by Fodor (1972). He argued that Vygotsky was wrong in assuming that most adult concepts (and their categorical instantiations) are definitional in nature, (i.e., conform to the classical view). He notes, as have others since the writings of Wittgenstein (1953), that most natural concepts cannot be represented by a set of attributes related by some logical rule, but rather are based on family resemblances that are at least analagous to the complexive structures observed by Vygotsky and Bruner et al. Consider the task of Bruner et al. in finding the common features among exemplars of a superordinate category. Fodor (p. 90) argues that for such superordinate concepts as *furniture* and *tableware* "there is no sensory attribute, and no Boolean function of sensory attributes, characteristic of all and only the instances that fall under the concept". If most of the natural concepts of adults are not definitional, it is difficult to see how the complexive groupings of the young child can be used as evidence supporting the notion that the young child and the adult represent their worlds in a qualitatively different manner. As Fodor (p. 90) summarized his view:

> If adult conceptualization is what Vygotsky thinks it is, and what the Vygotsky test presupposes that it is, the history of mental development is indeed the history of the child's gradual approximation of adult mastery of Boolean logic. If, on the other hand, adult concepts do not, in general, fit the Vygotsky model, if an adult concept isn't the sort of thing that Vygotsky supposes it to be, then there is less interest in the fact that children find it hard, and adults find it less hard, to perform with Vygotsky blocks.

Many theorists would now agree with Fodor that most concepts do not conform to the classical view. Their structure more closely approximates that of a family resemblance or prototype (for discussions of this view of concepts, see Fodor, 1972; Mervis & Rosch, 1981; Rosch, 1978; Smith & Medin, 1981; Wittgenstein, 1953). Of the remaining concepts, few have unequivocal classical definitions; these include, for example, such concepts as those that underlie kinship and mathematical terms as well as terms for geometrical figures (Armstrong et al., 1983). Concepts that underlie the meaning of natural-kind terms such as *gold* or *tiger* or *oak tree* may well have an essence or core that is a set of necessary and sufficient attributes, but these attributes remain in many cases to be determined by science and thus may not be incorrigible (Carey, 1982; Putnam, 1975; Quine, 1969; Schwartz, 1979). Even those that are known at present (e.g., *gold*) are, for the majority of us, certainly not part of the conceptual representations that determine our processes of categorization (Armstrong et al., 1983; Smith, Medin & Rips, 1984). What does seem to guide these processes of categorization and to constitute our internalized knowledge of natural-kind terms are sets of characteristic features with prototypic structures (Smith et al., 1984). If a prototypic structure truly describes the form of most adult concepts, our assertion that the conceptual structures and processes of categorization are of a kind in infants and adults gains credence.

Our view of the early development of categorization procedures and of their underlying conceptual structures is strongly nativistic. We believe this is necessary, as we, among others, are unable to imagine how experiential factors could be the sole determinants of these aspects of cognitive growth. For a nonatavistic position to hold, it would be necessary to describe the experiential principles that result in perceptual systems coming to categorize environmental information in early infancy well before this process provides functionally relevant information. In addition, it would be necessary to explain, especially in the domain of speech, how the actual physical categories and their likely prototypic structure are specified by experience well before these categories have linguistic significance.

Of course, there are difficulties with this simple view of conceptual development that become most evident when attempts are made to describe and bridge the difference between the concepts of infants and adults. One aspect of the problem lies in the fact that, as far as the data indicate, the categories of infants, and their presumed underlying conceptual structures, are sensory in nature, whereas the categories and concepts of adults are often far removed from the world of sensory data. One need only consider such concepts as *gold, pants,* or *justice* to realize that their definitional or characteristic attributes are in many instances not like the sensory-based attributes of the categories of infants. Nor can it be readily envisioned how the attributes of adult concepts can be constructed from the attributes innately available to infants. Nevertheless, a commonly, if often tacitly, held view is that the nontransducible attributes of adult concepts are somehow derived from the sensory primitives available to infants. Adequate (that is, testable) descriptions of the developmental process remain to be offered, however. In direct opposition to this approach, it has been assumed that the conceptual constructs of adulthood are themselves primitives and thus not decomposable, a position for which there is some empirical evidence (Fodor, Garrett, Walker, & Parkes, 1980). However, in that such a position requires the further assumption of an indefinite number of innately determined "primitive" concepts, it seems to offer little hope for providing a satisfying description of conceptual development.

"primitive" concepts, it seems to offer little hope for providing a satisfying description of conceptual development.

A very different approach to the problem of conceptual development has been to directly examine the changing nature of children's conceptual structures, within a metatheoretical framework that derives from recent philosophical discussions of conceptual change (Carey, 1982; Putnam, 1975; Quine, 1969). The early results of this endeavor are promising. For example, Carey (1982; 1985) has begun to show that the developmental changes in concepts are related to our developing naive theories of the world and how it functions. With the development of a naive theory of biology, for example, she has shown that a child's representation of such animal properties as eating and sleeping undergoes extensive reorganization. In addition, even by the age of 4 years, children begin to rely on rudimentary biological knowledge in addition to "an innate feature space" (Quine, 1969) in determining the characteristics of animals (for related findings, see Keil & Batterman, 1984). Of course, how the organizing concepts of our naive theories of the world develop and subsequently reorganize our original, sensory-based concepts remains to be determined, as does what is to be considered a conceptual primitive in this new framework. Along with this type of response to the problem of conceptual change, will be one, we believe, that continues to examine the processes of categorization in early infancy, but with greater effort devoted to uncovering higher levels of conceptual competence in young infants. Such a strategy, if successful, should narrow the apparent gap between the conceptual knowledge of infants and adults and thereby make the processes of transition less opaque. We are especially optimistic about the latter approach; after all, consider the progress that has been made in the study of infant cognition since the claims of Leach (1964), p.34; as cited by Rosch et al., 1976, p.383):

> The physical and social environment of a young child is perceived as a continuum. It does not contain any intrinsically separate "things." The child, in due course, is taught to impose upon this environment a kind of discriminating grid which serves to distinguish the world as being composed of a large number of separate things, each labeled with a name.

In light of the work of infant cognition researchers, such a view is no longer tenable.

ACKNOWLEDGEMENTS

Preparation of this paper was supported in part by grant HD 05331 from the National Institute of Child Health and Human Development to Eimas. We are grateful for the critical comments of Gregory Murphy, Einar Siqueland, and Joanne Miller on earlier versions of this paper.

REFERENCES

Abramson, A. S., & Lisker, L. (1970). Discriminability along the voicing continuum: Cross-language tests. In *Proceedings of the Sixth International Congress of Phonetic Science, Prague 1967* (pp. 569–573). Prague: Academia.

Abramson, A. S., & Lisker, L. (1973). Voice-timing perception in Spanish word-initial stops. *Journal of Phonetics, 1,* 1–8.

Armstrong, S. L., Gleitman, L. R., & Gleitman, H. (1983). What some concepts might not be. *Cognition, 13,* 263–308.

Aslin, R. N., Pisoni, D. B., Hennessy, B. L., & Perey, A. J. (1981). Discrimination of voice onset time by human infants: New findings and implications for the effect of early experience. *Child Development, 52,* 1135–1145.

Aslin, R. N., Pisoni, D. B., & Jusczyk, P. W. (1983). Auditory development and speech perception in infancy. In M. M. Haith & J. J.Campos (Eds), *Infancy and developmental psychobiology: Vol. 2, Handbook of child psychology* (4th edn., pp. 573–687). New York: Wiley.

Berlin, B., & Kay, P. (1969). *Basic color terms: Their universality and evolution.* Berkeley, CA: University of California Press.

Best, C. T., Morrongiello, B., & Robson, R. (1981). Perceptual equivalence of acoustic cues in speech and nonspeech perception. *Perception & Psychophysics, 29,* 191–211.

Bomba, P. C. (1984). The development of orientation categories between 2 and 4 months of age. *Journal of Experimental Child Psychology, 37,* 609–636.

Bomba, P. C., & Siqueland, E. R. (1983). The nature and structure of infant form categories. *Journal of Experimental Child Psychology, 35,* 294–328.

Bornstein, M. H. (1982). Perceptual anisotropies in infancy: Ontogenetic origins and implications of inequalities in spatial vision. In H. W. Reese & L. P. Lipsitt (Eds), *Advances in child development and behavior* (Vol. 19, pp. 77–123). New York: Academic Press.

Bornstein, M. H. (1983). Psychological studies of color perception in human infants: Habituation, discrimination and categorization, recognition and conceptualization. In L. P. Lipsitt (Ed.), *Advances in infancy research* (Vol. 1, pp. 1–40). Norwood, NJ: Ablex.

Bornstein, M. H. (1984). A descriptive taxonomy of psychological categories used by infants. In C. Sophian (Ed.), *Origins of cognitive skills: The eighteenth annual Carnegie Symposium on Cognition* (pp. 313–338). Hillsdale, NJ: Lawrence Erlbaum Associates Inc.

Bornstein, M. H., Kessen, W., & Weiskopf, S. (1976). Color vision and hue categorization in young human infants. *Journal of Experimental Psychology: Human Perception and Performance, 2,* 115–129.

Bourne, L. E., Ekstrand, B. R., & Dominowski, R. L. (1971). *The psychology of thinking.* Englewood Cliffs, NJ: Prentice-Hall.

Bower, T. G. R. (1974). *Development in infancy.* San Francisco: Freeman.

Bruner, J. S., Goodnow, J. J., & Austin, G. A. (1956). *A study of thinking.* New York: Wiley.

Bruner, J.S., Olver, R. R., & Greenfield, P. M. (1966). *Studies in cognitive growth.* New York: Wiley.

Bryant, P. E. (1969). Perception and memory of the orientation of visually presented lines by children. *Nature* (London), *224,* 1331–1332.

Bryant, P. E. (1973). Discrimination of mirror-images by young children. *Journal of Comparative and Physiological Psychology, 82,* 415–425.

Carey, S. (1982). Semantic development: The state of the art. In E. Wanner & L. R. Gleitman (Eds), *Language acquisition: The state of the art* (pp. 345–389). Cambridge: Cambridge University Press.

Carey, S. (1985). *Conceptual change in childhood.* Cambridge, MA: MIT Press.

Cohen, L. B., & Younger, B. A. (1983). Perceptual categorization in the infant. In E. K. Scholnik (Ed.), *New trends in conceptual representation: Challenges to Piaget's theory?* (pp. 197–220). Hillsdale, NJ: Lawrence Erlbaum Associates Inc.

Eimas, P. D. (1975). Speech perception in early infancy. In L. B. Cohen & P. Salapatek (Eds), *Infant perception* (Vol. 2, pp. 193–231). New York: Academic Press.

Eimas, P. D. (1985). The equivalence of cues in the perception of speech by infants. *Infant Behavior and Development, 8,* 125–138.

Eimas, P. D., Miller, J. L., & Jusczyk, P. W. (in press). On infant speech perception and the acquisition of language. In S. Harnad (Ed.), *Categorical perception.* Cambridge: Cambridge University Press.

Eimas, P. D., Siqueland, E. R., Jusczyk, P., & Vigorito, J. (1971). Speech perception in infants. *Science, 171,* 303–306.

Essock, E. A. (1980). The oblique effect of stimulus identification considered with respect to two classes of oblique effects. *Perception, 9,* 37–46.

Essock, E. A., & Lehmkuhile, S. (1982). The oblique effects of pattern and flicker sensitivity: Implications for mixed physiological input. *Perception, 11,* 441–455.

Essock, E. A., & Siqueland, E. R. (1981). Discrimination of orientation by human infants. *Perception, 10,* 245–253.

Fantz, R. L. (1964). Visual experience in infants: Decreased attention to familiar patterns relative to novel ones. *Science, 146,* 668–670.

Fitch, H. L., Halwes, T., Erickson, D. M., & Liberman, A. M. (1980). Perceptual equivalence of two acoustic cues for stop-consonant manner. *Perception & Psychophysics, 27,* 343–350.

Fodor, J. A. (1972). Some reflections on L. S. Vygotsky's "Thought and Language". *Cognition, 1,* 83–95.

Fodor, J. A., Garrett, M. F., Walker, E. C. T., & Parkes, C. H. (1980). Against definitions. *Cognition, 8,* 263–367.

Gelman, R. (1978). Cognitive development. *Annual Review of Psychology, 29,* 297–332.

Goldman, D., & Homa, D. (1976). Integrative and metric properties of abstracted information as a function of category discriminability, instance variability, and experience. *Journal of Experimental Psychology: Human Learning and Memory, 3,* 375–385.

Grieser, D. L., & Kuhl, P. K. (1983). The internal structure of vowel categories in infancy: Effects of stimulus "goodness". *Journal of the Acoustical Society of America, 74,* Supplement 1, S102(A).

Harris, P. L., Letendre, J. B., & Bishop, A. (1974). The young child's discrimination of obliques. *Perception, 3,* 261–265.

Homa, D., & Chambliss, D. (1975). The relative contributions of common and distinctive information on the abstraction from ill-defined categories. *Journal of Experimental Psychology: Human Learning and Memory, 1,* 351–359.

Homa, D., Cross, J., Cornell, D., Goldman, D., & Schwartz, S. (1973). Prototype abstraction and classification of new instances as a function of number of instances defining the prototype. *Journal of Experimental Psychology, 101,* 116–122.

Hull, C. L. (1920). Quantitative aspects of the evolution of concepts. *Psychological Monographs* (Whole No. 123).

Husaim, J. S., & Cohen, L. B. (1981). Infant learning of ill-defined categories. *Merrill-Palmer Quarterly, 27,* 443–456.

Jusczyk, P. W. (1981). Infant speech perception: A critical appraisal. In P. D. Eimas & J. L. Miller (Eds), *Perspectives on the study of speech* (pp. 113–164). Hillsdale, NJ: Lawrence Erlbaum Associates Inc.

Jusczyk, P. W. (1984). On characterizing the development of speech perception. In J. Mehler & R. Rox (Eds), *Neonate cognition: Beyond the blooming, buzzing confusion* (pp. 199–229). Hillsdale, NJ: Lawrence Erlbaum Associates Inc.

Kay, P., & McDaniel, C. K. (1978). The linguistic significance of the meanings of basic color terms. *Language, 54,* 610–646.

Keil, F. C., & Batterman, N. (1984). A characteristic-to-defining shift in the development of word meaning. *Journal of Verbal Learning and Verbal behavior, 23,* 221–236.

Kemler, D. G. (1981). New issues in the study of infant categorization: A reply to Husaim and Cohen. *Merrill-Palmer Quarterly, 27,* 457–463.

Knapp, A. G., & Anderson, J. A. (1984). Theory of categorization based on distributed memory storage. *Journal of Experimental Psychology: Learning, Memory, and Cognition, 10,* 616–637.

Kuhl, P. K. (1979). Speech perception in early infancy: Perceptual constancy for spectrally dissimilar vowel categories. *Journal of the Acoustical Society of America, 66,* 1668–1679.

Kuhl, P. K. (1980). Perceptual constancy for speech-sound categories in early infancy. In G. H. Yeni-Komshian, J. F. Kavanagh, & C. A. Ferguson (Eds), *Child phonology: Perception* (Vol. 2, pp. 41–66). New York: Academic Press.

Kuhl, P. (1983). Perception of auditory equivalence classes for speech in early infancy. *Infant Behavior and Development, 6,* 263–286.

Lasky, R. E., Syrdal-Lasky, A., & Klein, R. E. (1975). VOT discrimination by four-to-six-and-a-half-month-old infants from Spanish environments. *Journal of Experimental Child Psychology, 20,* 215–225.

Liberman, A. M., Cooper, F. S., Schankweiler, D. S., & Studdert-Kennedy, H. (1967). Perception of the speech code. *Psychological Review, 74,* 431–461.

Liberman, A. M., & Mattingly, I. G. (1985). The motor theory of speech perception revised. *Cognition, 21,* 1–36.

Lisker, L., & Abramson, A. S. (1964). A cross-language study of voicing in initial stops: Acoustical measurements. *Word, 20,* 384–422.

Lisker, L., & Abramson, A. S. (1970). The voicing dimension: Some experiments in comparative phonetics. In *Proceedings of the Sixth International Congress of Phonetic Sciences, Prague, 1967* (pp. 563–567). Prague: Academia.

Lisker, L., Liberman, A. M., Erickson, D. M., Dechovitz, D., & Mandler, R. (1977). On pushing the voice-onset-time (VOT) boundary about. *Language and Speech, 20,* 209–216.

Markman, E. M., Cox, B., & Machida, S. (1981). The standard object sorting task as a measure of conceptual organization. *Developmental Psychology, 17,* 115–117.

McClelland, J. L., & Rumelhart, D. E. (1985). Distributed memory representation of general and specific information. *Journal of Experimental Psychology: General, 114,* 159–188.

Medin, D. L., & Schaffer, M. M. (1978). A context theory of classification learning. *Psychological Review, 85,* 207–238.

Mervis, C. B., & Rosch, E. (1981). Categorization of natural objects. *Annual Review of Psychology, 32,* 89–115.

Miller, C. L., Younger, B. A., & Morse, P. A. (1982). The categorization of male and female voices in infancy. *Infant Behavior and Development, 5,* 144–159.

Miller, J. L., Connine, C. M., Schermer, T. M., & Kleunder, K. R. (1983). A possible auditory basis for the internal structure of phonetic categories. *Journal of the Acoustical Society of America, 73,* 2124–2133.

Miller, J. L., & Eimas, P. D. (1983). Studies of the categorization of speech by infants. *Cognition, 13,* 135–165.

Morse, P. A. (1972). The discrimination of speech and nonspeech stimuli in early infancy. *Journal of Experimental Child Psychology, 14,* 477–492.

Murphy, G. L., & Medin, D. L. (1985). The role of theories in conceptual coherence. *Psychological Review, 92,* 289–316.

Neumann, P. G. (1974). An attribute frequency model for the abstraction of prototypes. *Memory & Cognition, 2,* 241–248.

Oden, G. C., & Massaro, D. W. (1978). Integration of featural information in speech perception. *Psychological Review, 85,* 172–191.

Pisoni, D. B. (1973). Auditory and phonetic memory codes in the discrimination of consonants and vowels. *Perception & Psychophysics, 13,* 253–260.

Pisoni, D. (1978). Speech perception. In W. K. Estes (Ed.), *Handbook of learning and cognitive processes* (Vol. 6, pp. 167–233). Hillsdale, NJ: Lawrence Erlbaum Associates Inc.

Posner, M. I., & Keele, S. W. (1968). On the genesis of abstract ideas. *Journal of Experimental Psychology, 77*, 353–363.

Posner, M. I., & Keele, S. W. (1970). Retention of abstract ideas. *Journal of Experimental Psychology, 83*, 304–308.

Putnam, H. (1975). The meaning of meaning. In K. Gunderson (Ed.), *Minnesota studies in the philosophy of science* (Vol. 7, pp. 131–193). Minneapolis, MN: University of Minnesota Press.

Quine, W. V. (1969). Natural kinds. In W. V. Quine (Ed.), *Ontological reality and other essays* (pp. 114–138). New York: Columbia University Press.

Quinn, P. C. (1985). *Form categorization in early infancy.* Unpublished doctoral dissertation, Brown University, Providence, RI.

Quinn, P. C., & Bomba, P. C. (1986). Evidence for a general category of oblique orientations in 4-month-old infants. Manuscript submitted for publication.

Quinn, P. C., & Lehmkuhle, S. (1983). An oblique effect of spatial summation. *Vision Research, 23*, 655–658.

Quinn, P. C. Siqueland, E. R., & Bomba, P. C. (1985). Delayed recognition memory for orientation by human infants. *Journal of Experimental Child Psychology, 40*, 293–303.

Reed, S. K. (1972). Pattern recognition and categorization. *Cognitive Psychology, 3*, 382–407.

Repp, B. H. (1977). Dichotic competition of speech sounds: The role of acoustic stimulus structure. *Journal of Experimental Psychology: Human Perception & Performance, 3*, 37–50.

Repp, B. H. (1982). Phonetic trading relations and context effects: New experimental evidence for a speech mode of perception. *Psychological Bulletin, 92*, 81–110.

Repp, B. H. (1984). Categorical perception: Issues, methods, findings. In N. J. Lass (Ed.), *Speech and language: Advances in basic research and practice* (Vol. 10, pp. 243–335). New York: Academic Press.

Reznick, J. S., & Kagan, J. (1983). Category detection in infancy. In L. P. Lipsitt (Ed.), *Advances in infancy research* (Vol. 2, pp. 79–111). Norwood, NJ: Ablex.

Roberts, M., & Summerfield, R. (1981). Audiovisual presentation demonstrates that selective adaptation in speech perception is purely auditory. *Perception & Psychophysics, 30*, 309–314.

Rosch, E. (1973). Natural categories. *Cognitive Psychology, 5*, 328–350.

Rosch, E. (1975a). Cognitive reference points. *Cognitive Psychology, 1*, 532–547.

Rosch, E. (1975b). Universals and cultural specifics in human categorization. In R. W. Brislin, S. Bochner, & W. J. Lonner (Eds), *Cross-cultural perspectives on learning* (pp. 177–206). New York: Halsted Press.

Rosch, E. (1978). Principles of categorization. In E. Rosch & B. B. Lloyd (Eds), *Principles of categorization* (pp. 27–48). Hillsdale, NJ: Lawrence Erlbaum Associates Inc.

Rosch, E., & Mervis, C. B. (1975). Family resemblances: Studies in the internal structure of categories. *Cognitive Psychology, 7*, 573–605.

Rosch, E., Mervis, C. B., Gray, W. D., Johnson, D. M., & Boyes-Braem, P. (1976). Basic objects in natural categories. *Cognitive Psychology, 8*, 382–439.

Samuel, A. G. (1982). Phonetic prototypes. *Perception & Psychophysics, 31*, 307–314.

Schwartz, S. P. (1979). Natural kind terms. *Cognition, 7*, 301–315.

Sherman, T. L. (1985). Categorization skills in infants. *Child Development, 56*, 1561–1573.

Smith, E. E., & Medin, D. L. (1981). *Categories and concepts.* Cambridge, MA: Harvard University Press.

Smith, E. E., Medin, D. L., & Rips, L. J. (1984). A psychological approach to concepts: Comments on Rey's "Concepts and Stereotypes". *Cognition, 17*, 265–274.

Spelke, E. S. (1982). Perceptual knowledge of objects in infancy. In J. Mehler, M. Garrett, & E. Walker (Eds), *Perspectives on mental representation* (pp. 89–113). Hillsdale, NJ: Lawrence Erlbaum Associates Inc.

Spelke, E. S. (1985). Perception of unity, persistence and identify: Thoughts on infants' conceptions of objects. In J. Mehler & R. Fox (Eds), *Neonate cognition: Beyond the blooming, buzzing confusion* (pp. 409–430). Hillsdale, NJ: Lawrence Erlbaum Associates Inc.

Starkey, P., Spelke, E. S., & Gelman, R. (1983). Detection of intermodal numerical correspondence by human infants. *Science, 222,* 179–181.

Strauss, M. S. (1979). Abstraction of prototypical information by adults and 10-month-old infants. *Journal of Experimental Psychology: Human Learning and Memory, 5,* 618–632.

Strauss, M. S. (1981, April). *Infant memory of prototypical information.* Paper presented at the meeting of the Society for Research in Child Development, Boston, MA.

Streeter, L. A. (1976). Language perception of 2-month-old infants shows effects of both innate mechanisms and experience. *Nature, 259,* 38–41.

Summerfield, Q., & Haggard, M. (1977). On the dissociation of spectral and temporal cues to the voicing distinction in initial stop consonants. *Journal of the Acoustical Society of America, 62,* 435–448.

Vygotsky, L. S. (1962). *Thought and language* (E. Hanfmann & G. Vacar, Trans.). Cambridge, Mass.: MIT Press.

Werker, J. F., & Tees, R. C. (1984). Cross-language speech perception: Evidence for perceptual reorganization during the first year of life. *Infant Behavior and Development, 7,* 49–63.

Wertheimer, M. (1958). Principles of perceptual organization. In D. C. Beardslee & M. Wertheimer (Eds), *Readings in perception* (pp. 115–135). Princeton: Van Nostrand..

Williamson, A. M., & McKenzie, B. F. (1979). Children's discrimination of oblique lines. *Journal of Experimental Child Psychology, 27,* 533–543.

Wittgenstein, L. (1953). *Philosophical investigations* (G. E. M. Anscombne, Trans.). Oxford: Blackwell,

Wood, C. C. (1976). Discriminability, response bias, and phoneme categories in discrimination of voice onset time. *Journal of the Acoustical Society of America, 60,* 1381–1389.

IV THE OBJECT CONCEPT

13 The Construction of Reality

J. Piaget and R. Inhelder

The system of sensori-motor schemes of assimilation culminates in a kind of logic of action involving the establishment of relationships and correspondences (functions) and classification of schemes (cf. the logic of classes); in short, structures of ordering and assembling that constitute a substructure for the future operations of thought. But sensori-motor intelligence has an equally important result as regards the structuring of the subject's universe, however limited it may be at this practical level. It organizes reality by constructing the broad categories of action which are the schemes of the permanent object, space, time, and causality, substructures of the notions that will later correspond to them. None of these categories is given at the outset, and the child's initial universe is entirely centered on his own body and action in an egocentrism as total as it is unconscious (for lack of consciousness of the self). In the course of the first eighteen months, however, there occurs a kind of Copernican revolution, or, more simply, a kind of general decentering process whereby the child eventually comes to regard himself as an object among others in a universe that is made up of permament objects (that is, structured in a spatio-temporal manner) and in which there is at work a causality that is both localized in space and objectified in things.

Source: Piaget, J. and Inhelder, R. (1966). *The Psychology of the Child,* (translated by H. Weaver, published 1969). London: Routledge & Kegan Paul, pp. 14–19.

THE PERMANENT OBJECT

The first characteristic of this practical universe, which the child builds up during the second year, is that it consists of permanent objects. The universe of the young baby is a world without objects, consisting only of shifting and unsubstantial "tableaux" which appear and are then totally reabsorbed, either without returning, or reappearing in a modified or analogous form. At about five to seven months (Stage 3 of Infancy), when the child is about to seize an object and you cover it with a cloth or move it behind a screen, the child simply withdraws his already extended hand or, in the case of an object of special interest (his bottle, for example), begins to cry or scream with disappointment. He reacts, therefore, as if the object had been reabsorbed. It will perhaps be objected that he knows very well that the object still exists in the place where it has disappeared, but simply does not succeed in solving the problem of looking for it and removing the screen. But when he begins to look under the screen (see Stage 4), you can make the following experiment: hide the object in A to the right of the child, who looks for and finds it; then, before his eyes, remove and hide the object in B, to the left of the child. When he has seen the object disappear in B (under a cushion, say), it often happens that he looks for it in A, as if the position of the object depended upon his previous search which was successful rather than upon changes of place which are autonomous and independent of the child's action. In Stage 5 (nine to ten months), however, the object is sought in terms of its displacements alone, unless they are too complex (screens within screens), and in Stage 6 there appears a use of inferences successful in mastering certain combinations (picking up a cushion and finding nothing under it but another unexpected screen, which is then immediately removed).[1]

The conservation of the object is, among other things, a function of its localization; that is, the child simultaneously learns that the object does not cease to exist when it disappears and he learns where it does go. This fact shows from the outset that the formation of the scheme of the permanent object is closely related to the whole spatio-temporal and causal organization of the practical universe.

---

[1]These results, obtained by one of us, have since been confirmed by Th. Gouin-Décarie in Montreal (in ninety subjects) and by S. Escalona in New York. Escalona has noted that an object hidden in the hand is sought later than one hidden under an external screen (in other words, reabsorption without localization prevails over substantial and spatial permanence for a longer time). H. Gruber has made a study of the same problem in kittens. Kittens pass through approximately the same stages but reach a beginning of permanence as early as three months. The human infant, on this point as on many others, is backward in comparison to the young animal, but this backwardness bears witness to more complex assimilations, since later the human infant is able to go far beyond the animal.

SPACE AND TIME

To begin with the spatio-temporal structures, we observe that in the beginning there exists neither a single space nor a temporal order which contains objects and events in the same way as containers include their contents. There are, rather, several heterogeneous spaces all centered on the child's own body – buccal, tactile, visual, auditory, and postural spaces – and certain temporal impressions (waiting, etc.), but without objective coordination. These different spaces are then gradually coordinated (buccal and tactilo-kinesthetic, through sucking objects, for instance), but these coordinations remain partial for a long time, until the formation of the scheme of the permanent object has led to the fundamental distinction – which H. Poincaré wrongly thought was given from the outset[2] – between changes of state, or physical modifications, and changes of position, or movements constitutive of space.

Along with the behavior patterns of localization of and search for the permanent object, the displacements are finally organized (Stages 5 and 6) into a fundamental structure which constitutes the framework of practical space. This structure will later serve as the foundation, once it has been internalized, for the operations of Euclidean geometry. These displacements form what geometricians call a "group of displacements". Psychologically speaking, this group has the following characteristics: (1) a displacement AB and a displacement BC may be coordinated into a single displacement AC, which is still part of the system;[3] (2) every displacement AB may be reversed to BA, whence the behavior pattern of "return" to the point of departure; (3) the combining of the displacement AB with its reverse BA gives the null displacement AA; (4) the displacements are associative; that is, in the series $ABCD$, $AB + BD = AC + CD$. This means that by starting from A an identical point D may be reached by different paths (if the segments AB, BC, etc., are not along a straight line). When the child understands this property of space he can begin to solve "detour" problems.

---

[2]Poincaré had the great merit of foreseeing that the organization of space was related to the formation of the "group of displacements", but since he was not a psychologist, he regarded this group as a *priori* instead of seeing it as the product of a gradual formation.

[3]The path AC may not pass through B if AB and BC are not in a straight line.

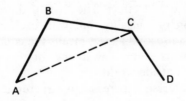

It is a late development (Stages 5 and 6 in the human infant) and is an activity understood by chimpanzees but unknown to hens, etc.

This organization of positions and of displacements in space goes together with the constitution of objective temporal series, since, in the case of the practical group of displacements, the displacements are effected physically, step by step, and one at a time, as opposed to the abstract notions which will later be constructed by thought and which will permit a general representation that is simultaneous and increasingly extra-temporal.

CAUSALITY

The system of permanent objects and their displacements is, moreover, indissociable from a causal structuration, for the property of an object is to be the source, the seat, or the result of various actions whose connections constitute the category of causality.

Causality develops in a similar manner as spatio-temporal schemes and becomes objective and adequate only at the end of a long evolution whose initial phases are centered on the child's own action, while he is still unaware of the spatial and physical connections inherent in the material causal schemes. As late as Stage 3, when the infant has already begun smiling at what he sees and manipulating objects according to various schemes (shifting, swinging, striking, rubbing, etc.), he still knows no other cause but his own action, and is not aware of the necessity of spatial contact. In the observation of the cord hanging from the top of the cradle, the baby does not locate the cause of the movement of the dangling rattles in the connection between the cord and the rattles, but rather in the global action of "pulling the cord", which is quite another thing. The proof is that he continues to pull the cord in an attempt to act upon objects situated two yards away, or to act upon sounds, etc. Similarly, other subjects in this third stage arch their bodies and fall back as a means of rocking their cradles, but also to act upon objects at a distance. Later an infant may squint in front of an electric light switch in order to turn on the light, etc.

This early notion of causality may be called magical-phenomenalist: "phenomenalist" because the phenomenal contiguity of two events is sufficient to make them appear causally related, and "magical" because it is centered on the action of the subject without consideration of spatial connection between cause and effect. The first of these two aspects recalls Hume's interpretation of causality, but with exclusive emphasis on the child's own action. The second aspect recalls the conceptions of Maine de Biran, but here there is neither awareness of the ego nor delimitation between self and the outside world.

However, as the universe is increasingly structured by the sensori-motor intelligence according to a spatio-temporal organization and by the formation of permanent objects, causality becomes objectified and spatialized: that is, the subject becomes able to recognize not only the causes situated in his own actions but also in various objects, and the causal relationships between two objects or their actions presuppose a physical and spatial connection. In the behavior patterns of the support, the string, and the stick (Stages 5 and 6), for example, it is clear that the movements of the rug, the string, or the stick are believed to influence those of the object (independently of the author of the displacement), provided there is contact. If the object is placed beside the rug and not on it, the child at Stage 5 will not pull the supporting object, whereas the child at Stage 3 or even 4 who has been trained to make use of the supporting object (or who has discovered its role by accident) will still pull the rug even if the object no longer maintains with it the spatial relationship "placed upon".

14 Phenomenal Identity and Form Perception in an Infant

T. G. R. Bower

Gestalt psychologists described in some detail the stimulus conditions which determine which parts of an array will be seen as units possessing "phenomenal identity." These same stimulus conditions, often called the Gestalt laws, were held to be effective determinants of form perception too. A previous study indicated that only one of the Gestalt laws, common fate, was an effective determinant of phenomenal identity in human infants of less than 16 weeks of age. The present study using a more powerful technique shows that another of the Gestalt laws, good continuation, is an effective determinant of phenomenal identity and form perception in infants of 36 days of age. A third variable, proximity, is not effective in this age range.

Perhaps the most primitive ability of any perceptual system is the ability to partial an array of stimulation into segregated units whose parts cohere with one another, remaining independent of the parts of other units. For vision, Koffka (1936) posed the problem as "Why is it that we see things rather than the spaces between them?" This is the problem of phenomenal identity. Gestalt psychologists, such as Koffka, treated it as a psychophysical problem, seeking to discover what properties of a visual array caused some segments to be seen as coherent units separable from the rest of the array. The resulting stimulus variables were entitled Gestalt laws. Perhaps it is the dignity of the title "law" which has sheltered these psychophysical formulations from further investigation, for little has been done with them since the pioneering Gestaltist investigations. In particular little has been

Source: *Perception and Psychophysics,* (1967). *2*, pp. 74–76.

done to investigate their origins, whether in phylogeny or ontogeny. Brunswik (1956) suggested that a process of correlation learning within the lifetime of an individual could explain the effectiveness of the Gestalt laws. Bower (1965) attempted to test this theory by testing the effectiveness of three laws with infants of various ages. Only one, common fate, the tendency to see segments which move together in phase as coherent, was effective with the younger infants. The result thus seemed to confirm Brunswik's empiricism against Gestalt psychologists' nativism. However, subsequent experiments have shown some flaws in the original. Bower (1965) found that infants are insensitive to pictorial information. The dynamic flow of information given in motion seems to be essential for them. It is thus possible that the apparent primacy of common fate resulted from no more than the fact that the display exemplifying it was the only one which involved motion. The displays exemplifying the others were presented as still projections on a screen so that not even head movements could produce motion gradients. Accordingly, the experiment was redone using solid models, which yield motion gradients during head movements, to exemplify the laws which were previously ineffective.

Six groups of four infants served as subjects. All of the infants were 36 days of age at testing. An operant conditioning technique was used. The technique used was modelled after a technique invented by Siqueland (1965). The operant response was a suck of high positive pressure. A sealed nipple was inserted in the infant's mouth. The resulting sucks were transduced and amplified by a Schwarzer polygraph. The output from the polygraph was fed into a Schwarzer amplitude discriminator, whose output controlled a counter and the display equipment described below. During the experiment the subject sat on his mother's or an experimenter's lap. The subject-holder was responsible for keeping the nipple in the subject's mouth. Fifteen inches from the subject's face at a 45° angle to his line of sight was placed a half silvered (30/30) mirror. Immediately behind the mirror at right angles to the line of sight was a translucent screen, behind which a motion picture projector was placed. Parallel to the subject's line of sight was a white peg-board which was used as a stimulus holder. The peg-board was illuminated by fluorescent tubes at top and bottom giving it a luminance of 52 ft.-L. Its edges were baffled so that the subject could see the stimulus only as reflected in the half-silvered mirror. The only other illumination in the room came from a dim corridor light. The output from the amplitude discriminator through a stepping switch extinguished the peg-board light and started the movie projector running for a 10-second period, at the end of which the projector stopped and the peg-board light came on again. The projector lamp was never off, so that a stopped frame of the movie was continuously visible behind the conditioned stimulus. For rest periods and stimulus changing both sets of lights were extinguished.

The movie shown was of an older child at play. The peg-board stimulus thus served as conditioned stimulus (CS), the high pressure suck as conditioned response (CR) and the 10-second movie presentations as reinforcement.

Two CS were used. The first was a black wire equilateral triangle, side 35 cm, thickness of wire 5 mm with a 7 cm diameter, 50 cm long, round, black rod placed over it. The second CS consisted of three 2.5 cm diameter black discs, mounted in a row with an interval of 5 cm between the left hand pair and 15 cm between the right hand pair.

Groups 1, 2, 3, and 4 were trained with the first CS, and the groups 5 and 6 with the second CS. The training procedure was the same for all groups. Daily 30–45 minute sessions were aimed at. The first session was spent in shaping the response, initially with continuous reinforcement, later with reinforcement on a variable ratio (VR) schedule on which every third response on average was reinforced. On the second day the VR3 schedule was maintained and a discrimination between presence and absence of the CS was formed. The Terrace (1963) fading procedure was used. The lights illuminating the peg-board were switched off for 1-second periods between responses. This period was gradually extended to 10 seconds. During these dark periods a response would not have been reinforced had one occurred. In fact, none occurred. The terminal minute of the second day was a discrimination test period. The peg-board lights were extinguished during this period. None of the infants emitted a single response during the test. This was taken as adequate evidence of discrimination.

The first 15 minutes of the third day were spent on a VR10 schedule. Thereafter 2 minutes of test trials were given. For 1 minute the CS was present without reinforcement, for the second minute a test stimulus was present, again without reinforcement. Half of the infants in each group viewed the presentations in the stated order, half in the reverse order. The test stimulus for each group is shown in Fig. 14.1. The reasoning guiding these choices is given below. After the 2 minutes of testing, 10 further minutes of training were given. Then a further 2 minutes of testing, with presentation order reversed for each infant, was given, followed by 3 further minutes of training on the VR10 schedule.

These experiments were designed to assess whether two of the Gestalt laws, good continuation and proximity, were effective in the infant subjects. The first CS was designed to assess the effects of good continuation. If infants, like adults, see contours, whose mathematical description in cartesian space is identical, as continuations of one another, then the infants should have seen this CS as a triangle with a bar over it. They should have seen the two visible segments of the triangle as continuations of one another, so that during testing the triangle (in Fig. 14.1) should have caused the minimal decrement in responding. If on the other hand, good continuation

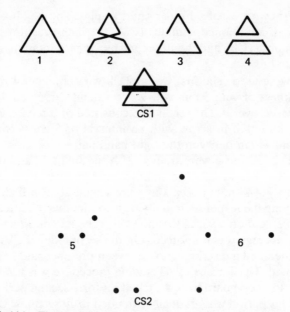

FIG. 14.1. The conditioning and test stimuli used in the experiments.

were not effective but if common fate were, if that is to say, the separation between bar and triangle were sufficient for head movements to produce different rates of displacement of their retinal projections, then they should have seen the display as an indeterminate figure with a bar over it; that is, they should have seen the top part of the triangle as connected with the bottom half, but been unable to specify the nature of the connection. If this were so the figures 1 and 2 of Fig. 14.1 should have been equally ineffective in suppressing responses. If again neither of these variables were effective, then 3 and 4 should have had the least effect, since they at least had no contours which were not present in the CS.

The second CS was designed to assess the effectiveness of the variable, proximity. The relevant Gestalt law may be stated as follows. In a visual field containing three or more identical elements, any pair of elements which are nearer to one another than either is to any other element will be seen as a unit. Thus the CS used here, labelling the dots a, b, c, should be seen as (ab), c, with a and b forming a single entity. If this variable were effective one should expect transfer stimulus 5 of Fig. 14.1 to produce less response decrement than transfer stimulus 6, since the former does not violate the unity of (ab) whereas transfer stimulus 6 does so.

The results are summarized in Table 14.1. As can be seen there, proximity had no effect on responding. The two transfer stimuli elicited equally few responses. There was no significant difference between them. The situation was quite different with good continuation which seemed to be highly

TABLE 14.1

Mean Response Rate per Min to:	CS	Test Stimulus
Group		
1	51.00	34.00
2	53.00	12.00
3	49.00	14.00
4	52.00	12.25
5	50.00	13.50
6	50.25	14.00

effective in that transfer stimulus a, which exemplified good continuation, elicited significantly more responses than any of the other three transfer stimuli ($p < 0.001$ by t-test), which in turn did not differ significantly from one another. Only on the hypothesis that good continuation is an effective variable can one comprehend this pattern of results.

The conclusions of the previous study must thus be revised. Proximity still seems ineffective but it does appear that good continuation can be an effective variable with young infants. It is worth noting that good continuation functioned here not only as a determinant of phenomenal identity, but also as a determinant of form perception. Not only did the infants "know" that the top of the triangle was connected to the bottom; they also knew the nature of the connection. This indicates a rather high degree of perceptual organization at this comparatively early age, rather more than most current theories of perceptual development would lead one to believe.

REFERENCES

Bower, T. G. R. (1965a). Phenomenal identity in infants. *Psychonomic Science, 3*, 323–324.

Bower, T. G. R. (1965b). Stimulus variables determining space perception in infants. *Science, 149*, 88–89.

Brunswik, E. (1956). *Perception and the representative design of psychological experiments.* University of California Press.

Koffka, K. (1936). *Principles of Gestalt psychology.* New York: Routledge.

Siqueland, E. (1965). Paper read at 1st conference on infancy. Cambridge.

Terrace, H. (1963). Discrimination learning with or without errors. *Journal of Experimental Analysis of Behaviour, 6*, 1–27.

15

Infant Search Errors: Stage of Concept Development or Stage of Memory Development

Elizabeth Ligon Bjork and E. Mark Cummings

An 8-to-12-month-old infant, having found an object hidden at a first location (A), will frequently continue to search at the A location when the object is moved, in full view of the infant, to a second location (B) and hidden there. In Piaget's (1954) theory of the way in which children acquire knowledge of the external world through actions, the occurrence of such $A\overline{B}$ (or Stage IV) search errors is considered to provide critical evidence that such infants are egocentrically concerned with their own actions and do not yet appreciate the systematic nature of spatial relationships or the permanence of objects. The present research, however, casts serious doubt upon the considerable theoretical significance that has been attached to the $A\overline{B}$ error by demonstrating that it occurs primarily as an artifact of the almost universally employed two-choice hiding task, which constrains all search errors made during B-hiding trials to be $A\overline{B}$ errors. In two experiments using less constrained hiding tasks, infants demonstrated no tendency to search incorrectly at the A location during B-hiding trials, and they produced a pattern of errors supportive of the notion that search errors result from a memory problem rather than from a conceptual one. A memory explanation is proposed to account for the present results as well as for search errors made throughout the sensorimotor period of development.

In nearly every area of psychology, the errors subjects make when performing different types of tasks are used to make inferences concerning possible underlying processes or structures. In the study of infants, the errors they

Source: *Memory and Cognition* (1984), *12*, pp. 1–19.

make while searching for hidden objects have served – since Piaget's (1954) original observations – as a rich data source for making inferences about the cognitive development of children.

One of the more intriguing and better known errors studied by Piaget (1954) and others is the so-called "A, not B" error, made by infants between the ages of 8 and 12 months. Around this age, infants become capable of finding a completely hidden object when it is hidden in one place, called the A location. However, when the object is then moved, in full view of the infant, to a second location, called B, and hidden there, infants frequently err by continuing to search for the object at location A – thus, the "A, not B" (or A$\bar{\text{B}}$) search error.

The AB error is well documented (Gratch & Landers, 1971; Piaget, 1954) and has been studied extensively (Bremner, 1978a, 1978b; Bremner & Bryant, 1977; Butterworth, 1975, 1976, 1977; Corter, Zucker, & Galligan, 1980; Evans & Gratch, 1972; Frye, 1980; Gratch, Appel, Evans, LeCompte, & Wright, 1974; Harris, 1973, 1974; Schuberth, Werner, & Lipsitt, 1978). The considerable attention given to the A$\bar{\text{B}}$ error occurs, in part, simply because of its intriguing nature, but primarily because of the critical role it plays in Piaget's (1954) theory of the way in which the child acquires knowledge of the external world through action.

In Piaget's (1954) theory, the occurrence of the A$\bar{\text{B}}$ error is a critical indicator that an infant is in Stage IV of the sensorimotor period of development. Indeed, the A$\bar{\text{B}}$ error frequently is referred to in the literature as "the Stage IV error," as "Piaget's Stage IV error," or as "Piaget's Stage IV object concept error," and the hiding task in which it has been observed, as "Piaget's Stage IV task." (Bremner, 1978b; Butterworth 1975, 1977; Evans & Gratch, 1972; Gratch et al., 1974). Stage IV is of particular importance because of its pivotal nature. In previous stages, infants are assumed not to have an awareness of the permanence of objects in space; that is, infants do not conceive of an object as something that continues to exist when it is out of sight. In Stage IV, however, external objects begin for the first time to have a permanence of their own for the infant – as testified by the infant's ability to find them when they are completely hidden in one location.

Even in Stage IV, however, the permanence of objects is assumed to remain closely tied to the infant's actions. When an object, successfully found in one location (A), is moved in full view of the infant from A to a new location (B) and is hidden there, the infant does not search for the object at B, but returns to A, where he or she has previously found or acted upon the object. That is, the object's existence and position in space are linked to or are partially defined by the infant's action; in a sense, the object exists for the infant as "the object that I find at location A". Thus, when the object is hidden or disappears from view at location B, the infant does not search for it at B but at A, since for the infant the object remains "at disposal in the place where the action has made use of it" (Piaget, 1954, p. 50). In Piaget's theory, then, the Stage IV infant's cognitions concerning space and objects are quite different from those of older individuals or adults; and, the A$\overline{B}$ error is regarded as critical evidence in support of this somewhat radical, but widely held, view of the infant's conception of objects and space.

Given the critical role played by the A$\overline{B}$ error in Piaget's (1954) theory of how the child acquires knowledge of the external world of objects and space, it is not surprising that this error has been extensively studied. What is surprising, however, is that investigators have not asked the most fundamental question regarding this behavior: namely, whether 8-to-12-month-old infants do, in fact, reliably search at the A location when erring during B-hiding trials. Research since Piaget has not adequately addressed this question because investigators studying the Stage IV error have, without exception, provided the infant with only two possible search locations (A and B) during B-hiding trials.[1] Given the constraints of this two-choice situation, if an overt error is made during a B-hiding trial, it must be a return-to-A error. There is no other location in which the infant can incorrectly search. Thus, a primary goal of the present research was to provide a satisfactory test of the occurrence of the A$\overline{B}$ error by presenting infants with at least one alternative location to A in which they can incorrectly search when the object is hidden at a second location (B).

A second purpose of the present research was to test whether the previous well-documented occurrence of the A$\overline{B}$ error in the two-choice situation might not stem from a memory problem rather than from a conceptual one. That is, incorrect searches at the A location could occur in the two-choice situation – not because the A location has a special significance to the infant, as assumed in Piaget's (1954) action-object interpretation of this error, but because on some B trials, infants have trouble remembering the object's new location and thus incorrectly search at A. In this view of infant search behavior, then, it is assumed that search errors arise not because the infant cannot conceptually understand the fundamental nature of objects and space, but, rather, because the infant cannot always precisely encode, store, or retrieve the currently correct location of an object as it is successively hidden in different spatial locations. If search errors largely stem from such memory problems, one might expect the infant's errors to reflect partial knowledge or retention of the object's new location. For example, in a situation in which there are more than two possible hiding

---

[1]Since aspects of the present research were first presented (Bjork & Cummings, Ref Note 1; Cummings & Bjork, Ref Note 4) several studies not directed at assessing the reliability of the Stage IV error but employing more than two locations in various types of search tasks have appeared in the literature (Rieser, 1979; Sophian & Sage, 1983; Wishart & Bower 1982). These studies are discussed further in the General Discussion section of the present paper.

locations, search errors might be expected to cluster around the object's currently correct hiding location or to form a spatial gradient stemming outward from the correct location.

An adequate answer to the first question raised above – whether 8-to-12-month-old infants will reliably make the A$\overline{B}$ error outside the constraints of a two choice hiding task – requires presenting infants with only one additional hiding location. However, to address our second question adequately – whether A$\overline{B}$ errors might stem from a memory problem rather than from a conceptual one – it is necessary to present more than three hiding locations. With only three hiding locations, it would not be possible to test the memory hypothesis's prediction of a spatial gradient of search errors stemming outward from the correct location. Thus, in order to address these two questions simultaneously, infants were presented with a Stage IV hiding task employing five possible hiding locations.

Two further theoretical points should be noted before the method of our first experiment is explained. First, Piaget (1954) did not specifically constrain infant search to A and B locations during B-hiding trials, but it is not clear that Piaget's infants understood that another legitimate search location existed during B-hiding trials. Second, whereas Piaget also considered the possibility that the A$\overline{B}$ error could occur due to memory failure or forgetting, he rejected this possibility in favor of the action-object explanation of the A$\overline{B}$ error. In fact, Piaget's interpretation of the A$\overline{B}$ error assumes that infants do not register or encode the new location (B) in which the object is hidden following their successful finding of it at the old location (A). Thus, although memory is involved in producing the A$\overline{B}$ error in Piaget's theory, the role of memory conceived by Piaget is very different from the role of memory being proposed here. In Piaget's theory, there is a failure of memory in that the new location is not registered by the infant; consequently, such information cannot in any way affect the infant's choice of search locations on B-hiding trials. In contrast, according to the role of memory we are suggesting, one would expect many of the infant's incorrect searches to reflect partial knowledge or retention of the object's new location.

EXPERIMENT 1

Method

Subjects.   The analyses for this study are based on the performance of 36 infants (18 males and 18 females), ranging in age from 8 months 10 days to 11 months 5 days, with a median age of 9 months 11 days. In terms of a frequency distribution of ages, there were 9 8-month-old infants, 21 9-month-old infants, 5 10-month-old infants, and 1 11-month-old infant. The infants were located through birth announcements in a local newspaper, such announcements being automatically published whenever a birth certificate is issued.

In addition to the above infants, six infants (3 males and 3 females; median age 9 months 12 days; age range from 8 months 25 days to 11 months 1 day; and located in the same manner) were tested in the present study but excluded from the data analyses. Four of the six infants were excluded because they were incorrect on all A trials (the data from such infants cannot be interpreted with respect to Piaget's 1954 prediction of A$\overline{\text{B}}$ errors, since for the A location to acquire a special significance for the infant, the infant must act upon the object at least once at the A location). An additional two infants had to be excluded because they became too upset to continue in the experiment.

Apparatus. A block of white foam rubber, 30 inches (76 cm) long, 12 inches (30 cm) wide, and 4 inches (10 cm) thick, served as the basic apparatus. Five holes, 5 inches (12.7 cm) high, 3 inches (7.62 cm) across, and 1.5 inches (3.81 cm) deep, were cut into the foam-rubber block. Each hole was 4.5 inches (11.43 cm) from the hole next to it, measured from center to center, or 1.5 inches (3.81 cm) from the hole next to it, measured from the two closest edges. Of these five holes, only the far left and far right holes were used as hiding locations, and these were 18 inches (45.72 cm) apart from center to center. Blue-felt pieces, slightly less than 3.75 inches (9.5 cm) wide and 8.75 inches (22.22 cm) long, were used as hiding covers. With the blue hiding covers in place, adjacent covers were separated by an intervening space of the white foam-rubber apparatus of slightly more than 1 inch.

A red plastic key or a red plastic octopus were used as search objects during warm up trials. During all of the experimental trials for a given subject, a single small rubber animal (a yellow duck or a blue bear) or a small red and yellow plastic rattle was employed as the hiding object. The rubber animal could be squeaked, and the rattle, which contained a single bell, could be shaken to attract the infant's attention before being hidden, but neither type of toy made any noise when moved toward or lowered into the hiding hole. Both types of toys fit entirely within the hiding hole so that the felt cover hiding the toy would lie flat on the apparatus.

Design and Procedure. The subjects were tested in their own homes on any convenient rug-covered floor. The infants were positioned directly in front of the middle hole of the apparatus. The infant's mother sat directly behind the infant on the floor, and the experimenter sat across from the infant on the opposite side of the apparatus. A second adult recorded the infant's responses and timed the delay from when the toy was hidden until the infant was allowed to search for it.

The infants were given four warm-up trials to familiarize them with the apparatus and with the task of retrieving toys from the apparatus. In two trials, the infant found a toy uncovered, and in two trials, the infant found a toy partially covered at the A location. All infants were able to perform the warm-up trials successfully.

Following the warm-up trials, the infants were given four experimental trials in which the toy was always completely hidden. The experimental trials began with the hiding of the toy two consecutive times at a first location (A). These trials were followed by two consecutive hidings of the same toy at a second hiding location (B). Only the far left and the far right holes served as hiding locations, and each was assigned to be the A or B location equally often. Furthermore, the infants were assigned at random to one of the two possible A-B hiding sequences: far left-far right or far right-far left.

During experimental trials, the experimenter shook or squeaked the toy, while holding it at a point just behind and above the middle hole of the apparatus, until the infant looked at the toy. The toy was then moved to the appropriate hiding location for that trial, lowered into the hole, and covered. This procedure was repeated if the infant stopped looking at the toy before it was covered. The infant was required to wait 3 seconds after the toy had been covered before searching for the toy. If the infant tried to reach for the toy before 3 seconds had elapsed, the mother would restrain the infant by gently holding his or her shoulders. After successfully finding the toy, the infant was allowed to play with it for a few seconds before the next trial was begun. If the infant searched unsuccessfully for the toy, the experimenter retrieved the toy for the infant before the infant could search further. The infant was then allowed to play with the toy for a few seconds before the start of the next trial.

Results and Discussion

In the present section, results are presented in the following general order: first, the overall correct search performance obtained across A and B trials; second, the analyses of search errors relevant to the prediction from Piaget's (1954) action-object account of infant search behavior; and finally, the analyses of errors relevant to the memory explanation's expectation of how search errors should be distributed.

Overall Correct Search Performance

A Trials. As a whole, infants were clearly able to search correctly for the hidden object on A-hiding trials. On the first A trial, 30 of the 36 infants (or 83%) searched for the object in its correct location, and on the second A trial, 31 of the 36 infants (or 86%) searched for the object in its correct location. Over the two A trials, 25 infants made no errors, and all 36 infants were correct on at least one A trial.

B Trials. On the first B-hiding trial, only 18 of the 36 infants (or 50%) correctly searched for the hidden object. On the second B-hiding trial, 25 infants searched correctly for the hidden object, with 10 infants making search errors and 1 infant failing to search. The drop in performance between the last A-hiding trial (86%) and the first B-hiding trial (50%) is significant by a sign test ($z = 2.92$, $p < 0.002$).

Action-Object Prediction

With respect to the fundamental question of whether 8–12-month-old infants will reliably make the $A\overline{B}$ error outside the constraints of the two-choice situation – in accordance with Piaget's (1954) action-object theory – the relevant data are as follows: On the first B-hiding trial, 18 search errors were made; however, only 1 of these errors was an A-returning error. All other incorrect searches occurred at locations in which the object had never been hidden and, thus, never acted upon.

On the second B-hiding trial, the pattern remained the same. Of the 10 overt search errors made, only 1 was an A-returning error, the remaining 9 being incorrect searches occurring at locations in which the object had never been hidden or acted upon by the infant.

In addition, analyses limited to only those infants who were correct on at least the last A-hiding trial or those infants who were correct on both A-hiding trials show the same pattern of results. There are 31 infants who qualified for the first set; of these, 16 searched correctly on the first B-hiding trial, 14 incorrectly searched in a location in which the object had never been hidden, and 1 returned to the A location to search for the hidden object. On the second B-hiding trial, 21 of these infants searched correctly, 9 incorrectly searched in a location in which the object had never been hidden, and 1 returned to the A location to search for the hidden object. Similarly, for the subset of 25 infants who were correct on both A trials, 16 searched correctly on the first B trial, 8 incorrectly searched in a location in which the object had never been hidden, and 1 returned to the A location to search for the hidden object. On the second B trial, 18 of these infants searched correctly, 6 incorrectly searched in a location in which the object had never been hidden, and 1 returned to the A location to search. In short, whether one looks at the behavior of all infants in the present experiment, or at the subset of infants who were correct on at least the last A-hiding trial, or only at those infants who were correct on both A-hiding trials, the pattern of results is the same.

In addition to showing no tendency to make A-returning search errors on B-hiding trials, the infants also showed no tendency to search at locations close to the A location when they erred during B-hiding trials. To illustrate, of the 18 search errors made on the first B trial, only 3 errors involved search at the A location or the hole closest to the A location; and on the second B trial, only 2 of the 10 overt search errors made involved search at the A location or the hole closest to the A location. In fact, across the two B-hiding trials, significantly more search errors occurred in the incorrect location farthest from the A location than occurred in the location closest to the A location ($p < 0.01$, binomial test).

Clearly, the patterns of errors obtained on both the first and second B-hiding trials of this experiment are inconsistent with the predictions of Piaget's (1954) action-object theory. In an unconstrained Stage IV hiding task, the infants demonstrated no tendency to return to the A location on B-hiding trials. This finding indicates that the A$\overline{\text{B}}$ error observed in previous Stage IV hiding tasks has occurred primarily as an artifact of providing the infant with only two clear search alternatives (A and B) during B-hiding trials. When the infants were not constrained by the experimental paradigm to return to the A location when they erred during B-hiding trials, the A location appeared to hold no special significance for the 8-to-12-month-old infants, in direct contradiction of Piaget's contention that at this stage of development the object conceptually remains at disposal in the location in which the infant's action has made use of it.

Memory Prediction

In order to evaluate the proposed role of memory in the production of infant search errors, it is necessary to analyze where infants search in relation to the actual location of the hidden object on any given trial. Such an analysis is presented in Table 15.1, which shows the number of search

TABLE 15.1
Frequency of Search at the Five Alternative Locations
During the A and B Trials of Experiment 1

Trial Number	Correct Hole	Search Location				Failures to Search
		Closest Hole				
		1st	2nd	3rd	4th	
A Trials						
1	30	4	2	0	0	0
2	31	5	0	0	0	0
B Trials						
1	18	8	7	2	1	0
2	25	7	1	1	1	1

Note – During B trials, the 4th closest hole is the A location. Maximum number of search attempts possible at any one location = 36.

errors made at each possible incorrect location as a function of its distance from the correct location on each A- and B-hiding trial.

As can be seen in the top half of Table 15.1, most infants searched either at or close to the correct hiding location on the first A-hiding trial, with this tendency increasing on the second A-hiding trial.

However, of more concern to the present memory hypothesis are the B-trial data shown in the bottom half of Table 15.1. There it can be seen that the prediction of a spatial gradient of errors stemming outward from the currently correct location of the object is rather dramatically upheld on the first B-hiding trial. On the second B-hiding trial, fewer incorrect searches occur, making a distribution analysis somewhat tentative. Nonetheless, the most frequent location of incorrect searches remains the location closest to the currently correct location of the hidden object.

It should be noted that in the context of the present experiment, the action-object hypothesis and the memory hypothesis make essentially opposite predictions concerning the direction of search attempts that should be observed in the present hiding task. The action-object hypothesis predicts that incorrect search attempts should be located at or near the A location on B-hiding trials; in contrast, the memory hypothesis predicts that search attempts should occur at or near the object's current location even on B-hiding trials. To test which of these predictions was correct, as well as the overall direction of search tendencies, the number of searches made at the B location and the location closest to the B location was compared with the number of searches made at the A location and the location closest to the A location during both the first and second B-hiding trials. (Searches at the middle hole were omitted from these analyses because it was not clear whether middle-hole searches indicated a tendency to search in the direction of the correct B location or in the direction of the A location.) These comparisons revealed no tendency for infants to search at or near the A location; instead, they revealed a significant tendency for infants to search at or near the currently correct location during both the first and second B-hiding trials ($z = 4.56$, $p < 0.001$, and $z = 4.94$, $p < 0.001$, respectively).

Thus, on both A and B trials, the distributions of search errors appear to reflect partial knowledge or retention of the current spatial location of the object, consistent with the assumptions of the present memory explanation of infant search behavior. We also feel that the significant drop in performance from the last A-hiding trial to the first B-hiding trial, as well as the poorer performance on the first B trial than on the first A trial, are consistent with the present proposal that infant search errors are primarily produced by a memory limitation rather than by a conceptual one. These aspects of the results are discussed in the General Discussion section following Experiment 2.

EXPERIMENT 2

Proponents of an object-action account of infant search behavior might want to argue that, because the infants in Experiment 1 did not make the $A\overline{B}$ error, they were not in what Piaget (1954) referred to as Stage IV, but were perhaps in some later stage in which object and action are no longer tied together so egocentrically as to produce the $A\overline{B}$ or Stage IV error.

There are several problems with this argument. First, although we realize that Stage IV is not defined as a particular age, but rather as a level of cognitive development, the present infants were of the exact average age (9 months) specified by Piaget (1954, p. 45) for the onset of Stage IV. Second, the present infants were of essentially the same mean age and age range as infants in the previous Stage IV studies that are considered to have documented the $A\overline{B}$ error (Butterworth, 1975, 1976; Evans & Gratch, 1972; Gratch et al., 1974; Harris, 1973). Third, and most importantly, a more advanced, Stage V infant should theoretically not make any errors on the Stage IV task (Piaget, 1954, pp. 66-67), whereas a majority of the infants in the present experiment made at least one B-trial error. Nevertheless, to dismiss such arguments and to demonstrate unambiguously that the infants of Experiment 1 were at the same level of cognitive development as the infants previously reported in the literature as making the $A\overline{B}$ error in two-choice hiding tasks, a second experiment was conducted. In Experiment 2, the same infants were tested for the occurrence of the $A\overline{B}$ error both in the traditional two-choice hiding task of previous Stage IV research and in the five-choice hiding task of Experiment 1. Thus, Experiment 2 allowed us to determine if the same infants who made $A\overline{B}$ errors in the traditional two-choice task and who, therefore, would be classified as Stage IV infants in accordance with the criteria of previous literature, would also make $A\overline{B}$ errors in a hiding task that did not constrain B-trial search errors to be returns to the A location.

Method

Subjects. The analyses for this study are based on the performance of 16 infants (6 females and 10 males), ranging in age from 8 months 10 days to 10 months 8 days and having a median age of 9 months 5 days. In terms of a frequency distribution of ages, there were 5 8-month-old infants, 10 9-month-old infants, and 1 10-month-old infant. The infants were located as in Experiment 1, by means of birth announcements in a local newspaper.

Five other infants (three males and two females: median age 9 months 17 days; age range from 9 months 3 days to 10 months 30 days; located in the same manner) were tested in the present study but were excluded from the data analyses. Three of these infants were excluded because they were incorrect on all A trials. The remaining two infants were excluded because they became too upset to continue in the experiment.

Apparatus.   The apparatus for the five-choice hiding task was identical to that used in Experiment 1; and, as before, only the far left and far right holes were used as hiding locations.

The apparatus for the two-choice hiding task was made from a block of white foam rubber identical in size and color to that for the five-choice hiding task. The two hiding holes cut into this block of foam rubber were also identical in dimensions to the holes of the five-choice apparatus, measuring 5 inches (12.7 cm) high, 3 inches (7.62 cm) across, and 1.5 inches (3.81 cm) deep. The two holes were separated by 9.5 inches (24.13 cm), measured from center to center, or 6.5 inches (16.51 cm), measured from the two closest edges. Separation between the two hiding locations in previous Stage IV studies has varied widely – for example, 4 inches (Harris, 1973), 7.87 inches (Butterworth, 1975), 11.02 inches (Bremner, 1978a; Bremner & Bryant, 1977), 12 inches (Evans & Gratch, 1972; Gratch et al., 1974), and 18 inches (Harris, 1974). Furthermore, these measurements generally have not been reported in such a way as to enable determination of whether they referred to separations measured from center to center or from the two closest edges of the hiding locations. Thus, the current separation distance was chosen so as to be roughly in the middle of the range of separations previously employed in two-choice hiding tasks.

Blue pieces of felt identical to those employed in Experiment 1 were used as hiding covers for both the two-choice and the five-choice apparatuses. The same red plastic key and red plastic octopus were used as search objects during the warm-up trials; and, during all of the experimental trials for a given subject, either one of the small rubber animals or the small red and yellow plastic rattle of Experiment 1 was employed as the hiding object.

Design and Procedure.   Most aspects of the testing procedure were the same as in Experiment 1. Infants were again tested in their own homes on any convenient rug-covered floor. They were positioned directly in front of the middle hole of the five-choice apparatus or equidistant between the two holes in the two-choice apparatus. The infant's mother sat directly behind the infant on the floor, and the experimenter sat across from the infant on the opposite side of the apparatus. A second adult recorded the infant's responses and timed the delay interval employed.

The warm-up trials were conducted in the same manner as in Experiment 1, and all infants were able to perform the warm-up trials successfully.

The experimental procedure was the same as that of Experiment 1, except that (1) one-half of the infants were tested first on the two-choice apparatus and then on the five-choice apparatus and one-half were tested first on the five-choice apparatus and then on the two-choice apparatus, and (2) the infants were given 3 A-hiding trials and 3 B-hiding trials in both the two-choice and the five-choice hiding task in order to get a somewhat better look at changes in performance over trials at the same location. (Although 4 or 5 trials at each location would probably have been better for this purpose, pilot work had indicated that 12 total trials was about the maximum number we could hope to conduct without stressing the infants.) As in Experiment 1, the hole used as the A or B location for each type of apparatus was counterbalanced across subjects, and a 3-second delay was imposed between the time the toy was hidden and the time the infant was allowed to search for it.

Results and Discussion

In the present section, results are presented in the following general order: first, analyses comparing search performance across the A and B trials for the two-choice versus the five-choice hiding task; and second, the analysis of search errors occurring on the five-choice task in relation to the correct location of the hidden object on each A and B trial.

Two-Choice Versus Five-Choice Search Behavior

A Trials. The frequencies of correct searches and types of search errors made during the three A-hiding trials on each type of apparatus are presented in Table 15.2, in which F denotes those locations in which the object has never been hidden. In general, infants were clearly able to search correctly for the hidden object on A-hiding trials in the two-choice task, with 13 of the 16 subjects (or 81%) searching correctly on the first A trial and 15 of the 16 subjects (or 94%) searching correctly on the second and third A trials. Over the three A trials, 12 infants made no errors. Of the remaining four, 3 made one A-trial error and 1 made two A-trial errors. All infants were correct on at least one A-hiding trial.

Initially at least, infants appear to have had slightly more difficulty on the five-choice task, with 10 of the 16 infants (or 63%) searching correctly on the first A trial and 11 (or 69%) searching correctly on the second A trial. However, by the third A trial, 14 (88%) of the subjects searched correctly. Over the three A-hiding trials, 7 infants managed to make no errors, 5 made one A-trial error, and 4 made two A-trial errors. However, all infants were correct on at least one A-hiding trial.

That infants could have more trouble on the initial A-hiding trials of a five-choice task than on those of a two-choice task is consistent with the present memory hypothesis. However, the present infants' performance on the first and second trials of the five-choice task was also poorer than that of the infants in Experiment 1. Two factors occur to us as possible reasons for this difference. First, the age composition of the two samples was somewhat different, with the Experiment 2 sample being slightly younger as a whole than the Experiment 1 sample. In Experiment 1, 17% of the infants were 10 to 11 months old, as compared with 6% of the Experiment 2 infants; and, 31% of the Experiment 2 infants were 8 months old, as compared with 25% of the Experiment 1 infants. Second, it seems likely that the poorer five-choice performance in Experiment 2 occurred because half of the infants had been tested on a two-choice task prior to being tested on the five-choice task and, thus, were quite likely to be somewhat fatigued. Indeed, 64% of the errors made on the first and second A-hiding trials were made by infants who performed the five-choice task following the two-choice task.

B Trials for all Infants. The frequencies of correct searches and types of search errors made during the three B-hiding trials for the two-choice and five-choice hiding tasks are presented in Table 15.3, in which F denotes those locations in which the object has never been hidden for that trial or for any preceding hiding trial. First, with respect to performance in the two-choice task, shown in the top half of Table 15.3, it is clear that many incorrect searches were made on the B-hiding trials and that these errors occurred at the A location; in short, they were traditional A $\overline{\text{B}}$ errors. Across the three B-hiding trials, a total of 14 such errors were made, with 9 occurring on the first B-hiding trial, 3 on the second, and 2 on the third. [It should perhaps be pointed out that the proportion of infants making

TABLE 15.2
Frequency of Correct Searches and Types of Search Errors
on A Trials in the Two-Choice and Five-Choice
Tasks of Experiment 2

Trial Number	*Response Type*		
	Correct Searches	*Incorrect Searches at F*	*Failures to Search*
	Two-Choice Hiding Task		
1	13	1	2
2	15	1	0
3	15	1	0
	Five-Choice Hiding Task		
1	10	6	0
2	11	5	0
3	14	2	0

Note – F denotes locations in which the object had not been hidden for that trial or any preceding hiding trial. Maximum correct on each trial = 16; chance = 8 on the two-choice task and 3.2 on the five-choice task.

an $A\overline{B}$ error on the first B trial in the present experiment (0.52) is comparable to the proportions previously observed in similar hiding situations (e.g., 0.58 in the "Same Toy Condition" of Evans & Gratch, 1972, and 0.52 in the "Object Hidden Condition" of Butterworth, 1977).]

Similarly, many incorrect searches were made on the B-hiding trials in the five-choice hiding task. In total, 21 incorrect searches (and 1 failure to search) occurred over the three B-hiding trials in the five-choice hiding task, with 10 occurring on the first B-hiding trial, 8 on the second, and 3 on the third. However, of these 21 overt search errors, only 1 was a return to the A location.

Furthermore, as in Experiment 1, the drop in performance between the last A-hiding trial and the first B-hiding trial is significant by a sign test ($z = 2.47, p < 0.01$).

B Trials for Infants Making $A\overline{B}$ Errors in the Two-choice Task. With respect to the primary question of Experiment 2, the most critical analysis involves only those infants who made at least one $A\overline{B}$ error in the two-choice hiding task and who, thus, would be Stage IV infants in accordance with previous research. In the present experiment, there were 10 infants making at least one $A\overline{B}$ error in the two-choice task, with 9 of these infants making an $A\overline{B}$ error on the first B trial. These same infants made a total of 15 B-trial errors in the five-choice task. Of these 15 errors, none was a return to the A location.

Thus, the answer to the primary question asked by Experiment 2 seems quite clear. The same infants who made the $A\overline{B}$ error on the traditional

TABLE 15.3
Frequency of Correct Searches and Types of Search Errors
on B Trials in the Two-Choice and Five-Choice
Tasks of Experiment 2

Trial Number	Correct Searches	Response Type		Failures to Search
		Incorrect Searches at A	Incorrect Searches at F	
Two-Choice Hiding Task				
1	5	9		2
2	13	3		0
3	13	2		1
Five-Choice Hiding Task				
1	6	1	9	0
2	8	0	8	0
3	12	0	3	1

Note – F denotes locations in which the object had not been hidden for that trial or any preceding hiding trial. Maximum correct on each trial = 16; chance = 8 on the two-choice task and 3.2 on the five-choice task.

two-choice hiding task and who, therefore, would be classified as Stage IV infants according to the criteria used in previous Stage IV research, did not do so in a hiding task involving more than two locations, that is, in a task that did not by its very nature constrain any overt search errors made during B-hiding trials to be $A\overline{B}$ errors. Although these infants made many B-trial errors on the five-choice task, they did not tend to be returns to the A location as would be predicted by the Piagetian action-object theory. The implications of these results seem unequivocal. The $A\overline{B}$ error, taken to indicate Stage IV of cognitive development in Piaget's (1954) theory of object-concept development, occurs primarily as an artifact of the previously employed two-choice hiding task, and, therefore, all theoretical conclusions based upon its occurrence are subject to question.

Distribution of Incorrect Searches

Although the main purpose of Experiment 2 was to ascertain whether the same infants who made $A\overline{B}$ errors in a two-choice task would also do so in a five-choice task, the five-choice data obtained in Experiment 2 can also be subjected to the same distance analysis used in Experiment 1 as a further test of the memory explanation of infant search behavior. The results of such an analysis are presented in Table 15.4, which shows the number of search errors made at each possible incorrect location as a function of its distance from the correct location on each A- and B-hiding trial.

The A-trial data, located in the top half of Table 15.4, show that, as in Experiment 1, most infants searched either at the correct hiding location or in the location next to it, with the tendency to search at the correct location steadily increasing over trials.

TABLE 15.4
Frequency of Search at the Five Alternative Locations
During the A and B Trials of Experiment 2

Trial Number	Correct Hole	Search Location				Failures to Search
		Closest Hole				
		1st	2nd	3rd	4th	
		A Trials				
1	10	4	2	0	0	0
2	11	4	1	0	0	0
3	14	2	0	0	0	0
		B Trials				
1	6	7	2	0	1	0
2	8	7	1	0	0	0
3	12	2	1	0	0	1

Note – Maximum number of search attempts possible at any one location = 16.

The B-trial data, shown in the bottom half of Table 15.4, also reveal the same pattern found in Experiment 1. On all three B-hiding trials, errors tend to form a spatial gradient stemming outward from the correct location of the object. On each trial, the majority of errors occur in the location closest to the correct location; and, across trials, search attempts can be seen to converge upon the correct location.

To test for the overall direction of search tendencies, the number of searches made at the B location and the location closest to the B location was compared with the number of searches made at the A location and the location closest to it across the three B-hiding trials. These comparisons revealed a significant tendency for infants to search at or near the currently correct location during all three B-hiding trials ($z = 2.73$, $p < 0.005$, $z = 3.76$, $p < 0.001$, and $z = 3.31$, $p < 0.001$, for the first, second, and third B trials, respectively).

Furthermore, if one considers only those infants who made at least one $A\overline{B}$ error in the two-choice task, the same trend is clearly present, with more infants searching at or near the correct location on each B trial of the five-choice task than at or near the A location ($z = 2.59$, $p < 0.005$, $z = 2.65$, $p < 0.005$, and $z = 2.65$, $p < 0.005$, respectively).

Finally, the higher frequency of A-trial errors occurring in the present study makes it possible to compare the types of errors occurring on A versus B trials. It seems clear that there is no qualitative difference between them; both A and B search errors tend to cluster around the currently correct location and to converge upon the correct location over trials, a result consistent with the current memory account of infant search behavior. In terms of the present memory account, the demands placed upon the information-processing skills of the infant by A and B trials are different in degree but not in kind, and, thus, the operation of the same underlying processes should determine the infant's performance on both types of trials. Differences between A- and B-trial performance will be further developed in the General Discussion section below.

Thus, Experiment 2 replicated the findings of Experiment 1 with respect to the location of incorrect search attempts on B-hiding trials. In addition, the A-trial errors obtained show the same distribution pattern as the B-trial errors. Hence, the present results both reconfirm and add new support to the proposed memory account of infant search behavior.

GENERAL DISCUSSION

Piaget's (1954) interpretation of the search behavior of 8-to-12-month-old infants as perseverative and, thus, indicative of a state of development in which the infant is unable to separate completely action from object has been called into question by the results of the present experiments. Although accorded great theoretical significance, the perseverative or $A\overline{B}$ search errors observed by Piaget and many others appear to occur primarily as an artifact of the two-choice hiding task employed by those researchers. When more than two search alternatives are provided, so that B-trial search errors are not constrained to be returns to the A location, infants do not demonstrate any tendency to search at the A location when erring during B-hiding trials, in direct contradiction of Piaget's action-object account of infant search errors.

General Support for a Memory-Based Explanation of Search Errors

In contrast, the proposed memory explanation of infant search behavior has been supported by the pattern of search performance observed in the present unconstrained hiding situation. According to this explanation, infants are capable both of understanding fundamental relations of objects and space and of storing in memory at least some information about the current location of an object as it is successively hidden in different spatial locations. Search errors occur because the information encoded and/or retrieved is not always precise enough to denote the specific current location of the object. Thus, when search errors occur, they should typically reflect partial knowledge or retention of the object's current location. In the context of the present situation, errors would be predicted (1) to cluster around the currently correct location on any given trial, forming a spatial gradient stemming outward from this location, and (2) to converge upon the correct location over trials at the same hiding location. Furthermore, any change in the task that places added demands on the infant's ability to process, store, or retrieve information should increase the number of search errors (as, for example, when the object's location is changed from an old (A) to a new (B) location).

Clearly, the pattern of errors obtained in the present two experiments has been consistent with these expectations of the memory explanation. On the A-hiding trials, errors formed a spatial gradient stemming outward from the correct location and converged upon the correct location over hiding trials at that same location. When the object was moved to a new location (B), there was a significant decrease in correct search performance, and the direction of search errors switched to the new location. Then, over trials at the new location, correct performance consistently increased, with search attempts steadily converging upon the new correct location, reaching A-trial levels by the third B trial in Experiment 2. At all times, the direction of search appeared to be influenced by information about the object's current location – not by information about previous action-locations involving the object.

The Lack of Specific Proactive Interference in the Present Five-Choice Tasks: A Problem for the Memory-Based Explanation?

Two aspects of B-trial performance observed in both of the five-choice tasks of the present two experiments warrant further discussion: (1) the significant drop in performance between the last A-hiding trial and the first B-hiding trial and (2) the poorer performance on the first B trial than on the first A trial.

The First B-Hiding Trial Versus the Last A-Hiding Trial

Whereas we see the drop in performance on the first B trial to reflect, at least in part, interference effects from the previous A trials on the encoding and retrieval processes occurring at B and, thus, to indicate the operation of a general type of proactive interference, there is no evidence in the present results for the operation of specific proactive interference – that is, specific response competition between A and B search responses as measured by intrusions of the A response when the B response is appropriate. Across the 52 first B trials on the five-choice tasks of the present two experiments, 28 errors were made, but only 2 of these, or 7%, were incorrect searches at the A location. By chance alone, one would expect 20% of the errors to occur at the A location.

Since, on the basis of research investigating memory for verbal material in adults, one might expect some evidence for the operation of specific proactive interference in producing the drop in performance from the last A- to the first B-hiding trial, the lack of such evidence in the present situation could be considered by some to create problems for a memory explanation of infant search behavior. However, we feel that the lack of such specific interference can be accounted for in terms of certain important differences between the present situation and the typical situation in which specific proactive interference is observed. In the present situation, both the spatial nature of the information that needed to be encoded and the nonverbal, or preverbal, nature of the subjects would seem to preclude the use of verbal encodings for this information. Hence, we assume that the present infants encoded the location of the object in spatial rather than verbal terms. In addition, since the physical A and B locations of the present five-choice apparatus were spatially quite distinct, it seems likely that the infant's functional memory codes for the A and B locations in the present situation were quite distinct. Thus, at the time of retrieval, the infant would have had little difficulty in discriminating the memory trace of the B location from that of the A location – a situation in which, drawing from the proactive-interference literature, one should expect little or no specific proactive interference or response competition between the A and B search responses. On the other hand, general interference effects from the just-previous series of A-hiding trials could have made encoding of the new B location more difficult, resulting in an initially poor or insufficient memory code for the B location. However, even when the memory code for the new B location was not sufficient to produce a correct search response or to differentiate the new B location from those alternative hiding locations most spatially similar to the new B location, it most likely still contained enough distinctive spatial information in the present situation to not be confusable with the trace of the spatially dissimilar A location and, thus, still directed the infant's search response to the general vicinity of the correct location. (See Crowder, 1976, pp. 211–216; and Gardiner, Craik, & Birtwistle, 1972, for a discussion of the role of retrieval discrimination as the basis for specific proactive interference in adult verbal memory studies.)

It is interesting that other studies designed to assess the role of proactive interference in the production of search errors made by another nonverbal organism – the rhesus monkey – have also found little or no evidence for the operation of specific proactive interference. In a study by Medin (1969), rhesus monkeys performed a task quite similar to the one performed by the present infants. The monkeys had to remember, for delay intervals of 0, 1, 2, 5, 10, or 20 seconds, behind which door in a 4 × 4 matrix of doors a food reward had been hidden. If proactive interference or response competition from the just-preceding trial is a principal source of forgetting in this situation, as seems to be the case in adult verbal memory studies (see Crowder, 1976, pp. 203–206; and Fuchs & Melton, 1974, for a discussion of sources of proactive interference effects), then a frequent type of error should have been searches at the location that had been correct on the just-preceding trial. However, an analysis of the location of incorrect search errors revealed little evidence for such specific proactive errors. In the Medin paradigm, one would expect 6.25% of the incorrect searches to occur by chance at the location of the previous hiding trial (specific proactive errors). For the two delay intervals most similar to those in the present study, 2 and 5 seconds, the percentages of errors that were such specific proactive errors were 8.9% and 7.6%, respectively. In addition, 83% of all these "specific proactive errors" occurred on trials in which the correct location on that trial happened to be adjacent to the location that had been correct on the preceding trial. Thus, in the Medin study, as in the present studies, the spatial similarity or closeness of an alternative location to the currently correct location of the object appears to have been a primary determiner of whether that location will be the locus of any incorrect search attempts.

In another series of experiments designed to test a proactive-interference analysis of errors, Fletcher, Garske, Barron, and Grogg (1968) found no evidence for the operation of specific proactive interference in producing the search errors of rhesus monkeys in the performance of two-choice hiding tasks. In fact, these authors concluded that even those search errors that appeared to be proactive-interference errors actually occurred as the result, and not the cause, of intratrial factors such as not attending and forgetting.

Our analysis of the drop in correct performance on the first B-hiding trial in the present five-choice situation has somewhat the same flavor as the Fletcher et al. (1968) analysis in that we see the decrement as arising, to a large extent, from general proactive-interference effects of the previous series of A-hiding trials that can be characterized as changes in the intratrial demand characteristics of the first B trial as compared with those of the last A trial. To illustrate, on all A trials, the infant must notice and encode only that the object is hidden at A. On the first B-hiding trial, the infant must first notice that the object is now being hidden in a different location and then come up with an encoding of that new location that will serve to differentiate it from the other possible locations in the present five-choice tasks, including the old A location. In short, the infant has more information to process on the first B trial than on the last A trial and, consequently, has less time or capacity to come up with a precise encoding of the object's location on the first B-hiding trial. Furthermore, an adequate encoding of the new B location must, in a sense, be more complex than the encoding of the A location, since the B location's encoding must both differentiate it from the other possible hiding locations and also include some sort of temporal or ordinal denotation that allows the infant to know that it is the most recent or last location of the object.

For all these reasons, even though the infant's initial encoding of the new B location would tend to contain some positional or spatial information about the object's new location, this information would frequently not be precise enough to differentiate the new B location from those alternative locations most spatially similar to it. On the other hand, in the context of the present task (for reasons discussed above), such an encoding would tend to not be confusable with the previous encoding of the spatially distinct A location, and, thus, the infant's attempts to retrieve the new B location of the object on the basis of such an encoding would not be seriously hampered by response competition from the memory trace of the previous A location. Hence, although the infant's initial encoding of the new B location would frequently not be sufficient to direct search to the precise new location of the hidden object, it should typically be sufficient to direct search at least to the general vicinity of the new location. (It also seems reasonable that, occasionally, an infant would not be able to encode even imprecise spatial information about the object's new location or, for some reason, not even notice or encode that the object had been moved to a new location on the first B trial. While the present data indicate that such events rarely happen, their occurrence could account for the few A-returning search errors observed in the present studies.) Over repeated trials at the new location, however, the information-processing demands would quickly become more like those of the preceding A trials, the infant's encoding of the new location should become more precise as well as less vulnerable to loss during the retention interval, and performance should rapidly return to A-trial levels.

It is important to point out that, although our analysis of first B-trial performance in the present five-choice tasks does not attribute the observed decrements to the operation of specific proactive interference or competition between A and B search responses, we do not, on the other hand, rule out specific proactive interference as one possible contributor to the infant's inability to retrieve the object's correct location in some task situations and, would, in fact, expect a greater influence of such specific retrieval competition in certain task situations. For example, if location A were to be made more similar than the other incorrect locations to location B or, if the hiding procedure used were one in which the infant's attention were to be directed to A or cues associated with A were reinstated at or just prior to the time the infant needed to retrieve information about the object's current location (Harris, 1973), specific proactive interference or retrieval competition between A and B responses might well act to reduce the infant's ability to retrieve the currently correct location information.

It could also be the case that specific proactive interference plays a larger role in producing forgetting on the first B trial in the typical two-choice task than in the present five-choice tasks, since, in two-choice hiding tasks, the A location is ipso facto the most similar alternative location to the correct B location. Furthermore, there would seem to be a real perceptual sense in which the A and B hiding locations of the present two-choice task, as well as those of other two-choice tasks, are more confusable or similar than the A and B hiding locations of the present five-choice tasks. In the latter case, the A and B locations are separated by other intervening locations, which could make their identity as opposite anchor or end locations more perceptually salient or noticeable, affording the infant more differential encoding cues for those locations.

On the basis of this difference between the typical two-choice task and the present five-choice tasks, we see the following tentative picture emerging to relate infant search behavior in the two types of situations. First, in both situations, infants are frequently able to encode and store some information about the object's new spatial location on the first B-hiding trial. However, for all the reasons discussed above, the information encoded is often not precise enough to differentiate the new B location from the location or locations most spatially similar or confusable with it, which, in the five-choice situation, are the alternative locations closest to the new B location and, in the two-choice situation, is the old A location. Thus, it could be that specific proactive interference or competition between A and B responses is largely responsible for the below-chance performance often observed on the first B trial of two-choice tasks, including that on the present two-choice task of Experiment 2, whereas the more generalized proactive-interference effects, discussed above, would be responsible for the drop in B-trial performance on multi-choice tasks, such as the present five-choice tasks.

It is important to remember, however, both in the case of the present two-choice task as well as in all previous two-choice tasks, that, on the basis of such tasks alone, one is no more entitled to attribute errors occurring at the A location to specific proactive interference than one is entitled to attribute errors at the A location to perseveration. On the other hand, since a memory explanation is also compatible with the results obtained in the unconstrained, multichoice situations of the present two experiments and the perseveration explanation is not, credence is lent to a specific proactive-interference explanation of A-location errors in the typical two-choice hiding task. In other words, the patterns of results obtained in the five-choice tasks of the present two experiments converge to support a memory explanation of search on two-choice tasks as well as on multichoice tasks.

The First B-Hiding Trial Versus the First A-Hiding Trial

In both of the present two experiments, as well as in most of the two-choice studies previously reported in the literature, first B-trial performance tends to be poorer than first A-trial performance. We feel that two factors are largely responsible for this common finding. First, the analysis presented above regarding first B-trial versus last A-trial performance also applies to first A-trial versus first B-trial performance. That is, just as the intratrial-demand characteristics of the first B trial are different and greater than those of the last A trial, they are also different and greater than those of the first A trial. On all A trials, including the first, the infant must notice and encode only that the object is hidden at A. On the first B trial, however, the infant must first notice that the object is being hidden at a new location and then encode that new location in a way that both differentiates it from the other locations and denotes it as the most recent location of the object. In other words, on the first B trial, as opposed to the first A trial, updating demands as well as encoding demands are placed on the infant. Thus, there is more information that must be processed and stored on the first B trial than on the first A trial, and, consequently, the infant's encoding of the object's location on the first B trial should typically be less precise.

A second factor that we feel must contribute to the common finding of better first A-trial than first B-trial performance is the typically employed procedure of conducting warm-up trials in the hiding location that is to be the A location in the experimental trials. Thus, by the time the infants are presented with the first actual A trial, they have already had considerable practice in retrieving the toy from that location, a factor that should, in terms of the present memory explanation, give the infants a considerable encoding advantage on the first A trial as compared with the first B trial. There is substantial evidence in both of the present two studies, as well as in others in the literature, that correct search performance increases with repeated hidings of the object at the same location.

In light of the present analysis, one might well ask why we did conduct our warm-up trials in that location that was to become the A location of the experimental trials. We did so because that is the procedure that has been used in most previous two-choice Stage IV studies, and we wished to depart as little as possible from all aspects of previously employed procedures, except for the use of more than two hiding locations. Why previous studies have typically used this procedure is hard to say, but since memory was not considered to be a primary factor in producing infant search errors, the potential memorial consequences of such a procedure would not have been considered.

A Memory-Based Interpretation of Past and Future Results

Although the present memory explanation accounts for several aspects of the observed search behavior, it does so at a general level and needs to be developed in further detail. At present, the explanation makes two basic contentions: (1) that infants do not suffer from an inability to separate the actual spatial locations of objects from the locations of actions performed upon these objects, and (2) that infants can effectively encode, store, and retrieve information concerning the current spatial locations of objects in their environment. Another way of stating the latter contention is that infants have the ability to update their memories regarding the current location of objects in their environment. Whether infants always make use of this ability and under what circumstances it is more or less effective are, of course, separate issues. Furthermore, the ways in which encoding, storage, and retrieval processes may be different or limited in the infant, as compared with the adult, and what the relative roles of these processes are in producing both successful and incorrect search behavior in the infant remain to be clarified. For example, it may turn out that infants have more trouble with one process than another at different points in their development. Perhaps storage capacity remains relatively constant throughout development and from individual to individual, whereas encoding and retrieval processes are more subject to individual patterns of development through exposure to different types of experiences that lead the infant to develop encoding and retrieval strategies of varying degrees of effectiveness. In addition, we feel that the relative effects of these processes on performance are likely to vary as a function of the nature or demands of the particular task to be performed – for example, the type of cues that are potentially available for encoding the object's location, or the type of distraction or interference occurring between hiding and search.

Some light can already be shed on these issues by examining the findings of previous research in terms of the present memory analysis. For example, several studies (Bremner, 1978a, 1978b; Butterworth, 1979, Ref Note 2) have found that in two-choice hiding tasks, search performance is improved when covers of two different colors are used on a hiding apparatus of uniform color, but not when the covers are the same color and each side of the apparatus has a different color. The differential effects of these two stimuli can be explained in terms of their potential to be noticed and used as encoding cues by the infant. The cloth covers are picked up and handled by the infants as they perform the search task, making these items highly salient stimuli in the infants' immediate surround and, consequently, more likely to be used by the infants as cues for encoding the hidden object's location.

A similar interpretation can be made of Bremner's (1978a; Experiment 2) finding that infants make fewer search errors when the spatial relationship of a hidden object to the infant changes owing to movement of the infant rather than to movement of the object. As Bremner suggested, the movement of the infants could alert them to the fact that a change is taking place. We would further suggest that this movement alerts the infant to the need to encode the object's location in terms of a cue that will remain stable or invariant with respect to rotation. When such a cue is readily available – such as salient black and white covers – the infants' search errors are dramatically reduced. Acredolo and Evans (1980) also showed that 6-, 9-, or 11-month-old infants are better able to keep track of positions in space when landmarks are provided. Similarly, Rieser (1979) demonstrated that 6-month-old infants can encode and remember spatial-location information in terms of gravitational and landmark cues when such cues are made available. These results point to insufficient encoding as the primary source of infant search errors. Note, however, that it is not the case that infants are unable to encode the spatial location of the object effectively; rather, the constraints of the task are usually such that little in the way of good encoding cues are available to the nonverbal infant – that is, external cues about a given location that can be encoded and, when retrieved, can be used by the infant to differentiate that location from another. When such external cues are made available (such as salient black and white covers), the infant can take advantage of these cues to encode more effectively the correct location of the hidden object.

Other studies reported in the literature can also be interpreted as supporting or being consistent with the current account of infant search behavior. For example, Gratch et al. (1974) and Harris (1973) found that, in order to produce search errors during B-hiding trials, it was necessary in the two-choice hiding task to insert a delay between the time the object was hidden and the time the infant was allowed to search for the object. Fox, Kagan, and Weiskopf (1979) also showed a critical effect of delay on the frequency of B-trial errors. Webb, Massar, and Nadolny (1972), using a three-choice hiding paradigm involving 14- and 16-month-old infants, concluded that the high incidence of correct searches obtained when the 16-month-old infants were given a second opportunity to search for objects indicated that at least some information about the object's current location had been stored in memory. In research both with 9-month-old infants performing slightly different three-, five-, and six-choice visible-hiding tasks and with 12-to-14-month-old infants performing a five-choice invisible-displacement task, we have found patterns of search errors essentially identical to the ones observed in the present five-choice visible-displacement tasks. (See Cummings & Bjork, 1981; 1983b; for further details of this research.)

In other research with older infants, Sophian and Sage (1983) recently examined the performance of 13- and 21-month-old infants across a series of search tasks, including visible-displacement tasks that utilized three possible hiding locations. In this innovative study, Sophian and Sage found that when infants made errors on the visible-displacement tasks, those errors were just as likely to be at the location in which the object had not been hidden on that trial, designated the control location by Sophian and Sage, as at the location in which the object had first been hidden on that trial (i.e., the A location), designated the relevant-but-incorrect location by Sophian and Sage. Although this result is not directly comparable, owing to slight differences in the hiding procedures used by Sophian and Sage, it is certainly concordant with our finding of no tendency on the part of 9-month-old infants to make A-returning search errors when not forced to do so by the constraints of the two-choice hiding paradigm.

Sophian and Sage (1983) interpreted their finding of no difference in the likelihood of errors occurring at the control location versus the relevant-but-incorrect location on visible-displacement problems as indicating an inability or failure on the part of the infants to identify the relevant locations in these tasks, that is, the two locations that were actually involved in the hiding problem on a given trial. Beyond the issue of whether this interpretation entails acceptance of the null hypothesis, we feel that a better and more parsimonious interpretation of this finding is that it reflects a limitation of memory rather than an inability to identify or comprehend which two of the three possible locations were actually involved in the hiding problem presented on any given trial.

Again, our reasons for asserting a memory interpretation of this finding stem from an information-processing analysis of the task situation with which the infants in this study were faced. More specifically, in the Sophian and Sage (1983) study, each infant was presented with five different types of hiding tasks in succession. Furthermore, within each type of hiding task, at least three trials were presented to each infant such that the initial hiding was performed equally often in each of the three possible locations and, if the problem involved a second location, all possible pairings of first and second locations were used equally often. In other words, which location happened to be the control location and which location happened to be the relevant-but-incorrect location changed from trial to trial on the same problem type for each infant. From an information-processing point of view, then, this counterbalancing scheme created a hiding-task situation that would place tremendous updating demands on the infant's memory and one in which potent interference effects would be operating from one trial to the next. Given these up-dating demands, trying to keep track of which two locations happened to be relevant on each trial and then choosing between them would be a less efficient and more demanding strategy in terms of the memory load it would place on the infant than would simply trying to note and remember in which location the object was ultimately left and then searching there, which, in fact, is the strategy that Sophian and Sage suggested the infants in their study seemed to have adopted. It is important to note, however, that adoption of such a strategy does not imply that the infants were unable to identify the two relevant locations on each trial. Thus, while Sophian and Sage's interpretation is not inconsistent with the data, we feel that it goes beyond what is called for by the data and that the present memory interpretation is a more parsimonious interpretation of their finding.

Another point we would like to make with respect to the Sophian and Sage (1983) study relates to the concern these authors expressed with respect to their finding of a relatively low performance level on even their simple single-hiding problem, the task in which the object was hidden in only one location and then the infant was allowed to search for it. As Sophian and Sage pointed out, the average performance level of their 13-month-old infants on this task was considerably poorer (56% correct) than the performance level of 9-month-old infants on similar problems, for which they gave as an example the A-hiding trials in previous two-choice tasks. As Sophian and Sage suggested, one reason for the lower performance level in their study may have been the use of a three-alternative hiding task. Although possibly a contributing factor, the average performance levels of the 9-month-old infants on the A trials of the present five-choice hiding tasks, which were 86% and 73% correct in Experiments 1 and 2, respectively, argue that the presence of three alternatives could not be the entire reason for the poor performance of Sophian and Sage's 13-month-old infants. Instead, we feel that their procedure of changing the position of the correct or ultimate hiding location of the object on each successive trial of a given problem type was probably the major reason for this finding.

To be more specific, we suspect that this procedure created, in essence, an analog to the Brown-Peterson task of the adult verbal memory literature (Brown, 1958; Peterson & Peterson, 1959). In a Brown-Peterson task, in which subjects are asked to remember similar types of items on each trial (say, three consonants), recall performance tends to be perfect on Trial 1 and then drops off rapidly, reaching asymptotic performance level over three to six trials (Fuchs & Melton, 1974; Keppel & Underwood, 1962; Loess, 1964). Furthermore, if after asymptotic performance level has been reached, the type of items to be remembered is changed (say, from consonants to digits), recall performance tends to recover (Wickens, Born, & Allen, 1963). Thus, our conjecture that Sophian and Sage's (1983) procedure created an analog to the Brown-Peterson task implies that the low performance level they observed on the single-hiding problem could be due to the fact that this performance level was arrived at by averaging across the three trials presented to each subject. Although Sophian and Sage did not present single-trial performance data, we suspect that first-trial performance would be higher and more similar to previously reported performance levels than that obtained by averaging across the three trials. Furthermore, Sophian and Sage's procedure of switching from one type of hiding container to another between problem types could be analogous to switching from one type of material to another in the adult task, thus allowing performance levels to recover, which, in turn, would account for why no effect of the order of problem type was obtained and why the overall level of performance based on data only from the first problem type that each infant received was about the same as the overall level of performance based on all the data.

Although Sophian and Sage (1983) were rightfully concerned with the question of whether their method of testing the same infant across a series of different problem types might raise problems of carry-over effects from one problem type to another, their analyses ignored the possibility of carry-over effects from one trial to the next within a given problem type. From the perspective outlined above, however, memorial inter-trial carry-over effects were probably potent and cannot be ignored if a proper understanding of infant search behavior in such tasks is to be understood. Our point here, and a recurring thesis throughout the present paper, is that without subjecting the various tasks we use in infant research to an information-processing analysis that, among other considerations, attempts to recognize the various demands such tasks place on the infant's memory, we can easily be misled in our interpretation of the infant's behavior on such tasks.

In addition to the supportive evidence from the studies discussed above, the plausibility of a memory explanation for infant search behavior is enhanced by recent evidence (Fox et al., 1979; Kagan & Hamburg, 1981) of significant increases in memory-related functions in the last half of the 1st year of life – a period in which the infant's performance on object-permanence tasks also rapidly improves (Gratch & Landers, 1971). Finally, in a recent discussion of the development of memory in infancy, Schacter and Moscovitch (in press) also argued compellingly for a major role of memory in producing the traditional $A\overline{B}$ error.

On the other hand, some results previously obtained in two-choice hiding tasks seem to be at odds with the present memory explanation of infant search behavior. In particular, Butterworth (1977) and Harris (1974) reported that infants err even when the object is visible during B-hiding trials – a finding that, on the surface, at least, appears to be inconsistent with the notion that B-trial errors are primarily produced by memory failures.

In Harris' (1974) experiment, infants first received three pretest A trials in which a car, located behind a transparent barrier, was pushed down a track to one of two transparent doors, which the infants could open to retrieve the car. Infants then received, in courterbalanced order, one A trial, in which the car was pushed to the same door as before, and one B trial, in which the car was pushed to the opposite door, but now both doors were locked. On both A and B trials, most infants first approached the door behind which the car was visible, but, on finding it locked, then approached the opposite or empty door; thereafter, they vacillated between the two locked doors. Because infants approached the visibly empty A door on B-test trials, Harris ruled out a memory explanation of the $A\overline{B}$ error. However, this interpretation does not take into account two important aspects of the infants' behavior. First, on B-test trials, most infants first approached the door behind which they could see the car (i.e., the B door) and, only after finding it locked, did they then approach the visibly empty A door. Second, and most tellingly, on A-test trials, infants also approached the visibly empty B door after finding the A door locked. That is, approaching the empty door was not peculiar to B test trials. Thus, a more plausible interpretation, which would be consistent with both A- and B-trial performance, is that infants saw and comprehended where the car was on both types of trials and were merely trying all possible strategies to gain access to it. Hence, we feel that Harris' results are more reasonably attributed to problem-solving strategies and are largely irrelevant to a memory explanation of infant search errors.

In Butterworth's (1977) experiment, infants were tested in three types of two-choice hiding tasks: (1) the standard Stage IV task, in which the object was completely hidden at A and B (OH); (2) one in which the object was covered by a transparent cover at A and B (OC); or (3) one in which the object was not covered at A and B (OV). In all three conditions, infants made more errors on the first B-hiding trial than on the first A trial, which in the OC and OV conditions might be considered as being inconsistent with a memory explanation of infant search errors. However, in all three conditions, B trials presented infants with a completely different problem from that presented on previous A trials, due to the introduction of a 3-second delay between hiding and search. During this delay, the sudden introduction of which was probably frustrating or at least distracting to the infants, it is quite possible that some infants looked away from B after the object was hidden and then failed to look back at the time of search. Moreover, consistent with a memory explanation of infant search errors, infants in the OV condition were generally correct, whereas performance in the OH condition was significantly worse (chance level). On the other hand, Butterworth's finding of no significant difference in the number of errors made in the OH and OC conditions is puzzling. If the object was still completely visible when covered by the transparent Perspex covers used in the OC condition, then one would expect performance in this condition to be essentially like that in the OV condition. It may be that the act of lowering the transparent cover over the object was distracting in some way, thus increasing the likelihood that infants would look away from B after the object was hidden and then fail to look back at the time of search. Another possibility is that, except from a certain vantage point that was not assumed by all infants at the time of search, the toy was not clearly visible through the transparent cover. Clearly, further research is needed to determine the source of difficulty in this condition.

A recent experiment by Willatts (1979) might also seem to pose a problem for a memory explanation of infant search errors. In Willatts's experiment, 4- and 5-month-old infants were given five 20-second trials in which they could reach for an object placed to either the left or right of their midline (the A trials). Then, for half of the infants in each age group (the experimental groups), the object was moved to the opposite side of the midline (i.e., a B trial), and for the other half (the control groups), the object remained in the same place (i.e., another A trial). Willatts took two behavioral measures: (1) manipulation of the object or moving of the infant's hand through the region of space previously occupied by the object and (2) fixation of the object or of the location in which the object had previously been located. Willatts found no differences in these measures between the 5-month-old experimental and control groups, but the 4-month-old experimental group reached more into the empty place (the spot in which the object had been on the previous A trials) than did the same-age control group (the corresponding spot on the opposite side for them) and fixated the empty spot more than did the controls. However, the 4-month-old experimental group also fixated the object far more than they fixated the empty place (i.e., the previous A location). In fact, of the 20 seconds of observation time, the experimental infants fixated the empty place for an average of only 1.4 seconds, which was possibly about the amount of time that would be necessary to look at that spot and determine that the object was no longer there or even perhaps that there was not another object there as well. On the other hand, the 4-month-old experimental infants spent less time, overall, reaching than did their controls and spent as much time reaching into the empty place as they did reaching into the place with the object. Thus, although the 4-month-olds were able to identify the object's new position visually, they did not seem able to use this information to control their reaching behavior. Such reaching errors had disappeared in the 5-month-olds. As Willatts suggested, this disappearance in reaching errors could occur because 5-month-old infants have learned that an object can exist in a variety of places, or it could occur because the infants have improved in their reaching skills. Perhaps the 4-month-old infants are unable to inhibit a previously successful action or cannot rapidly substitute one reach for another. Thus, although the infant is fixating the new location of the object, it cannot inhibit the reaching response that previously brought the object into contact with its hands. Indeed, the fact that the 4-month-old experimental infants spent less time, overall, reaching than did their corresponding controls might be an indication of some sort of interference or mutual inhibition between the two reaching responses. Although Willatts stated that his findings did not indicate whether the object-concept or the motor-skills explanation was appropriate, we would argue that only the motor-skills explanation is consistent with both the fixation and the reaching data.

Using a paradigm in which different types of intervening tasks were introduced during a 90-second interval between A- and B-hiding trials, Frye (1980) evaluated various explanations of the A$\overline{\text{B}}$ errors. To test Harris's (1973) proactive-interference explanation of A$\overline{\text{B}}$ errors, Frye compared B-trial performance when this interval was filled with a distracting activity with performance in a no-activity (control) condition, arguing that proactive interference should be reduced in the distraction condition compared with that in the control condition, and that, thus, if proactive interference produces A$\overline{\text{B}}$ errors, there should be fewer search errors in the former condition. Frye found no difference in first-trial B performance between the distraction and control conditions and, thus, argued against a proactive-interference explanation of A$\overline{\text{B}}$ errors. However, as argued by Schacter and Moscovitch (in press), and as it also appears to us, this finding is at best inconclusive with respect to the role of proactive interference in producing search errors, since, as described by Frye, there seems to have been little difference in the actual activities taking place during the 90-second interval between the A and B trials in these two conditions. Although infants in the distraction condition were given a doll with which to play during this interval and infants in the control condition were not, Frye reported that if infants in the control condition became restless or bored, which in a 90-second interval probably happened frequently, the experimenter made a special effort to engage the infant in play – an activity that would seem to be equally as distracting to the infant as, if not more so than, playing with a doll.

Infant Memory and Egocentrism

The present results and memory-based explanation also have important implications for recent accounts of infant search behavior in terms of egocentrism. Several investigators (Acredolo & Evans, 1980; Bremner, 1978b; Butterworth, 1977) have explained infant search behavior by suggesting that infants use either an objective or an egocentric frame of reference to guide search. The infant's selection of spatial location codes is thought to depend, in part, upon the characteristics of the task situation, including the nature of the spatial-location cues available. Whereas the notion that task demands and the availability of different types of spatial-location cues should affect the infant's search performance is consistent with the present memory account, our position with respect to the infant's use of egocentric versus objective or allocentric cues to encode spatial information is somewhat different from that of these researchers, which seems to be that the infant's predominant means of conceptualizing space are egocentric in nature and that encoding spatial information in terms of egocentric codes is a basic tendency that can be overridden or suppressed only in certain situations. In contrast, we feel more comfortable with the notion that egocentric codes are but one of several types of codes available to the infant for processing and encoding spatial information. Furthermore, rather than viewing egocentric encoding as a preferred or dominant method of encoding information, we see it as being more like a strategy of last resort. That is, we feel that egocentric codes would tend to be used or relied upon only in the absence or unavailability to the infant of other salient and more reliable objective cues for processing and encoding spatial information.

In addition, although we feel that egocentric cues can certainly be used by the infant and probably are used both by the infant and by the adult individual in certain situations, we do not feel that it is necessary to draw upon the concept of egocentrism, or the notion that the infant's predominant means of conceptualizing space are egocentric, in order to account for infant search errors. The primary basis for our position is that there is little compelling evidence that the infant's predominant mode of search is egocentric. Two-choice tasks artifactually constrain all infant search errors to be "egocentric". In the unconstrained tasks used in the present research, infants gave no evidence of employing egocentric spatial-location codes. Furthermore, in one of the few studies to address the issue of egocentric encoding and also to employ more than a two-choice task, Rieser (1979) obtained results indicating that even 6-month-old infants can encode and remember spatial information in terms of geocentric and landmarks cues when such cues are made available.

Rieser's (1979) procedure in this study was to first train 6-month-old infants to look toward one of four possible doors for a visual reward when they were cued by a signal bell. After reaching a specified learning criterion, infants were tested in one of six conditions. In each testing condition, the infant was first passively rotated 90 degrees; what varied in each condition was the type of information available for keeping track of the location of the previously rewarded door. When only minimal, passive-movement information could be used to keep track of the previously rewarded door's location, the infants looked predominantly at the egocentric door. However, when gravitational information was available for encoding and keeping track of the previously rewarded door's location in geocentric terms, infants looked predominantly at the geocentric (or correct) door. From the pattern of results obtained across conditions, Rieser concluded that 6-month-old infants can encode and remember spatial information in terms of egocentric, geocentric, or landmark cues but that the egocentric code exerts a stronger influence on the 6-month-old infant's visual search than does either of the other types of codes.

Although we agree with the first part of this conclusion, we feel that the second part is not yet warranted. First, the latter part of this conclusion seems not to give enough weight to the finding that in the condition in which gravitational information was available for encoding the rewarded door's location, the infants looked pre-dominantly at the geocentric door. In other words, in the condition in which salient information was available for encoding the location of the correct door in geocentric terms, the infants' visual search was guided more by the geocentric code than by the egocentric code. Second, Rieser (1979) seemed largely to come to the latter part of the conclusion above because, in the condition in which the geocentric and egocentric doors were both marked by patterns (Condition E-G patterned),[2] infants looked more at the egocentric door, whereas in the condition in which the geocentric and an irrelevant door were both patterned (Condition

---

[2]There is a discrepancy between the textual and schematic (Figure 1) descriptions of Condition E-G patterned in Rieser (1979). The present discussion assumes the textual description to be correct and is consistent with it.

I-G patterned), infants looked more at the geocentric door. To Rieser, this pattern of results indicated that the egocentric code is stronger than the geocentric code in guiding visual search. However, from an information-processing point of view, a comparison of these conditions did not constitute an adequate test of the primacy of the egocentric code. In the E-G patterned condition, the egocentric door was not only patterned similarly to the geocentric door, but was also spatially adjacent to it, whereas in the I-G patterned condition, the irrelevant door, which was patterned similarly to the geocentric door, was also the door most spatially distant from the geocentric door. Thus, in the former condition, the egocentric door was confusable with the geocentric door in two ways, whereas in the latter condition, the irrelevant door was confusable with the geocentric door in only one way. In other words, a spatial-adjacency or spatial-similarity variable had been confounded with the egocentric/irrelevant-door variable in these two conditions. Given this problem and the finding of the present two studies of a major role of spatial adjacency or similarity in determining the locus of search errors, it seems best to reserve judgment as to the relative potency of egocentric and geocentric codes in guiding the 6-month-old infant's visual search. At present, we see Rieser's results as being compatible with the notion that infants tend to rely on egocentric codes to remember spatial information only when other salient and more reliable cues are not available for encoding and remembering such information.

In another study investigating whether infants code spatial-location information in geographic or egocentric terms, Wishart and Bower (1982) used a procedure somewhat similar to Bremner's (1978a) and Rieser's (1979), in which, after an infant watched as an object was hidden in one of two or one of three containers sitting on a table, either the infant or the table, or both, were rotated, and the infant's task was to keep track of the location of the container in which the object had been hidden. Three groups of infants were tested: a cross-sectional group (12 to 24 months), a longitudinal group (12 to 24 months), and an accelerated group (8 to 20 months). Whereas the results from Wishart and Bower's two-container task suffer from the interpretation problems of all two-choice search tasks and, thus, do not shed any light on the question of the prevalence of egocentric errors in infant search behavior, the results of their three-container task are not similarly confounded. With respect to this point, it is interesting to note that, although on the one hand, Wishart and Bower themselves argued that the results of their two-container series were largely uninterpretable, since, without a viable "other" response, any search response must have been either egocentric or geographic, they then do not fully make use of this observation in interpreting the results of their three-container series. To illustrate, in all three groups of infants, the geographic response was by far the most predominant reponse and, in two of the groups (longitudinal and accelerated), the frequencies of the "egocentric" and "other" errors were essentially equal. Despite this finding, Wishart and Bower concluded that egocentric responding continues well into the second half of the 2nd year of life. In other words, they seemed to ignore the message yielded by the pattern of search with respect to "other" responses in interpreting their results. One could equally well argue that the infants in these two groups either remembered the location of the correct container or guessed, choosing randomly between the two other containers. Furthermore, on the basis of these results, one would be as justified to conclude that "other" responding continues well into the 2nd year of life as to conclude that "egocentric" responding does. Given no evidence of a tendency on the part of these infants to search at the "egocentric" location rather than at the "other" location, there is no basis for assuming that infants have a tendency to respond egocentrically.

Furthermore, in the one condition in which infants appear to have been making slightly more "egocentric" errors than "other" errors at several of the testing ages (the cross-sectional condition), there may have been a biasing effect operating to produce more responses that would be labeled by Wishart and Bower (1982) as "egocentric" than ones that would be labeled as "other". From Wishart and Bower's description of the three-container series, it would seem that on 8 of the 12 trials presented to each infant, the object could be found in either the near or the far center position after rotation. However, it also appears that the "other" container never ended up in the center position after rotation, whereas the "egocentric" container was in the center position on 4 of the 12 trials. Thus, on trials in which the infant had lost track of the correct container's location, the infant might be biased toward searching in the near or far center position, which would spuriously produce more "egocentric" responses than "other" responses. Since this bias would only come into play on trials in which the infant had forgotten the correct location, its effects would be more prevalent in the cross-sectional group of infants than in the other two groups and, thus, could have contributed to what appears to be a slight prevalence of "egocentric" responses over "other" responses in that group. In any event, although this nonequivalence in the possible locations of the "correct", "egocentric", and "other" containers presents an interpretation problem for all three groups of subjects, the obtained pattern of results can be accounted for by the information-processing/memory explanation of search behavior that we are advocating without resorting to the concept of egocentrism. Furthermore, an egocentric explanation seems untenable, as well as unnecessary. Two of the three groups of infants gave no evidence of egocentric responding, and the apparent "egocentric" responding of the third is largely uninterpretable because of the biasing problem discussed above. In addition, even without this interpretation problem, an egocentric account would still be faced with the difficult task of explaining why only one of the three groups of infants showed any preference for egocentric responding.

Thus, although we applaud Wishart and Bower's (1982) use of a three-choice task and find their discussion of the interpretation problems presented by all two-choice studies to agree with the argument that we are making here and have made elsewhere (Cummings & Bjork, 1981, 1983a; Bjork & Cummings, Ref Note 1), we see little or no compelling evidence in their study to support the contention that egocentric responding persists well into the second half of the 2nd year of life or that the infant tends to make spatial judgements or encode spatial information on the basis of self-referents.

In conclusion, we feel that infant search behavior can be explained without appeal to the notion that the infant's predominant means of conceptualizing space are those of egocentrism. Although egocentric codes are certainly available to the infant, as they are, for that matter, to the adult, we see little convincing evidence in the literature that they are the infant's preferred or dominant means of encoding and remembering spatial information. Our position is that the findings of studies that have been interpreted as supporting the infant's egocentric conception of space can be better and more parsimoniously accounted for in terms of an information-processing analysis of the task and of the demands the task places on the infant's ability to process, store, and retrieve spatial information. Finally, it should be noted that other researchers are questioning the usefulness of egocentrism as an explanatory concept (Cox, 1980).

A Memory-Based Interpretation of Other Search Errors

The present memory explanation for the search behavior of 8-to-12-month-old infants gains further credence when one considers the ability of such a memory model to account for search errors assumed to be characteristic of other stages in Piaget's (1954) sensori-motor period. In Stage I (birth to 1 month) and Stage II (1 to 4 months), infants fail to search for an object at all when it is hidden from view. Piaget attributed this behavior to the infant's egocentric concern for his or her own actions without regard to objects. We feel that this behavior would be more parsimoniously described in terms of the current memory analysis as a reflection of extremely limited encoding skills and/or memory storage in young infants.

Piaget (1954) suggested that, in Stage III (4 to 8 months), objects have permanence for the infant only as an extension of the immediate action in progress. Thus, for example, the infant at this stage is able to find a partially covered but not a fully covered object because "the child sees a fragment of the object and the action of grasping thus set in motion bestows a totality on the thing perceived" (Piaget, 1954, p. 35). Again, it seems to us that a simpler explanation of this behavior is to assume that infants are able to find the partially covered but not the totally covered object because, in the former situation, they are provided with a memory aid or retrieval cue (i.e., the visible part of the object) for the object's current location. Visual-tracking studies (e.g., Bower, 1974) have also been interpreted as providing support for a memory, as opposed to an object-concept, explanation for infant search behavior in this period, but the evidence is ambiguous (Meicler & Gratch, 1980), and it may be that the visual-tracking paradigm is too fraught with methodological problems to address adequately this issue (Muller & Aslin, 1978).

During Stage V (12 to 18 months), infants find a directly hidden object (visible displacement) easily, but they have difficulty when the object is first concealed inside a larger object or a container before it is hidden (invisible displacement). According to Piaget (1954), the infant's difficulty in the latter situation arises because the invisible-displacement task causes "the habits of preceding stages to reappear through temporal displacement" (Piaget, 1954, p. 66). In contrast, the proposed memory model would expect the infant to make more search errors in the invisible-displacement task because of the greater load such a task places on the infant's memory in comparison with that of the visible displacement task. In the invisible-displacement task, the infant must first notice and remember that the toy has been concealed in another, larger container and then the infant must notice and remember the location to which this larger container is moved.

Furthermore, the invisible-displacement procedure can be thought of as functioning essentially like a distractor activity in a memory or recall task. That is, before searching for the hidden object, the infant must somehow realize that the object is no longer concealed in the larger container. In the typical invisible-displacement task, the infant must search the larger container to know that the object has been removed from it. Thus, the task demands of the invisible-displacement procedure both increase the processing and memory load on the infant and require the infant to engage in a distracting activity just prior to retrieving information concerning the most likely last location of the hidden object. These changes in task demands should increase the difficulty of encoding, retaining, and/or retrieving precise location information, and, according to the memory explanation, more search errors should occur. However, the predicted search errors would not be of the type predicted by Piaget's (1954) action-object account, which assumes that Stage V infants faced with the invisible-displacement task will revert to behavior appropriate to an earlier stage of object-concept development; namely, they will make $A\overline{B}$, or Stage IV, errors. In contrast, the current memory account would expect the increased search errors to reflect partial knowledge of the object's likely new spatial location.

It remains, of course, to substantiate or insubstantiate the validity of the above memory explanations of infant search errors. However, we feel that conceiving of the infant as a less mature or less effective processor of information than the adult individual is a promising theoretical framework, one that is a formidable alternative to the more radical Piagetian view of the infant as a being with concepts that are fundamentally different from those of the adult. In addition, a demonstration that the "object permanence" errors made throughout the sensorimotor period arise from memory limitations or failures without regard to the infant's ability to separate object from action would have profound repercussions for Piaget's (1954) account of cognitive development, since a cornerstone of Piaget's theory is the notion that infants are initially egocentrically concerned only with their own actions and only gradually come to appreciate the significance of objects distinct from action.

CONCLUSION

In conclusion, the present research has provided a needed and critical test of perseverative search in infant behavior and has shown that the $A\overline{B}$ search error held to be characteristic of 8-to-12-month-old infants and indicative of Stage IV in Piaget's (1954) sensorimotor period of development occurs primarily as an artifact of the two-choice search tasks employed by past researchers. Consequently, the considerable theoretical significance that has been attached to the occurrence of the $A\overline{B}$ error is subject to serious question and needs to be reexamined in the light of the present findings.

More specifically, the patterns of search errors obtained in the present unconstrained five-choice search tasks, on both single A and B trials as well as across trials, clearly indicate that infants between the approximate ages of 8.5 and 10.5 months are capable of storing in memory some information concerning the current location of an object as it is hidden in successive spatial locations. There is no evidence that infants revert, owing to a failure to assimilate information about a new hiding location of an object, to the first and/or previous location in which they acted upon the object. At least by the age of 9 months, then, infants appear to appreciate the substantive permanence of objects and the reality of distinct positions in space.

Finally, the failure of Piaget's (1954) action-object theory to account for search errors obtained in an unconstrained situation, combined with the success of the proposed memory explanation to predict the pattern of search errors obtained in such a situation, implies that a memory model, such as the one outlined in the present paper, might better account for search errors made throughout the sensorimotor period. The development of such a model would take a far less radical view of the infant than the one suggested by Piaget, being guided by a conception of the infant as simply a more limited or less efficient processor of information than the adult individual.

ACKNOWLEDGEMENTS

Authorship in the present paper is equally shared. The research reported was supported by Research Committee Grants 4-574069-09528-7 and 4-574069-19900-7 from the University of California, Los Angeles. The paper was presented in part at the meeting of the Psychonomic Society, Phoenix, Arizona, November 1979.

The authors are indebted to Janet Matsunaga and Cheryl Maisel for their assistance in the collection of data and to three colleagues, Patricia Greenfield, Alice Healy, and Lynne Reder, for their support and encouragement during this research. The authors also wish to thank Daniel Schacter and two anonymous reviewers for many perceptive and valuable comments leading to numerous improvements in the final version of the present paper.

John W. Hagen served as Guest Editor for this manuscript.

REFERENCE NOTES

1. Bjork, E. L., & Cummings, E. M. (1979, November). *The "A, not B" search error in Piaget's theory of object permanence: Fact or artifact?* Paper presented at the meeting of the Psychonomic Society, Phoenix, Arizona.
2. Butterworth, G. (1979, March). *Logical competence in infancy: Object permanence or object concept?* Paper presented at the meeting of the Society for Research in Child Development, San Francisco.
3. Cummings, E. M., & Bjork, E. L. (1977, April). *Piaget's Stage IV object concept error: Evidence of perceptual confusion, state change, or failure to assimilate?* Paper presented at the meeting of the Western Psychological Association, Seattle.

REFERENCES

Acredolo, L. P., & Evans, D. (1980). Developmental changes in the effects of landmarks on infant spatial behavior. *Developmental Psychology, 16*, 312–318.
Bower, T. G. R. (1974). *Development in infancy.* San Francisco: Freeman.
Bremner, J. G. (1978a). Egocentric versus allocentric spatial coding in nine-month-old infants: Factors influencing the choice of code. *Developmental Psychology, 14*, 346–355.
Bremner, J. G. (1978b). Spatial errors made by infants: Inadequate spatial cues or evidence of egocentrism? *British Journal of Psychology, 69*, 77–84.
Bremner, J. G., & Bryant, P. E. (1977). Place versus response as the basis of spatial errors made by young infants. *Journal of Experimental Child Psychology, 23*, 162–177.
Brown, J. (1958). Some tests of the decay theory of immediate memory. *Quarterly Journal of Experimental Psychology, 10*, 12–21.
Butterworth, G. (1975). Object identity in infants: The interaction of spatial location codes in determining search errors. *Child Development, 46*, 866–870.
Butterworth, G. (1976). Asymmetrical search errors in infancy. *Child Development, 47*, 864–867.
Butterworth, G. (1977). Object disappearance and error in Piaget's Stage IV task. *Journal of Experimental Child Psychology, 23*, 391–401.

Corter, C. M., Zucker, K. J., & Galligan, R. F. (1980). Patterns in the infant's search for mother during brief separation. *Developmental Psychology, 16,* 62–69.

Cox, M. V. (1980). (Ed.) *Are young children egocentric?* New York: St. Martins Press.

Crowder, R. G. (1976). *Principles of learning and memory.* Hillsdale, N.J: Lawrence Erlbaum Associates Inc.

Cummings, E. M., & Bjork, E. L. (1981). The search behavior of 12 to 14 month-old infants on a five-choice invisible displacement hiding task. *Infant Behavior and Development, 4,* 47–60.

Cummings, E. M., & Bjork, E. L. (1983a). Perseveration and search on a five-choice visible displacement hiding task. *Journal of Genetic Psychology, 142,* 283–291.

Cummings, E. M., & Bjork, E. L. (1983b). Search behavior on multi-choice hiding tasks: Evidence for an objective conception of space in infancy. *International Journal of Behavioral Development, 6,* 71–87.

Evans, W. F., & Gratch, G. (1972). The Stage IV error in Piaget's theory of object concept development: Difficulties in object conceptualization or spatial localization? *Child Development, 43,* 682–688.

Fletcher, H. J., Garske, J. P., Barron, T., Grogg, T. M. (1968). Intertrial and intratrial determinants of delayed responses of monkeys. *Journal of Comparative and Physiological Psychology, 65,* 66–71.

Fox, N., Kagan, J., & Weiskopf, S. (1979). The growth of memory during infancy. *Genetic Psychology Monographs, 99,* 91–130.

Frye, D. (1980). Stages of development: The Stage IV error. *Infant Behavior and Development, 3,* 115–126.

Fuchs, A. F., & Melton, A. W. (1974). Effects of frequency of presentation and stimulus length on retention in the Brown-Peterson paradigm. *Journal of Experimental Psychology, 103,* 629–637.

Gardiner, J. M., Craik, F. I. M., & Birtwistle, J. (1972). Retrieval cues and release from proactive inhibition. *Journal of Verbal Learning and Verbal Behavior, 11,* 778–783.

Gratch, G., Appel, K. J., Evans, W. F., LeCompte, G. K., & Wright, N. A. (1974). Piaget's Stage IV object concept error: Evidence of forgetting or object conception? *Child Development, 45,* 71–77.

Gratch, G., & Landers, W. F. (1971). Stage IV of Piaget's theory of infant's object concepts: A longitudinal study. *Child Development, 42,* 359–372.

Harris, D. L. (1973). Perseverative errors in search by young children. *Child Development, 44,* 28–33.

Harris, D. L. (1974). Perseverative search at a visibly empty place by young infants. *Journal of Experimental Child Psychology, 18,* 535–542.

Jackson, E., Campos, J. J., & Fischer, K. W. (1978). The question of decalage between object permanence and person permanence. *Developmental Psychology, 1,* 1–10.

Kagan, J., & Hamburg, M. (1981). The enhancement of memory in the first year. *Journal of Genetic Psychology, 138,* 3–14.

Keppel, G., & Underwood, B. J. (1962). Proactive inhibition in short-term retention of single items. *Journal of Verbal Learning and Verbal Behavior, 1,* 153–161.

Loess, H. (1964). Proactive inhibition in short-term memory. *Journal of Verbal Learning and Verbal Behavior, 3,* 362–368.

Medin, D. L. (1969). Form perception and pattern reproduction by monkeys. *Journal of Comparative and Physiological Psychology, 68,* 412–419.

Meicler, M., & Gratch, G. (1980). Do 5-month-olds show object conception in Piaget's sense? *Infant Behavior and Development, 3,* 265–282.

Muller, A. A., & Aslin, R. N. (1978). Visual tracking as an index of the object concept. *Infant Behavior and Development, 1,* 309–319.

Peterson, L. R., & Peterson, M. J. (1958). Short-term retention of individual verbal items. *Journal of Experimental Psychology, 58*, 193–198.

Piaget, J. (1954). *The construction of reality in the child.* New York: Basic Books.

Rieser, J. J. (1979). Spatial orientation of six-month-old infants. *Child Development, 50*, 1078–1087.

Schacter, D. L., & Moscovitch, M. (in press). Infants, amnesics, and dissociable memory systems. In M. Moscovitch (Ed.), *Infant memory,* New York: Plenum Press.

Schuberth, R. E., Werner, J. S., & Lipsitt, L. P. (1978). The Stage IV error in Piaget's theory of object concept development: A re-consideration of the spatial localization hypothesis. *Child Development, 49*, 744–748.

Sophian, C., & Sage, S. (1983). Developments in infants' search for displaced objects. *Journal of Experimental Child Psychology, 35*, 143–160.

Webb, R. A., Massar, B., & Nadolny, T. (1972). Information and strategy in the young child's search for hidden objects. *Child Development, 43*, 91–104.

Wickens, D. D., Born, D. G., & Allen, C. K. (1963). Proactive inhibition and item similarity in short-term memory. *Journal of Verbal Learning and Verbal Behavior, 2*, 440–445.

Willatts, P. (1979). Adjustment of reaching to change in object position by young infants. *Child Development, 50*, 911–913.

Wishart, J. G., & Bower, T. G. R. (1982). The development of spatial understanding in infancy. *Journal of Experimental Child Psychology, 33*, 363–385.

V EARLY SOCIAL BEHAVIOUR

16 Early Person Knowledge as Expressed in Gestural and Verbal Communication: When do Infants Acquire a "Theory of Mind"?

Inge Bretherton, Sandra McNew, and Marjorie Beeghly-Smith

The child's image of the world is mirrored twice, once directly and again as a representation of the representation of others. His image of himself is also mirrored twice, once with direct knowledge of his internal states and again by his representation of his behavior in the eyes of others. Each image extends and modifies the other. (Shields, 1978)

INTRODUCTION

During the first year of life, infants come to know about objects by man- ipulating, shaking, banging, finding, hiding, pushing, pulling, throwing, stacking, and nesting them. By acting on objects, infants discover – paradox- ically – that objects have properties that are independent of the infant's action, that objects continue to exist in space and time whether the baby perceives them or not, and that objects can sometimes act without being acted upon (a toy car can roll down an incline without being pushed). Infants also discover that one object can act indirectly on another, making it possible to obtain one object (for example, a necklace) by means of another (the cloth on which it rests). During the first year of life, infants also come to know about people by interacting with them in everyday routines and games, discovering that people can act without being acted upon, that they are agents who continue to exist in time and space indepen-

Source: M. E. Lamb and L. R. Sherrod, (Eds) *Infant Social Cognition*. Hillsdale, N. J.: Lawrence Erlbaum Associates Inc, pp. 333–373.

dent of the infant's perception. Further, babies discover that a person can also be used as a means to an end – as a social tool through whom the infant can obtain a desired action by using a communicative gesture such as pointing. Person permanence and object permanence (Bell, 1970; Jackson, Campos, & Fischer, 1978) and social and nonsocial tool use (Bates, Camaioni, & Volterra, 1975; Bates, Benigni, Bretherton, Camaioni, & Volterra, 1979) seem to develop more or less in step with one another, suggesting that the same underlying processes may come into play in the acquisition of object and person knowledge. Or do they?

We believe, in common with a number of other researchers (Bruner, 1977; Newson, 1977; Shields, 1978; Shotter, 1978; Trevarthen & Hubley, 1978) and philosophers (Habermas, 1972; Hamlyn, 1974), that there are fundamental differences between person knowledge and object knowledge even though both types of knowledge are constructed by a child through feedback from his or her own actions. The differences are evident both in the way in which person knowledge and object knowledge are acquired (through dialogue with a person, compared to acting upon an object) as well as in what is acquired (knowledge of physical laws, as compared to knowledge of others and of oneself as a psychological agent with intentions, beliefs, emotions, and the ability to communicate). For example, a baby playing with a rattle obtains *interesting effects* (noises, visual and tactile stimulation) depending only on the skill with which he or she manipulates the toy. From people, on the other hand, a baby receives a *reply* to his or her action by a more experienced partner who treats the baby's action as socially meaningful behavior. For example, when a mother responds to her baby's cry as if it were a communicative signal, she allows the baby to discover eventually that crying (and other behaviors) can be used as communicative signals. Mothers thus provide a scaffold (Wood, Bruner, & Ross, 1976) within which babies can begin to make sense of their own and their mothers' actions. As Hamlyn (1974, p. 34) phrases it: "The child could come to have the idea of what a person is only *via* and in the context of *being* a person; and for this to have any real sense the child must be treated as a person".

In dialogue, infants very early discover the rudiments of turn taking (Stern, 1977), how to achieve affective synchrony in interaction with others (Brazelton, Koslowski, & Main, 1974), the capacity to predict the behavior of others and the capacity to *influence* another's behavior intentionally. Even 3-month-old infants can recognize their ability to make a partner repeat his or her behavior by repeating their own behavior (Rheingold, Gewirtz & Ross, 1959). Later, around 7 months of age, babies tend to repeat the antics that lead an adult to laugh, seeming to anticipate further laughter (Bates et al., 1975). Both examples qualify as *intentional behavior designed to influence other persons,* but not yet as *intentional communication* as the term is used in this paper.

Intentional communication as well as a host of other new achievements become possible as the result of a far-reaching discovery on the part of the infant, which dramatically alters the nature of his or her relationship to other human beings. Infants come to recognize not only that others possess agency (can activate themselves) and resemble them physically, but that others are like them *psychologically* and yet distinct from them (see also Lewis & Brooks-Gunn, 1979, for a discussion of this point). It is this discovery that makes experiential sharing or intersubjectivity possible (Trevarthen & Hubley, 1978). Whereas the capacity of intersubjective sharing is prefigured in the neonate's ability to imitate facial expressions (Meltzoff & Moore, 1977), to show empathetic distress (Hoffman, 1975), and to adapt to the micro- and macrorhythms of the caregiver (Sander, 1977), it truly blossoms around 9 months, as demonstrated by the following list of capacities that emerge between then and 12 months, inspired by a similar list by Trevarthen and Hubley (1978). All of the examples except those specifically acknowledged were collected in a study jointly undertaken by Bates, Benigni, Bretherton, Camaioni, and Volterra (1979):

1. Obeys simple gestural or verbal requests such as "Give me the cup" said with an outstretched open palm extended to the baby. Begins to make gestural requests.
2. Points to objects (first without [later with] checking whether the addressee is attending) and follows the pointing gesture of an adult (Murphy & Messer, 1977).
3. Reliably turns his or her regard in the same direction as that of an adult (Scaife & Bruner, 1975).
4. Requests adult help to obtain an object or to "fix" it.
5. Shakes head or says "no-no" in refusal, also occasionally in self-reproof.
6. Shows manners by appropriate waving or saying "hi" and "bye-bye" and by saying "thank you" when handing over, or being handed, an object.
7. Begins to use conventional labels for objects such as balls, bottles, and teddy bears. Also requests labels with "Whassa?" Begins to name persons and pets.
8. Demonstrates affection in the learned form of hugging and kissing. Kisses, hugs, and pats favorite dolls and teddy bears.
9. Initiates, with appropriate gestures, games such as peekaboo and pattycake.

10. Plays at carrying out adult activities such as mopping the floor, driving the car (turning the steering wheel), telephoning, reading books, putting on clothes, brushing and combing hair, dancing and singing.
11. Imitates conventional actions with objects (driving a car), but resists imitating counterconventional use (drinking from a car) (Killen & Uzgiris, 1978).

The emergence of these behaviors is difficult to explain unless one assumes that the child has come to recognize the psychological similarity as well as the separateness of self and others (a rudimentary form of identification) and is operating within a shared meaning system that he or she has developed through interaction with another person.

In later childhood, the knowledge that others are more than self-activating agents, but persons who perceive, feel, and intend in much the same way as the children themselves can be applied in complex social situations where the other persons' feelings, viewpoints, thoughts, and intentions may *differ* from one's own (i.e., role taking, see Flavell, Botkin, & Fry, 1968, for a review). But before children can conceive of others as having *different* viewpoints, they must first recognize that *others can have viewpoints and other mental processes at all* (Flavell, 1974).

Thus, the young child's psychological model of persons may at first not be very much concerned with possible differences of viewpoint, but rather with the similarity of self and others. Shields (1978, pp. 553–554), in discussing the minimum psychological model required for intentional communication and preceding the role-taking skills of preschool children, proposed the following dimensions:

1. Persons have identity over time despite changes in location, behavior and appearance.
2. Persons are self-moving or animate, and influence over the course of their behavior has to be negotiated by invoking interest or a shared frame of constraint.
3. Persons identify each other and can react to each other.
4. Persons can see, feel, hear, touch and smell, i.e., they have a perceptual field.
5. Persons intend their actions.
6. Persons conceptualize and construct their world in roughly similar ways.
7. Persons have moods and states such as anger and fear, and also wants, likes and dislikes.
8. Persons can send and receive messages based on gestures and words which are related to context in stable ways.
9. Persons have an action potential, i.e., things they can and can't do.

10. Persons can retain previous experience and structure their present behavior by it.
11. Persons can replicate previous behaviors in new contexts.
12. Persons share sets of rules about what is appropriate within particular frames of action.

Is Shield's model a realistic one? There are many windows into a child's person knowledge, and therefore many different ways in which Shield's model could be tested: through the observation of dyadic interaction, the study of symbolic play, and the study of intentional communication through gesture and word. In this paper, we focus on the last topic, but we do so in full awareness that verbal and gestural communicative skills do not represent the sum total of a young child's person knowledge. Knowledge that can be mapped onto a communicative medium does, however, have special status by being more shareable than the private knowledge of imagery and more explicit than the observable knowledge expressed in action. In his early work, Piaget was criticized (Flavell, 1963) for investigating young children's understanding through interviews instead of asking children to act out solutions to problem situations. Although it is interesting that children *can* understand and solve a problem at the level of doing (without being able to give a coherent verbal account of their actions), communicable knowledge – especially communicable knowledge of others and the self as perceiving, intending, feeling, cognizing, and moralizing beings – is, we believe, an extremely important aspect of person knowledge in its own right. It is both an indicator of present knowledge available for linguistic symbolization and communication, and it probably also facilitates the further acquisition of such knowledge. This remains true even if verbally expressible person knowledge is not the first and only form of such knowledge that a child possesses.

The data with which we are buttressing our arguments come from many published sources, but also include data that were collected by us as part of a larger joint project with Elizabeth Bates on the prerequisites to language and the emergence of symbols. In this study 32, middle-class Boulder, Colorado infants were observed in the presence of their mothers at 10½ and 13 months. Twenty-seven of these infants were seen again at 20 months (with an additional three infants to bring the sample size up to N = 30) in a number of structured and unstructured situations at home and in the laboratory. An extensive interview of the mother was also conducted at each age. We have in the past found interviews to be reliable (i.e., to correlate strongly with comparable observational data), provided we confined our questions to the present and provided we asked the mother to supply concrete examples of behavior. The latter procedure is very effective at eliminating potential misunderstandings (see also Bates et al., 1979). The data presented here are taken from the maternal interview and from a comprehension test of emotion labels. The sample is referred to as the Boulder Sample.

PERSON KNOWLEDGE VIEWED THROUGH THE WINDOW OF GESTURAL AND VERBAL COMMUNICATION

Babies appear to communicate intentionally from about 9 months of age (Bates et al., 1975, 1979); that is, they begin at this age to use conventional gestures (and sometimes sounds) such as giving, showing, pointing, requesting, shaking the head "no" or saying "no-no-no," waving "bye-bye", saying "hi," clapping the hands in applause, and so forth. Table 16.1 shows how many such communicative conventions had already been mastered by the Boulder Sample at 10½ and 13 months.

What makes such gestural and vocal conventions communicative? Instead of straining to reach an unattainable object, a baby who is attempting to communicate a request will reach toward the object without straining, open and close the hand while intermittently glancing up at mother's face, perhaps with an imperative "eheheh". Functional reaching and grasping behavior gradually becomes abbreviated and ritualized as it turns into a communicative gesture. Similarly, the arms-up gesture emerges out of cooperation with the mother: As the mother extends her arms toward the baby in order to pick him or her up, the baby responds by lifting its arms. Later, the baby may start to raise the arms as soon as mother enters the room in the morning in the *expectation* of being picked up. Eventually, an infant comes to use the arms-up gesture communicatively, that is, the child spontaneously approaches his or her mother in order to *request* a pick-up (Edwards, 1978). Other gestures, like waving "bye-bye", are not ritualizations of actions in context, but have to be acquired through imitation.

Before the advent of conventional communication, the baby is already engaging in behavior designed to influence adults, but intentional communication requires more than this. Bates (1979, p. 36) writes:

> Intentional communication is signaling behavior in which the sender is aware, *a priori*, of the effect that the signal will have on his listener, and he persists in that behavior until the effect is obtained or failure is clearly indicated. The behavioral evidence that permits us to infer the presence of communicative intentions include (1) alternations in eye contact between the goal and the intended listeners, (2) augmentations, additions, and substitution of signals until the goal has been obtained, and (3) changes in the form of the signal toward abbreviated and/or exaggerated patterns that are appropriate only for achieving a communicative goal.

Implicit in Bates' definition is the fact that the infant recognizes a partner's capacity to *understand* a message. In other words, the infant attributes an internal state of *knowing* and *comprehending* to the mother as he or she communicates, and thus must have what Premack and Woodruff (1978, p. 515) have called a "theory of mind". According to these authors, an organism is said to have a theory of mind if:

> he imputes mental states to himself and others (either to conspecifics or to other species) as well. A system of inferences of this kind is properly viewed as a theory, first, because such states are not directly observable and second, because the system can be used to make predictions specifically about the behavior of others. . . Purpose or intention is the state we impute most widely; several other states are not far behind, however. They include all those designated by the italicized term in each of the following statements: John *believes* in ghosts; He *thinks* he has a fair chance of *winning*; Paul *knows* that I don't *like* roses; She is *guessing* when she says that; I *doubt* that Mary will come; Bill is only *pretending*. This list is in no way exhaustive.

TABLE 16.1

Percentage of Children in the Boulder Sample Using Conventional Gestures in Communication at 10½ and 13 Months (According to Maternal Report)

Convention	Used at 10½ Months	Used at 13 Months
Communicative Gestures and Sounds		
Shows an object	66%	94%
Gives an object	75%	100%
Requests an object by pointing	9%	50%
Requests an object with outstretched arm, accompanied by grasping motions and/or ritual sound	9%	66%
Requests object by banging on or shaking container	0%	25%
Requests pick up with arms-up gesture	100%	97%
Refuses with head shake	33%	44%
Refuses by saying "no," "nanana," etc.	25%	28%
Affirms with head nod	0%	9%
Requests attention by pointing and visual check to adult	34%	69%
Greetings		
Waves bye or hi (mostly bye)	59%	69%
Says bye-bye or bye	6%	34%
Says hi	19%	65%
Affective Expression		
Kisses	9%	84%
Hugs	50%	75%
Applauds self	not known	53%
Joins in applause with others	not known	78%

Even the ability to impute internal states to self and others is, in and of itself, not enough. In order to communicate intentionally, a baby must have recognized that his or her mind can be *interfaced* with that of a partner (Bretherton & Bates, 1979). This interfacing is possible only because both partners: (1) share a *framework of meaning*; (2) share an *interfacible medium* (language or conventional gestures) into which underlying intentions can be encoded by the speaker and from which they can be decoded into something corresponding to the speaker's underlying intentions by the addressee. The notion of interface has, surprisingly, been taken for granted by philosophers concerned with the transmission of meaning. For example, according to Grice (1968) as rephrased in our terms, a baby who means something by his or her gesture or utterance would like his or her mother: (1) to understand the meaning or content of his or her communication; (2) to either act upon it or at least acknowledge its receipt. That the production of mutually comprehensible messages is possible is simply taken for granted by Grice.

When suggesting that infants as young as 9 months of age have something as outlandish as a theory of interfacible minds, we do not mean to suggest that they are *aware* of using such a theory, nor that they can impute *any* mental state, nor that their inferences are likely to be as sophisticated as those ascribed to naive adult psychologists by Heider (1958). Let us make this clear by way of an analogy. When at around age 2, babies begin to use syntax in the construction of utterances, their knowledge of syntactic rules is only implicit. Late in the third year of life, however, some young children start correcting the speech of younger siblings and even come up with simple etymological explanations (Clark, 1978). They have become aware of some of the rules underlying language. Similarly, a baby's use of a theory of interfacible minds remains at first implicit and fairly rudimentary. It becomes somewhat more explicit as children gain experience with repairing misfired nonverbal messages, a phenomenon that has been noted but not systematically studied in infants. A particularly striking example is reported by Rubin and Wolf (1980, p. 18) in a longitudinal study of J., who was 12 months at the time of the following observation:

J. has been playing in his room. There he found his jack-in-the-box sitting on the table with a block resting on its lid. He cranked the handle, the jack popped up, sending the block flying off behind a shelf. J. wants to make this grand event happen again, but he has lost his block. He runs to the kitchen, calling out his father's name. He pulls his father back into the room and points behind the shelf, saying "there, there." His father has a hard time understanding and tries several guesses, pulling out first one favorite book, then another. J., somewhat exasperated, at last takes his father's hand in his own, places them both on top of the jack-in-the-box, makes a kind of explosive noise, and moves his and his father's hand in an arc toward the bookcase. J. then reaches his own hand down behind the bookcase, making somewhat conventionalized effort sounds to signal reaching. Still looking at his father, he says something like "block".

Such heroic efforts at communicating are hard to explain unless one assumes that the child knows that one's intentions can be transmitted to another via messages which implies that the child has a theory of interfacible minds. It is especially noteworthy that J. did not assume that because he himself knew that he wanted the block, his father must automatically know it too (the egocentric position). He seemed to assume, however, that by making his father see and experience the situation from *his* (J.'s) viewpoint, he could somehow convey his meaning.

That at least some very young children can demonstrate simple role-taking skills in their communications is illustrated also by the example of Jacqueline Piaget (Piaget, 1954, p. 297) at 16½ months:

Jacqueline has just been wrested from a game she wants to continue and placed in her playpen from which she wants to get out. She calls, but in vain. Then she clearly expresses a certain need, although the events of the last ten minutes prove that she no longer experiences it. No sooner has she left the playpen then she indicates the game she wishes to resume!

Thus we see how Jacqueline, *knowing* that a mere appeal would not free her from her confinement, has *imagined* a more efficacious means, *foreseeing* more or less clearly the sequence of actions that would result from it (italics added).

Not only did Jacqueline know that she could communicate her wish to get out of the playpen, she could also envisage which type of presumed need on her part would be most effective in getting her parents to act as she wished, an attempt at deception with all the hallmarks of role-taking skill.

The recognition that self and others are objectively and subjectively similar but distinct is *implicit* in intentional communication when it first emerges. It becomes *explicit* in three aspects of language development during the subsequent 2 years. The three aspects to be discussed in turn are: (1) the establishment of one-to-one correspondence between the physical self and the physical other as shown in language through comprehension and then production of labels for corresponding body parts; (2) reference to self and other by personal names as well as the mastery of pronouns, which because of their deictic properties require simple role-taking skills; (3) the verbal expression of mental states imputed to self and other (perception, physiological states, affects, cognitions, and moral judgments).

Self and Other: the Labeling of Body Parts

In his book *Play, Dreams and Imitation in Childhood* (1962), Piaget gives very detailed descriptions of his children's struggles with imitation, especially when they could not see themselves perform the actions that they were trying to replicate. Thus Lucienne, at 11 months, first opened and closed her fist, and then later her mouth in response to Piaget's demonstration of opening and closing the eyes. Only 3 months later did she finally master the correct movement. Laurent also started by confusing mouth with eyes, although he required only 1 month to achieve correct imitation after his first erroneous attempt at imitating eye opening and closing. Jacqueline struggled from 11½ to 12½ months before she was able to touch her index finger to her forehead like the model and not her eye instead.

Piaget (1962, Pp. 42–43) theorizes that the idea of one-to-one correspondence of invisible bodily (facial and head) features is acquired through the use of indices:

> Although the child cannot picture his own mouth (and does not need to do so) he understands through the sound he hears that the movements he sees made by the mouths of others are concomitant with a certain tactilo-kinesthetic impression in his own mouth. In other words, thanks to the index, the child assimilates the visual and auditory model to the auditory motor schema with which he is familiar in himself, and imitation becomes possible through accommodation to this schema. The sound then becomes unnecessary, whereas if it were a signal it would have to persist as a stimulus, or, in case of transfer, itself be produced as a result of visual perception. When a silent, visual suggestion does in fact produce a vocal motor response (obs. 30) it is only transitory, and the sound very soon disappears.

The index can be established also via direct tactile comparison, as when babies explore their own and the model's mouth with their fingers.

Thus, there is evidence that the recognition of which *invisible* body parts on oneself correspond to which *visible* body parts on another human being is no easy achievement. We believe, however, that Piaget may have underestimated the contribution of language in the establishment of this one-to-one correspondence. Although we did not ask the mothers of the Boulder Sample how often they played body-part-labeling games with their infants, we did ask which labels the infants comprehended at 10½ and 13 months as well as how the mother inferred comprehension. Very frequently the answer turned out to be that the baby indicated comprehension by pointing to the correct part on self or other in response to the question: "Where's your nose, ears, eyes? Where's Mommy's nose, ears, eyes?" Interestingly, the body parts best known in comprehension at 10½ and 13 months and most frequently labeled at 20 months are precisely the head and facial features for which one-to-one correspondence is most difficult to discover (see Table 16.2).

When do children also find out that one sees with the eyes, hears with the ears, tastes with the mouth and tongue, and smells with the nose?

TABLE 16.2
List of Body-Part Labels Understood by the Boulder Sample
At 10½ and 13 Months and Produced at 20 Months
(Percentage of Sample)

Body Part	Comprehended at 10½ Months (N = 32)	Comprehended[a] at 13 Months (N = 32)	Labeled at 20 Months (N = 30)
Head Area			
Nose	10%	22%	67%
Eye(s)	3%	25%	60%
Hair	3%	6%	60%
Ear(s)	3%	3%	57%
Mouth	3%	19%	47%
Teeth	–	–	43%
Face	–	–	23%
Cheek(s)	–	–	20%
Tongue	3%	–	13%
Beard	–	–	3%
Chin	–	–	3%
Eyebrow(s)	–	–	3%
Head	–	3%	3%
Neck	–	3%	3%
Shoulder-Arm Area			
Hand(s)	3%	–	37%
Finger(s)	–	3%	30%
Arm(s)	–	–	20%
Elbow	–	–	7%
Shoulder	–	–	3%
Thumb	–	–	3%
Wrist	–	–	3%
Trunk Area			
Tummy (Belly)	3%	12%	37%
Bellybutton	–	3%	33%
Penis	–	12% (of males)	47% (of males)
Bottom (Butt)	–	–	13%
Back	–	–	7%
Chest	–	–	3%
Leg Area			
Feet (foot)	3%	25%	40%
Toes	3%	9%	37%
Knee(s)	–	–	30%
Leg(s)	–	–	23%

[a]Only two infants produced body-part labels at 13 months.

When do they discover that sight can be excluded by covering the eyes, sounds by covering the ears, and smell by holding the nose? There is no systematic information except for vision, although Yarrow and Waxler (1977) mention a child who held her hand over her ears during a parental quarrel, and Piaget (1962) describes Jacqueline, who at the age of 28 months, pulled her doll's hair away from the ears in order to make her listen to music.

In a study of two-year olds, Masangkay, McCluskey, McIntyre, Sims-Knight, Vaughn, and Flavell (1974) found that quite young children could accurately specify the object in an array of four at which an adult was gazing. Lempers, Flavell, and Flavell (1977) corroborated these results and also showed that 18- to 24-month olds when required to *prevent* an adult from seeing an object hit upon the idea of turning the adult away from the object. It was more difficult for children of this age to "fix it" so that an adult or doll with closed eyes could see an object (the child had to open the adult's eyes or turn the doll from a prone to a supine position).

Learning to label body parts on self and others and learning to label the associated sensory activities (seeing, smelling, hearing, tasting) are presumably instrumental in drawing young children's attention to the correspondence of their own to other people's sensory organs and associated perceptions, even though nonverbal cues may also be of help in establishing the correspondence.

Self and Other: Names and Pronouns

Using first-, second-, and third-person pronouns requires more than the discovery of a one-to-one correspondence between self and other selves, as observed in the acquisition of body-part labels. *I* and *you, my* and *your* are deictic words; that is, they point from a speaker to an addressee. Their correct usage therefore requires simple role-taking skills, because the reference shifts depending on who is speaker and who addressee. Personal pronouns are mastered earlier than other deictic word pairs, such as *come*, and *go, here* and *there, this* and *that*, which have a directional or distance component as well as a deictic component pointing to a speaker or addressee (Clark & Sengul, 1978).

Most of the Boulder Sample had begun to produce the labels Mommy or Daddy at 13 months (69% produced Mommy, 69% produced Daddy, and 81% produced Daddy or Mommy). On the other hand, only 10% of the children could say a version of their own name at this age on request or in response to seeing their image in a mirror. They did not use it to refer to themselves in communication. By 20 months, the situation had changed dramatically in some respects. Mother and father were still addressed as Mommy and Daddy, but 60% of the children could now say their names, although only 23% used their own names to refer to themselves in communication (i.e., Betty night-night). On the other hand, 75% had mastered at least one first-person pronoun, and all of these were used in communication. Table 16.3 lists the pronouns acquired, as well as how many children produced one, two, three, and four first-person pronouns. It also provides examples of how the pronouns were used in multiword utterances. The pronoun "I" only appeared in two-word or multiword utterances in this sample (we did not count formulaic uses such as a slurred "Iyuvyou" at bedtime). In spite of the fact that first-person-pronoun use was so frequent, only two children had started to address others as "you".

We know from other sources that children are often confused about the use of first- and second-person pronouns (Stern & Stern, 1928; Bloom & Lahey, 1978; Clark & Sengul, 1978). There are even examples in the literature of children who consistently refer to themselves as "you" (Halliday, 1975), but we do not know how long such errors usually last and whether they appear more frequently in complex rather than simple utterances. The children in the Boulder Sample seemed to have chosen the strategy of acquiring the first person pronouns for self-reference while still addressing others by name, using the principle of mastering one thing at a time. There are occasional anecdotes illustrating the reasoning process that some children go through in the process of acquiring correct pronouns. For example, Cathy (25 months) systematically inquired about ownership of the potty: "Is this my potty?". . ."Is it Tara's potty?". . ."Is it Mommy's potty?". . ."Is it Daddy's potty?" before finally concluding "It is OUR potty". The strategy of personal pronoun use deserves much more systematic study. Every time a child acquires the use of these pronouns, he or she rediscovers the person knowledge already built into the language, thus mastering the naïve psychology of roles, i.e., who is relating to whom and in what way as speaker, addressee, and bystander.

TABLE 16.3
First-Person Pronouns Used by the Boulder Sample (According to Maternal Interview)

No. of Pronouns	No. of Children Using Pronouns at 20 Months	Type of Pronouns	Examples of Pronoun Use in Multiword Utterances
0	6	–	–
1	6	5 mine or my 1 me	mine toy me out
2	6	4 me/my 2 my/mine	my baby
3	10	4 I/my/mine 3 I/me/mine 2 me/my/mine 1 I/me/mine	I'm hungry
4	6	6 I/me/my/mine	

Self and Other: Imputing Mental States

The mere fact that infants engage in intentional communication requires, as we suggested earlier, that they impute mental states to themselves and to others. But can one be more specific about *which* states are imputed? By using the technique of "rich interpretation" (interpreting communicative behavior within its total context; see Bloom, 1970; Brown, 1973), one can infer that a child who habitually uses vocalizations to request objects or actions probably imputes auditory perception to others and that a child who systematically uses manual gestures such as pointing probably imputes vision to others. Furthermore, a child who habitually bangs on a container while looking back and forth from the container to mother (requesting what is inside) probably imputes shared *knowledge* and *memory* to the mother. A young child who takes a security blanket to a crying playmate probably imputes *distress* and knows that this state is changeable (Hoffman, 1975). It is from the consistency with which children engage in such behaviors, as well as from associated cues such as tone of voice and facial expression, that an observer may infer that the children are imputing specific mental states to themselves and to others. With the child's acquisition of first words, the observer's inferential task becomes thankfully somewhat easier. A child who says "no" as her mother reaches for a toy probably imputes *wanting* to her mother; a child who says "there ball" to his brother is probably imputing *shared perception*; a child who says "man cry" (Main, Weston, & Wakeling, 1979) to a crying clown in a sad tone of voice seems to be imputing *distress*; a child who takes a toy to her mother saying "fix" imputes *ability* and *knowledge* to the mother that the child does not have herself. A child who says "horsie all gone" when driving past a field that used to contain horses or a child who asks "where Daddy?" when his father is not present is fairly obviously imputing *memory* to his partner. Piaget (1954, p. 347) reports a particularly striking example of the latter:

> OBS. 173a. At 1;6(15) Jacqueline weeps while calling her mother. I imitate her, repeating, "Mama, Mama," in a tearful tone, and she laughs. Two days later, at 1;6(17); we play at reproducing the sounds of animals and Jacqueline inserts this memory into the game: "How does the goat go?" "Meh." "And the cow?" "Moo." "And the dog?" "Voovoo." "And Jacqueline?" "Mama." This final answer is given by imitating exactly the tone of the other day and with a *meaningful smile,* which demonstrates clearly that Jacqueline is *alluding* to a past behavior pattern and is not making up a new game (italics added).

The onset of language makes it easier for researchers and mothers to infer what the child is implicitly imputing because the messages become more precise. But, when do children begin to label states or processes of perception, physiological deprivation, affect, cognition, and moral judgement explicitly? In an attempt to probe the first emergence of a variety of internal-state labels, we interviewed the mothers of the Boulder Sample (see Table 16.4). The mother was first asked whether the child produced the particular label at all, and then whether she or he used it to refer to her/himself, to others, or to pictures and representations of others. For each use, the mother was requested to supply a concrete example. Labels that describe affect expression (kiss, cry) as well as psychological labels (love, happy, sad, mad, scared) were included on the assumption that reference to emotional behavior would precede labels for emotional states. However, labels of emotional expression *were* assumed to have strong connotations of emotional state and, conversely, the psychological labels to have strong connotations of emotional expression (at 13 months many mothers used the expression "give Mommy love" to request a hug). Some of the perceptual labels included in the questionnaire could be projected inward to refer to a mental state of self or other, or, they could be projected outward to describe the state of an object. When an object is described as "cold" for example, the child refers to perceived property, but the coldness is presumed to reside in the object (outward projection). If a child refers to feeling cold herself, she is labeling a perceptual state (the feeling of coldness resides in herself). The frequencies given in the table for hot, cold, wet, dry, dirty, good, and bad always refer to labels applied to a person rather than to a thing being hot (such as a stove) or bad (such as food). There are other potential uses such as "the ice feels cold" or "the milk tastes bad" in which the perceptual quality is emphasized, but we did not ask about perceptual verbs in this preliminary study.

As expected, the concrete expressive labels (cry, kiss) were indeed mastered by a large number of infants at 20 months, but note that not one child produced the label "smile" even though a number of children could apply the corresponding psychological label "happy" appropriately. Perhaps the smile is not so distinct behaviorally as tears, a puckered face, and the sound effects that one labels "crying". Sadness may be more tied to one of its behavioral referents, namely "crying", than happiness is to "smiling".

In addition to "happy", a small but not negligible number of children referred to themselves and/or others as hungry thirsty, tired, sad, mad, and scared (all psychological rather than behavioral labels). The word "hot" was produced by almost all children in the sample to refer to stoves or liquids, but much more rarely to refer to a perceptual state. A larger number of children spoke of themselves as "cold", particularly in the form "brr-cold," a fact that might relate to the season during which the data were collected. The perception of pain (or inference of pain in others) is labeled very frequently, but as yet more often by the conventionalized pain-cry "ouch" than the adult term "hurt", although one child said "hurt" when her mother called out "ouch" in pain. Despite the fact that many children

TABLE 16.4
Number of Children in the Boulder Sample Who Used the Following Internal-State Words at 20 Months (According to the Maternal Report)

State Word	Applied to Self	Applied to Other Persons	Applied to Doll or Picture
Perceptual			
Cold and Brr-cold	8	2	0
Brr	3	1	0
Hot	5	0	0
Wet	14	4	0
Dry	5	1	0
Hurt	9	4	0
Ouch, Owie	21	9	1
Physiological			
Hungry	4	0	0
Thirsty	3	0	0
Sleep	7	7	5
Sleepy	4	4	0
Tired	2	0	0
Night-night, Bye-bye (to mean sleepy or sleeping)	11	6	4
Emotional			
Positive			
Happy	5	1	0
Smile	0	0	0
Funny	1	2	0
Kiss	14	13	4
Love	11	6	2
Emotional			
Negative			
Sad	0	2	1
Cry	4	13	8
Mad (Angry)	0	1	1
Scared	2	0	0
Dirty (Disgust)	12	8	1
Yuck (Ick, etc.)	12	6	0
Gross	1	0	0
Messy	0	0	0
Phtew	1	0	0
Ability			
Hard (difficult)	2	1	0
Moral			
Good	12	4	0
Nice	7	10	2
Gentle	3	2	0
Bad	6	7	1
Naughty	0	0	1
No-no (meaning bad)	2	0	1

already used the adult labels "tired", "sleepy", an equal number extended the meaning of the bedtime greeting "night-night" to refer to the state of sleeping as well as to the feeling of sleepiness.

The meaning of mental state and its correlated external expression are intertwined in the early use of these labels. Do they therefore only refer to external behavior? We do not think so. There is indirect evidence that words such as "sleepy" carry state meaning. For example, a child who says "tired" when her eyes are not closed and she is not lying down is *informing* her mother of an internal state that the mother may already have inferred from the child's sluggishness or whining.

In addition to interviewing the mothers of the Boulder Sample about their infants' production of internal-state labels, we conducted a comprehension test for emotion labels. The infants were shown a book containing nine pairs of test pictures that had been pretested during another study of preschool children (Blackmon, personal communication) with filler items to retain the baby's interest. Pictures of children and infants, each showing a distinct emotion, were presented in pairs as follows: sad-happy, happy-mad, sad-happy, crying-smiling, happy-serious, sad-mad, happy-sad, and sad-happy. For each emotion pair, the tester would point and say: "Here's a baby (boy, girl) and here's another baby (boy, girl). Can you show me the happy (sad, mad, crying, smiling) baby (boy, girl)?" The book was shown twice, asking first for one, then for the other expression. Because this test was part of a large correlational study, the pictures were presented in the same order to all children, but randomized with respect to which emotion (positive or negative) was requested first and where the first target picture was located (right or left page). Had responses been entirely random – and most children recognized that they were required to point to a picture – about 50% correct responses could have been expected overall. Because the pictures were presented in pairs, random responding would have resulted in 25% correct identifications of both members of a pair, 25% incorrect identifications of both members of a pair, and 50% correct identifications of one picture in a pair. For the whole sample, we found significantly more instances of correct pointing to *both* members of a pair than incorrect pointing to *both* members ($X^2(1) = 6.9$, $p < 0.01$), but this result was largely due to one sad – happy pair that was identified correctly by 40% of the children. Only four children correctly identified four picture pairs out of nine. Thus, it appears that comprehension is not far ahead of the production of emotion labels in 20-month-old infants.

Spontaneous production of labels (not counting echoing) also concurred during this comprehension test. Most instances of labeling involved the word "cry," a result that corroborates the mothers' report about the frequent use of that word (see Table 16.4). Twelve of the children (six boys and six girls) spontaneously labeled pictures of sad children as "he cry," "crying," "baby cry", "uh-oh, cry", sometimes with wiping of tears, imitation of crying noises, and kissing the baby picture. Only in two cases did this happen as an echoing response when the child was asked to point to the crying baby (see pair 5); *in no case was a mad or happy face labeled as crying*. Saying "uh-oh" and kissing and wiping the tears of the child in the picture could be interpreted as evidence for concern (and therefore as evidence that the word had affective as well as behavioral connotations).

The findings on internal-state labeling by 20-month olds led us to conduct a literature search for examples of internal-stage language in young children up to 36 months of age. Only utterances for which the context was also supplied were included, and our major sources were: (1) Stern and Stern (1928) who describe the language development of their three children as well as quoting from other contemporary diaries; (2) a series of studies by Bloom and her colleagues (Bloom, 1970, 1973; Bloom & Lahey, 1978; Bloom, Lightbown, & Hood, 1975; Hood & Bloom, 1979). In addition, we collaborated with Lynn Tracy who for 8 weeks collected utterances made by her 25–26-month-old daughter, Cathy (Cathy's mother had, incidentally, *not* noticed that Cathy had begun to use words labeling internal states and processes until she began to write down Cathy's utterances systematically). The results of our compilation are summarized in Table 16.5 according to six categories (perception, physiology, emotion, volition and ability, cognition, and moral judgment).

A large number of the utterances containing emotion labels came from data collected or reported by parents (Stern & Stern, 1928; the Boulder Sample; Cathy's mother) rather than from direct observations made by researchers. This bias in the collection of utterances makes it difficult to draw quantitative conclusions about the data.

[. . .]

We were not only interested in the variety of labels used (although we think it impressive), but in whether the children applied the label to others as well as to themselves. Table 16.5 shows that many internal-state labels were indeed applied to others (statements about seeing, wanting, hunger fatigue and feeling pain), although we discovered more instances of self-labeling than other-labeling. Only a developmental study could show whether self-labeling generally precedes other labeling. Note that Table 16.4 lists a few examples to the contrary in 20-month-old infants (the verb *cry* was used by more children to label others, and *mad* was used by two children about their mother, but not to label their own state). Whether a label is first applied to the self or to another may depend on the individual label, but *when* a label is appropriately applied both to self and others by the same child, we have evidence that psychological one-to-one correspondence has been achieved for that label, and that the state can be symbolically represented.

TABLE 16.5
Summary of Internal-State Words Used by Children up to 36 Months

Type of Internal-State Word	Age First Reported (in Months)	Applied to Self	Applied to Other	Applied to Doll or Picture	Negated, Used in Past or Future Tense or Question	Used in Causal Sentence
Perceptual						
See, look	11	X	X	X	X	X
Watch	24	X	X			X
Hear	14½	X	X		X	
Listen	22		X			
Taste	26	X	X		X	X
Feel (to touch)	24½	X				
Cold	20	X	X	X	X	X
Freezing	25	X			X	X
Hot	20	X				X
Warm	25			X		
Hurt	20	X	X	X		X
Ouch, boo-boo	18½	X	X			X
Physiological						
Hungry	20	X		X	X	
Starving	25	X				
Thirsty	20	X			X	
Sleep	20	X	X	X	X	X
Sleepy	20	X				
Tired	17	X			X	
Awake, wake up	28		X	X	X	X
Emotional						
Positive						
Happy, pleased	20	X	X	X	X	
Fun	25	X			X	
Funny	20	X	X			
Feel (emotional)	25	X	X		X	
All right	25		X		X	
Nice	20	X	X			
Like	22½	X	X		X	
Love	20	X				
Hug	20	X		X		
Kiss	20	X	X	X	X	
Negative						
Sad	20	X	X	X		
Mad	20	X	X	X	X	X
Scared	20	X			X	
Scary	20	X	X	X		
Dirty	20	X	X	X		X
Messy	20	X	X			
Bad (feeling)	20	X	X			
Cry	17	X	X	X	X	X

Table 16.5 (*continued*)

Table 16.5 (continued)

Type of Internal-State Word	Age First Reported (in Months)	Applied to Self	Applied to Other	Applied to Doll or Picture	Negated, Used in Past or Future Tense or Question	Used in Causal Sentence
Volition and Ability						
Want	20	X	X	X	X	X
Need	22	X	X			X
Have to	25	X			X	
Can	20	X	X		X	X
Hard	20	X	X			
Cognition						
Know	15	X			X	X
Think	23½	X	X		X	
Remember	26	X			X	
Believe	26	X			X	
Maybe	33	X				
May	33	X				
Seem	29	X				
Understand	28		X			
Pretend	29	X	X	X		
Moral Judgment						
Good	20	X	X			
Bad, naughty	20	X	X	X		
May	25	X			X	
Let	25		X		X	
Supposed to	25	X	X		X	
Must	34	X				

Note: The table indicates the age at which each word was first used, whether it was applied to self and/or others, and the types of utterance. The data were obtained from the Boulder Sample, a pilot study, and various published sources.

In addition to noting the person to whom the label is applied, we were also interested in the extent to which a child could use a label *outside* the situation in which the particular emotion or state was felt or experienced. If a child says "me hungry", he or she is talking about a state presently being experienced. But if a child says "I was hungry", he or she is talking about past experience. The first statement could be replaced by pointing at food and making a peremptory sound; the second statement could not. The second type of statement indicates that the child cannot only label the state when it occurs, but can use it for the symbolic manipulation of knowledge and for the symbolic sharing of such knowledge outside the narrow context of the experience itself. The same is true of statements in which a state is denied ("Me no hungry") or couched in the future tense ("I will be hungry"). (See Table 16.5 for how frequently such statements were found in the literature.)

Another extremely important aspect of knowledge and communication about the internal states of self and others is the attribution of cause and effect (including as cause or effect a person's internal state and behavior). Table 16.6 illustrates that causal utterances about the internal states of self and others appear almost as early as internal-state labeling itself. Note that almost half of the statements that we collected were made by children under 26 months of age.

TABLE 16.6

Child Utterances About the Possible Cause or Resolution (Termination) of
Internal States Experienced by Self and Others

State	Utterance	Age	State of Self	State of Other
Perceptual States				
SEE	"Want out/see wow-wow."	22½	X	
	"Seen enough today/Go night-night again". (also under WANT)	27		X
WATCH:	"I left it open, because I wanna watch it (TV)."	31	X	
COLD:	"Brr-cold. Get jacket."	20	X	
	"Cold. Cold feet. Put heater up."	21	X	
	"Baby blanket – cold." (about doll)	23		X
	"Close (window) – so Bubi doesn't freeze."	26½	X	
HOT:	"If I get too hot, I sweat."	33	X	
HURT:	"Head-ouch-cut."	17	X	
	"Doctur hurt Mommy/stone-stick." (threat)	20		X
	"Christy fell down/hurt self."	24½	X	
	"I'm putting medicine on the lamb's leg cause he had a boo-boo." (pretend play)	31½		X
Physiological States				
SLEEP:	"Daddy sleep. Mustn't shout, Daddy finish sleeping – me can shout again.	31		X
TIRED:	"Tired, tired? Chair-yes? Sit."	21½	X	
WAKE UP:	"Don't ring the bell either. Jenny will wake up."	35		X
Emotional States				
SAD:	"Her eyes are crying – her sad."	26		X
	"I'm sad I popped it." (balloon)	25	X	
	"Goes train. We sad." (about father's trip)	30	X	X
	"Today (we will) both go on trip. Else (should) not be sad. . . . (because we will) come back."	33		X
HAPPY:	"Günther made Mommy happy."	31		X

(Table 16.6 *continued*)

Table 16.6 (continued)

State	Utterance	Age	State of Self	State of Other
PLEASED:	"He pleased of (about) Hilde."	33		X
MAD:	"If I cry I'm mad. If you cry I'll be mad."	26	X	X
SCARE:	"That doesn't scare me." (scare is causative)	20	X	
	"Those ladies scare me."	25	X	
DIRTY:	"Baby/splash/dirty."	20½		X
BAD:	"Daisy gone. No more in garden. (I feel) bad."	25½	X	
CRY:	"Baby cry/hurt/breast." (Baby needs to be fed)	17		X
	"Don't say shhh to me. I wanna cry."			
	(also under MAD and WANT)	26	X	
States of Volition and Ability				
WANT:	"(Child is) crying/want Mommy."	24½		X
	"I want to go door see my Mommy."	25½	X	
	(also under SEE and CRY)			
NEED:	"You need a stool to climb up."	25½		X
CAN:	"Can't. Too hard."	20	X	
	"The door is open so I can get in."	33	X	
	"When I was a little girl I could go 'geek-geek' like that, but now I can go 'this is a chair.' "	34	X	
	"Now you can try one/cause I teached you."			
	(also under KNOW)	35		X
Cognitive States				
KNOW:	"Could you read this to me, cause I don't know how."	35½	X	
States of Moral Obligation				
MUST:	"Doll is going to sleep. Must be quiet."			
	(also under SLEEP)	34	X	

Hood and Bloom (1979) also analyzed causal utterances produced by children in their second and third years. They found that the majority of causal statements made by the children in their sample were concerned with the activities and internal states of people ("I want to go door see my Mommy"), rather than with the behavior of physical objects ("Cup fall so it broke"). Physical objects obey the laws of what Aristotle has called efficient causality (direct push, gravity, etc.) whereas persons usually influence each other via what Aristotle has called final causality (will, motivation). As scientists, we know much more about efficient causality in the domain of physical reality than about final causality as it is exercised in personal interaction. Yet it appears, on the basis of Hood and Bloom's findings, that psychological causality is much more salient for young children than physical causality. Moreover, our own inventory of causal statements would suggest that children are as interested in explaining others' internal states as they are in explaining their own.

Lastly, the fact that young children sometimes *question* others about their internal states ("Are you alright?"), or question one person about the internal state of a third ("Is Tara mad at me?") indicates awareness that the states of others are not always easy to infer. The same is true of statements indicating uncertainty such as "I think that man is going camping" or "He may want to play with the truck". It appears that at a very young age children are *beginning* to realize that the interfacing of minds has to be achieved through communication, that intersubjectivity is not automatic. Thus, young children are neither radical egocentrists, nor radical behaviorists.

CONCLUSIONS

From a theory of interfacible minds, which is *implicit* in infants' first attempts at intentional communication at the end of the first year, young children progress to an *explicit, verbally expressible* theory of mind that begins to emerge at the end of the second year. At this stage in their development, children become capable of exchanging verbal information about internal states as experienced by themselves and by others and the fact that they do so allows us to make a number of inferences about the state of their person knowledge.

Let us now return to the 12-point person model proposed by Shields (1978) as a minimum prerequisite for the occurrence of communication and for the later development of role-taking skills. The data on the development of language and communication that we have presented lend support to each of Shields' 12 points and to two additional points of our own. In their language, children between 12 and 36 months of age *explicitly* (as well as implicitly) express the knowledge:

1. that persons have identity over time despite changes in location: by talking about "daddy at work"; persons have identity despite changes in behavior, state, and appearance by commenting on "daddy sleeping," "mommy mad.";
2. that persons are self-moving or animate: by making requests for actions or objects; influence over the course of their behavior has to be negotiated by "look," "watch," "listen.";
3. that persons identify each other: and can react to each other by naming and correctly using personal pronouns;
4. that persons see, hear, smell, feel (touch), feel temperature, and feel pain: by using the appropriate labels for these experiences; persons have a perceptual field by asking "did you see?", or commenting "I can't see," "want to see," "daddy didn't hear";

5. that persons intend their actions: by "I want," "you want," "baby wants," "I'm going to.";
6. that persons conceptualize and construct their world in roughly similar ways: through language itself, but also by asking questions or stating "I know,""you know.";
7. that persons have moods and states such as joy, anger, sadness, and fear as well as likes and dislikes: (mad) by words denoting these feelings and states: "mom" "K. likes me," "I love K..";
8. that persons can send and receive messages based on gestures and words: that are related to context in stable ways by using the medium of language for communication: the messages are sometimes successfully, sometimes unsuccessfully, received by "understand," "daddy didn't hear";
9. that persons have an action potential: by commenting "I can," "I know how," "I don't think I can"; some persons have a higher action potential than others by "only daddy can," "now you can try cause I taught you";
10. that persons can retain previous experience and structure their present behavior by it: through requests for repetition and words like remember; that people can sometimes forget previous experience or knowledge by "I don't remember";
11. that persons can replicate previous behavior in new contexts: by "pretend that. . .," "I known how. . .," "You can. . .";
12. that persons share a set of rules about what is appropriate behavior within particular frames of action: by "you supposed to," "good boy," "bad girl," and polite language like "hi," "bye," "please," "thank you";
13. that interpersonal behavior is regulated by reciprocal consent: using words such as "let," "may," "may not";
14. that the internal states of others are not always unambiguously expressed and have to be inferred: by "Is T. mad at me?" "Moo. Dyahear?"

There can be no question that very young children have a fairly sophisticated model of others and of themselves as psychological beings, even though they still make many errors of attribution and find it difficult to manipulate many aspects of their person knowledge simultaneously, as required in the traditional egocentrism tests (see Flavell et al., 1968).

But is the capacity to talk about internal states related to interpersonal functioning? It would seem reasonable to suppose that being able to give verbal expression to one's states should facilitate interaction and lead to the acquisition of further knowledge through feedback (having one's misconceptions corrected). Until the research results are in, however, we cannot be sure that this is so.

Furthermore, it is likely that were we to look, we would discover individual differences in the extent to which children talk about the perceptions, intentions, feelings, thoughts, and activities of persons and the degree to which they talk about the properties of physical objects. In play, analogous differences have been noted by Shotwell, Wolf and Gardner (1979), who observed that some children prefer to reenact person-related events in symbolic play (dramatists), and others explore the structure of the physical world in combinatorial play (patterners). Clarke-Stewart (1973) found boys at 20 months to be more object-oriented and girls to be more person-oriented. Are these differences also reflected in the vocabulary of the children? What we have in mind is slightly different from the expressive-referential dichotomy described by Nelson (1973) when she studied the acquisition of the first 50 words. Some of her subjects used language as a tool for *regulating* interaction (expressive) and some to talk *about* the object world (referential). We are instead interested in whether there are children who specialize in *analyzing* the social rather than the object world – in infant psychologists versus infant physicists. Does preference for combinatorial play go with a more sophisticated object vocabulary and preference for symbolic play go with a more articulated internal-state vocabulary?

If individual differences such as these are found to exist, where do they originate? Are they associated with the child's temperament (and related cognitive style) or with the harmoniousness of mother-child interaction? Or are they perhaps more specifically related to how often internal-state words are mentioned by adults in the child's environment and *when* a state is labeled (while the child is experiencing it or attending to someone else experiencing it)? These and many other research questions remain to be answered.

ACKNOWLEDGMENTS

During the writing of this paper, the authors were supported by a grant from the Spencer Foundation. The research reported in this paper was funded by a grant from the National Science Foundation (BNS76–17624) and a grant from the Spencer Foundation to E. Bates and I. Bretherton. We would like to express our appreciation to the mothers and infants of the Boulder Sample and to Vicki Carlson, Karlana Carpen, Andy Garrison, Cecilia Shore, and Carol Williamson who helped with the data collection and analysis. We also thank Lynn Tracy for recording her daughter's internal-state utterances.

REFERENCES

Bates, E. (1979). Intentions conventions and symbols. In E. Bates et al. (Eds), *The emergence of symbols; Cognition and communication in infancy.* New York: Academic Press.
Bates, E., Benigni, L., Bretherton, I., Camaioni, L., & Volterra, V. (1979). Cognition and communication from 9–13 months: Correlational findings. In E. Bates *et al.* (Eds), *The emergence of symbols: Cognition and communication in infancy.* New York: Academic Press.

Bates, E., Camaioni, L., & Volterra, V. (1975). The acquisition of performatives prior to speech. *Merrill-Palmer Quarterly, 21(3)*, 205–226.

Bell, S. M. (1970). The development of the concept of object as related to infant-mother attachment. *Child Development, 41*, 291–313.

Bloom, L. (1970). *Language development: Form and function in emerging grammars.* Cambridge, Mass.: MIT Press.

Bloom, L. (1973). *One word at a time.* The Hague: Mouton.

Bloom, L., & Lahey, M. (1978). *Language development and language disorders.* New York: Wiley.

Bloom, L., Lightbown, P., & Hood, L. (1975). Structure and variation in child language. *Monograph of the Society for Research in Child Development*, No.2.

Brazelton, T. B., Kozlowski, B., & Main, M. (1974). *The origins of reciprocity: The early mother-infant interaction.* In M. Lewis & L. A. Rosenblum (Eds) *The effect of the infant on its caregiver.* New York: Wiley.

Bretherton, I., & Bates, E. (1979). The emergence of intentional communication. In I. Uzgiris (Ed.) *New directions for child development* (Vol. 4). San Francisco: Jossey-Bass.

Brown, R. (1973). *A first language: The early stages.* Cambridge, Mass.: Harvard University Press.

Bruner, J. S., (1977). Early social interaction and language acquisition. In H. R. Schafer (Ed.) *Studies in mother-infant interaction.* New York: Academic Press.

Clark, E. (1978). Awareness of language: Some evidence from what children say and do. In A. Sinclair, R. T. Jarvella & W. T. M. Levelt (Eds) *The child's conception of language.* New York: Springer-Verlag.

Clark, E. V., & Sengul, C. J. (1978). Strategies in the acquisition of deixis. *Journal of Child Language, 5*, 457–475.

Clarke-Stewart, K. A. (1973). Interactions between mothers and their young children: Characteristics and consequences. *Monographs of the Society for Research in Child Development, 37*, No. 153.

Edwards, D. (1978). Social relations and early language. In A. Lock (Ed.) *Action, gesture and symbol.* New York: Academic Press.

Flavell, T. H. (1963). *The developmental psychology of Jean Piaget.* New York: Van Nostrand.

Flavell, T. H. (1974). The development of inferences about others. In T. Mischel (Ed.), *Understanding other persons.* Totowa, N.J.: Rowam & Littlefield.

Flavell, T. H., Botkin, P. T., & Fry, C. L. (1968). *The development of role-taking and communication skills in young children.* New York: Wiley.

Grice, H. P., (1968). Utterer's meaning, sentence-meaning, and word-meaning. *Foundation of Language, 4*, 1–18.

Habermas, T. (1972). *Knowledge and human interests.* London: Heinemann.

Hamlyn, D. W. (1974). Person-perception and our understanding of others. In T. Mischel (Ed.), *Understanding other persons.* Oxford: Blackwell.

Halliday, M. A. (1975). *Learning how to mean: Explorations in the development of language.* London: Edward Arnold.

Heider, F. (1958). *The psychology of interpersonal relations.* New York: Wiley.

Hoffman, M. L. (1975). Developmental synthesis of affect and cognition and its implications for altruistic motivation. *Developmental Psychology, 11*, 607–622.

Hood, L., & Bloom, L. (1979). What, when and how about why: A longitudinal study of early expressions of causality. *Monograph of the Society for Research in Child Development, 44*, Serial No. 181.

Jackson, E., Campos, J. J., & Fischer, K. W. (1978). The question of decalage between object permanence and person permanence. *Developmental Psychology, 14*, 1–10.

Killen, M., & Uzgiris, I. (1978, March). *Imitation of actions with objects: The role of social meaning.* Paper presented at the International Conference on Infant Studies, Providence, R. I.

Lempers, T., Flavell, E., & Flavell, T. H. (1977). The development in very young children of tacit knowledge concerning visual perception. *Genetic Psychology Monographs, 95,* 3–53.

Lewis, M., & Brooks-Gunn, J. (1979). Toward a theory of social cognition: The development of self. In I. Uzgiris (Ed.), *New directions for child development (Vol. 4).* San Francisco, Jossey-Bass.

Main, M., Weston, D., & Wakeling, S. (1979, March). *"Concerned attention" to the crying of an adult actor.* Paper presented at the Biennial Meeting of the Society for Research in Child Development, San Francisco.

Masangkay, Z., McCluskey, K., McIntyre, C., Sims-Knight J., Vaughn, B., & Flavell, E. (1974). The early development of inferences about the visual percepts of others. *Child Development, 45,* 357–366.

Meltzoff, A., & Moore, M. K. (1977). Imitations of facial and manual gestures by human neonates. *Science, 198,* 75–78.

Murphy, C. M., & Messer, J. D. (1977). Mothers, infants and pointing: A study of a gesture. In H. R. Schaffer (Ed.), *Studies in mother-infant interaction.* New York: Academic Press.

Nelson, K. (1973). Structure and strategy in learning to talk. *Monographs of the Society for Research in Child Development, 48,* Serial No. 149.

Newson, T. (1977). An intersubjective approach to the systematic description of mother-infant interaction. In H. R. Schaffer (Ed.), *Studies in mother-infant interaction.* New York: Academic Press.

Piaget, J. (1954). *The construction of reality in the child.* New York: Basic Books.

Piaget, J. (1962). *Play, dreams and imitation in childhood.* New York: Norton.

Piaget, J. (1963). *The origins of intelligence in children.* New York.

Premack, D., & Woodruff, G. (1978). Does the chimpanzee have a theory of mind? *The Behavioral and Brain Sciences, 1,* 516–526.

Rheingold, H. L., Gewirtz, J. L., & Ross, H. W. (1959). Social conditioning of vocalization in the infant. *Journal of Comparative and Physiological Psychology, 52,* 68–73.

Rubin, S., & Wolf, D. (1980). The development of maybe: The evolution of roles into narrative. In E. Winner (Ed.) *New directions for child development (Vol. 6).* San Francisco: Jossey-Bass.

Sander, L. W. (1977). The regulation of exchange in the infant-caregiver system and some aspects of the context-content relationship. In M. Lewis & L. A. Rosemblum (Eds) *Interaction, conversation and the development of language.* New York: Academic Press.

Scaife, M., & Bruner, J.S. (1975). The capacity for joint visual attention in the infant. *Nature, 253,* 265–266.

Shields, M. M. (1978). The child as psychologist: Construing the social world. In A. Lock (Ed.), *Action, gesture and symbol.* New York: Academic Press.

Shotter, T. (1978). The cultural context of communication studies: Theoretical and methodological issues. In A. Lock (Ed.), *Action, gesture and symbol.* New York: Academic Press.

Shotwell, J., Wolf, D., & Gardner, H. (1979). Exploring early symbolization: Styles of achievement. In B. Sutton-Smith (Ed.), *Play and learning.* New York: Gardner Press.

Stern, C., & Stern, W. (1928). *Die Kindersprache: Eine psychologische und sprachtheoretische Untersuchung.* (4th ed.). Leipzig: Barth.

Stern, D. (1977). *The first relationship: Infant and mother.* Cambridge, Mass.: Harvard University Press.

Trevarthen, C., & Hubley, P. (1978). Secondary intersubjectivity: Confidence, confiding and acts of meaning in the first year. In A. Lock (Ed.), *Action, gesture and symbol*. New York: Academic Press.

Wood, D., Bruner, J. S., & Ross, G. (1976). The role of tutoring in problem solving. *Journal of Child Psychology and Psychiatry, 17,* 89–100.

Yarrow, M. R., & Waxler, C. Z. (1979). The emergence and functions of prosocial behaviors in young children. In B. Sutton-Smith (Ed.), *Play and learning*. New York: Gardner Press.

VI CONTINUITY

17 Continuity in Mental Development from Infancy

Marc H. Bornstein and Marian D. Sigman

In this reading we document moderate continuity in mental development beginning in infancy and extending into childhood. Psychological opinion in the past has tended to favor discontinuity theories of cognitive development from infancy. In recent years, however, the foundations on which discontinuity positions were originally established have themselves come under question and new findings grounded in new assessment procedures have appeared, necessitating revision of opinion on this significant psychological and developmental issue. Our reading has several aims. We first review briefly the bases for contemporary discontinuity theories of mental development. Second, we present current findings that support the alternative proposition of continuity: Recent research demonstrates that infants who more efficiently encode visual stimuli or more efficiently recollect visual or auditory stimuli tend to perform more proficiently on traditional psychometric assessments of intelligence and language during childhood. Third, we scrutinize the assessment methods from which these continuity results derive. Fourth, we offer several models that help to explain the continuity findings. Fifth, we discuss critically the origins and the maintenance of continuity in mental development as it is coming to be conceptualized currently. Finally, we reflect on implications of continuity for the future of infant assessments specifically and for theories of early mental development generally.

Source: *Child Development*, (1986), *57*, pp. 251–274.

THE QUESTION OF CONTINUITY IN
COGNITIVE DEVELOPMENT

The assessment of cognitive competence early in life and the prediction of mature cognitive stature from early performance are compelling and abiding topics of infancy studies. These two issues have justly provoked wide research attention in the past. On the basis of a half-century of inquiry, it was commonly believed that there is little or no association between cognitive performance in infancy and cognitive performance later in childhood and in adulthood. In the light of contemporary data, however, our interpretation of infant cognition and our understanding of growth in mental development from infancy warrant reformulation. In this essay we undertake such a reevaluation.

Since early in this century, standardized developmental tasks – the classic sequences, scales, and schedules of infant testing – have provided invaluable descriptions of the normative course of early human ontogenesis (Brooks-Gunn & Weinraub, 1983, provide a summary). The questions of defining mental ability in infancy and of assaying stability in mental development from infancy have usually been addressed through initial developmental testing in infancy followed up longitudinally into childhood with more traditional psychometric assessments of intelligence. For example, Bayley (1949) retested a cohort of 27 children from 3 months to 18 years of age and then correlated their Bayley test scores (at several points in infancy and early childhood) with their intelligence test scores in young adulthood (at 18 years). No correlation between testings over the first 4 years of life and intelligence in maturity obtained. Only after children reached about 5 years of age did Bayley find that the correlation between child scores and eventual adult scores rises to 0.60, attaining a peak of about 0.90 between 11 and 18 years. These early findings have been widely replicated (Honzik, 1983; Kopp & McCall, 1980). Although the predictive power of developmental tests administered to infants older than 12 months is somewhat greater than that of tests administered in the first year (Wilson, 1983), and longitudinal relations appear to be stronger for certain populations, such as high-risk infants (Cohen & Parmelee, 1983; Siegel, 1983), correlations between traditional developmental measures administered in the first year of life and childhood intelligence tests have regularly proven uniformly low (Fagan & Singer, 1983; Kopp & McCall, 1980).

From these data, several global "discontinuity" hypotheses about normal cognitive growth have emerged: (1) that there is no general intelligence factor, g; (2) that if g exists, it is not a fixed or stable attribute; and (3) that if g exists, whatever it is in infancy, it is very different from whatever it is in maturity and further, that it does not follow automatically that to be intelligent at one age is to be intelligent at another (for summaries, see

Eysenck & Kamin, 1981; Kopp & McCall, 1980; Lewis, 1983; Vernon, 1980). Although these popular interpretations of early mental development differ, they have two important factors in common. They derive from the same general data set, and, based on that data set, they reject continuity in mental development from infancy. However, this data set can be challenged – not for lack of quality in the data themselves but because of how mental ability was initially conceived, operationalized, and standardized in infant tests. For instance, the Bayley Scales of Infant Development (Bayley, 1969) largely tap sensory and motor capacities, such as reaching, grasping, and orienting,[1] that bear little conceptual relation to measures included in traditional psychometric tests of intelligence administered in childhood. In short, what has been asked of children at different ages changes, and so on reflection we have had little cause to expect task performance in infancy to be related to intellectual performance in childhood.

As a consequence, our understanding of continuity in mental development has been restricted, and the continuity hypothesis has proved to be an inadequate test. There has been continuing need to identify and apply new measures to the assessment of cognitive functioning in infancy. This general need to expand infant tests operationally was noted by several investigators in the past, including Fagan (1975), Fantz and Nevis (1967), Lewis (1971), McCall (1971), and Wechsler (1963). To wit, assessments of the predictive validity of intelligence ought ideally to embrace information-processing skills in infancy in psychometrically sound ways that are relatively free of motor limitations. As if in response to this exigency, two classes of information-processing measures applied in the first year of life – decrement and recovery of attention – have been examined recently, and both have been found to show moderate but significant levels of continuity with measures of cognitive competence in childhood.

AN INFORMATION-PROCESSING ORIENTATION TO INFANT COGNITIVE COMPETENCE: EVIDENCE FOR CONTINUITY

Attention has long been conceived as an "avenue to the study of cognitive development" (McCall, 1971); indeed among experts in educational testing attention has traditionally been construed as definitional to intelligence (see Stankov, 1983, for a review). Two measures of attention have been identified as potential indexes of mental ability in infancy. They are the *decrement of attention* that infants manifest to an aspect of the environment that is unchanging, and the *recovery of attention* that infants demonstrate

---

[1]For example, at 4 months the Mental Development Index and the Psychomotor Development Index of the Bayley Scales correlate at 0.70.

to an aspect of the environment that is novel. Decrement of attention, frequently referred to as "habituation" or "total fixation time," is usually indexed by the amount or rate of decay in looking or by the cumulative amount of looking infants show to a repeated or a constant stimulus. Greater decrements, quicker decays, or relatively lesser amounts of cumulative looking are generally interpreted as more efficient styles of information processing. Recovery of attention, frequently referred to as "novelty preference" or "response to novelty," is indexed by the relative amounts of looking infants pay to novel over familiar stimuli. The term "novelty preference" is usually used when novel and familiar stimuli are compared simultaneously after a familiarization period, and "response to novelty" when novel and familiar are shown individually and successively after familiarization or habituation. Relatively greater amounts of looking at novel stimuli, or reciprocally lesser amounts of looking at familiar stimuli, are generally interpreted as more efficient information processing.

At this time, both measures have associated with them moderate levels of psychometric reliability as well as moderate levels of concurrent and predictive validity for cognitive functioning. Concerning reliability, Bornstein and Benasich's (in press) recent review documents the reliability of habituation. Aggregating over six sets of conditions in five separate studies, they calculated the mean test-retest reliability of habituation to be 0.44 (Bornstein & Benasich, in press; Fenson, Sapper, & Minner, 1974; Miller et al., 1979; Pêcheux & Lécuyer, 1983; Riksen-Walraven, 1978). Aggregating over four sets of conditions in two separate studies, we can similarly calculate the mean test-retest reliability of recovery to be 0.46 (Bornstein & Benasich, in press; Fagan & McGrath, 1981; see also Mundy, Seibert, Hogan, & Fagan, 1983). These stability levels prevail despite several significant potential sources of variance (Cohen & Cohen, 1983), including procedural variations across studies (e.g., Bornstein, 1985a), distractions that may be internal or external to the infant (e.g., Freedle, 1971; Gardner & Karmel, 1983), and variations that may intrude on observer judgment (e.g., Ames, Hunter, Black, Lithgow, & Newman, 1978). Of course, the reliability of measures of attention can also be expected to vary with infant age, methodological regimen, stimulus, test-retest interval, and dependent measure.

Regarding concurrent validity, infants and young children who demonstrate efficient decrement tend also to prefer complexity (Greenberg, O'Donnel, & Crawford, 1973), to show advanced sensorimotor development (Johnson & Brody, 1977), to explore their environment rapidly (Fenson, Sapper & Minner, 1974; Messer, Kagan, & McCall, 1970; Pêcheux & Lécuyer, 1983), to play in relatively sophisticated ways (Kagan, 1971; Riksen-Walraven, 1978), to problem solve quickly and attain concepts efficiently (Lewis, Goldberg, & Campbell, 1969), and to excel at oddity identification, picture matching, and block configuration (Miller, Spiridigliozzi,

Ryan, Callan, & McLaughlin, 1980). In adults, learning rate correlates with IQ; that is, given equivalent opportunities, intelligent individuals learn more in shorter amounts of time (Bloom, 1976; Durkin, 1966; Glaser & Rosner, 1975). Similar associations obtain between recovery and diverse cognitive skills (for a review, see Fagan & Singer, 1983). Further, infants who are expected to differ in intelligence later in life show commensurate individual differences in decrement as well as recovery of attention. Perinatal risk adversely affects decrement (Friedman, 1975; Lewis et al., 1969; Sigman, Kopp, Littman, & Parmelee, 1977) as it does recovery (Caron & Caron, 1981; Rose, 1980; Rose, Gottfried, & Bridger, 1979; Sigman, 1977; Sigman & Parmelee, 1974; Siqueland, 1981), just as trisomy-21 adversely affects both decrement (Barnet, Ohlrich, & Shanks, 1971; Cohen, 1981) and recovery (Cohen, 1981; Miranda & Fantz, 1974). Indeed, the consensus that decrement and recovery of attention entail stimulus information processing underpins the widespread acceptance and use of these measures as techniques to study perception and cognition in infancy (e.g., Banks & Salapatek, 1983; Olson & Sherman, 1983).

Beyond their reliability and concurrent validity, both decrement and recovery of attention in infants have now been found to possess moderate predictive validity for mental functioning in childhood. Table 17.1 summarizes results of several recent studies and documents that infants who show efficient decrement or recovery of attention in the first 6 months of life tend to perform proficiently on traditional assessments of cognitive competence, including standardized psychometric tests of intelligence and measures of language ability, in later childhood between 2 and 8 years of age. To examine the effect size of this relationship (Cohen, 1977), we submitted the decrement and recovery data, separately and together, to meta-analysis (Glass, McGaw, & Smith, 1981; Mullen & Rosenthal, 1985; Rosenthal & Rosnow, 1984). Taking eight independent groups from the decrement data set and 11 from the recovery data set (omitting predictions closer in time where two or more were available as well as larger correlations where two tests were reported on the same sample), we calculated that decrement in infancy and cognition in childhood share (r^2) 15% of common variance, that recovery and cognition share 22%, and that the overall common variance shared by the infancy and childhood measures was 18%.

These findings raise three points about infant cognitive processes. First, decrement and recovery of attention probably reflect central mental capacities. Although studies of decrement and recovery of visual attention have dominated research investigations to date, auditory recovery in infancy is equally predictive, supporting the conclusion that this phenomenon is modality independent and probably centrally controlled.

Second, decrement and recovery of attention may be related. The ways in which this is so have only begun to submit to description, however. The two seem to follow a similar ontogenetic course (Haith, Goodman,

TABLE 17.1

Two Measures of Attention in the First Half-Year of Life in Relation to Several Measures of Cognitive Competence in the Second Year of Childhood and Later: Longitudinal Studies

Authors[a] and Year	N	Infancy		Childhood		
		Measure	Age (Months)	Measure	Age (Years)	Correlation[b]
				Decrement: Habituation and Fixation Time		
Bornstein, 1984, 1985a	20	Amount	4	WPPSI ($N = 14$)	4	0.54
Bornstein, 1985b	18	Index[c]	5	RDLS-R	2	0.55
Lewis & Brooks-Gunn, 1981	22	Amount	3	Bayley	2	0.61
Miller et al., 1979	29	Amount	2–4	Language comprehension	3.3	0.39
Sigman, 1983	96[d]	Fixation time[e]	(Term)	Stanford-Binet	5	−0.29
Sigman, Cohen, Beckwith, & Parmelee, 1986	58[d]	Amount	4	Stanford-Binet	5	0.44
	96[d]	Fixation time[e]	(Term)	WISC-R ($N = 56$)	8	0.28
				WISC-R ($N = 91$)	8	−0.36
Slater, Cooper, Rose, & Perry, 1985	21	Index[f]	1.5–6.5	WPPSI ($N = 16$)	4.5	−0.63
				BAS ($N = 16$)	4.5	−0.77

Study	N	Measure	Age	Test	Age	r
Bornstein, 1984	20	Recognition memory	4	WPPSI ($N = 14$)	4	0.54
Caron, Caron, & Glass, 1983	31	Response to novelty	5–6	Stanford-Binet	3	0.42
Fagan & McGrath, 1981	35	Novelty preference	7	Language scales	3.8	0.41
	19	Novelty preference	5	PPVT	4.3	0.33
	20	Novelty preference	4–5	Language scales	6.5	0.66
	19	Novelty preference	5	Language scales	7.5	0.46
Lewis & Brooks-Gunn, 1981	22	Response to novelty	3	Bayley	2	0.52
	57	Response to novelty	3	Bayley	2	0.40
O'Connor, Cohen & Parmelee, 1984	28[d]	Auditory response to novelty	4	Stanford-Binet	5	0.60
Rose & Wallace, 1985	35[d]	Novelty preference	6	Stanford-Binet ($N = 14$)	2.8	0.66
				Stanford-Binet ($N = 17$)	3.3	0.45
				WISC-R ($N = 19$)	6	0.56
Yarrow, Klein, Lomonaco, & Morgan, 1975	39	Novelty preference	6	Stanford-Binet	3.6	0.35

[a] Authors are listed in alphabetical order.
[b] All correlations are significant at $p < 0.05$; direction and nature of the correlation depend on the measures.
[c] Latent variable of baseline, slope, and amount.
[d] Sample consists of or includes preterm infants: testing carried out at corrected age.
[e] One trial or first trial.
[f] Mean of total fixation time, duration of first fixation, average fixation duration, and average trial duration.

wyn, & Montgomery, 1982; see also Hunter, Ames, & Koopman, 1983; Lewis & Brooks-Gunn, 1981; Rose & Slater, 1983). Moreover, they moderately intercorrelate. Bornstein and Ruddy (1984) measured both habituation decrement and response to novelty in the same sample of 20 4-month-olds and found that the two measures correlated, $r = 0.45$, $p < 0.03$. Likewise, Sigman (1983) measured visual attention at term, and O'Connor, Cohen, and Parmelee (1984) measured response to novel auditory stimuli 3 months later in the same sample of 47 babies, and these investigators also found that the two measures correlated, $r = -0.42$, $p < 0.05$. Decrement and recovery may be universally related; however, the magnitude of their interassociation will likely depend on many factors, especially how each is measured, for example, since methodological choice could attenuate variance in one or both measures and hence the degree of association between the two.

Third, decrement and recovery of attention seem to predict childhood cognitive competence more accurately than do traditional infant developmental tests. Table 17.2 summarizes relations reported between childhood cognitive outcomes and infant developmental test scores in comparison with infant attention measures. Whereas traditional infant tests account for between 0% and 8% of the variance in childhood intelligence (median = 2%), at this time the attention measures account for between 8% and 59% (median = 21%).

Importantly, these values are likely to underestimate the predictive validity of the infant attention measures on account of their still relatively poor reliability. If we make the assumption that a true construct of attention in infants predicts a true construct of cognition in children, but that we possess only imperfect measures of each, we can estimate the correlation between hypothetical constructs by correcting for attenuation of reliability (Cohen & Cohen, 1983, p.69). Extreme caution must be exercised in interpreting attenuation-corrected coefficients; they are not the same as obtained coefficients. This evaluation involves three correlations. The median obtained predictive correlation is 0.46 (see Table 17.1); the reliability coefficient of attention measures is 0.45 (see above); and Wechsler (1963, p.22) reported a reliability of 0.96 for the Preschool and Primary Scale of Intelligence at 4.5 years (the average age of longitudinal follow-up culled in Table 17.1). Therefore, the attenuation-corrected validity coefficient between infant attention and childhood intelligence can be calculated at 0.70. This evaluation leads to the conclusion that attention might share as much as half of common variance with childhood intelligence if error attributable to low reliability of infant attention measures did not attenuate predictive validity. As the precision of measurement of attention in infancy improves, as floor and ceiling effects in the distributions of attention variables are removed, and as new methods of assessment of attention and other infor-

TABLE 17.2
Median Correlations Between Two Kinds of Infant Scores and Childhood Cognitive Competence

	Developmental Test Scores[a]						Attention Scores				
	Normal			High Risk			Normal			High Risk	
	Age at Follow-up (Years)			Age at Follow-up (Years)			Age at Follow-up (Years)			Age at Follow-up (Years)	
Infant Test (Months)	3	4-5	6+	3	4-5	6+	2-3	4-5	6+	3-5	6+
0–4	0.04 (4)	0.06 (2)	0.07 (3)	0.14 (2)	0.08 (4)	0.07 (2)	0.46 (2/3)	0.54 (2/2)	0.66 (1/1)	0.44 (2/1)	0.32 (1/1)
5–7	0.25 (14)	0.20 (5)	0.06 (6)	0.27 (5)	0.24 (13)	0.28 (3)	0.42 (3/3)	0.41 (2/3)	0.46 (1/1)	0.55 (1/1)	0.56 (1/1)

Note – Figures in parentheses refer to the number of studies included/the number of samples included.
[a] Development Test scores are reproduced from Fagan and Singer (1983).

257

mation-processing capacities in infants are applied in longitudinal analyses of cognitive development, the predictive validity of infancy measures ought to increase concomitantly. Still, we wish to note explicitly that at present infant attention fails to account for a large proportion of the variance in childhood cognitive performance.

The results of the several research programs summarized in Table 17.1 substantiate a continuity perspective of mental development from infancy. Information processing measured in the first half-year of life correlates moderately with selected cognitive competences assessed in childhood. The findings apply across at least two infant information-processing capacities (decrement and recovery of attention), across at least two modalities (vision and audition), and across at least two different populations of infants (healthy full-terms and at-risk preterms). Finally, these findings apply across a small spectrum of childhood cognitive competences subsumed under the rubric of psychometric intelligence and verbal proficiency.

These findings of continuity plot new directions and raise new questions for the study of early mental development. What exactly are these infant information-processing measures? How can continuity be modeled? Whence do individual differences in information-processing capacities arise in infancy? How is continuity maintained from infancy through childhood? And what implications have these findings generally for our understanding of the nature of mental development? In the next sections, we attempt to address these questions.

MEASUREMENT OF COGNITION IN INFANCY AND CHILDHOOD

The procedures used to assess attention decrement and recovery in infants are hardly new, and their application in infancy studies has been long-standing in investigations of perception. However, their service in the field of cognition and intelligence is relatively novel, as most of the reports cited in Table 17.1 date from the 1980s. Because the continuity implication of the positive longitudinal correlations is revisionist, we believe that these measures merit close scrutiny. What are the methods used to assess decrement and recovery of attention? How are they operationalized? Have these measures explicit or identifiably implicit meaning related to cognition? And what is the nature of the criterion ability they predict?

Decrement of attention

Several different paradigms have been employed to assess decrement; the two most prominent are fixed-trial(s) and infant-control habituation procedures. In the fixed-trial(s) version (Fantz, 1964), a stimulus is presented to the infant for a predetermined number of discrete exposure periods of predetermined duration with or without interstimulus intervals. In the infant-control version (Horowitz, Paden, Bhana, & Self, 1972), a stimulus is presented to the infant for as long as the infant looks, and presentations continue from the infant's initial or baseline level of looking until the infant reaches a predetermined habituation criterion (commonly two or three consecutive looks, each less than 50% of the mean of the infant's initial two or three looks).

The two habituation procedures have different comparative merits for longitudinal assessments. The fixed-trial(s) method was introduced first and has maintained wide popularity, although it is subject to compelling criticisms. Because stimulus presentation is experimentally determined, infant looking times are markedly influenced by parameters of the regimen (e.g., trial length, number of trials, intertrial-interval length, and so on) above and beyond the infant's attending to (processing information in) the stimulus. For example, infants still looking at the moment of stimulus offset can have their inspection times artificially truncated. Under this habituation procedure, therefore, infants may not be exposed equally to a stimulus for reasons that have little to do with their processing information in the stimulus; consequently their actual decrement scores may vary artifactually, infusing longitudinal relations with noise (see also Cohen & Gelber, 1975). The infant-control method, which is of more recent vintage, gives stimulus presentation over to the infant and so attempts to meet these criticisms. If infants have equal exposure opportunity to a stimulus, the variance in their decrement scores should more accurately reflect true differential processing capabilities. In addition, this procedure permits sensitive tracking of the individual course of habituation and equating infants for a common asymptote of habituation. However, infant behavior must be monitored on line, and the possibility of false judgments of the termination of individual looks (Ames et al; 1978) or chance satisfaction of the habituation criterion (e.g., Bertenthal, Haith, & Campos, 1983; Bogartz, 1965) are ever present. Further attention may decline because of processing but also because of fatigue or state change. Pretest-posttest controls and dishabituation trials are often used to guard against this possibility (Bornstein, 1983a).

The fixed-trial(s) and infant-control procedures permit the determination of several quantitative dependent measures of habituation, including initial looking time, slope of decay, and accumulated looking time and trials through criterion. A popular summary statistic of the past was amount of habituation, determined as a negative value according to McCall and Kagan's (1970, p. 94) formula:

$$\frac{(\text{total duration of last 2 looks}) - (\text{total duration of first 2 looks})}{(\text{total duration of first 2 looks})}.$$

It is also possible to determine qualitative patterns of habituation. Three prominent modes are exponential decrease, increase-decrease, and fluctuating (see Bornstein, 1985a; McCall, 1979). These measures of habituation have served as the infancy correlates in assessments of cognitive continuity (Table 17.1). Several of them are interdependent, conceptually similar, and, in practice, correlated. Ruddy and Bornstein (1982) habituated 20 4-month-olds over 15 trials and found that habituation amount and trials to criterion were significantly correlated, $r = -0.78, p < 0.0001$. However, the measures are not redundant. For example, one infant might descend over 11 trials from 10- to 4-second average looks, whereas another infant might descend over six trials from 10- to 4-second average looks; both infants habituate an equivalent amount, but the two differ in rate. It remains to be seen if the partial residuals among measures (e.g., the 40% of variance unaccounted for) are predictive of outcome. Clearly, the choice of dependent measure, as the choice of procedure, has important implications for continuity assessments; in the hypothetical case, rate yields variation, whereas amount of habituation yields no variation and would contribute to a spuriously low predictive correlation.

Recovery of attention

A second class of infant behavior that predicts childhood cognition is recovery of attention to a novel stimulus relative to a familiar one. Recovery has been operationalized in terms of the infant's preference for a new stimulus or, reciprocally, lack of preference for a familiar stimulus. In the typical recovery paradigm, an infant is familiarized with one stimulus during the simultaneous presentation of two examples of that stimulus over a fixed duration (usually 60 seconds); after familiarization, the infant is tested (usually twice for 10 seconds each time) with the familiar stimulus paired with a novel stimulus. Novelty preference percentages are determined according to the formula:

$$\frac{(\text{mean duration looking at the novel stimulus})}{(\text{mean duration looking at the novel stimulus}) + (\text{mean duration looking at the familiar stimulus})} \times 100.$$

Novelty preference reliably greater than 50% indicates discriminative recovery and constitutes the major infant correlate in the continuity assessments enumerated in Table 17.1.

Like decrement scores, recovery scores are subject to some procedural question. Two principal concerns can be identified. First, the familiarization procedure is formally a habituation regimen of one fixed trial and is therefore subject to its criticisms. For example, during familiarization the investigator exercises control over the duration of stimulus presentation but not over infants' exposure times to the stimulus. As a consequence, individual infants may view the study stimulus for unequal amounts of time, and variance in recovery may reflect happenstantial stimulus exposure across babies as opposed to infants' differential information processing. This state of affairs could contribute to unreliable or variable recovery scores. Group correlations of study time with degree of recovery mitigate this criticism (Fagan & Singer, 1983), and extended familiarization times are usually provided to allow all infants minimal study time. When recovery is assessed after infant-control habituation, the investigator has brought every infant to the same habituation criterion; as a consequence, however, variance in response to novelty might be attenuated (DeLoache, 1976). On these considerations, it remains to be determined what kind of tests of recovery the two paradigms provide for subsequent prediction of individual differences in outcome.

Second, true recovery needs to be distinguished from the threat of spontaneous regression (Bertenthal et al., 1983). Infants not looking at the end of familiarization could return to a higher level of looking on account of random fluctuation rather than reaction to a new stimulus. Adopting conservative familiarization criteria, adding suppression trials, retesting with the familiar stimulus, or instituting no-change control comparisons have proven useful countermeasures to this criticism. In their absence, the interpretation of recovery is suspect.

Verbal intelligence

Inspection of Table 17.1 reveals that verbal ability and psychometrically measured intelligence, which is itself heavily verbal in nature, are the forms of childhood cognition most often reported in outcome studies of decrement or recovery of attention in infancy. Why is language capacity so often the criterion variable documented? Some investigators may have limited themselves to testing verbal intelligence alone; others may have reported associations with language because, of several abilities assessed, language was the only criterion measure to show a significant relation with infant attention measures. Without detailed knowledge of how many measures were employed in these studies and how many of these measures were independent or mutually exclusive, it is difficult to certify that the pattern of findings in Table 17.1 does not reflect a Type I error. However, the consistency and similarity of findings across studies militate against the criticism that these may be random effects. Further, three reports seem to substantiate a special relation between attention scores and language abilities. Bornstein (1984,

1985b) found that habituation predicted children's intelligence test performance but not their visual discrimination learning, and Slater, Cooper, Rose, and Perry (1985) observed that habituation predicted children's Wechsler test verbal scores much better than their performance scores. In a similar vein, J. F. Fagan (personal communication, 1984) reported that recovery predicted children's language scores but not their recognition memory.

Verbal proficiency is a so-called crystallized form of intelligence (Cattell, 1971; Horn, 1976, 1979, 1980) that reflects both information acquisition, as is implicated in attention decrement, and memory, as is implicated in attention recovery, over and above its prerequisites in perceptual processing. In an influential series of analytic papers aimed at identifying the determinants of verbal ability, Hunt has argued that intelligence tests indirectly measure information processing by directly assessing the products of information processing. Thus, better information processing skills early in life might lead to increased acquisition of vocabulary as psychometrically assessed (Hunt, 1978, 1983). Hunt hypothesized, for example, that the development of verbal ability might depend, in part, on "the speed with which the internal representations of STM and intermediate term memory . . . can be created, integrated, or altered" (Hunt, Lunneborg, & Lewis, 1975, p. 197).

Assessments of verbal abilities are also especially psychometrically sound. Systematic analysis of statistical properties of the Wechsler scales, including the WISC-R and the WAIS-R (see Wechsler, 1974, 1981), shows that verbal IQ has greater split-half reliability, greater short-term stability, lower standard error of measurement, higher correlation with full-scale IQ, and better longitudinal continuity than does performance IQ. Furthermore, on each of these dimensions of comparison, vocabulary subscales are, with only minor exceptions, consistently the best of the dozen-odd subscales on each test. Though vocabulary is not as stable in the WPPSI, it is still among the best subscales in that test as well. The increasing structural consistency of verbal IQ with age may be significant for prediction since, as the data in Table 17.2 suggest, the correlation between attention measured early in infancy and verbal IQ measured in childhood seems to increase, in violation of the simplex structure of longitudinal correlation (Guttman, 1966, p. 477), as though infant attention were being tested against better and better representatives of its true childhood analog. However, the number of studies involved is small, and this observation warrants confirmation or disconfirmation in future tests.

Overview

Several observations follow from our examination of measures of attention in infancy as associated with measures of verbal intelligence in childhood. First, the predictive relations we have described are apparently reasonably robust, despite gross variations in procedures and in the measures themselves. Second, the longitudinal results so far attained may be construed as underestimates of the potential association between ability in infancy and proficiency in childhood since improved procedures and measures in infancy ought commensurately to improve obtained predictive validity. Third, this point leads to the conclusion that the psychometric adequacy of common decrement and recovery measures has not yet itself received adequate attention. Finally, in both decrement and recovery a central cognitive process is inferred from overt behavior, but the overt behavior is all that we have to go on. Therefore, the nature of what is continuous is critical to our argument, and it is to this question that we now turn.

MODELS OF COGNITIVE CONTINUITY

Table 17.1 documents a moderate degree of continuity, that is, a correlation in performance, from early infancy through middle childhood between behaviors we hypothesize broadly to entail cognition. What possible models might help to explain cognitive continuity in the child? We propose three:

Model 1: Continuity of Identical Behavior $(X \rightarrow X)$
Model 2: Continuity of Underlying Process $(X \rightarrow X')$
Model 3: Continuity of Developmental Status $(X \rightarrow Y)$.

Each of these models assumes that children are tested at two times, and that children's performance is distributed at each age tested.

Continuity of Identical Behavior states that performance on behavior X at time 1 ought to correlate with performance on behavior X at time 2 if the identical behavior is being assessed. Suppose, for example, that the same measure of habituation or of recognition memory were equally applicable in infancy and in childhood. If there is continuity, then habituation or recognition performances at the two times ought to correlate. Continuity of Underlying Process argues that performance on X at time 1 ought to correlate with performance on X' at time 2 if X and X', though different behaviors, reflect the same underlying process that is continuous. Suppose, for example, that habituation stood for encoding in infancy and that verbal proficiency stood for encoding in childhood. Though not identical, habituation might correlate with verbal proficiency because encoding, their shared underlying process, is continuous. Continuity of Developmental Status proposes that performance on X at time 1 ought to correlate with performance on Y at time 2 if X and Y, which are wholly different behaviors, are tied, in that they follow the same developmental trajectories, though displaced in time. Suppose, for example, that infants differed in terms of how habituation matured and that children differed in terms of how verbal proficiency matured; habituation and verbal proficiency could then correlate, not because the two are themselves identical or even conceptually related competencies, but because children's maturational status is stable and is correlated to both.[2]

How can these models account for continuity between attention (decrement or recovery) in infancy and cognition (intelligence or verbal proficiency) in childhood? Clearly, attention in infancy and verbal intelligence in childhood are not identical, and therefore the longitudinal correlation between the two does not exemplify Continuity of Identical Behavior. The correlation is between different measures and therefore may reflect the second or third models of continuity. Let us first consider Continuity of Underlying Process. What are some candidate underlying processes that attention and cognitive competence may share? One is general, namely, intelligence; a second is more specific, namely, mental representation; and a third includes components thought to be integral to intelligence, namely, motivation and the capacity to regulate state of arousal.

Could the longitudinal correspondence between infancy and childhood reflect continuity in general intelligence? Available data do not support this hypothesis, though it may not be ruled out. If general intelligence underlies the longitudinal correlation, we could deduce that because different childhood abilities intercorrelate so as to yield the construct of intelligence, decrement or recovery in infancy ought to correlate not only with verbal proficiency but also with other interrelated childhood abilities. Empirical investigation so far casts doubt on the hypothesis that the longitudinal correlation between infancy and childhood is carried by global intelligence. In childhood, verbal intelligence correlates with discrimination learning (e.g., Bornstein, 1984, 1985b), with performance intelligence (e.g., Slater et al., 1985), and with recognition memory (e.g., Ellis, McCartney, Ferretti, & Cavalier, 1977; Harris & Fleer, 1972); however, between infancy and childhood, decrement correlates with verbal intelligence but does not correlate with discrimination learning (Bornstein, 1984, 1985b) or with performance IQ (Slater et al., 1985), and recovery correlates with verbal intelligence but does not correlate with recognition memory (J. F. Fagan, personal communication, 1984).[3] Because studies of the concurrent validity of decrement and of recovery (reviewed earlier) indicate that in childhood

---

[2]The examples we supply here are intended to illuminate differences among these three models, though they certainly do not address all questions raised by the models. Can X and X' always be told apart, so that Continuity of Identical Behavior is always distinguishable from Continuity of Underlying Process? We think not. Can the nature of the behavior in Continuity of Developmental Status be specified so that Y is always identifiably different from X, or might Y sometimes be an age-adjusted X? We admit so.

[3]Reciprocally, this comparison suggests that attention decrement and recovery in infancy cannot be taken to be early versions of discrimination learning or recognition memory, respectively, since these seemingly matched pairs of behaviors fail to correlate over time.

each is related to diverse cognitive functions, improved infant measures may yield more robust patterns of longitudinal association in the future, and so the general intelligence argument continues to merit investigation.

The predictive correlation could alternatively reflect Continuity of Underlying Process that is more specific than general intelligence. We have inferred that infant looking times stand for central cognitive functions. It is presumed that decrement and recovery entail two processes that involve encoding stimulus information and subsequent comparison of new stimulation. Thus a more specific candidate phenomenon common to decrement and recovery is mental representation.

Mental representation is pervasive in everyday elementary information processing, and it subsumes subprocesses as diverse as detection, discrimination, identification, categorization, concept formation, problem solving, and retrieval (Hunt, 1983; Sternberg, 1985). Representation has likewise been implicated in language acquisition; it is argued that to derive or to use a concept linguistically (e.g., "chair") depends on the abstraction of a representation of the concept usually based on experience with multiple instances of the concept (e.g., "rocking chair," "Barcelona," "high-chair," and so on). (For more extensive discussions, see e.g., Anglin, 1977; Fodor, 1975; Kosslyn, 1980; Macnamara, 1982; Rosch & Lloyd, 1978; Smith & Medin, 1981.) If mental representation constitutes a specific capacity common to the two infant measures and also underpins childhood verbal intelligence, then continuity in individual differences in establishing such representations, or in hierarchies of aptitude or reliance on abilities related to representation, could stand as the candidate underlying process being tapped in the longitudinal studies we have tabulated. Of course, "mental representation" still needs to be specified further. The infant especially efficient in attention who becomes a verbally able child must have cognitive skills or interests in a particular form of mental representation that support the specific linkage. Mental representations may assume analog forms (e.g., pictures, holograms, tape recordings, 3-D models, and so on), or symbolic forms (e.g., linked list structures, conceptual graphs, verbal codes, and so on), or propositional forms (e.g., abstract concepts, networks, associative structures, and so on). (For more complete discussions, see Anderson, 1980; Block, 1981; Lindsay & Norman, 1977; Mandler, 1983; Paivio, 1979; or Posner, 1973.) We can only speculate about the nature of representation in the mental life of the infant. It could be that imagery alone, for example, qualifies as a continuous underlying process. Mental representation could alternatively take the form of "schemata," as suggested by Piaget.

Finally, Continuity of Underlying Process could be sustained by an unchanging component of intelligence, such as motivation or self-regulation. Many experts include motivation in overarching constructs of intelligence (see, e.g., Scarr, 1981; Yarrow, Morgan, Jennings, Harmon, & Gaiter,

1982; Zigler, Abelson, & Seitz, 1973). In discussing both the philosophy and administration of his psychometric scales in the WISC-R manual, Wechsler (1974; p.6), for example, was careful to define intelligence as a global multidetermined and multifaceted entity that does not singularly equate with intellectual ability but rather embraces conative and nonintellectual factors. "Intelligent behavior . . . may also call for one or more of a host of aptitudes (factors) which . . . involve not so much skills and know-how as drives and attitudes. . . . They include such traits as persistence, zest, impulse control, and goal awareness."

On this account, attention could reflect in part the infant's motivation to explore new environments, and intelligence could reflect in part the child's motivation to explore new testing materials and tasks as well as to perform well during testing. The infant with strong motivation to explore new environments might turn away sooner from repeated stimuli in the habituation procedure and look longer at novel stimuli during the recovery procedure than the infant whose motivation is weaker. The child with strong motivation to explore new tasks and to perform during testing might persist longer during learning situations and during intelligence assessment. Attention in infancy and intelligence in childhood could in this way relate to one another longitudinally (e.g., Berg & Sternberg, in press; Yarrow, Klein, Lomonaco, & Morgan, 1975). Motivation could have direct or indirect influences on continuity. The more direct influence, as described, would be in shaping attention in infancy and task persistence in childhood. The indirect influence would be in modifying learning throughout infancy and childhood so that the infant who preferred novel environments would learn more in early life and would consequently score higher on the childhood tests of verbal proficiency and intelligence. Sigman, Cohen, Beckwith, and Topinka (1986) measured attention in 37 4-month-postnatal preterm infants and later measured persistence in the same children at 24 months of age. Infants who looked less at the constant stimulus at term persisted at a puzzle task at 2 years of age, $r = -0.38$, $p < 0.05$. Moreover, the more persistent 2-year-olds had higher scores on the Binet Scale at 5 years of age, $r = 0.37$, $p < 0.05$. Infant attention and subsequent intelligence may partly reflect a linkage through continuity in motivation.

Motivation and cognition are integrated constructs, but, like height and weight, exceptions clearly show that the two possess a degree of independence. Children who are overachievers or underachievers plainly demonstrate that intelligence and motivation are separable. Just as there is need to see motivation as a part of cognition, there is longstanding recognition of their disassociability. Wechsler (1974; p.6) also wrote in the WISC-R manual that "nonintellective factors are necessary ingredients of intelligent behavior; they are not, however, substitutes . . . for other basic abilities. No amount of drive will develop a dullard into a mathematician any more than good intentions alone will suffice to make a person a saint." In general, children's intelligence test performance embraces pure cognitive abilities as well as factors like motivation, and motivation to focus attention in infancy could be continuous with the motivation to stay on task in childhood.

The capacity to regulate state of arousal, and thereby to initiate, sustain, and inhibit attention, is a second characteristic that is plausibly related to cognitive performance at different ages and equally plausibly continuous in development. Certainly, arousal, attention, and intelligence share variance under normal circumstances (Gardner & Karmel, 1983). Like motivation, the capacity to regulate state in the infant could have either direct or indirect influences on continuity between infant attention and childhood intelligence. The infant who is able to modulate arousal may develop into the child who is able to cope with the stress of testing situations. Alternatively, or in addition, the capacity for state regulation may modulate the young child's capacity to learn so that that child could learn more in growing and would therefore score higher on IQ tests.

The third model, Continuity of Developmental Status, states that the longitudinal correlation between two manifestly different behaviors could be understood to be meaningful if both matured at the same rates in different children but at different times in the life cycle, and if some a priori theoretical linkage could be established between the two. Suppose that all infants possess a cognitive capacity on which they are distributed in terms of maturational standing, and suppose that as children they possess a wholly separate cognitive capacity on which the same standings obtain. If developmental standing were a constant, as is plausible, the infant who is ahead on one would be the child who is ahead on the other, and children's scores on the two cognitive tasks would correlate over time as they grew up. Unlike Continuity of Identical Behavior or Underlying Process, the two capacities would not have to be identical or even conceptually similar for continuity to obtain. The lack of stability from traditional infant developmental scales to childhood intelligence tests tends to argue against Continuity of Developmental Status and suggests that attention and cognition must share in some yet unidentified theoretical base.

To adjudicate empirically among these models of continuity, at least on an exploratory basis, attention and a variety of other developed and developing capacities, such as sensorimotor skills, as well as motivation and the capacity for self-regulation, would need to be assessed in infancy. Then in childhood, attention and a variety of other sorts of developed and developing capacities, such as verbal intelligence and, again, motivation and self-regulation, would need to be assessed. Continuity of Identical Behavior predicts specifically that the infants who attend efficiently will be the children who attend efficiently; Continuity of Similar Process predicts more broadly that conceptually linked, though not necessarily identical, processes, such as attention and verbal skills, will correlate over time; and Continuity of Developmental Status most broadly predicts that correspondingly emerging cognitive schemata will correlate. Moreover, these predictive associations ought to obtain when motivation and self-regulation – as well as third mutually related variables – are partialed out of the regression of intelligence on attention.[4]

In constructing such an experiment, a further issue must be borne in mind. Consider Continuity of Identical Behavior. If we assessed the exact same behavior X at two times (adjusted by age for developmental status and adjusted by difficulty for cognitive level), then the correlation between X and X would essentially set an upper limit on what we take to be "continuity". However, if X at any time is already advanced to an asymptote or is automatic with respect to performance and is not distributed, then the correlation between infant and child will constitute a flawed test of continuity. Appropriately adjusted measures of, say, recognition memory might correlate; but to expect recognition in early infancy (a distributed response) to relate to older children's reading recognition of their own names (an automatic response) may not be meaningful. That is, X's must be distributed at both ages.

THE ORIGINS AND MAINTENANCE OF
COGNITIVE CONTINUITY FROM INFANCY

Because this reading focuses on individual differences in early infancy, questions inevitably arise of how continuity of such individual differences originates and how it is maintained. The controversy that swirls around the origins of intelligence is magnificent and, in magnitude, is matched only by the complexity of the issue and by the enormity of our ignorance. We know that cognitive growth proceeds as a continuous organism-environment transaction, but beyond that the dynamics of mental development are poorly understood. Here we treat select data on the origins and maintenance of attention in infancy, data that are directly relevant to our thesis, and we do not presume to resolve any larger issues.

---

[4]This discussion proceeds on the assumption that the longitudinal correlations reflect continuity of *cognition*. However, it could be that some psychological characteristic that is not cognitive in itself but is nevertheless related both to attention in infancy and to intelligence test performance in childhood is developmentally continuous and thereby carries the infant-to-child correlation. Simply put, attention and intelligence could be independent constructs whose association is fortuitously mediated by a common third variable. In correlating attention and intelligence, have we been thus misled on the question of cognitive continuity? Although the issue of noncognitive factors needs to be entertained seriously, we believe that the similarity and consistency of results in the context of so many diverse tests of the continuity hypothesis militate against this interpretation.

The fact that individual differences in decrement and recovery of attention date from the earliest months of life logically suggests that some cognitive ability reflects biogenetic expression in conjunction with experience in an environment that is quick and sure in its effect. Infants' performance on standardized developmental tests (e.g., the Bayley) has been linked to their genetic endowment (Wilson, 1983) just as has childhood IQ (e.g., Bouchard & McGue, 1981; Rose et al., 1980; Rose, Harris, Christian, & Nance, 1979; cf. Eysenck & Kamin, 1981), at least when measured by conventional methods. Do genetics contribute to patterns of attention in infancy? Although newborns habituate and recover, and they show individual differences in doing so (e.g., Slater, Morison, & Rose, 1984), which is suggestive, there are virtually no data that address the question directly. Moreover, there is only uncertainty about the most common operational translations of the question, as, for example, the psychological relation between parental IQ and infant attention or the sociological index that sometimes stands in for parental IQ, namely, educational level. Decrement was tentatively associated with parental education (and SES) by Lewis (e.g., Lewis et al., 1969) and by McCall (e.g., McCall, Hogarty, Hamilton, & Vincent, 1973), but McCall (1979) later repudiated this link. Fagan and Singer (1983) failed to find a consistent relation between maternal education and infant novelty preference (the two correlated in one sample, $r = 0.34$, $p < 0.05$, but not in another); and neither O'Connor et al. (1984) nor Rose and Wallace (1985) found maternal education to be correlated with infant recovery. It is important to note that, in whatever way they are commonly interpreted, these SES data are removed from any potential genetic contribution by two steps, that is, from SES to intelligence and from intelligence to genetics. Thompson and Fagan (1983) reported that parental intelligence correlated with 7-month recognition memory. Sigman and Cohen (1985) also reported that maternal IQ correlated with attention at term for a sample of preterm infants. Of course, intelligence is potentially confounded with rearing pattern in these studies.

The absolute dependence of individual differences in infancy on genetic endowment seems unlikely and would be very difficult to confirm. Infants' attention scores are distributed even in samples where pertinent characteristics of parent populations are relatively homogeneous. Significantly, how maternal IQ may relate to infant attention is inevitably mixed with how mothers behave toward their infants. Familial socioeconomic status is related to childhood IQ (McCall, 1977, 1981), although it must be that aspects of parental rearing style rather than social class status per se constitute the relevant proximal and effective influences. All the studies in Table 17.1 have involved babies with at least 3 months postpartum experience in the family, and of course infants' experiences even at this tender age may affect their cognitive performance. For example, maternal contingent behavior is concurrently related to habituation in 3-month-olds (Lewis & Goldberg, 1969) as is maternal responsivity to habituation in 5-month-olds (Bornstein & Tamis, 1986); frequency of maternal encouraging attention to properties, objects, and events in the environment is concurrently related to habituation in 4-month-olds (Bornstein, 1984, 1985b); and caretaker verbal and social interaction is concurrently related to fixation time in 4-month-postnatal preterm girls (Sigman & Beckwith, 1980). The direction of influence in these associations still needs to be unpacked: newborn differences may affect parental behavior, just as parents might socialize cognitive styles in their young infants (e.g., Belsky, Goode, & Most, 1980; Bornstein, 1985b; Riksen-Walraven, 1978; Slater et al., 1984).

What forces would maintain cognitive continuity from infancy? Continuity in information processing performance might wholly or in part reflect temporal stability in the child's social, didactic, or material environment. The classic development curves have demonstrated increasing continuity in observed IQ beginning at about 5 years of age. It could be that continuity in schooling spawns and supports continuity in measured intelligence beginning at this time. Cognitive continuity beginning in infancy could also be maintained by external means. There is reasonable evidence of continuity in many caretaker activities with infants. For example, Bornstein and Ruddy (1984) found that the extent to which mothers engage in didactic practices, encouraging their infants to attend to properties, objects, and events in the environment, is rather stable between 4 and 12 months, $r = 0.62$, $p < 0.001$, and Bornstein and Tamis (1986) recently found the same to be true even earlier, between 2 and 5 months, $r = 0.52$, $p < 0.01$. These particular maternal activities not only maintain positive concurrent associations to habituation at 4 months but they also independently predict language outcome at 1 year and intelligence test performance at 4 years (Bornstein, 1984, 1985b). Beckwith and Cohen (1983, 1984), Clarke-Stewart (1973), Coates and Lewis (1984), Olson, Bates, and Bayles (1984), Papoušek, Papoušek, & Bornstein (1985), and Russell (1983), among others, have documented similarly high levels of consistency in cognitively reinforcing caretaker activities over the early months and years of children's lives.

Demonstrations of stability in caretaker activity by no means prove that continuity in the environment maintains continuity in the infant; the two may reflect wholly independent but parallel phenomena. Factors in the infant that are separate from caretaker characteristics or that actually provoke caretaker action could equally well maintain children's cognitive standing. Wilson's (1983) comparative studies of epigenetic synchronies in mental development in monozygotic and dyzygotic twins support the hypothesis that babies can bring a certain stability to their own performance, the potential of twin "contrast effects" notwithstanding. According to Wilson, the increasing concordance and parallel courses of cognitive growth among monozygotic, relative to dyzygotic, co-twins point to intrinsic scheduling of a genetic program in intellectual development. In addition, infants engage their parents. For example, Bornstein (1985b) found that infant attention style at 4 months influenced the frequency of maternal didactics at 1 year; that is, young babies who habituated more efficiently had mothers who encouraged them more in toddlerhood.

At present we can conclude very little about the origins and maintenance of individual differences in infant cognitive functioning beyond what logic dictates. Parents doubtlessly transmit some talents genetically to their offspring, but parents also act with their offspring or provide for their offspring in ways that differentially influence their infants' performance. Infants, too, for their part may provoke their parents to act in specific ways with them. As Scarr and Weinberg (1983) point out, demonstrating either an environmental or a genetic basis for an infant characteristic is virtually impossible in populations of children reared in natural families because genetic endowment and environmental influence are completely confounded. As a consequence, these several considerations of origins and maintenance of continuity unfortunately fail to help us adjudicate among the different models of continuity because the origins and maintenance of cognition are ineluctable products of interpersonal transaction.

Additional comparative study of the earliest information-processing capacities in infants seems warranted. Several strategies recommend themselves. First, multiple estimates of cognitive and educational characteristics of parents in heterogeneous samples could be assessed to determine direct relations between parent abilities or activities and newborn performance, independent of socioeconomic characteristics. Second, the course of development of attention could be pursued in children in whom species-specific genetic errors, such as Down's syndrome, are observed. Third, particular caretaker activities associated with enhanced infant attention measures could be manipulated in experimental studies designed to assess whether and how infant information processing can be externally influenced.

FUTURE CONSIDERATIONS IN THE ASSESSMENT OF COGNITIVE CONTINUITY

The studies summarized in Table 17.1 support the idea of moderate continuity in early cognitive development. The initiation and application years ago of new procedures to measure infant perception have had a propitious impact on our understanding of the nature of the mental life of the child. Because theoretical preferences, as much as empirical results, will guide future developments in this field, we urge several considerations.

First, we believe that infant attention, measured in terms of decrement or recovery, ought not to be considered a cognitive index independent of experimental considerations of stimulus, method, state, and subject population. Statements to the effect that "habituation absolutely predicts IQ" or "novelty preference predicts IQ better than habituation" are not meaningful. One need only imagine applying a stimulus that yields no individual variability in habituation to realize that habituation per se is not an absolute predictor, just as one need only imagine contrasting a novelty stimulus that does not differentiate among infants with a habituation stimulus that does to realize that one type of measure will not predict better than another under all circumstances. A habituation stimulus to which infants show equally efficient or inefficient decline, or a novel stimulus that is easily discriminated or is indiscriminable from a familiar stimulus, may elicit equivalent amounts of looking from all babies. Such stimuli would produce floor and ceiling effects that eliminate variance from habituation and novelty preference measures alike. In turn, restriction of variance will spuriously diminish any predictive correlation.

Further, systematic methodological variations ought to provide critical information about the robustness of these measures. Consider the delay between decrement and recovery. Assessments of recovery after only a brief delay might evoke discrimination, whereas assessments after considerable delay might evoke memory. Does one more consistently predict cognition? In childhood, immediate recognition memory is thought to be more powerfully related to intelligence than is delayed recognition (Ellis et al., 1977). Parametric studies may show that these infant measures have different upper limits in the proportion of variance they share with childhood performance. Moreover, state gates information processing in infancy, just as do the organizing effects of external stimuli (Gardner & Karmel, 1983), and so attention will be a product of the combined effect of several factors. For the moment we have only the fact that certain methodological choices made years ago now show that decrement and recovery of attention in infancy possess moderate predictive validity for childhood intelligence.

The psychometric adequacy of infant measures used to investigate continuity requires additional documentation. Useful indexes must yield distributions in infant performance as well as substantial short-term reliability since the latter places a ceiling on validity. As we demonstrated, the predictive value of infant measures will be enhanced in the degree to which they are refined to improve their psychometric soundness. (Note, however, that reliability can be expected to interact with characteristics of the stimulus, procedure, and infant population.) In support of this point, Slater et al. (1985) recently reported that only infant measures that showed good test-retest reliability and consistent change with age predicted childhood cognitive performance.

We may ask whether extant measures of decrement and recovery exhaust potential predictors or even constitute the best predictors available. Consider, for example, the potential of a new measure of "recognition-reexamination," namely, infants' looking at the familiar stimulus in a retest compared to their looking at the same stimulus at the end of familiarization, perhaps even subsequent to the intervening presentation of a novel stimulus.[5] It could be that a low level of looking on retest indicates recognition, whereas a high level indicates forgetting, and that recognition ability is predictive. Alternatively, longer looking on retest might reflect the infant's interest in reexamining characteristics of the familiar stimulus in comparison with those of the intervening novel stimulus; this result would imply a cognitively sophisticated strategy based on discrepancy theory (McCall & McGhee, 1977). In one report of this measure, Bornstein (1984) found that retest sensitivity correlated concurrently with habituation decrement at 4 months, $r = 0.44$, $p < 0.03$, and predictively with WPPSI performance at 4 years, $r = 0.54$, $p = 0.02$. These positive correlations support the reexamination hypothesis: babies who habituate efficiently tend to study the habituation stimulus on re-presentation; it may be that these infants encode the intervening novel stimulus in the test efficiently and then spend more time comparing novel and familiar (Martin, 1975).

This reexamination measure still builds on traditional and straightforward approaches of decrement and recovery. It is also desirable to develop new estimators of infant cognitive ability. Consider infants' habituation in a concept-formation paradigm or their ability to abstract invariance. In a concept study, infants must habituate to multiple variants of a class of stimuli; in the abstraction of invariance test that follows, infants must recognize a new instance of the same class (Bornstein, 1983b). Infant capacity in either of these variants of habituation and recovery may prove predictive of later cognitive function. Consider, too, infants' ability at crossmodal transfer, the availability in one modality of information about a stimulus acquired via experience with the same stimulus in a different modality. Cross-modal transfer seems to require mental representation, that is, the visual recognition of a stimulus previously felt but not seen gives strong evidence of some sort of central coding of stimulus information (Stoltz-Loike & Bornstein, 1985). On these grounds, cross-modal transfer may illuminate cognitive differences among infants that predict later competencies as clearly or more clearly than simple decrement or recovery of attention (Rose, 1981, 1984). Furthermore, intersensory integration has been hypothesized to function as ontogenetically prerequisite to language

---

[5]This measure contrasts with recovery (i.e., infants' novelty preference for an arbitrary new stimulus compared to a familiar stimulus). Responsiveness to the habituation stimulus following the introduction of a novel stimulus is termed "dishabituation" in the animal literature (Tighe & Leaton, 1976, p. 332).

development (Birch & Lefford, 1963; Ettlinger, 1967; Geschwind, 1965a, 1965b).

A significant question that arises in entertaining the possibility of new infant measures concerns whether different infant predictors might interrelate and thereby reflect a common underlying construct of infant mind. To date, mostly single measures of decrement and recovery of attention have been used in investigating continuities (Table 17.1). Nevertheless, an important assumption of this line of research is that some central cognitive process is being assessed, if necessarily indirectly, by the surface manifestations of decrement or recovery of attention. Put another way, infant measures are "observed" variables, and the cognitive process(es) they presumably stand for are unmeasured "latent" variable(s). Observed measures do not faithfully mirror underlying processes, however. At minimum they are characterized by variance that may be partitioned into components shared with the latent construct and components ascribable to measurement error. Latent variable modeling permits an assessment of the interrelations among unmeasured latent variables and observed variable indicators (Bentler, 1980; Jöreskog, 1978). This analysis accomplishes the partitioning of observed measurements into true and error components so that the true "error-corrected" scores alone may be considered in relation to one another. The latent variable approach could be applied to evaluate whether infant variables – habituation, novelty preference, and cross-modal transfer, for example – interrelate and coalesce as a unified underlying cognitive construct. In turn, it would be possible to test whether that latent construct is a better predictor of child competence than are the individual infant measures. We have reported that habituation and novelty preference correlate to some degree, and this finding suggests that the two may compose a latent construct in infants. However, the obtained correlations were low. It is reasonable, therefore, to entertain an alternative hypothesis, namely, that decrement and recovery are unrelated and represent different, conceptually distinct, cognitive processes. For example, habituation may reflect information analysis or encoding, as novelty preference may reflect retrieval. The degree to which these different processes are correlated has implications both for the view of mental representation as a coherent construct of infant mind and for prediction.

Assessments of infant and child thus far brought to bear on the question of continuity in cognition may represent an upper limit of measurement. However, the infant procedures that we have focused on were developed years ago – in the infancy of this discipline and often, admittedly, with different goals in mind – and they may not be the most sophisticated or appropriate to address questions about mental development. A similar criticism holds for the outcome measures that have been applied to assess cognition in childhood. At minimum, increased diversity and a better matching of infant and child assessments warrant experimental attention. Such matching promises to substantiate continuity. For instance, it seems important to evaluate how relatively well-matched the infant measures might be to conceptually similar childhood tests of fluid intelligence, such as nonverbal problem solving characteristic of the Raven's Progressive Matrices Test, in contrast to tests of crystallized intelligence or acquired information and knowledge characteristic of vocabulary (Cattell, 1971; Guilford, 1967, 1979; Horn, 1976, 1979, 1980). In a similar vein, it might be profitable to explore prediction to componential forms of intelligence (e.g., Hunt, 1983; Sternberg, 1985). Further, alternative infant assessments, such as habituation to concepts and abstraction of invariance, should be observed in relation to the development of basic naming since concept formation and abstraction are common general components of proficiency in both (Anglin, 1977; Brown, 1973; Caron & Caron, 1981; Macnamara, 1982; Nelson, 1979; Slobin, 1974). Independent of what is measured, and whether or not different infant abilities are related to one another, the exploration of new measures at each age is desirable (Scarr, 1981). Further, since multivariate approaches more appropriately assess multiple simultaneous processes, a composite of multiple measures ought to possess predictive power greater than any single measure. Most studies to date, as Table 17.1 shows, have unfortunately relied on individual infant indexes.

The measures of cognition available to infant and to child testing today still only faintly estimate actual cognitive competence. Moreover, those measures represent only a selected few among the variety of performance capacities that describe children at either age. "Intelligence" is not a unitary construct. It can express itself in many ways (Gardner, 1984), as there are multiple subtypes even to its psychometric instantiation (Guilford, 1967, 1979; Hunt, 1983). The kinds of intelligence thus far included as the outcome criteria of infancy studies represent a limited variety, albeit an important one because of their recognized cultural value to communication and literacy and to academic achievement, work performance, and social attunement (National Research Council, 1982). These measures may or may not best represent intelligence, however, or even best represent that kind of intelligence we have targeted. Further, most investigators have estimated competence correlations based on the infant's performance at one time in relation to the child's performance as just one other time. How a child performs at either time (on a given measure) may reflect the child's worst, average, or best effort. We do not know which performance – nor have we solid reason to select among the three – may "best estimate" the individual child. In short, our actual predictive measures are necessarily several steps removed from the ultimate constructs we seek, namely, true infant and child cognitive competencies.

A final caveat. Table 17.1 documents a fairly consistent psychological finding given the diversity of measures, populations, and laboratories over which continuity has now been determined. Nevertheless, obtained correlations show that the current infant measures still predict only a relatively small proportion of the variance in the child outcome measures. In addition, the limits of these effects require further investigation. For example, Lewis and Brooks-Gunn (1981) reported that a 3-month habituation measure predicted 2-year Bayley scores in one infant group but not in another. The same qualifications obviously hold for the variety of factors directly associated with these effects. For example, Fagan and Singer (1983) reported that parental education correlated with 7-month novelty preference in one infant sample but not in a second. Such variation tells us that the comprehensive study of continuity in mental development from infancy is only beginning.

CONCLUDING COMMENTS

We have argued that individual differences in mental performance in infancy are developmentally continuous in a moderate degree at least through childhood. The evidence we have marshalled in support of this proposition has emerged from studies conducted independently in different laboratories, using different, though conceptually related, measures of information processing in infants, usually indexed by decrement and recovery of attention, to predict cognitive proficiency in childhood, usually indexed by performance on standard psychometric tests of intelligence and especially verbal ability. These new findings contravene long-held opinions that instability or discontinuity characterizes normal cognitive development. We find it telling that these particular patterns of attention in infants have become established as manifestations of cognition in early life, namely, how rapidly and completely infants construct schemas of their visual and auditory worlds and how resistant to decay or interference those schemas may be. As Rheingold (1985) observed, mental development proceeds through transformations of novelty into familiarity. For the infant, each thing in the world begins as new, and development progresses by rendering the new known; in turn, what is known sets the occasion for recognizing what is new and thus provides the basis for further mental development. The two are reciprocal processes and clearly situated within the individual. For infants, as we plainly know, both the familiar and the novel exert attraction. From the newfound significance of these processes we believe that three important implications follow.

First, we have observed that these initial studies of continuity succeeded largely on account of follow-up to infant procedures of decrement and recovery of attention that were novel years ago. Though these effects now seem to be consistent, we have noted that the correlations reported to date are only moderate. Nonetheless, this literature has quite a happy aspect. The measures that were applied to infants years ago were not the most sophisticated, sensitive, or refined; yet, years later and against historical prediction, child assessments not even matched to the infant measures have been found to share upwards of 50% of common variance. Thus, current data may actually set a lower bound of longitudinal assessment. New, more sophisticated composite infant and child measures will, we believe, enhance predictive associations. We therefore urge a renewal of longitudinal study and recommend the application of additional improved measures in infancy as well as multiple measures of cognitive competence in childhood so as to characterize cognitive continuity correctly and comprehensively.

Second, the analyses we have presented indicate that interactional and possibly material factors may influence the development of attention in infancy. On this account, we also exhort further study of diverse forms of caretaking near to the beginning of life so as to specify to the degree possible the impetus and supports to continuity in cognitive competence.

Our final point is a scientific cum political one. It was the impression of some of our predecessors, based on the data available to them years ago, that infancy might play little or no role in determining the eventual cognitive performance of the child and, therefore, that individuals could sustain neglect in infancy if remediation were later made available. We recognize that intervention can successfully influence the later course of cognitive growth, and we acknowledge that current infant measures leave unaccounted much variance in mature cognition. Nonetheless, the data we have gathered and the hypothesis of continuity that they support spotlight a significant role for infancy in cognitive development.

ACKNOWLEDGEMENTS

This paper was written during the authors' tenure as Professeurs Invités at the Laboratoire de Psychologie Expérimentale et E.P.H.E. (3ème section, associé au CNRS), Paris, Marc H. Bornstein was supported by a Research Career Development Award HD00521 and research grants HD17423 and HD20559 from the National Institute of Child Health and Human Development and by a J. S. Guggenheim Foundation Fellowship. Marian D. Sigman was supported by the Department of Psychiatry, UCLA School of Medicine, and by research grants from the National Institute of Child Health and Human Development HD17662 and the National Institute of Mental Health MH33815. We thank H. Bornstein, J. Gaughran, B. Karmel, M. E. Lamb, P. Mundy, K. Nelson, A. Parmelee, C. Stangor, C. Tamis, and N. Yirmiya for comments.

REFERENCES

Ames, E.W., Hunter, M. A., Black, A., Lithgow, P. A., & Newman, F. M. (1978). Problems of observer agreement in the infant control procedure. *Developmental Psychology, 14,* 507–511.

Anderson, J. R. (1980). *Cognitive psychology and its implications.* San Francisco: W. H. Freeman.

Anglin, J. M. (1977). *Word, object and conceptual development.* New York: Norton.

Banks, M. S., & Salapatek, P. (1983). Infant visual perception. In M. M. Haith & J. J. Campos (Eds) P. H. Mussen (Series Ed), *Handbook of child psychology: Vol. 2, Infancy and developmental psychobiology* (pp. 435–571). New York: Wiley.

Barnet, A. B., Ohlrich, E. S., & Shanks, B. L. (1971). EEG evoked responses to repetitive auditory stimulation in normal and Down's syndrome infants. *Developmental Medicine and Child Neurology, 13,* 321–329.

Bayley, N. (1949). Consistency and variability in the growth of intelligence from birth to eighteen years. *Journal of Genetic Psychology, 75,* 165–196.

Bayley, N. (1969). *Bayley Scales of Infant Development,* New York: Psychological Corp.

Beckwith, L., & Cohen, S. E. (1983). *Continuity of caregiving with preterm infants.* Paper presented at the meeting of the Society for Research in Child Development, Detroit.

Beckwith, L., & Cohen, S. E. (1984). Home environment and cognitive competence in preterm children during the first five years. In A. Gottfried (Ed.) *Home environment and early cognitive development* (pp. 235–271). New York: Academic Press.

Belsky, J., Goode, M. K., & Most, R. K. (1980). Maternal stimulation and infant exploratory competence: Cross-sectional, correlational, and experimental analyses. *Child Development, 51,* 1163–1178.

Bentler, P. M. (1980). Multivariate analysis with latent variables: Causal modeling. *Annual Review of Psychology, 31,* 419–456.

Berg, C. A., & Sternberg, R. J. (in press). Response to novelty: Continuity versus discontinuity in the developmental course of intelligence. In H. W. Reese (Ed.), *Advances in child development and behavior.*

Bertenthal, B. I., Haith, M. M., & Campos, J. J. (1983). The partial-lag design: A method for controlling spontaneous regression in the infant-control habituation paradigm. *Infant Behavior and Development, 6,* 331–338.

Birch, H. H., & Lefford, A. (1963). Intersensory development in children. *Monographs of the Society for Research in Child Development, 28*(5, Serial No. 89).

Block, N. (Ed.) (1981). *Imagery,* Cambridge, MA: M.I.T. Press.

Bloom, B. S.. (1976). *Human characteristics and school learning.* New York: McGraw-Hill.

Bogartz, R. S. (1965). The criterion method: Some analyses and remarks. *Psychological Bulletin, 64,* 1–14.

Bornstein, M. H. (1983a). Perceptual development. In M. H. Bornstein & M. E. Lamb (Eds) *Developmental psychology: An advanced textbook* (pp. 81–131). Hillsdale, NJ: Lawrence Erlbaum Associates Inc.

Bornstein, M. H. (1983b). A descriptive taxonomy of psychological categories used by infants. In C. Sophian (Ed.) *Origins of cognitive skills* (pp. 313–338). Hillsdale, NJ: Lawrence Erlbaum Associates Inc.

Bornstein, M. H. (1984). *Infant attention and caregiver stimulation: Two contributions to early cognitive development.* Paper presented at the International Conference on Infant Studies, New York.

Bornstein, M. H. (1985a). Habituation of attention as a measure of visual information processing in human infants: Summary, systematization, and synthesis. In G. Gottlieb & N. A. Krasnegor (Eds) *Measurement of audition and vision in the first year of postnatal life: A methodological overview* (pp. 253–300). Norwood, NJ: Ablex.

Bornstein, M. H. (1985b). How infant and mother jointly contribute to developing cognitive competence in the child. *Proceedings of the National Academy of Sciences (U.S.A.).*

Bornstein, M. H., & Benasich, A. A. (in press). Infant habituation: Assessments of short-term reliability and individual differences at 5 months. *Child Development.*

Bornstein, M. H., & Ruddy, M. (1984). Infant attention and maternal stimulation: Prediction of cognitive and linguistic development in singletons and twins. In H. Bouma & D. G.

Bouwhuis (Eds) *Attention and performance X: Control of language processes* (pp. 433–445). London: Lawrence Erlbaum Ltd.

Bornstein, M. H., & Tamis, C. (1986). *Origins of cognitive skills in infants.* Paper presented at the International Conference on Infant Studies, Los Angeles.

Bouchard, J. J., & McGue, M. (1981). Familial studies of intelligence: A review. *Science, 212,* 1055–1059.

Brooks-Gunn, J., & Weinraub, M. (1983). Origins of infant intelligence testing. In M. Lewis (Ed.) *Origins of intelligence* (pp. 25–66). New York: Plenum.

Brown, R. (1973). *A first language.* Cambridge, MA: Harvard University Press.

Caron, A. J., & Caron, R. F. (1981). Processing of relational information as an index of infant risk. In S. L. Friedman & M. Sigman (Eds) *Preterm birth and psychological development* (pp. 219–240). New York: Plenum.

Caron, A. J., Caron, R. F., & Glass, P. (1983). Responsiveness to relational information as a measure of cognitive functioning in non-suspect infants. In T. Field & A. Sostek (Eds) *Infants born at risk: Physiological, perceptual, and cognitive processes* (pp. 181–209). New York: Grune & Stratton.

Cattell, R. (1971). *Abilities: Their structure, growth, and action.* Boston: Houghton Mifflin.

Clarke-Stewart, K. A. (1973). Interactions between mothers and their young children: Characteristics and consequences. *Monographs of the Society for Research in Child Development,* 38 (6–7, Serial No. 153).

Coates, D. L., & Lewis, M. (1984). Early mother-infant interaction and cognitive status as predictors of school performance and cognitive behavior in six-year-olds. *Child Development, 55,* 1219–1230.

Cohen, J. (1977). *Statistical power analysis for the behavioral sciences.* New York: Academic Press.

Cohen, J., & Cohen, P. (1983). *Applied multiple regression/correlation analysis for the behavioral sciences.* Hillsdale, NJ: Lawrence Erlbaum Associates Inc.

Cohen, L. B. (1981). Examination of habituation as a measure of aberrant infant development. In S. L. Friedman & M. Sigman (Eds.) *Preterm birth and psychological development* (pp. 241–253). New York: Academic Press.

Cohen, L. B., & Gelber, E. R. (1975). Infant visual memory. In L. B. Cohen & P. Salapatek (Eds) *Infant perception: From sensation to cognition* (pp. 347–403). New York: Academic Press.

Cohen, S. E., & Parmelee, A. H. (1983). Prediction of five-year Stanford-Binet scores in preterm infants. *Child Development, 54,* 1242–1253.

DeLoache, J. S. (1976). Rate of habituation and visual memory in infants. *Child Development, 47,* 145–154.

Durkin, D. (1966). *Children who read early.* New York: Teachers College Press.

Ellis, N. R., McCartney, J. R., Ferretti, R. P., & Cavalier, A. R. (1977). Recognition memory in mentally retarded persons. *Intelligence, 1,* 310–317.

Ettlinger, G. (1967). Analysis of cross-modal effects and their relationship to language. In F. L. Darley & C. H. Milliken (Eds.) *Brain mechanisms underlying research and language* (pp. 53–60). New York: Grune & Stratton.

Eysenck, H. J., & Kamin, L. (1981). *Intelligence: The battle for the mind.* London: Pan.

Fagan, J. F. (1975). Infant recognition memory as a present and future index of cognitive abilities. In N. Ellis (Ed.) *Aberrant development in infancy* (pp. 187–201). Hillsdale, NJ: Lawrence Erlbaum Associates Inc.

Fagan, J. F. (1984). *Infants' attention to visual novelty and the prediction of later intellectual deficit.* Paper presented at the International Conference on Infant Studies, New York.

Fagan, J. F., & McGrath, S. K. (1981). Infant recognition memory and later intelligence. *Intelligence, 5,* 121–130.

Fagan, J. F., & Singer, L. T. (1983). Infant recognition memory as a measure of intelligence. In L. P. Lipsitt (Ed.) *Advances in infancy research* (Vol. 2, pp. 31–78). Norwood, NJ: Ablex.

Fantz, R. L. (1964). Visual experience in infants: Decreased attention to familiar patterns relative to novel ones. *Science, 146,* 668–670.

Fantz, R. L., & Nevis, S. (1967). The predictive value of changes in visual preferences in early infancy. In J. Hellmuth (Ed.) *The exceptional infant* (Vol. 1, pp. 349–414). Seattle: Special Child Publications.

Fenson, L., Sapper, V., & Minner, D. G. (1974). Attention and manipulative play in the 1-year-old child. *Child Development, 45,* 757–764.

Fodor, J. (1975). *The language of thought.* Cambridge, MA: M.I.T. Press.

Freedle, R. (1971). A stimulus similarity scale for temporal measures of attention in infants and children. *Developmental Psychology, 4,* 240–247.

Friedman, S. (1975). Infant habituation: Process, problems, and possibilities. In N. Ellis (Ed.) *Aberrant development in infancy: Human and animal studies* (pp.217–239). New York: Halstead.

Gardner, H. (1984). *Frames of mind: The theory of multiple intelligences.* New York: Basic.

Gardner, J. M., & Karmel, B. Z. (1983). Attention and arousal in preterm and full-term neonates. In T. Field & A. Sostek (Eds), *Infants born at risk* (pp. 69–98). New York: Grune & Stratton.

Geschwind, N. (1965a). Disconnexion syndromes in animals and man (Part I). *Brain, 88,* 237–294.

Geschwind, N. (1965b). Disconnexion syndromes in animals and man (Part II). *Brain, 88,* 585–644.

Glaser, R., & Rosner, J. (1975). Adaptive environments for learning: Curriculum aspects. In H. Talmage (Ed.) *Systems of individualized education* (pp. 84–135). Berkeley, CA: McCutchan.

Glass, G., McGaw, B., & Smith, M. L. (1981). *Meta-analysis in social research.* Beverly Hills, CA: Sage.

Greenberg, D. J., O'Donnell, W. J., & Crawford, D. (1973). Complexity levels, habituation, and individual differences in early infancy. *Child Development, 44,* 569–574.

Guilford, J. P. (1967). *The nature of human intelligence.* New York: McGraw-Hill.

Guilford, J. P. (1979). Intelligence isn't what it used to be; What to do about it. *Journal of Research and Development in Education, 12,* 33–44.

Guttman, L. (1966). Order analysis of correlation matrices, In R. B. Cattell (Ed.) *Handbook of multivariate experimental psychology.* Chicago: Rand McNally.

Haith, M. M., Goodman, G. S., Goodwyn, M., & Montgomery, L. (1982). *A longitudinal study of infants' visual scanning and discrimination of form.* Paper presented at the International Conference on Infant Studies, Austin, TX.

Harris, G. J., & Fleer, R. E. (1972). Recognition memory for faces by retardates and normals. *Perceptual and Motor Skills, 34,* 755–758.

Honzik, M. P. (1983). Measuring mental abilities in infancy: The value and limitations. In M. Lewis (Ed.) *Origins of intelligence in infancy and early childhood* (pp. 67–105). New York: Plenum.

Horn, J. L. (1976). Human abilities: A review of research and theory in the early 1970's. *Annual Review of Psychology, 27,* 437–485.

Horn, J. L. (1979). The rise and fall of human abilities. *Journal of Research and Development in Education, 12,* 59–78.

Horn, J. L. (1980). Concept of intellect in relation to learning and adult development. *Intelligence, 4,* 285–319.

Horowitz, F. D., Paden, L., Bhana, K., & Self, P. (1972). An infant-controlled procedure for studying infant visual fixations. *Developmental Psychology, 7,* 90.

Hunt, E. B. (1978). Mechanics of verbal ability. *Psychological Review, 85,* 109–130.

Hunt, E. B. (1983). On the nature of intelligence. *Science, 219,* 141–146.

Hunt, E. B., Lunneborg, C., & Lewis, J. (1975). What does it mean to be high verbal? *Cognitive Psychology, 7,* 194–227.

Hunter, M. A., Ames, E. W., & Koopman, R. (1983). Effects of stimulus complexity and familiarization time on infant preferences for novel and familiar stimuli. *Developmental Psychology, 19,* 338–352.

Johnson, D., & Brody, N. (1977). Visual habituation, sensorimotor development, and tempo of play in one-year-old infants. *Child Development, 48,* 315–319.

Jöreskog, K. G. (1978). Structural analysis of covariance or correlation matrices. *Psychometrika, 43,* 443–477.

Kagan, J. (1971). *Change and continuity in infancy.* New York: Wiley.

Kopp, C. B., & McCall, R. B. (1980). Stability and instability in mental performance among normal, at-risk, and handicapped infants and children. In P. B. Baltes & O. G. Brim (Eds) *Life-span development and behavior* (Vol. 4, pp. 33–61). New York: Academic Press.

Kosslyn, S. M. (1980). *Image and mind.* Cambridge, MA: Harvard University Press.

Lewis, M. (1971). Individual differences in the measurement of early cognitive growth. In J. Hellmuth (Ed.) *The exceptional infant* (Vol. 2, pp. 172–210). New York: Brunner/Mazel.

Lewis, M. (Ed.) (1983). *The origins of intelligence.* New York: Plenum.

Lewis, M., & Brooks-Gunn, J. (1981). Visual attention at three months as a predictor of cognitive functioning at two years of age. *Intelligence, 5,* 131–140.

Lewis, M., & Goldberg, S. (1969). Perceptual cognitive development in infancy: A generalized expectancy model as a function of the mother-infant interaction. *Merrill-Palmer Quarterly, 15,* 82–100.

Lewis, M., Goldberg, S., & Campbell, H. (1969). A developmental study of information processing within the first three years of life: Response decrement to a redundant signal. *Monographs of the Society for Research in Child Development, 39*(9, Serial No. 133).

Lindsay, P. H., & Norman, D. A. (1977). *Human information processing: An introduction to psychology.* New York: Academic Press.

Macnamara, J. (1982). *Names for things.* Cambridge, MA: M.I.T. Press.

Mandler, J. M. (1983). Representation. In J. H. Flavell & E. M. Markman (Eds), P. H. Mussen (Series Ed.), *Handbook of child psychology: Vol. 3. Cognitive development* (pp. 420–494). New York: Wiley.

Martin, R. M. (1975). Effects of familiar and complex stimuli on infant attention. *Developmental Psychology, 11,* 178–185.

McCall, R. B. (1971). Attention in the infant: Avenue to the study of cognitive development. In D. N. Walcher & D. L. Peters (Eds), *Early childhood: The development of self-regulatory mechanisms* (pp. 107–137). New York: Academic Press.

McCall, R. B. (1977). Childhood IQ's as predictors of adult educational and occupational status. *Science, 197,* 482–483.

McCall, R. B. (1979). Qualitative transitions in behavioral development in the first two years of life. In M. H. Bornstein & W. Kessen (Eds) *Psychological development from infancy: Image to intention* (pp. 183–224). Hillsdale, NJ: Lawrence Erlbaum Associates Inc.

McCall, R. B. (1981). Early predictors of later I.Q.: The search continues. *Intelligence, 5,* 141–147.

McCall, R. B., Hogarty, P. S., Hamilton, J. S., & Vincent, J. H. (1973). Habituation rate and the infant's response to visual discrepancies. *Child Development, 44,* 280–287.

McCall, R. B., & Kagan, J. (1970). Individual differences in the infant's distribution of attention to stimulus discrepancy. *Developmental Psychology, 2,* 159–170.

McCall, R. B., & McGhee, P. E. (1977). The discrepancy hypothesis of attention and affect in infants. In I. C. Uzgiris & F. Weizmann (Eds) *The structuring of experience* (pp. 179–210). New York: Plenum.

Messer, S. B., Kagan, J., & McCall, R. B. (1970). Fixation time and tempo of play in infants. *Developmental Psychology, 3,* 406.

Miller, D. J., Ryan, E. B., Aberger, E., McGuire, M.D., Short, E. J., & Kenny, D. A. (1979). Relationships between assessments of habituation and cognitive performance in the early years of life. *International Journal of Behavioral Development, 2,* 159–170.

Miller, D. J., Spiridigliozzi, G., Ryan, E. B., Callan, M. P., & McLaughlin, J. E. (1980). Habituation and cognitive performance: Relationships between measures at four years of age and earlier assessments. *International Journal of Behavioral Development, 3,* 131–146.

Miranda, S. B., & Fantz, R. L. (1974). Recognition memory in Down's syndrome and normal infants. *Child Development, 45,* 651–660.

Mullen, B., & Rosenthal, R. (1985). *BASIC meta-analysis: Procedures and programs.* Hillsdale, NJ: Lawrence Erlbaum Associates Inc.

Munday, P. C., Seibert, J. M., Hogan, A. E., & Fagan, J. F. (1983). Novelty responding and behavioral development in young, developmentally delayed children. *Intelligence, 7,* 163–174.

National Research Council. (1982). *Ability tests: Uses, consequences, and controversies.* Washington, DC: National Academy Press.

Nelson, K. (1979). The role of language in infant development. In M. H. Bornstein & W. Kessen (Eds) *Psychological development from infancy: Image to imitation* (pp. 307–337). Hillsdale, NJ: Lawrence Erlbaum Associates Inc.

O'Connor, M. J., Cohen, S., & Parmelee, A. H. (1984). Infant auditory discrimination in pre-term and full-term infants as a predictor of 5-year intelligence. *Developmental Psychology, 20,* 159–170.

Olson, G. M., & Sherman, T. (1983). Attention, learning, and memory in infants. In M. M. Haith & J. J. Campos (Eds), P. H. Mussen (Series Ed.) *Handbook of child psychology: Vol. 2. Infancy and developmental psychobiology* (pp. 1001–1080). New York: Wiley.

Olson, S. L., Bates, J. E., & Bayles, K. (1984). Mother-infant interaction and the development of individual differences in children's cognitive competence. *Developmental Psychology, 20,* 166–179.

Paivio, A. (1979). *Imagery and verbal processes.* Hillsdale, NJ: Lawrence Erlbaum Associates Inc.

Papoušek, M., Papoušek, H., & Bornstein, M. H. (1985). The naturalistic vocal environment of young infants: On the significance of homogeneity and variability in parental speech. In T. M. Field & N. Fox (Eds) *Social perception in infants* (pp. 269–297). Norwood, NJ: Ablex.

Pêcheux, M. G., & Lécuyer, R. (1983). Habituation rate and free exploration tempo in 4-month-old infants. *International Journal of Behavioral Development, 6,* 37–50.

Posner, M. I. (1973). *Cognition: An introduction.* Glenview, IL: Scott, Foresman.

Rheingold, H. L. (1985). Development as the acquisition of familiarity. *Annual Review of Psychology, 36,* 1–17.

Riksen-Walraven, J. M. (1978). Effects of caregiver behavior on habituation rate and self-efficacy in infants. *International Journal of Behavioral Development, 1,* 105–130.

Rosch, E., & Lloyd, B. B. (Eds). (1978). *Cognition and categorization.* Hillsdale, NJ: Lawrence Erlbaum Associates Inc.

Rose, D. H., & Slater, A. M. (1983). Infant recognition memory following brief stimulus exposure. *British Journal of Developmental Psychology, 1,* 221–230.

Rose, R. J., Boughman, J. A., Corey, L.A., Nance, W. E., Christian, J. C., & Kang, K. W. Data from kinships of monozygotic twins indicate maternal effects on verbal intelligence. *Nature, 283,* 375–377.

Rose, R. J., Harris, E. L., Christian, J. C., & Nance, W. E. (1979). Genetic variance in nonverbal intelligence: Data from the kinships of identical twins. *Science, 205,* 1153–1155.

Rose, S. A. (1980). Enhancing visual recognition memory in infants. *Developmental Psychology, 16,* 85–92.

Rose, S. A. (1981). Lags in the cognitive competence of prematurely born infants. In S. L. Friedman & M. Sigman (Eds) *Preterm birth and psychological development* (pp. 255–269). New York: Academic Press.

Rose, S. A. (1984). *Cross-modal transfer as a predictor of later mental development.* Paper presented at the Gatlinburg Conference on Research in Mental Retardation and Learning Disabilities, Gatlinburg, TN.

Rose, S. A., Gottfried, A., & Bridger, W. (1979). Effects of haptic cues on visual recognition memory in full-term and preterm infants. *Infant Behavior and Development, 2,* 55–67.

Rose, S. A., & Wallace, I. F. (1985). Visual recognition memory: A predictor of later cognitive functioning in preterms. *Child Development, 56,* 843–852.

Rosenthal, R., & Rosnow, R. L. (1984). *Essentials of behavioral research: Methods and data analysis.* New York: McGraw-Hill.

Ruddy, M., & Bornstein, M. H. (1982). Cognitive correlates of infant attention and maternal stimulation over the first year of life. *Child Development, 53,* 183–188.

Russell, A. (1983). Stability of mother-infant interaction from 6 to 12 months. *Infant Behavior and Development, 6,* 27–37.

Scarr, S. (1981). Testing for children: Assessment and the many determinants of intellectual competence. *American Psychologist, 36,* 1159–1166.

Scarr, S., & Weinberg, R. A. (1983). The Minnesota Adoption Studies: Genetic differences and malleability. *Child development, 54,* 260–268.

Siegel, L. S. (1983). Correction for prematurity and its consequences for the assessment of the very low birth weight infant. *Child Development, 54,* 1176–1188.

Sigman, M. (1977). Early development of preterm and full-term infants: Exploratory behavior in eight-month-olds. *Child Development, 47,* 606–612.

Sigman, M. (1983). Individual differences in infant attention: Relations to birth status and intelligence at five years. In T. Field & A. Sostek (Eds) *Infants born at risk: Physiological, perceptual, and cognitive processes* (pp. 271–293). New York: Grune & Stratton.

Sigman, M., & Beckwith, L. (1980). Infant visual attentiveness in relation to caregiver-infant interaction and developmental outcome. *Infant Behavior and Development, 3,* 141–154.

Sigman, M., & Cohen, S. E. (1985). *Infant attention in relation to intellectual abilities in childhood.* Paper presented at the International Society for the Study of Behavioral Development, Tours, France.

Sigman, M., Cohen, S. E., Beckwith, L., & Parmelee, A. H. (1986). Infant attention in relation to intellectual abilities in childhood. *Developmental Psychology.*

Sigman, M., Cohen, S. E., Beckwith, L., & Topinka, C. (1986). *Task persistence in two-year-olds in relation to subsequent attentiveness and intelligence.* Paper presented at the International Conference on Infant Studies, Los Angeles.

Sigman, M., Kopp, C. B., Littman, B., & Parmelle, A. H. (1977). Infant visual attentiveness in relation to birth condition. *Developmental Psychology, 13,* 431–437.

Sigman, M., & Parmelee, A. H. (1974). Visual preferences of four-month-old premature and full-term infants. *Child Development, 45,* 959–965.

Siqueland, E. R. (1981). Studies of visual recognition memory in preterm infants: Differences in development as a function of perinatal morbidity factors. In S. L. Friedman & M. Sigman (Eds) *Preterm birth and psychological development* (pp. 271–288). New York: Academic Press.

Slater, A., Morison, V., & Rose, D. (1984). Habituation in the newborn. *Infant Behavior and Development, 7,* 183–200.

Slater, A., Cooper, R., Rose, D., & Perry, H. (1985). *The relationship between infant attention and learning, and linguistic and cognitive abilities at 18 months and at 4½ years.* Paper presented at the International Society for the Study of Behavioral Development, Tours, France.

Slobin, D(1974). *Psycholinguistics.* Glenview, Ill: Scott, Foresman.

Smith, E., & Medin, D. (1981). *Categories and concepts.* Cambridge, MA: Harvard University Press.

Stankov, L. (1983). Attention and intelligence. *Journal of Educational Psychology, 75,* 471–490.

Sternberg, R. J. (1985). *Beyond IQ: A triarchic theory of human intelligence.* Cambridge: Cambridge University Press.

Stoltz-Loike, M., & Bornstein, M. H. (1985). *The roles of imagery, language, and metamemory in cross-modal transfer in children.* Unpublished manuscript, New York University.

Thompson, L., & Fagan, J. F. (1983). *A family study of infant recognition memory.* Paper presented at the 13th Annual Meeting of the Behavioral Genetics Association, London.

Tighe, T. J., & Leaton, R. N. (1976). *Habituation: Perspectives from child development, animal behavior, and neurophysiology.* Hillsdale, NJ: Lawrence Erlbaum Associates Inc.

Vernon, P. E. (1980). *Intelligence: Heredity and environment.* San Francisco: W. H. Freeman.

Wechsler, D. (1963). *Wechsler Preschool and Primary Scale of Intelligence.* New York: Psychological Corp.

Wechsler, D. (1974). *Wechsler Intelligence Scale for Children – Revised.* New York: Psychological Corp.

Wechsler, D. (1981). *Wechsler Adult Intelligence Scale – Revised.* New York: Psychological Corp.

Wilson, R. (1983). The Louisville Twin Study: Developmental synchronies in behavior. *Child Development, 54,* 298–316.

Yarrow, L. J., Klein, R. P., Lomonaco, S., & Morgan, G. A. (1975). Cognitive and motivational development in early childhood. In B. X. Friedlander, G. M. Sterritt, & G. E. Kirk (Eds) *Exceptional infant* (Vol. 3, pp. 491–502). New York: Brunner/Mazel.

Yarrow, L. J., Morgan, G. A., Jennings, K. D., Harmon, R. J., & Gaiter, J. L. (1982). Infants' persistence at task: Relationships to cognitive functioning and early experience. *Infant Behavior and Development, 5,* 131–142.

Zigler, E., Abelson, W. D., & Seitz, V. (1973). Motivational factors in the performance of economically disadvantaged children on the Peabody Picture Vocabulary Test. *Child Development, 44,* 294–303.

18 The Importance of Simply Growing Older

Jerome Kagan

Most psychologists believe habits die hard, and that experience etches an indelible mark on the mind that is not easily erased. Psychological growth during the early years is thought to be under the strong influence of external events. The psychological structures established then are thought to last at least into early adolescence. This hypothesis owes part of its popularity to Freud.

I was certain that this was true, and set out to find the form of those initial structures, and the earliest time one might foresee a child's future. But, during a search that has lasted 15 years, I observed some children living in an isolated Indian village on Lake Atitlan, in the highlands of north west Guatemala, I saw listless, silent, apathetic infants; passive, quiet, timid three year olds; but active, gay, intellectually competent eleven year olds. There is no reason to believe that living conditions in this village have changed during the last century. So it is likely that the alert eleven year olds were, a decade earlier, listless, vacant-staring infants. That observation has forced me to question the strong form of the continuity assumption.

Take passivity as an example. Very few of the young children in this Indian village tried to establish dominance over other children. They kept this passivity until they were five or six years old. However, by eight, some of the children had begun to dominate. These dominant children's early disposition was less important in determining their behaviour than their physical size, strength and competence in valued skills.

Source: *New Society,* 14 June 1973, pp. 610–12. This reading is condensed from a paper delivered to the American Association for the Advancement of Science conference in December 1972.

Thus, it seems that the continuity of the psychological disposition does not stem from some neurological structure within the individual, separate from external pressures. The group of scientists who have championed stability – I have been among them – envisage a small box of different coloured gems in the brain, with names like "intelligent", "passive", "irritable" or "withdrawn", engraved upon them. This belief in a distinct and unchanging mosaic of core traits – an identity – is fundamental to western thought and is reflected in the psychological writings of Erik Erikson and the novels of popular Western writers. Only Herman Hesse, among the more gifted modern western novelists, fails to make out the case for personal identity. The heroes of his *Siddharta, Magister Ludi* and *Narziss and Goldmund* are not trying to discover "who they are", but are seeking serenity. Each appreciates the relevance of setting in that journey. Hesse's prejudice for the philosophy of the East is probably one reason why he gives the theme of identity secondary status.

My own observations were made in various settings in Guatemala. One location was three subsistence-farming villages in eastern Guatemala inhabited by Ladinos (i.e. Spanish speaking people of mixed Indian and Spanish parentage). The villages are fairly isolated, with between 800 and 2,500 inhabitants. The families live in small thatched huts of bamboo or adobe, with a dirt floor and no separate sanitation. Children rarely have books, pencils, paper or pictures before going to school. Even in school, the average child has no more than a thin notebook, with ruled pages, and a stub of pencil.

The second location was the more isolated Indian village of San Marcos. This is on the shores of Lake Atitlan, in the north west mountainous region of Guatemala. It had 850 inhabitants. The Indians of San Marcos have no easy access to a city, and are psychologically more detached than the inhabitants of the three other villages. Their isolation is due not only to geography, but also to the fact that few of the women, and no more than half of the men, speak reasonable Spanish.

During his first ten to twelve months, the San Marcos baby spends most of his life in the small, dark interior of his hut. Women do not work in the field. So the mother usually stays close to the home and spends most of her day preparing food – typically tortillas, beans and coffee – and perhaps doing some weaving. If she travels to a market to buy or sell, she usually leaves her baby with an older child or relative. The baby is close to the mother – held on her lap, enclosed on her back in a coloured cloth, sitting on a mat, or sleeping in a hammock. The mother rarely allows the baby to crawl on the dirt floor of the hut. She feels that the outside sun, air and dust are harmful.

The baby is rarely spoken to or played with. The only objects available for play, besides his own clothing and his mother's body, are oranges, ears of corn and pieces of wood or clay. These babies differ from American children of the same age by their extreme fearfulness, minimal smiling, and, above all, extraordinary quietness. Some, with pale cheeks and vacant stares, were almost like tiny ghosts. Many would not respond to tape-recorded speech, or smile or babble when I spoke to them. They would hesitate for over a minute before reaching for an attractive toy.

An American woman who lived in the village made separate 30-minute observations in the home on twelve babies of eight to 16 months old. On average, the babies were spoken to, or played with, 6 per cent of the time. The maximum was 12 per cent. Colleagues of mine found the comparable average for American middle class homes was 25 per cent, with a maximum of 40 per cent. The sounds the Guatemalan babies made (which lasted about 6 per cent of the time) were usually grunts, going for less than a second, and not the prolonged babbling typical of middle class American homes. The babies cried very little, because the slightest irritability led the mother to nurse her child at once. Nursing was the single, universal therapeutic treatment for all infant distress, whether caused by fear, cold, hunger, or cramps. Observations of homes in the other three villages confirmed those in San Marcos.

One reason why the Guatemalan mothers behave this way may be that it is abundantly clear to every parent that all their children begin to walk by 18 months, to talk by age three, and to perform some adult chores by age ten – despite the listless, silent quality of infancy.

We could not do any formal laboratory testing of the San Marcos children. But we could in the three Ladino villages. Though infants in the Ladino villages were slightly more alert than the Indian children of San Marcos, living conditions and rearing practices were so similar that I assume the San Marcos infants would have behaved rather like the Ladino children. In these laboratory experiments, the Guatemalan mother and child came to a special laboratory equipped with a chair and a stage. This simulated the setting in our Harvard laboratories. We were therefore able to give tests to cross-cultural groups of 84 American and 80 Guatemalan babies, who were aged five and a half months, seven and a half months, nine and a half months and eleven and a half months. There were ten to twenty-four infants from each culture at each age-level.

The first test was of cognitive growth. We wanted to establish concretely what the difference at these ages was between American middle class children and Guatemalan village children.

Each child was shown a two-inch wooden orange block for six or eight successive trials, followed by three or five trials in which a one-and-a-half inch orange block was presented. Three of the original two-inch blocks were then presented. In a test with lights, the child was shown eight or ten repetitions of a sequence in which a hand moved an orange rod in a semi-circle, until it touched a bank of three light bulbs. These were lighted on contact between the rod and the bulbs. In the next sequence, of five repetitions, the hand appeared, but the rod did not move, and the lights lit after a four-second interval. Following this, the original light-bulb sequence was repeated three times.

During the tests, two observers noted how long the infant attended to the event; whether it made any sound or smiled; and if it fretted or cried. The Guatemalan infants were less attentive than the Americans on both tests. The differences between them were greater at the two older, than at the two younger ages. We concluded that since the Ladino infants appeared somewhat more mature than the San Marcos children, it is possible that the American infants were three or four months advanced in cognitive function over the San Marcos children during the first year and a half of life.

But we needed to check to see if the apparent slowing of cognitive growth in the Guatemalan child is stable or whether he recovers. When the San Marcos Indian child starts to move around, at about 15 months, he leaves the dark hut, plays with other children, and *provides himself* with cognitive challenges that demand answers. All the San Marcos children have this marked break in experience between their first and second birthdays. How does this make a difference to older Guatemalan and American children?

We gave memory, perception and conceptual tests to children in San Marcos and in the Ladino villages, and two different groups of the children from Guatemala City. One of the Guatemala City groups was at a day-care centre for very poor children. The second group were middle class children attending nursery school, who resembled middle class Americans in both family background and opportunity.

We gave a recall test with twelve objects to two of the samples of Guatemalan children: 80 from a Ladino village, and 55 from San Marcos. The Ladinos were between five and seven years old, equally balanced for age and sex. The 55 Indians were aged between five and twelve years old (26 boys and 29 girls).

The twelve miniature objects to be recalled were common to village life – a pig, a hat, a knife, for example. And they could be clustered conceptually (animals, clothing, utensils). Recall and conceptual clustering both increased with age. Yet no five or six year olds in the Ladino village went to school. School for the others consisted of little more than semi-organised games. Moreover, none of the children in San Marcos had ever left the village, and the five and six year olds usually spent most of the day within a 500 yard radius of their homes. Hence, *school attendance, and contact with books and a written language, do not seem to be pre-requisites for recall and conceptual clustering in young children.*

The recall and cluster scores in Guatemala closely resembled those reported for middle class American children by L. F. Appel and his colleagues in 1971. The cultural similarity in recall tests also held for tests of recognition memory. In a separate study, children aged five, eight and eleven from the Ladino villages, and from Cambridge, Massachusetts, were shown 60 pictures of objects, some familiar and some unfamiliar. After delays of various lengths, each child was shown 60 pairs of pictures, one of which was old and the other new, and asked to decide which one he had seen. The five and eight year old Americans performed no better than the Guatemalans. But there was no cultural difference for the eleven year olds (see Table 18.1). Thus, recall and recognition seem to be basic cognitive functions that, in fact, mature in a regular way in any natural environment.

In perception tests, the rural five and six year olds were about three years behind the middle-class Guatemala City children. But no five or six year old was completely incapable of solving any of these problems. The differences reflected the fact that the rural children had difficulty with two or three of the harder items. This was the first time, we think, that many rural children had ever seen a two-dimensional drawing. Nonetheless, these children solved seven or eight of the twelve test items.

The perceptual competence of the San Marcos children is confirmed by their performance on a test administered in both San Marcos and Cambridge, called Perceptual Inference. The children (60 Americans and 55 Guatemalans, from five to twelve years of age) were shown a schematic drawing of an object and asked to guess what that object might be if the drawing were completed. The child was given a total of four clues for each of 13 items. Each of the clues added more information. The child had to guess an object from an incomplete illustration, and to make an inference from minimal information.

Figure 18.1 shows how this worked out in the case of a fish. Though the San Marcos children did slightly worse, the difference for the children over seven was not significant. Figure 18.1 shows the results.

TABLE 18. 1

Percentage of Correct Responses in Recognising Pictures after Delays

Age	Americans			Guatemalans		
	5	8	11	5	8	11
Delay	%	%	%	%	%	%
0	92.8	96.7	93.3	58.4	74.6	85.2
24 hours	86.7	95.6	96.7	55.8	71.0	87.0
48 hours	87.5	90.3	93.9	61.4	75.8	86.2

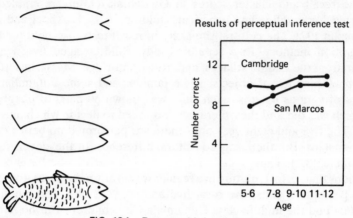

FIG. 18.1.   Perceptual inference test.

Familiarity with the test objects governed the child's success. All the San Marcos children had seen hats, fish and corn, and these items were rarely missed. By contrast, the American children often failed these items. No San Marcos child not attending school, and therefore unfamiliar with books, correctly guessed the book-related items. The majority of those children who did go to school guessed them correctly.

These findings, of course, have marked implications for educational problems in such countries as America (or Britain). There is a tendency to regard the poor test performances of badly-off minority-group six year olds in the United States as a sign of a permanent, and perhaps irreversible, defect in intellectual ability. But our findings, and others that confirm them, suggest that children differ in the age at which basic cognitive competences emerge; and that "experience"– not necessarily schooling – influences the time of emergence. Poor city or country children may be between one and three years behind middle class children in some of the problem-solving skills which Piaget has characterised as the stage of "concrete operation". But these skills eventually appear by the age of ten or eleven. The common practice in the United States of arbitrarily setting seven years – the usual time of school entrance – as the age when children are to be classified as competent or incompetent, confuses differences in the rate of maturation with permanent, qualitative differences in intellectual ability. This practice is as logical as classifying children as permanently sexually fertile or infertile, depending on whether or not they have reached physiological puberty by their thirteenth birthday.

Our Guatemalan data are not the first of their kind to be reported. Their importance lies in the fact that the San Marcos eleven year olds performed so well, considering the poverty and extreme isolation of their environment.

There is a message, therefore, not only for those who set too much store by IQs; but also for those who expect too much from environmental factors, as opposed to biological maturation.

Early environmental experiences have an important influence on intellectual development. But that influence seems to be more reversible and more temporary than many have surmised, if the child is put in a facilitating environment. Support for this comes from recent studies by Harlow and his colleagues. Several years ago, Harlow's group demonstrated that though monkeys reared in isolation for the first six months displayed abnormal, and often bizarre, social behaviour they could, if the experimenter were patient, solve the complex learning problems normally administered to monkeys born normally in the wild. The prolonged isolation did not destroy their cognitive competence.

From Locke's *Essay on Understanding* to Skinner's *Beyond Freedom and Dignity*, we in the West have seen the perfectibility of man as vulnerable to the vicissitudes of the objects and people who block, praise, or push him. We have resisted giving the child any compass of his own. The mind, like the nucleus of a cell, has a plan for growth and can transmute a new flower, an odd pain, or a stranger's unexpected smile, into a form that is comprehensible.

We need not speak of joy in this psychological mastery. Neither walking nor breathing are performed in order to experience happiness. The maturation I have written about occurs because each physiological system or organ naturally exercises its primary function. The child explores the unfamiliar and attempts to match his ideas and actions to some previously acquired representation because these are basic properties of mind. The child has no choice.

REFERENCES

Appel, L. F., et al., (1971). *The development acquisition of the distinction between perceiving and memory* (unpublished manuscript).

Harlow, H. F., Schlitz, K. A., & Harlow, M. K. (1969). The effects of social isolation on the learning performance of rhesus monkeys. In C. R. Carpenter (Ed.), *Proceedings of the Second International Congress of Primatology, Vol. 1*. New York: Karger.

Author Index

Abelson, W.D., 266
Abramson, A.S., 147, 149–150
Abramson, L., 111
Acredolo, L.P., 200, 207
Ainsworth, M.D.S., 29, 35
Allen, C.K., 203
Als, H., 111
Amatruda, C., 3, 12
Ambrose, J.A., 60
Ames, E.W., 252, 256, 259
Ames, L.B., 7
Anderson, J.A., 141n, 152
Anderson, J.R., 265
Anger, D., 115
Anglin, J.M., 265, 275
Antonovsky, H.F., 25
Appel, K.J., 178
Appel, L.F., 289
Arai, S., 32, 35
Armstrong, S.L., 133, 154–155
Arnold, W.R., 60
Aronson, E., 101
Ashton, R., 120
Asling, R.N., 148, 212
Athavale, V.B., 35
Austin, G.A., 131, 153
Ayres, B., 25

Babu, E, 29
Bahrick, E., 99
Baldwin, J.M., 55
Banks, M.S., 253
Bardet, C., 29, 31
Barnet, A.B., 253
Barron, T., 195–196
Barry, H., III, 25
Barton, S., 4
Bates, E., 220–221, 223–226
Bates, J.E., 270
Bateson, G., 24
Batterman, N., 156
Baurière M., 111
Bayles, K., 270
Bayley, N., 12, 15, 36, 250–251, 269
Beach, F.A., 87
Beaton-Williams, L., 117
Beckwith, L., 254, 266, 270
Beeghley-Smith, M., ix, 219–243
Bell, R., 111
Bell, S.M., 220
Belsky, J., 270
Benasich, A.A., 252
Benigni, L., 220–221
Bentler, P.M., 274
Berg, C.A., 266

Berlin, B., 142
Berlyne, D.E., 75
Bertenthal, B.I., 98, 259, 261
Bertoncini, J., 111
Bertucci, M., 88
Best, C.T., 150
Bhana, K., 259
Bierman, J.M., 32
Birch, H.H., 274
Birns, B., 4
Birtwistle, J., 195
Bishop, A., 145
Bjork, E.L., 177–214
Black, A., 252
Blackmon, 235
Block, N., 265
Bloom, B.S., 253
Bloom, L., 231–232, 236, 240
Blount, B.G., 25
Boehm, J., 16
Bogartz, R.S., 259
Bolles, R.C., 66
Bomba, P.C., 136–138, 139n, 141, 144–145
Born, D.G., 203
Born, W.S., 100
Bornstein, M.H., ix, 133n, 143, 145, 249–277
Botkin, P.T., 222
Bouchard, J.J., 269
Bourne, L.E., 153
Bovet, M.C., 36
Bower,T.G.R., 9–10, 96, 99, 101–102, 105, 119, 132, 171–175, 179n, 209–212
Brackbill, Y., 60, 66
Brazelton,T.B., 25, 27–8, 32, 111, 220
Breeze, K.W., 8
Bremner,J.G., 178, 187, 200, 207, 209
Bretherton, I., ix, 219–243
Bridger, W., 253
Brody, D., 14
Bordy, N., 252
Brooks-Gunn, J., 221, 250, 254–256, 276
Broughton, J.M., 9, 101
Brown, J., 203

Brown, R., 232, 275
Brown, R.E., 35
Bruner, B.M., 15
Bruner, J.S., 10, 15, 131, 152–154, 220–221
Brunswik, E., 172
Bryant, G.M., 12
Bryuant, P.E., 145, 178, 187
Bühler, K., 51, 56
Burnett, C.N., 9
Burns, P., 117
Burnside, H.L., 7–8
Butterfield, E.C., 116
Butterworth, G., 95–103, 178, 186–187, 190, 200, 204–205, 207
Bystroletova, G.N., 60

Cairns, G.F., 116
Caldwell, B.M., 28
Callan, M.P., 253
Camaioni, L., 220–221
Camp, B.W., 12
Campbell, B.A., 26, 87–88, 91
Campbell, H., 252
Campos, J.J., 92, 220, 259
Carey, S., 152, 155–156
Carlson, V.R., 120
Carns, M.L., 16
Caron, A.J. and R.F., 120, 125, 253, 255, 275
Casaer, P., 8
Casati, I., 36
Castle, P., 9
Cattell, R.B., 262, 275
Cavalier, A.R., 264
Chambliss, D., 135–136
Chasdi, E.H., 25
Chee, F.K.W., 15, 32
Child, I.L., 24–25
Chisholm, J.S., 26
Choudhuri, N., 35
Christian, J.C., 269
Chu, F., 100
Cicchetti, D., 101
Claparède, E., 51, 56
Clark, D.L., 15, 17, 32
Clark, E., 226, 230–231

Clarke, A.M. and A.D.B., 26
Clarke-Stewart, K.A., 243, 270
Clifton, R.K., 59, 66
Coates, D.L., 270
Coates, L., 88
Coghill, G.E., 53
Cohen, J., 252–253, 256
Cohen, L.B., 92, 139–141, 253, 259
Cohen, P., 252, 256
Cohen, S.E., 250, 254–256, 266,
  269–270
Coll, C., 28
Collier, G.A., 25, 28, 32
Condon, W.S., 116
Connine, C.M., 150
Connolly, K.J., viii, 3–17
Cooper, F.S., 147
Cooper, L., 9
Cooper, R., 254, 262
Corballis, M.C., 11
Corman, H.H., 36–37
Cornell, D., 135
Corter, C.M., 178
Cousins, D.B., 116
Cox, B., 154
Cox, M.V., 211
Craik, F.I.M., 195
Cravioto, J., 32
Crawford, D., 252
Cross, J., 135
Crowder, R.G., 195
Cummings, E.M., 177–214
Curti, M.W., 35
Cutting, J.E., 98

D'Andrade, R.G., 25
Dang, L., 35
Das, V.K., 31
Dasen, P.R., 29, 36
Davenport, R.K., 75
Davies, K.J., 12
Day, R.H., 106
Dean, R.F.A., 15, 27–29, 33
DeCasper, A.J., 111–117
DeChateau, P., 111
Dechovitz, D., 149
Delgado, H., 28

De Licardie, E., 32
DeLoache, J.S., 261
De Lucia, C.A., 71–76
Demany, L., 105–109
De Vries, M.W., 25, 28
Di Franco, D., 10
Dixon, S., 27
Dodds, J.B., 12
Dodwell, P.C., 10
Dominowski, R.L., 153
van Doorninck, W.J., 12
Du Bois, C., 26
Durkin, D., 253
Durojaiye, 29

Earle, D.C., 123
Easton, T.A., 16
Edwards, D., 224
Eimas, P.D., 111, 131–156
Eisenberg, R.B., 111, 116
Ekstrand, B.R., 153
Elliott, J.M., 11
Ellis, N.R., 264, 272
Engle, P., 28
Enright, M., 87–92
Erickson, D.M., 149–150
Erikson, E., 286
Escalona, S.K., 36–37, 166n
Essock, E.A., 144, 152
Ettlinger, G., 274
Evans, D., 200, 207
Evans, W.F., 178, 186–190
Eysenck, H.J., 251, 269

Fagan, J.F., 250–253, 255, 257,
  261–262, 264, 269, 276
Fagen, J.W., 87–92
Faladé, S., 29, 35
Falmagne, J.-C., 35
Fantz, R.L., 37, 83, 123, 134, 251, 253,
  258
Fenson, L., 252
Ferek, J.M., 88
Ferretti, R.P., 264
Fifer, W.P., 111–117
Finley, G.E., 37–38
Fischer, K.W., 220

Fisher, E., vii
Fitch, H.L., 150
Fitzgerald, H.E., 60, 66
Flavell, E., 230
Flavell, T.H., 222–223, 230, 242
Fleer, R.E., 264
Fletcher, H.J., 195–196
Fodor, J.A., 152, 154–155, 265
Forbes, E.J., 59–60
Fox, N., 201, 204
Fox, R., 98
Fraise, P., 105
Francis-Williams, J., 12
Frankenburg, W.K., 12
Freedle, R., 252
Freedman, D., 14, 26–27
French, F.E., 32
Frenkel, E., 35
Freud, S., 285
Friedlander, B., 111
Friedman, S., 253
Fry, C.L., 222
Frye, D., 178, 206–207
Fuchs, A.F., 195, 203

Gaiter, J.L., 265
Galligan, R.F., 178
Gardiner, J.M., 195
Gardner, H., 243, 275
Gardner, J.M., 252, 267, 272
Garrett, M.F., 155
Garske, J.P., 195–196
Geber, M., 15, 27–31, 33, 35
Gekoski, M.J., 88, 91
Gelber, E.R., 92, 259
Gelman, R., 134n, 154
Geschwind, N., 274
Gesell, A., 3, 5, 11–12, 16
Gewirtz, J.L., 83, 220
Gibson, E.J., 96, 99–100, 120, 128
Gibson, J.J., 95–96
Gitlin, M., 32
Glaser, R., 253
Glass, G., 253
Glass, P., 255
Gleitman, L.R. and H., 133
Goldberg, S., 29, 36–37, 252, 270

Goldman D., 135, 140
Goode, M.K., 270
Goodman, G.S., 253
Goodnow, J.J., 131, 153
Goodwyn, M., 253
Gottfried, A., 253
Gottlieb, G., 117
Gouin-Décarie, Th., 166n
Gower, E.C., 10
Graham, F.K., 28, 66
Granrud, C.E., 97
Grantham-McGregor, S.M., 35
Gratch, G., 178, 186–187, 190, 201,
    204, 212
Greenberg, D.J., 252
Greenfield, P.M., 152
Grice, H.P., 226
Griesel, R.D., 29
Grieser, D.L., 150
Griffiths, J., 27
Grogg, T.M., 195–196
Guilford, J.P., 275
Guttman, L., 262

Habermas, T., 220
Haggard, M., 149
Haidvogl, M., 13
Haith, M.M., 253, 259
Halliday, M.A., 231
Halpern, F., 35
Halton, A., 10
Halverson, H.M., 9, 11
Halwes, T., 150
Hamburg, M., 204
Hamilton, J.S., 269
Hamlyn, D.W., 220
Harkness, S., 25–26
Harlow, H.F. and M.K., 291
Harmon, R.J., 265
Harris, D.L., 178, 186–187, 197, 201,
    204, 206
Harris, E.L., 269
Harris, G.J., 264
Harris, M., 24
Harris, P.L., 145
Hatano, G., 37
Hawke, W.A., 35

Headrick, M., 66
Heider, F., 226
Hein, A., 10
Held, R., 9–10
Hellebrandt, F.A., 16
Hennessy, B.L., 149
Hess, E.H., 117
Hesse, H., 286
Hetzel, B.S., 14
Hindley, C.B., 14–15
Hoffman, M.L., 221, 232
von Hofsten, C., 10, 96, 101
Hogan, A.E., 252
Hogarty, P.S., 269
von Holst, E., 53
Homa, D., 135–136, 140–141
Honzik, M.P., 250
Hood, L., 236, 240
Hooker, D., 10
Hoorweg, J., 14
Hopkins, B., 28, 31–32
Horn, J.L., 262, 275
Horowitz, F.D., 259
Hoving, K.L., 88
Hubley, P., 220–221
Hugon, J., 27
Hull, C.L., 66, 132, 153
Humphrey, T., 11
Hunt, E.B., 262, 265, 275
Hunt, J.McV., 37, 80–81
Hunter, M.A., 252, 256
Husaim, J.S., 139–140

Inhelder, B., viii, 29, 36, 51–57, 165–169
Ishikawa, J., 32
Ivanans, T., 32, 35

Jackson, E., 220
Janes, M.D., 30
Jansson, G., 96
Jassik-Gershenfeld, D., 111
Jaynes, J., 87–88, 91
Jennings, K.D., 265
Johansson, G., 95–96, 98, 102
Johnson, D., 252
Johnson, E., 9

Jöreskog, K.G., 274
Julia, H., 117
Jusczyk, P.W., 147–148, 151
Kagan, J., ix, 26, 32, 37–8, 92, 133n, 135, 201, 204, 252, 259, 285–291
Kagia, J., 29
Kamin, L., 251, 269
Kandoth, W.K., 35
Kardiner, A., 24
Karmel, B.Z., 252, 267, 272
Katz, 32
Kaul, K.K., 31, 35
Kay, P., 142–143
Kaye, H., 4
Kaye, K., 112n
Kearsley, R.B., 37–8
Keefer, C.H., 27
Keele, S.W., 135–136, 139n
Keil, F.C., 156
Kellman, P.J., 97–98
Kember, D.G., 139
Kennel, J.H., 111
Keppel, G., 203
Kessen, W., 143
Khoka, E.W., 37
Kilbride, J.E., 29–30, 34–5
Kilbride, P.L., 29, 34
Killen, M., 222
Klaus, M.H., 111
Klein, R.E., 28, 32, 37–38, 149
Klein, R.P., 255, 266
Kleunder, K.R., 150
Knapp, A.G., 141n, 152
Knoblock, H., 36
Koffka, K., 105, 171
Koga, Y., 35
Kohen-Raz, R., 35
Köhler, W., 51, 56
Kolb, S., 30
Konner, M.J., 27, 29–30, 32, 36, 38–39
Koopman, R., 256
Kopp, C.B., 37, 250–251, 253
Korner, A.F., 117
Koslowski, B., 10, 27, 220
Kosslyn, S.M., 265
Kotelchuck, M., 37
Koza, C., 35

Krachkovskaia, M.V., 60
Kraemer, H.C., 29
Kravitz, H., 16
Kreutzberg, J.R., 15, 32
Kron, R.E., 116
Kuhl, P.K., 100, 146, 150
Kumari, R., 35

Lagerspetz, K., 30
Lahey, M., 231, 236
Lambert, W.W., 25
Lampe, J.M., 12
Landau, R., 26
Landauer, T.K., 26
Landers, W.F., 178, 204
Lasky, R.E., 10, 28, 38, 149
Lavallée, M., 29, 36
Layne, O, Jr, 38
Leach, 156
Leaton, R.N., 273n
Leboyer, F., 31
Lechtig, A., 28
LeCompte, G.K., 178
Lécuyer, R., 252
Lee, D., 101
Lefford, A., 274
Lehmkuhle, S., 144, 152
Leiderman, G.F., 29, 34–35
Leiderman, P.H., 29–31, 34–35
Lempers, T., 230
Lester, B.M., 28, 37
LeTendre, J.B., 145
Le Vine, R.A., 25
Lewis, J., 262
Lewis, M., 29, 35, 221, 252–256
    269–270, 276
Lézine, I., 36
Liberman, A.M., 147, 149–150
Liddicoat, R., 29, 35
Lightbown, P., 236
Lindhagan, K., 10
Lindsay, P.H., 265
Lindsley, O.R., 72
Lintz, L.M., 60
Lipsitt, L.P., 60, 116, 178
Lisker, L., 147, 149–150
Lithgow, P.A., 252

Littman, B., 253
Lloyd, B.B., 265
Lock, A., vii
Locke, J., 291
Loess, H., 203
Lomonaco, S., 255, 266
Lucas, D., 87–92
Lundberg, A., 13
Lunneborg, C., 262
Lusk, D., 29, 35

McCall, R.B., 250–252, 259–260, 269,
    273
McCartney, J.R., 264
McClelland, J.L., 141n, 152
McCluskey, K., 230
McDaniel, C.R., 98, 142–143
McDonnell, P.M. 10–11
MacFarlane, A., 117
McGaw, B., 253
McGhee, P.E., 273
McGrath, S.K., 252, 255
McGraw, M.B., 7–8
McGue, M., 269
Machida, S., 154
McIntyre, C., 230
McKenzie, B.F., 105–109, 145
McLaughlin, J.E., 253
Macnamara, J., 265, 275
McNemar, Q., 14
McNew, S., ix, 219–243
Mactutus, C.F., 88
Main, M., 220, 232
Mandler, J.M., 265
Mandler, R., 149
Markman, E.M., 154
Marquis, D.P., 60
Marshall, F.B., 35
Martin, R.M., 273
Martinez, S., 38
Martorell, R., 28
Masangkay, Z., 230
Massar, B., 201
Massaro, D.W., 150
Massé, G., 29, 35
Matarazzo, K.G., 28
Mattingly, I.G., 150

Maurer, D., 106
Mead, M., 24
Medin, D.L., 131, 133, 137n, 152, 154–155, 195, 265
Megaw-Nyce, J., 99
Mehler, J., 111
Meicler, M., 212
Melton, A.W., 195, 203
Meltzoff, A.N., 100, 221
Melvish, E., 111
Menzel, E.W., 75
Mervis, C.B., 133, 136, 154
Messer, J.D., 221
Messer, S.B., 252
Miles, M., 111
Miller, D.J., 252, 254
Miller, J.L., 146–150
Minner, D.G., 252
Minton, C., 38
Miranda, S.B., 123, 253
Monckeberg, F., 14
Montgomery, L., 256
Moore, M.K., 9, 100–101, 221
Moreigne, F., 29
Morgan, G.A., 255, 265–266
Morgan, M.J., 11
Morison, V., 119–128, 269
Morrongiello, B., 150
Morse, P.A., 116, 146
Moscovitch, M., 204, 206
Moss, H.A., 26
Most, R.K., 270
Muir, D.W., 10
Mullen, B., 253
Muller, A.A., 212
Mundy, P.C., 252
Mundy-Castle, A.C., 29
Munroe, R.L. and R.H., 25
Murphy, C.M., 221
Murphy, G.L., 133
Murray, M., 9

Nadolny, T., 201
Naidr, J., 29
Nance, W.E., 269
Neligan, G., 14
Nelson, K., 243, 275

Neumann, P.G., 140–141
Nevis, S., 251
Newcombe, R.G., 12
Newman, F.M., 252
Newson, T., 220
Nolan, E., 37
Norman, D.A., 265
Nygard, M., 30

Oates, J., vii–ix
Obrist, P.A., 66
O'Connor, M.J., 255–256, 269
Oden, G.C., 150
O'Donnell, W.J., 252
Ohrlich, E.S., 253
Okonji, M.O., 29
Olshen, R., 9
Olson, G.M., 253, 270
Olver, R.R., 152
Othenin-Girard, C., 36
Owsley, C.J., 99

Paden, L., 259
Paivio, A., 265
Palti, H., 32
Papoušek, M. and H., 270
Paraskevopoulos, J., 37
Parke, R., 83
Parkes, C.H., 155
Parkin, J.M., 27–28
Parmelee, A.H., 250, 253–256
Parsons, P.J., 88, 92
Pasamanick, B., 36
Patel, N.V., 31, 35
Pavlov, I.P., 54
Paxson, L.M., 25
Pêcheux, M.G., 252
Perey, A.J., 149
Perry, H., 254, 262
Peterson, L.R. and M.J., 203
Pharoah, P.O.D. 14
Phatak, P., 31–32, 35
Piaget, J., viii–ix, 9, 16, 36–37, 51–57, 80, 84, 165–169, 177–180, 182, 184, 186, 191–193, 211–214, 223, 227–228, 230, 232, 290
Pisoni, D., 145, 147–150

Poincaré, H., 167
Poole, H.E., 29–30
Pope, M.J., 101
Porges, S.W., 59–60, 66–67
Posner, M.I., 135–136, 139n, 265
Premack, D., 225
Prescott, J.W., 25
Proffitt, D.R., 98
Prudham, D., 14
Puri, B., 35
Putnam, H., 155–156

Quine, W.V., 155–156
Quinn, P.C., 131–156

Ramarasaona, Z., 29, 35
Ramey, C.T., 77–84
Ramsey, D.S., 92
Rebelsky, F., 25, 36
Reed, S.K., 137n
Reinhardt, M., 36
Repp, B.H., 147, 149–150
Retschitzki, J., 29, 36
Reznick, J.S., 133n, 135
Rheingold, H.L., 220, 276
Riccio, D.C., 88
Richards, F.M., 12
Richardson, K., vii
Rieser, J., 179n, 200, 208–209
Riksen-Walraven, J.M., 252, 270
Rips, L.J., 155
Robbins, M.C., 29
Roberts, J.M., 25
Roberts, M., 150
Robey, J.S., 25, 28, 32
Robson, R., 150
Rogers, C.M., 75
Rogoff, B., 32, 37
Ronch, J., 4
Rosch, E., 133, 136, 139n, 142,
    144–145, 154, 156, 265
Rose, D.H., 123, 126, 254, 256, 262,
    269
Rose, R.J., 269
Rose, S.A., 253, 255, 269, 273
Rosenblith, J.F., 14
Rosenthal , R., 153

Rosner, J., 253
Rosnow, R.L., 253
Ross, G., 220
Rovee-Collier, C.K., 87–92
Rubin, S., 226
Ruddy, M., 256, 260, 270
Ruff, H.A., 10
Rumelhart, D.E., 141n, 152
Rupp, N., 116
Russell, A., 270
Ryan, E.B., 253

Sage, S., 179n, 201–203
Salapatek, P., 253
Sameroff, A.J., 59, 71
Samuel, A.G., 150
Sander, L.W., 116–117, 221
Sapper, V., 252
Scaife, M., 221
Scarr, S., 265, 271, 275
Scarr-Salapatek, S., 33
Schachtel, E.G., 87
Schacter, D.L., 204, 206
Schade, M., 16
Schaffer, M.M., 137n
Schermer, T.M., 150
Schickendanz, D., 37
Schlitz, K.A., 291
de Schonen, S., 11
Schuberth, R.E., 178
Schwartz, S.P. 135, 155
Scrutton, D.R., 9
Seibert, J., 252
Seitz, V., 266
Self, P., 259
Sellers, M.J., 37–38
Senecal, M.J., 29
Sengul, C.J., 230–231
Sepkoski, C., 28
Shanks, B.L., 253
Schankweiler, D.S., 147
Sharma, N.L., 31
Shaw, R.E., 96
Sheldon, S., vii–ix
Shephatia, L., 35
Sherman, T., 253
Sherman, T.L., 139, 141

Sherrington, C.S., 16
Shields, M.M., 220, 222–223, 241
Shirley, M.M., 8
Shotter, T., 220
Shotwell, J., 243
Siegel, L.S., 250
Siegman, M.D., ix, 37, 249–277
Simonian, K., 32
Sims-Knight, J., 230
Singer, L.T., 250, 253, 257, 261, 269, 276
Siperstein, G., 116
Siqueland, E.R., 71–6, 116, 136–138, 139n, 141, 144, 147–148, 172, 253
Skinner, B.F., 291
Slater, A.M., 119–128, 254, 256, 262, 264, 269–270, 272
Slobin, D., 275
Smilansky, E., 35
Smith, E.E., 131, 137n, 152, 154–155, 265
Smith, M.L., 253
Smith, R.S., 32
Sokolov, E.N., 67
Solomons, G., 12, 15, 32
Solomons, H.C., 15, 32
Sonnad, L., 35
Sophian, C., 179n, 201–203
Spear, N.E., 26, 87–8, 92
Spelke, E.S., 37, 97–8, 100, 134n
Spetner, N.B., 98
Spiridigliozzi, G., 252
Spiro, M.E., 25
Ssengoba, C.M.E.B., 29, 31
Stamback, M., 36
Stamps, L., 59–68
Stanfield, J.P., 14
Stankov, L., 251
Starkey, P., 134n
Statham, L., 9
Stechler, G., 117
Steggerda, M., 35
Stein, P.S.G., 17
Stern, C. and W., 231, 236
Stern, D., 220
Sternberg, R.J., 265–266, 275
Stoltz-Loike, M., 273

Strandvik, C., 30
Strauss, M.S., 140-141
Streeter, L.A., 148
Studdert-Kennedy, H., 147
Stutterer, J.R., 66
Sullivan, M.W., 87–92
Summerfield, P., 149
Summerfield, R., 150
Super, C.M., viii, 15, 23–40
Sutherland, D.H., 9
Sykes, M., 123
Syrdal-Lasky, A., 149

Takahashi, K., 37
Takahashi, M., 38
Tamis, C., 270
Tees, R.C., 149, 152
Terrace, H., 173
Thelen, E., 16–17
Theunissen, K.B., 35
Thoman, E.B., 117
Thomas, M.A., 98
Thompson, L., 269
Tighe, T.J., 273n
Tolman, E.C., 66
Topinka, C., 266
Toshima, K., 32
Touwen, B.C.L., 5, 8–9, 13, 16
Trevarthen, C., 220–221
Triandis, L., 25
Tronick, E., 27–8, 111
Twitchell, T., 11
Tynes, D.M., 91

Ueda, R., 12
Uklonskaya, R., 35
Underwood, B.J., 203
Užgiris, I.C., 37, 80–1, 222

Valantin, S., 29
Varkevisser, C.M., 29–30
Vaughn, B., 230
Vernon, P.E., 251
Vigorito, J., 147–148
Vincent, J.H., 269
Vincent, M., 27
Vinter, A., 100

Volterra, V., 220–221
Voorhees, S., 12
Vouilloux, P.D., 27, 29–30, 35
Vurpillot, E., 105–109
Vygotsky, L.S., 152–154

Wakeling, S., 232
Walker, A.C., 99, 120
Walker, E.C.T., 155
Wallace, I.F., 255, 269
Walter, G.F., 60
Walters, C.E., 36
Walters, R., 83
Warren, N., 15, 27–9
Warren, W.H., 96
Watson, J.S., 77–84
Waxler, C.Z., 230
Webb, R.A., 66, 201
Wechsler, D., 251, 256, 262, 266
Weinberg, R.A., 271
Weinraub, M., 250
Weiskopf, S., 143, 201
Werker. JF. 149, 152
Werner, E.E., 15, 32
Werner, J.S., 178
Wertheimer, M., 99, 134n
Weston, D., 232
White, B.L., 9
Whiting, B., 24
Whiting, J.W.M., 24–26
Wickens, D.D., 203

Willatts, P., 205–206
Williamson, A.M., 145
Wilson, R., 250, 269–270
Wilson, R.S., 66
Wise, S., 111
Wishart, J.G., 179n, 209–211
Wittgenstein, L., 154
Wolf, D., 226, 243
Wolf, M., 25
Wolff, P.H., 112n
Woo, S.L.Y., 9
Wood, C.C., 147
Wood, D., 220
Woodruff, G., 225
Wright, N.A., 178
Wug de Leon, E., 32
Wyke, B., 15

Yamada, Y., 38
Yarbrough, C., 28
Yarrow, L.J., 255, 265–266
Yarrow, M.R., 230
Younger, B.A., 141, 146
Yule, W., 12

Zelazo, N.A., 30
Zelazo, P.R., 15, 30, 37–38
Zern, D., 25
Zigler, E., 266
Zloto, R., 32
Zucker, K.J., 178

Subject Index

Accommodation, 53
African infants
    mental development, 34–36, 38
    motor behaviour, 27–31
Anthropology, 24–25 *see also* Culture
Asian infants
    mental development, 35, 37–38
    motor behaviour, 31–32
Assimilation, 52–53
Attention, 37–39
    decrement, 258–260
    recovery, 260–261

Body, labelling of parts of, 228–230
Bonding, 111–117
Botswana, 29–30, 32, 36, 38

Categorization, 131–156
    issues, 151–156
    speech, 146–151
    vision, 134–146
Causality, 168–169
Cognition, 250–251
    measurement of, 258–263
    see also Continuity
Communication, 219–243
    labelling body parts, 228–230
    mental states, 232–241

names, pronouns, 230–231
    person knowledge, 224–227
Concept development, *vs*. memory
    development, 177–214
Conditioning
    memory reactivation, 87–92
    response-contingent stimulation,
    77–84
    temporal, of heart rate response,
    59–68
    visual reinforcement, 71–6
Continuity in mental development,
249, 277
    assessment of, 271–277
    cognition measurement, 258–263
    cognitive development, 250–251
    information-processing approach,
    251–258
    maturation, 285–291
    models of, 263–268
    origins and maintenance of, 268–271
Culture, 23–40
    attention, 37–39
    integration of infancy, 24–26
    mental states at birth, 33–34
    motor behaviour, 27–32
    Piaget's theory, 36–37
    psychometric tests, 34–36

Dot patterns, perception, 135–140

Egocentrism, 207–211
Encounters in perception, 100–102
Environment, and maturation, 285–291
Events
   biological motion, 98–99
   encounters, 100–102
   in perception, 96–98
   intersensory, 99–100

Faces, perception of, 38, 140–142

Gestalt theory, 171–172
Guatemala, 28, 32, 37–39, 285–291
Gusii infants, 27–28

Heart rate, temporal conditioning of, 59–68
Hue perception, 142–144

Ifaluk infants, 25
Indian infants, 31–32, 35, 37
'Infancy', 23–24
Intelligence, verbal, 261–262
Ivory Coast, 29, 36

Japan, 32, 35, 38

Kenya, 23–24, 29–30, 32
Kipsigis, 23–24, 30, 32
Kwoma infants, 25
!Kung San infants, 30, 32, 36, 38

Lateralisation of function, 11
Learning
   memory reactivation, 87–92
   response-contingent stimulation, 77–84
   sensori-motor level 51–57
   temporal conditioning of heart rate responses, 59–68
   visual reinforcement, 71–76
   see also Bonding

Maturation, 285–291 see also
Continuity; Motor skills

Measurement of cognition, 258–263
   attention decrement, 258–260
   attention recovery, 260–261
   verbal intelligence, 261–262
Memory
   development, vs. concept development, 177–214
   reactivation of, 87–92
Mental development
   continuity in, 249–277
   cross-cultural studies, 33–39
Mental states, 232–241
Mexico, 25, 28, 32, 38
Mother, voice preference for, 111–117
Motion, and perception, 98–99
Motor skills, 3–17
   biological substrate, 15–17
   cross-cultural research, 26–32
   maturation, 4–7
   patterns, sequences, 7–11
   timing, variations, 11-15

Names, 230–231
New Guinea, 25

Object concept
   phenomenal identity and form perception, 171–175
   Piaget's theory, 165–169
   search errors, 177–214
Orientation perception, 144–146

Perception
   categorization, 131–156
   'dynamic', 95–96
   events and encounters, 95–103
   phenomenal identity, 171–175
   preference for mother's voice, 111–117
   rhythm, 105–109
   shape constancy and slant, 119–128
Person knowledge, 224–227
Phenomenal identity, 171–175
Psychometric tests, 34–36
Puerto Rican infants, 28

Reaching, 9–11
Reactivation of memory, 87–92

Reflexes, 15–17, 27–28 *see also*
Conditioning
Reinforcement, visual, 71–76
Response-contingent stimulation,
77–84
Rhythm perception, 105–109

Search, 177–214
Sensori-motor level, 51–57
Shape, constancy of, 119–128
Slant, perception of, 119–128
Social behaviour, 219–243
Speech, categorization of, 146–151
Stereotypes, 16–17
Sucking
   preference for mother's voice,
   111–117

visual reinforcement of, 71–76

Temporal conditioning of heart rate
responses, 59–68

Uganda, 27–29, 33–34

Verbal intelligence, 261–262
Vision categorization, 134–146
   dot patterns, 135–140
   faces, 140–142
   hue, 142–144
   orientation, 144–146

Walking, 8–9

Zambia, 29, 36
Zinacantecans, 25, 28